THIRD EDITION

WHY STATES MATTER

An Introduction to State Politics

GARY MONCRIEF
BOISE STATE UNIVERSITY

PEVERILL SQUIRE
UNIVERSITY OF MISSOURI

ROWMAN & LITTLEFIELD
Lanham • Boulder • New York • London

Executive Editor: Traci Crowell
Assistant Editor: Deni Remsberg
Higher Education Channel Manager: Jonathan Raeder
Interior Designer: Pro Production Graphic Services

Credits and acknowledgments for material borrowed from other sources, and reproduced with permission, appear on the appropriate pages within the text.

Published by Rowman & Littlefield
An imprint of The Rowman & Littlefield Publishing Group, Inc.
4501 Forbes Boulevard, Suite 200, Lanham, Maryland 20706
www.rowman.com

6 Tinworth Street, London SE11 5AL, United Kingdom

British Library Cataloguing in Publication Information Available

Library of Congress Cataloging-in-Publication Data
Names: Moncrief, Gary F., author. | Squire, Peverill, author.
Title: Why states matter : an introduction to state politics / Gary Moncrief, Peverill Squire.
Description: Third edition. | Lanham, Maryland : Rowman & Littlefield, 2020. | Includes
   bibliographical references and index.
Identifiers: LCCN 2019052735 (print) | LCCN 2019052736 (ebook) | ISBN 9781538136140
   (cloth) | ISBN 9781538136157 (paperback) | ISBN 9781538136164 (epub)
Subjects: LCSH: State governments—United States.
Classification: LCC JK2408 .M64 2020 (print) | LCC JK2408 (ebook) | DDC 320.473—dc23
LC record available at https://lccn.loc.gov/2019052735
LC ebook record available at https://lccn.loc.gov/2019052736

Brief Contents

Contents

Boxes, Figures, and Tables

BOXES

FIGURES

TABLES

Preface

ON THE DAY WE WROTE THIS PREFACE to the third edition of *Why States Matter*, two headlines from the *New York Times* illustrated several of the book's themes. The first headline, on the front page, reported, "Trump to Revoke California's Authority to Set Stricter Auto Emission Rules." The second, smaller headline on page A14 noted that "New Mexico Announces Plan for Free College for State Residents."

The first headline was, indeed, big news. It described a clash between the federal government and the largest state government. More precisely, it describes a federal administrative action to limit a state's authority to establish environmental regulations that are stricter than those imposed by the administration of President Trump. Note that this was an executive action, not a congressional action. Note also that the attorney general of California said he would challenge the action in federal court. This is an example of what federalism in today's world often looks like: executive action (not congressional action) at the national government level and state resistance, led by the state attorney general. It is not a coincidence that the president of the United States and the attorney general of California are from opposing political parties.

The second headline reported an innovative effort on the part of one state, New Mexico, to address an important state issue: the cost of education at public institutions. It is unlikely that many readers of the *New York Times* noticed that article. After all, it appeared in the paper's back pages, in a smaller headline font. It was not about confrontation between two governmental titans—the federal government and the state of California. Instead, it was about New Mexico, a small, poor state, seeking to find a solution to a local problem. Whether the policy is successful, or even is fully implemented, remains to be seen. But the article points out what is often true about the states: they experiment with a variety of policy solutions that directly affect their citizens and that may be adopted by other states if they appear successful.

While national government decisions get the bulk of media attention, the actions of state governments also impact Americans' daily lives. Moreover, as citizens, we often can have more direct influence on policies at the state and local level than those generated at the national level. We hope that this book helps readers understand why states matter, and why we need to pay greater attention to state and local elections and the actions of our state and local governments.

We are grateful to the people at Rowman & Littlefield for helping bring this third edition to fruition and thank Jon Sisk and Traci Crowell for their continued support. We also express our great gratitude to our colleagues who reviewed or adopted the previous editions of *Why States Matter* and who provided advice and suggestions for this edition, including John Hanley (University of Central Florida), Dave Price (Santa Fe College), Jaclyn Kettler (Boise State University), Andrew Kolin (Hilbert College), John Bertalan (University of South Florida), Nicole Shoaf (Missouri Southern State University), and Dave Claborn (Howard Payne University). As always, our greatest thanks go to our families, especially Heidi and Janet for their support and patience as we disappeared to the office on campus or the study at home to work on this and other projects.

Finally, it is perhaps an appropriate time to revisit an acknowledgment we made years ago in a different book. Our mentors included four giants of their generation of political scientists: Malcolm Jewell, Donald Matthews, Nelson Polsby, and Ray Wolfinger. We are privileged to have learned from them.

About the Authors

GARY MONCRIEF is University Foundation Professor Emeritus of Political Science at Boise State University. He received his undergraduate degree in political science from the University of California, Santa Barbara, and his PhD degree from the University of Kentucky. He is the coauthor or editor of six books, including *Who Runs for the Legislature?* (2001), *Reapportionment and Redistricting in the West* (2012), and *State Legislatures Today* (third edition, 2019). He has worked with the Council of State Governments, the National Conference of State Legislatures, and the State Legislative Leaders Foundation and was a consulting scholar with the Eagleton Institute of Politics, Rutgers University.

PEVERILL SQUIRE is Professor of Political Science and holds the Hicks and Martha Griffiths Chair in American Political Institutions at the University of Missouri. Among the books he has authored are *The Rise of the Representative: Lawmakers and Constituents in Colonial America* (2017) and *The Evolution of American Legislatures: Colonies, Territories and States, 1619–2009* (2012). He has served as senior editor of *Legislative Studies Quarterly*, chair of the American Political Science Association's Legislative Studies Section, and cochair of the International Political Science Association's Research Committee of Legislative Specialists. In 2018, he was given the Career Achievement Award by the American Political Science Association's State Politics and Policy Section.

1

Making a Case for the States

★ ★ ★

THE TWO WORLDS OF WENDOVER

The Great Basin is the largest desert in the United States. It is about five hundred miles wide, flanked by Salt Lake City on the east and Reno on the west. In between is mostly sage brush, salt flats, and mineral deposits, and remarkably few people. In fact, once the traveler leaves the outskirts of Salt Lake City heading west, there are no towns at all for more than one hundred miles. The first town one encounters is Wendover, founded in 1907 as a watering station for the Western Pacific Railroad. Wendover is on the Utah side of the Utah-Nevada border. But when Nevada legalized gambling in 1931, an adjacent town developed on the Nevada side: West Wendover.

In many ways the two towns are a single, intertwined community. A majority of the Wendover workforce "commutes" a couple of hundred yards across the border to work in the casinos, motels, and restaurants in West Wendover. But by simply walking across the invisible state line, one walks into a very different policy world. The obvious difference is gambling. On the Nevada sign of the line are several large casinos; there are none on the Utah side. Even a state-run lottery is illegal in Utah; only five other states do not permit lotteries. Interestingly, the *parking lots* for two of the biggest West Wendover casinos are on the Utah side of the border (largely because the property is cheaper and the property taxes are lower on the Utah side). So, as the patron walks from the parking lot to the casino, she crosses over the state line.

In 2016, Nevadans voted to legalize the recreational use of marijuana, and in 2018 the West Wendover city council granted a license to a large marijuana retailer who planned to open a retail store in late 2019.[1] And, because Utah controls liquor and beer sales through state-owned liquor stores, Nevada's more lenient liquor laws mean there are retail liquor stores in West Wendover.[2] The *Salt Lake Tribune* reports that over four million people visit West Wendover every year, and most of them are from Utah. As the West Wendover mayor admits, "People come out here to let their vices run free."[3] Such is the nature of state policy differences!

But the public policy contrasts between these two states go well beyond attitudes toward recreation, as shown in table 1.1. Utah has an individual income tax and a state corporate income tax. Nevada has neither. Utah imposes a tax on food; Nevada does not. Nevada authorizes Medicaid eligibility to a family of three if their income is as high as $28,676; in Utah the same family would only be eligible if their income was below $20,780.[4]

The Wendover case is just one of many instances of neighboring communities in different states with consequential policy differences. Take as another example LaCrosse, Wisconsin, and LaCrescent, Minnesota. Separated only by the width of the Mississippi River, the residents of these two cities share the same physical world—the same climate and geography. What is not the same for these residents is their public policy world. In the last decade, the state government of Wisconsin cut income taxes, reduced collective bargaining rights for public employees, decreased public school spending, and declined to expand Medicaid. At the same time, Minnesota increased some business taxes, raised the income tax rate for high-income earners, expanded the right to unionize to include in-home child care workers, increased per-student K–12 spending, expanded Medicaid coverage, and created a state-based health exchange.[5] These two states, which for generations were so similar in ethnicity, economic base, and ideology that they were described as "cousins" or "two peas in a pod," are now following divergent policy paths.[6] As one political scientist observes, Minnesota and Wisconsin "have begun a natural experiment that compares the agendas of modern progressivism and the new right."[7] Knowingly or otherwise, the citizens of LaCrosse and LaCrescent are part of that experiment.

Among other contrasting pairs are New Hope, Pennsylvania, and Lambertville, New Jersey; Sunland Park, New Mexico, and El Paso, Texas; Bristol, Tennessee, and Bristol, Virginia; and Kansas City, Kansas, and Kansas City, Missouri. To varying degrees, border towns across the United States are subject to different state laws than their neighbor right across the state line. And like Wendover and West Wendover, residents in these cities can live in dramatically different policy worlds. Take, for another example, Lewiston, Idaho, and Clarkston, Washington. Separated only by the width of the Snake River (about four hundred yards), citizens in one state (Washington) have legal access to both medical and recreational marijuana, doctor-assisted suicide for the terminally ill, labor union–friendly laws, and a state-mandated minimum wage of at least $12 per hour from a state (Idaho) with none of those policies.[8]

Clearly, states differ in important ways, meaning that they matter. When it comes to voting, taxes, environmental regulation, social services, education, criminal justice, political parties, property rights, gun rights, marriage and divorce laws, and just about anything else other than national defense, the state

Table 1.1.   Wendover, Utah, versus West Wendover, Nevada, 2019

	Utah	Nevada
State income taxes		
Rate range	4.95%	None
Number of brackets	1 (flat rate)	None
State corporate tax rate	4.95%	None
State sales tax rate	5.95%	6.85%
Sales tax on food	3.0%	None
Sales tax on prescription drugs?	None	None
Sales tax on nonprescription drugs?	5.95%	6.85%
State gas tax	$.30 per gallon	$.23805 per gallon
Cigarette taxes	$1.70 per pack	$1.80 per pack
Beer tax	$.4129 per gallon	$.16 per gallon
Sales tax also applied?	Yes	Yes
Marijuana laws	Medical use allowed	Recreational use allowed
Prostitution laws	Illegal	County option (legal in Elko County)
Gaming laws		
Casinos allowed	No	Yes
Sports betting allowed	No	Yes
Smoking allowed		
In bars	No	Yes
Private worksites	No	No
Restaurants	No	No
Medicaid eligibility limit (parents in a family of three)	100% of federal poverty rate	138% of federal poverty rate
Motorcycle helmet mandatory?	Only for riders under 21 years old	All riders
Hand-held cellphone use while driving	Allowed	Prohibited

Box 1.1	States in the Headlines

"OKLAHOMA KEEPS UP OPIOID FIGHT AGAINST BIG PHARMA AFTER $270 MILLION PURDUE DEAL."
https://www.washingtonexaminer.com/business/oklahoma-keeps-up-opioid-fight-with-big-pharma-after-purdue-deal

"UTAH STARTING $2.5M DEBT FORGIVENESS PROGRAM FOR TECH GRADS"
https://www.apnews.com/3741ad419cc54b2eafb36afb1746e221

"WASHINGTON BECOMES FIRST STATE TO LEGALIZE HUMAN COMPOSTING"
https://www.seattletimes.com/seattle-news/washington-becomes-first-state-to-legalize-human-composting/

"ALABAMA GOVERNOR SIGNS ABORTION BAN INTO LAW"
https://www.npr.org/2019/05/14/723312937/alabama-lawmakers-passes-abortion-ban

"MAINE LEGALIZES MEDICALLY ASSITED SUICIDE"
https://thehill.com/policy/healthcare/448245-maine-legalizes-medically-assisted-suicide

"AMID MEASLES OUTBREAK, NEW YORK ENDS RELIGIOUS EXEMPTIONS FOR VACCINES"
https://www.governing.com/topics/health-human-services/tns-new-york-ends-religious-exemptions.html

"MICHIGAN IS FIRST STATE TO BAN VAPING PRODUCTS"
https://www.usnews.com/news/best-states/articles/2019-09-04/michigan-gov-whitmer-bans-flavored-e-cigarettes

in which one resides makes a difference, often a big difference. This idea—that states matter—is the fundamental idea behind this book. So much attention is paid by the media to the national government and what the president and Congress are doing—or not doing—that it is easy to lose sight of the fact that states are different, their policies are different, and these differences have a real, direct effect on the everyday lives of their citizens. Indeed, a strong case can be made that, as one Republican official recently commented, "the real action is happening in the states."[9] For example, look at box 1.1, which provides a sampling of headlines from stories about state policymaking. All of these stories appeared in a six-week period and most of them involve just one policy area: health care, broadly defined. On any given day one can find multiple stories about state policymaking on a wide variety of issues.

While Washington has been politically gridlocked for the last decade, it is increasingly the states that are the first to address the problems and uncertainties induced by emerging technologies. Telemedicine, fantasy sports waging, ballot selfies, flavored e-cigarettes, and self-driving vehicles are just a few recent examples. It is the states—or at least some states—that are blazing the policy trail on these new issues.

Moreover, state politicians now take great pride in not being like their Washington counterparts. A report from a group of political scientists who spent time in ten state capitals noted,

> There was one attitude that pervaded every state capitol we visited. It was usually expressed as, "We are not D.C." The specter of congressional gridlock is such that it spurs states to attempt to act differently from Congress. "We're here to get things done," said a Maine leader in specific comparison to Congress. An Iowa senator took pride in his chamber by saying, "The Senate has a desire to do things differently from D.C. In 2013 and 2014 there was lots of cooperation. In 2013 we passed a property tax reform, health reform—there were many grand bargains made. One success led to the next success. We all felt good about not being like D.C."[10]

State leaders are also repulsed by the negative side of Washington politics. Following an ugly incident in the West Virginia Capitol, the Republican Speaker of the House took to the chamber floor to lament, "We have allowed national level politics to become a cancer on our state, to become a cancer on our Legislature, to invade our chamber in a way that frankly makes me ashamed."[11]

The message of this book is twofold. First, state (and local) governments make critical policy decisions that affect Americans every day. Second, because of this, citizens enjoy the ability to exert meaningful influence on policymaking, probably to a much greater degree at the state (and local) level than at the national level. The sheer scale and inertia of policymaking at the national level is daunting. But citizens in every state can make an impact at the state capitol, the county commission, the school board meeting, or city hall. But to exercise that ability, they have to recognize how many important policy decisions are made outside of Washington. And that idea motivates this book.

THE HISTORICAL CONTEXT

To claim that states matter does not require us to argue that they matter in quite the same way as in the past. It would be foolish to believe that states hold the same position relative to the national government that they did in 1790. Clearly, the world has changed over the last two centuries.

We think it foolish to even argue that states *should* hold precisely the same position as they did in 1790; after all, hardly anything in the world is as it was in 1790. Certainly, the international role of the U.S. government was far different than today. The role of all governments was much smaller then; there were few large cities, virtually no public education, little in the way of health or welfare policies, and few roads built and maintained by the government.[12] Industrialization had not yet occurred on a significant scale. The vast majority of labor and commerce in the United States was associated with farming and maritime trade. Many people died of diseases that today are controllable. The average life span was about forty-five years, compared to about seventy-nine years today. The infant mortality rate (well below 1 percent today) was as high as 15 percent in 1790.

The first U.S. Census, conducted in 1790, indicated the total population of the thirteen states was 3.9 million, which is barely more than 1 percent of the population of the United States today. Of that 3.9 million, the largest urban area was New York City, with a population of 33,131.[13] Today, there are more than a thousand cities in the United States with a population greater than New York City in 1790.[14] In fact, by 2019 fifteen metropolitan areas in the United States each had a population greater than that of the entire country in 1790.[15]

Of the 3.9 million people counted in the 1790 census, almost seven hundred thousand were slaves. We know this because one of the six questions on the first U.S. Census specifically asked about the number of slaves in the household.[16] Obviously, American society was different than today.

The usual estimate is that roughly 90 percent of the workforce was employed in agriculture at that time, while today less than 2 percent works in that sector. The population was small, residing almost entirely on family farms and homesteads, with considerably less economic interdependence than we find today. The role of government—all governments, regardless of national, state, or local level—was limited. And the relationship between these levels of government differed. Scholars often characterize the original relationship between the states and the federal government as one of "dual federalism"— by which they mean the national and state governments operated in separate policy spheres. For the most part, however, both spheres were small.

From the founding it was unclear exactly what the relationship between the national and state governments ought to be. The Articles of Confederation—the first system under which the nation operated—gave the states the upper hand. But that system failed, leaving open the question of how the different levels of government were to relate. When the Constitution was adopted, there was still considerable uncertainty. There were those, such as Alexander Hamilton, who argued forcefully for a nationalist perspective—contending that the primary constituents of the new system were the people and that it was "the people" as a collection of individuals who were sovereign grantors of authority to the new government. Under this view, the national government would hold a pre-eminent position. A second view was that the federal system was agreed to by the states themselves, not individuals. In this view, the states were the sovereign grantors of authority to the new government and as such retained the ultimate sovereignty themselves. Proponents of this view saw the federal system as an agreement—a compact—of sovereign states. Obviously, this tug between two views—the nationalist and the compact—is still with us today. In 2010, governors or legislatures in several states invoked the "compact theory" as they argued that states had the constitutional authority to reject the newly enacted federal health care law, more commonly referred to as "Obamacare." Their legal claims were largely unsuccessful, but they highlight the fact that such arguments have been central to many of the most historic moments in the country's history.

James Madison, one of the key architects of the new system, argued that both the nationalist and the compact theories were correct—or at least they were partially and equally correct. Madison described the system as a "compound republic." As Martha Derthick noted, "It is a pity that Madison's term *compound republic* did not survive in our political language for it conveys the complicated and ambiguous intent of the framing generation and helps to make comprehensible what otherwise is bewildering to the modern citizenry."[17]

Madison's compound republic was a system that "sought to assemble majorities of two different kinds: one composed of individual voters, the other, of the states as distinct political societies."[18] The individual voters, by forming an "association of people, under a constitution of government, uniting their power" provide the nationalist perspective.[19] The states, as "distinct political societies" forming together, provide the compact perspective.

We will explore the various interpretations and mutations of federalism in greater detail in chapter 2. For now, it is enough to note that whatever the "proper" federal relationship was at the time the Constitution was ratified, it has changed substantially over our history. Certainly, the Civil War resulted in a different version of federalism than that which had existed previously.

But the most dramatic changes in the federal relationship occurred in the twentieth century. The expansive roles undertaken by the national government during the Great Depression of the 1930s and the civil rights era of the 1960s were particularly important in redefining the nature of American federalism. But the changes do not end there; the U.S. Congress and the U.S. Supreme Court continued to redefine the acceptable reach of national power through most of the century.[20]

If, during this time, the national government usurped some policymaking roles that had traditionally been left to the states, it was largely in reaction to the states' weakness in exercising their responsibilities and inability to meet the needs of their citizens. Robert Allen, in a pointed criticism of the states in the middle of the twentieth century, wrote, "Since 1930, state government has dismally failed to meet responsibilities and obligations in every field. . . . The federal government has not encroached upon state government. State government has failed."[21]

To put it bluntly, it was largely the states' own fault they lost power relative to the national government. This is an important point to recognize; in many instances the states were failing their citizens. Most were unwilling or unable to devise modern revenue systems until forced to do so by the economic collapse wrought by the Great Depression. And when states did change, it was often too little too late to have a meaningful effect, leaving the national government's "New Deal" programs to carry the burden.[22] As former North Carolina governor Terry Sanford wrote in 1967, "Out of the ordeal of the depression came damaging blows to the states. From the viewpoint of the efficacy of state government, the states lost their confidence, and the people their faith in the states; the news media became cynical, the political scientists neglectful, and the critics became harsh."[23] Borne of this era was a dramatic expansion of federal aid to the states, a phenomenon referred to as "fiscal federalism." Between 1930 and 1980, fiscal federalism was central to redefining the relationship between the states and national government. We will examine the issue of federal aid and fiscal federalism in greater detail in chapter 3.

Furthermore, many states had neglected to redistrict their legislatures for decades, leaving rural interests with disproportionate political power. State officials were poorly paid; state government was poorly staffed and poorly rated. In the most hyperbolic muckraking tradition, one journalist wrote in mid-century that "state government is the tawdriest, most incompetent, and most stultifying unit of the nation's political structure. In state government are to be found in their most extreme and vicious forms all the worst evils of misrule in the country."[24] Among the evils attributed to state governments he specifically identified "low-grade and corrupt Legislatures."[25]

Meanwhile, under the revived rubric of "States' Rights," government officials of the southern states resisted a national desire to end segregation and ensure civil rights for racial minorities, especially African Americans. It was an ugly time, pitting citizen against citizen, and the national government against some of the state governments. As one historian put it, "By the 1950s and 1960s, the only time state action made headlines was when a racist governor stood in the schoolhouse door."[26]

It is easy to dismiss the bulk of the twentieth century as a "lost era" for the states. But some argue that, despite the obvious shortcomings of the states, they were doing innovative work at various times during the century.[27] Starting with the "reapportionment revolution" of the 1960s and 1970s, and facilitated by reformist-minded groups like the Citizen's Conference on State Legislatures, the National Conference of State Legislative Leaders, the Eagleton Institute of Politics at Rutgers University, the Ford Foundation, Carnegie Corporation, and the Twentieth-Century Fund, state governments were pressed to modernize and to improve their institutional and policymaking capacities.[28] Some of this story is told in greater detail in chapter 5. For now, it is worth noting that state governments generally—and state legislatures in particular—became more capable policymaking institutions during the modernizing period often known as the "legislative professionalization revolution" in the 1960s and 1970s.[29]

To put it simply, out of all the turmoil, state governments were pushed to become much more capable governing partners in the federal system. This may not often be recognized by the media or even by members of Congress. But apparently the general public recognizes it on some fundamental level, as evidenced by the fact that surveys consistently demonstrate a higher level of trust for state government than national government. A September 2019 Gallup poll indicated that a far larger proportion held a favorable view of their state government (63 percent) than of the federal government (39 percent).[30]

Arguably most telling, however, is a question posed at three points in time over the last eighty years. When asked, "Which theory of government do you favor: concentration of power in the state government or concentration of power in the federal government," 56 percent of respondents in 1936 chose the federal government. As we will see in chapter 2, having a majority take this stance in the middle of the Great Depression does not come as a surprise because at that time state governments were unable to respond to the economic crises, leaving the governing field to the federal government. When the question was asked again in 1981 during the first year of the Reagan administration, 56 percent of respondents preferred to concentrate power in state governments. Virtually the same response was given in 2016, with 55 percent of respondents opting for power to be at the state level. Thus, for more than a generation Americans have expressed a clear preference for state government.[31]

RED STATES, BLUE STATES, AND BIG SORTS

Red state, blue state is part of today's political lexicon. It developed from the desire in the visual media for a simple way to show how states were voting in the presidential election. Why? Because the presidential election is determined by the Electoral College and the vote units in the Electoral College are the states. If presidential elections were not decided in blocks of state units, perhaps no one would have conceived of red and blue states.

Nonetheless, the "red state, blue state" characterization works quite well for a growing number of states, as the division of partisans across them is becoming more lopsided. In other words, political polarization is real and growing in many states. The authors of one book on the subject put it this way: "Geography matters politically. States are not merely organizational entities. . . . States have real, significant cultural and political differences. And despite the homogenizing tendencies of national media, drastically lower transportation costs, and a franchised economy, regional differences have not gone away."[32] In other words, changes in technology, mobility, and mass consumerism have not eliminated state differences. Some argue, in fact, that the differences are growing as technology and mobility allow people to live where they want.[33]

All of this is important because our behaviors as citizens are constrained or encouraged far more by state laws than they are by the federal laws. As two political scientists note, "State boundaries have taken on great meaning partly because of the social and economic practices that are legally permitted or prohibited within them."[34] States are important because they help structure civil society, and as a result of this fact, civil society is not the same in all states. Simply stated, politically, it matters where a person lives.

In his book *The Big Sort: Why the Clustering of Like-Minded America Is Tearing Us Apart*, Bill Bishop wrote that "people do not live in states. They live in communities." This is not an entirely accurate statement, of course. One look at a driver's license confirms that people do live in states. What Bishop meant was that people choose to live in particular communities, or particular neighborhoods that just happened to be in a particular state. His argument is that people are "sorting" themselves by their religious and civic attitudes into like-minded local "tribes."[35] Indeed, "tribalism" or "political tribalism" is a current description of today's politics in the United States.

There is growing evidence that people are self-sorting. Political bloggers Harry Enten and Nate Silver find "the data is enough to suggest that the people moving away from a region are ideologically distinct from those who continue to live there. . . . Instead, movers have more in common with their new neighbors; liberals are attracted to liberal regions, and conservatives to conservative regions."[36]

Political scientists report something similar; they find that the correlation between ideology and party affiliation among the general public is growing in strength state by state. We have long known that party elites (elected officials and leaders) are polarizing at the state level. These more recent results suggest that as long as party elites are polarized, "the mass electorate will continue to sort and the macro-level manifestation of that are redder red states and bluer blue states."[37]

Perhaps this would not matter much if the political parties themselves were not so "tribal" in terms of their politics these days. But they are. As a leader of one of the most important associations of elected state officials said recently, "This is the most hyper-polarized, hyper-partisan time we've seen in generations, and nobody can deny that."[38] And that fact surfaces in everyday life. A *New Yorker* cartoon a few years ago showed two people conversing at a cocktail party, with one saying to the other, "I try not to judge people by the actions of their state government."[39] Most Americans today get the joke.

THE CONTEMPORARY CONTEXT

It is interesting that in this time of globalization there remain dissimilarities among the states on a wide range of economic, demographic, cultural, and other dimensions. We are reminded that states do indeed represent different mixes of people, characteristics, and cultures and that is, in Elazar's phrase, "what transforms each state into a civil society, possessing a political system that is in some measure autonomous."[40] California has a population of forty million, Texas almost thirty million. There are roughly twenty million residents of New York and twenty-one million in Florida. Meanwhile, there are five states (Delaware, North and South Dakota, Vermont, and Wyoming) each with a population under nine hundred thousand. As you can imagine, states as governing units face different policy and administrative demands.

States vary in many other meaningful ways. California's economy, measured as state gross domestic product, would rank fifth or sixth in the world ahead of those of France and the United Kingdom. In contrast, Vermont's would rank 102nd, just ahead of Estonia.[41] Per capita income varies widely across the states; Mississippi's is about half of Connecticut's. Of course, the source of state wealth differs; some states have been blessed with valuable natural resources while others have not. The proportion of college-educated individuals is much higher in some states than others (which is an important variable in explaining per capita income). The incidence of death by opioid overdose has been ten times higher in West Virginia and Ohio than in Montana or Nebraska.[42] Racial and ethnic makeups vary. Frequency of church attendance differs; regular church attendance is much higher in the southern states (as well as Utah) than in the Pacific Northwest and New England states. A 2016 Pew Research Center poll found that more than 70 percent of residents in Alabama, Mississippi, Tennessee, Louisiana, Arkansas, and South Carolina said that religion was very important in their lives, while less than 40 percent of the people in Maine, Vermont, Massachusetts, and New Hampshire made that claim.[43] The depth of religious meaning to one's daily life is known as "religiosity" and has been linked to very specific policy preferences on issues such as abortion and same-sex marriage.

Given all of this variation, can any state be thought to be representative of the nation? One attempt to answer this question produced surprising answers. Looking at fifty-one different indicators, the most representative state was Kansas, followed by Oregon and Delaware. Isolating just economic variables, Iowa was the most representative, followed by Oregon and Georgia.[44]

The key point here is that the states are not just fifty varieties of vanilla. They differ geographically, demographically, culturally, and economically. All of this adds up to the realization that the people in the different states have somewhat different political and social values—different civil societies. Indeed, these contrasts may be even more apparent today than they were a generation or two ago. To some extent, sorting may contribute to this. And the political stalemate often evident at the national level because of the split in power between the two major parties means states, where because of sorting usually one party is in control, are left with greater latitude to pursue their own policy agendas on many issues. Just like nature, policymaking abhors a vacuum and the states have been willing and politically able to fill that vacuum. As the *Wall Street Journal* observed, "with gridlock in Washington, lobbyists turn to statehouses." And they do so because that is where many of the important policy decisions are being made today.[45]

With red and blue states pursuing different policy agendas, we are likely to see very different policies from one state to another—much like we saw in

Nevada and Utah. As one federalism expert recently noted, "Policy debates that previously played out primarily at the national stage are increasingly devolving to state capitols, resulting in a patchwork of policies and an increasingly fragmented federalism."[46]

"Meanwhile," says Bill Bishop, "in states and cities where the Big Sort has resulted in increasingly larger majorities, there has been an explosion of innovation and legislation. Federal leadership has been replaced by a wild display of federalism, as like-minded communities put their beliefs into law."[47] Some states, notably Kansas and North Carolina, have adopted conservative policies, while others such as California and Illinois have moved to a liberal agenda.

We are likely to see further divergences in state policies, as more states fall under one political party's control. For the past decade we have had more states with unified control of government (that is, the governor, the state senate, and the state house all controlled by the same party) than at any time since 1962. After the 2014 election, the number of unified state governments declined from a historic high of thirty-eight to twenty-nine (thirty if we were to count Nebraska, which is officially nonpartisan but in practice is a unified Republican government). After the 2018 election, the number of unified states was thirty-six, more than 70 percent of all states. Figure 1.1 shows these trends since 1960.

In 1960, 63 percent of the states operated under unified government; in 1962 the figure reached 65 percent (thirty-two states). But over the next forty

Figure 1.1   Number of States with Unified Government, 1960–2018

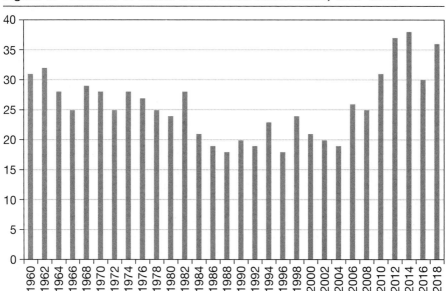

years there was a steady decline in the number of states with unified government, as southern states and some northeastern states began the slow process of partisan realignment. Fewer than half of the states experienced unified government in any given electoral cycle between 1984 and 2006. In other words, divided government became the norm. Starting around 2006, however, a new and dramatic trend occurs. There is a clear increase in the percentage of states with unified government.

And it is not simply that states are now more apt to have unified governments. In many states the majority party enjoys unchallenged dominance. In January 2020, Democrats controlled over 85 percent of the state legislative seats in Hawaii and Rhode Island, while the Republicans held at least 80 percent of the seats in each chamber in Idaho and Wyoming. The proportion of legislative chambers in which one party dominates is very high today.[48] For example, in 2019, the majority party held at least 60 percent of the seats in both chambers of the legislature in at least thirty-one states—over two-thirds of the seats in both chambers in eighteen states. Although party competition can still be found in some states, many clearly tilt heavily in one party's favor. Given that Republicans dominate in some states while the Democrats are in clear control in others, we can expect contrasting approaches to governance to emerge. And that is exactly what we have seen in the past few years.

Meanwhile, as more and more states are controlled by one party (unified government), we see a different situation at the national level. Table 1.2 shows the trends. Over the past three decades, we have experienced divided government at the national level much more. In ten of the fifteen biennial periods, divided government was the norm. The only exceptions are the 1993–1994 biennium (the first two years of the Clinton administration), four and a half years during the George W. Bush years, the first two years of the Obama administration, and the first two years of the Trump presidency. In other words, in a thirty-year period, the national government had a unified regime for about ten and a half years. Divided government has been the norm, existing over 65 percent of the time.

It is the combination of divided national government and increased unified state governments that makes the contemporary period one in which states do indeed matter, and why citizens need to be aware of it. Furthermore, as table 1.2 shows, the number of unified Republican (GOP) states and the number of unified Democratic states shifts over time (see columns 4 and 5). There have been many more Republican-controlled states since 2011. Finally, it is worth noting that when there is unified government at the national level, the "out party"—the party not in control at the national level—always gains more unified states when the unified national regime collapses (see column 6). This is another important point about why states matter; they serve as the source for rebuilding the out party. We will have more to say about this in subsequent chapters.

Table 1.2. Unified and Divided Governments in a Federal System, 1991–2020

Years	The national government	Total number of unified states	Unified GOP states	Unified Dem. states	Out-party pickup at state level
1991–1992	DIVIDED	18	3	15	
1993–1994	*Dem. Unified*	21	3	18	
1995–1996	DIVIDED	23	15	8	+12 GOP
1997–1998	DIVIDED	19	13	6	
1999–2000	DIVIDED	23	14	9	
2001–2002	DIVIDED*	21	13	8	
2003–2004	*GOP Unified*	16	10	6	
2005–2006	*GOP Unified*	20	12	8	
2007–2008	DIVIDED	25	10	15	+7 Dem
2009–2010	*Dem Unified*	26	9	17	
2011–2012	DIVIDED	32	21	11	+12 GOP
2013–2014	DIVIDED	36	24	12	
2015–2016	DIVIDED	29	22	7	
2017–2018	*GOP Unified*	34	26	8	+7 Dem
2019–2020	DIVIDED	36	21	15	

*For the first four months of the 2001–2002 cycle, Republicans held unified government, from late January until May 2001. On May 24, 2001, Vermont Senator Jeffords changed his party affiliation from Republican to Independent. This party switch effectively changed Senate party control from Republican to Democrat, thus ending the four-month period of unified Republican government. The remainder of the cycle (twenty months) was a period of divided government.

Source: Calculations by authors.

THE FEDERAL GOVERNMENT AND THE FUTURE

There is little doubt that the federal budget will be under enormous pressure for the foreseeable future. Of the major economic powers in the world (the Group of Twenty [G20]), the United States currently has the fourth-highest debt to gross domestic product (GDP) ratio. The nonpartisan Congressional Budget Office estimates that over the next ten years the federal debt will reach more than $28 trillion and the national debt-to-GDP ratio will be greater than at any time since the end of World War II.[49] Moreover, as the baby boom generation retires, federal budget obligations to social insurance programs like Medicare and Social Security mean that in the absence of substantial structural changes to those programs the debt will necessarily increase, putting even greater pressure on the federal budget. One of the implications for the states is that they are likely to experience a decline in federal aid to programs outside of those associated with health care. In other words, in the future states are likely to have to deal with more problems by relying only on their own financial resources.

This is not going to be a painless transition. One option for state policy-makers will be to increase taxes—almost never a popular option among the voting public. Another choice will be to cut back or completely eliminate some programs. In some cases, this means eliminating programs relied on heavily by the poor and most vulnerable segments of society, another option that the public usually resists. A third alternative will be for states to try innovative—some might say "radical"—solutions by drastically changing the way that services are provided and the manner in which costs are borne. Major changes to education, corrections, welfare, and transportation can be expected. For the American states, the next decade will be a time of significant changes. Those changes will not look the same from one state to another. But change is nothing new to the states.

A NEED FOR CITIZEN AWARENESS

Sometimes state governments fail their citizens. Ask the people of Flint, Michigan, who learned in late 2015 that their water was tainted. To be fair, it appears that all levels of government—local, state, and federal—had a hand in the tragedy that resulted in over six thousand children being exposed to lead poisoning due to a severely contaminated water supply.

But the role of Michigan state officials is central to the story. Under state authority, the governor had appointed an emergency manager of Flint who then authorized the switch in the municipal water source that resulted in the contamination problem. Complaints from Flint residents and warnings from a local pediatrician and a Virginia Tech civil engineer who tested the water went unheeded by city and state officials. Ultimately, several managers in the Michigan Department of Environmental Quality resigned or were dismissed. The governor issued apologies for the state's role in creating this crisis. Petitions to recall the governor circulated.

State governments make a multitude of decisions that affect their residents. Sometimes their actions—or inactions—can have serious long-term consequences. As one observer pointed out, "State and local governments have a huge influence on citizens' daily lives. They spend tax dollars. They decide how school operate and what constitutes a crime. And yet, few people seem to care these days."[50]

A survey conducted at Johns Hopkins University during the 2018 political campaign (when most states held elections for state legislature and state-wide offices) found that about half of those surveyed did not know what was the largest expenditure in the state budget or whether the state had a bicameral or unicameral legislature. Over one-third did not know the name of their governor. One of the researchers lamented, "It's a bit discouraging to discover how little citizens know about the states that govern them."[51]

Part of the problem is that media attention to state and local politics is not what it used to be. The traditional business model for media outlets like local newspapers became unsustainable, and many of them reduced the size of their reporting staff or went out of business altogether. Across the states, the number of full-time statehouse reporters was cut by more than 35 percent in a fifteen-year period.[52]

These changes create problems for our political system because it is essential that citizens pay attention to what their state officials are doing in order to be able to hold those officials accountable for their actions.[53] Unfortunately, accountability at the state level appears to be waning. For example, about 40 percent of state legislators do not face competition in the general election. And even if there is an opposing candidate, only a small percentage of races are truly competitive. Furthermore, voters in such elections appear to be remarkably ill-informed. Less than half of citizens know which party controls their state legislature. Voters also appear to choose state legislative candidates not on the basis of state or local issues but on the basis of their reaction to the president's performance.[54] If state legislators are being held accountable for anything at all, it is for things the national government may have done, not what they did at the state level.[55]

Part of our task in writing this book is to make the case that states matter as governing institutions. If we are convincing in this argument, perhaps the reader will recognize that all of us as citizens have an obligation to pay closer attention to those institutions and to hold them accountable.

In the remainder of this book we discuss some key areas in which states matter and ways in which changes have occurred. In chapter 2, we start at the beginning by discussing the adoption of the U.S. Constitution, the establishment of the federal system, and the continual tug between national and state influences on policymaking. We will also see how federalism has played out differently in other countries. Some of the most important and least understood aspects of state governments are their fiscal systems. That is, how they raise revenue and decide how to spend it. State fiscal systems is a complicated topic, but one that is critical for students and citizens of the states to grasp. We tackle this crucial topic in chapter 3. Budgets fundamentally define what a state can and cannot do in terms of policy. State budgets also have a significant impact on what local governments can achieve.

Chapter 4 examines how the basic structures of state government developed and makes the case for why these governments are important in specific policy arenas. While states are clearly constrained by the U.S. Constitution, U.S. Supreme Court decisions, and actions by the president, the Congress, and the federal agencies, there are plenty of areas in which states have authority to chart their own courses.

As mentioned earlier, states face major challenges in the immediate future. Much of the burden to meet these challenges falls on the institutions of state government—the executive, legislative, and judicial branches. Chapter 5 demonstrates how these instruments of state government, which were so inadequate sixty years ago, are much better prepared to take on increased responsibilities today. The overall capacity of the states to govern effectively is much greater today than two generations ago.

In chapter 6 we make the case that states are significant policymakers in many areas to impact Americans' daily lives. For example, state governments make most of the relevant decisions about publicly funded schools, at both the K–12 level and higher education. Often states are out in front of the national government in developing innovative, imaginative solutions to public problems. In some cases, they are way ahead of the national government. And in many instances, the variation in public policy from one state to another is substantial and impactful.

Chapter 7 focuses on the role of local governments in the United States, and the relationship between local governments and their state governments. That relationship is increasingly strained, especially for larger cities, in many states because of the vast gulf in partisanship and problems between them and the surrounding rural areas.

One of the ways that states matter most is in the electoral arena. Unfortunately, this is not often appreciated by the general public, except when incredibly close contests expose the reality. Chapter 8 provides an explanation of the critical role states play in national electoral politics. We also discuss the various instruments of direct democracy that play a critical role in some state policymaking but that are nonexistent at the national level. Some of the innovative policies discussed in chapter 6 are driven by the referendum and initiative processes that exist in many states. We also discuss the important topic of redistricting and the nature of partisan gerrymandering in the states.

Finally, in chapter 9, we conclude with an assessment of how the world of state government and politics is changing and why states will remain important for the foreseeable future—that is, why states matter.

2

States and the Federal System

States matter because:

- ★ They are an essential part of the federal system.
- ★ They still have primary responsibility for policymaking in many issue areas.
- ★ They employ more government workers than the national government.
- ★ They have authority to define the nature of local government operations.
- ★ Citizens look to the states when there is a stalemate at the national level.
- ★ They provide a political refuge for the party not in control at the national level.

IN THE SPRING OF 2016 in North Carolina, a skirmish broke out between city, state, and national government over "the bathroom bill." It is a story that touches several of the important themes of this book, including the relationship between local and state governments, the tension inherent in federalism, and the polarizing effect of many issues in today's politically charged environment.

The story began on February 22, when hundreds of citizens showed up to a Charlotte city council meeting. On the agenda was a proposed change to the city's existing nondiscrimination ordinance; the change would extend protections against discrimination to lesbian, gay, bisexual, and transgender (LGBT) individuals. Included in the protections would be a specific stipulation that a transgender individual had the right to use the bathroom of the sex with which they identified, not necessarily the sex to which they were assigned at birth. While there were a variety of protections provided in the proposed amendment, it was this particular policy aspect that drew the most attention—so much so that the ordinance (and subsequent legislative reaction) became known as "the bathroom bill."

As reported in the state's largest newspaper, "After more than three hours of impassioned public comment . . . Charlotte City Council approved new legal protections for gay, lesbian and transgender people—a decision that will likely provoke a battle with the General Assembly, which could nullify the city's historic vote."[1] Indeed, within a matter of weeks the North Carolina state legislature (officially known as the General Assembly) acted. As one newspaper account held, "In a one-day specially convened session Wednesday, North Carolina's legislature passed a sweeping law that reverses a Charlotte ordinance . . . [and] also nullified local ordinances around the state that would have expanded protections for the LGBT community."[2] The bill was designated as House Bill 2 (HB2) and was signed by the governor almost immediately after its passage by the legislature on March 23. Essentially, HB2 reaffirmed the statewide definition of classes of people who are protected from discrimination. That definition did not include sexual orientation. The state law under HB2 prevented local governments from establishing their own, more inclusive standards. In other words, the state of North Carolina not only nullified the actions of the City of Charlotte, it prohibited all local governments in North Carolina from passing similar ordinances.

On May 4, 2016, the national government intervened, with the U.S. Justice Department (under President Obama's administration) announcing that it considered HB2 a violation of the 1964 Civil Rights Act. The Justice Department informed North Carolina governor Pat McCrory that unless the law was rescinded, North Carolina stood to lose millions—perhaps hundreds of millions—of dollars in federal funding.[3] Four days later, the governor sued the U.S. Justice Department, arguing that the federal agency had exceeded its authority because the U.S. Congress had never passed a law extending civil rights protections to transgender individuals.[4] "It's the federal government being a bully," exclaimed Governor McCrory. The U.S. Justice Department responded that same day with a countersuit, saying the North Carolina law required "public agencies to follow a facially discriminatory policy."[5] Several days later, the U.S. Departments of Justice and Education sent letters to public school districts in all fifty states arguing that transgendered individuals were protected under the federal 1964 Civil Rights Act and providing guidance on how to implement these protections as they apply to public school bathrooms. By May, eleven states had filed legal briefs in support of North Carolina's challenge to the national government.[6]

Furthermore, a number of businesses and organizations announced they would cancel plans to expand their operations in North Carolina as a protest against HB2. The Associated Press estimated the economic impact of the threatened boycotts over the next decade to be more than $3 billion.[7] Amid these concerns, the legislature repealed HB2 and replaced it with a less sweeping version (HB 142) by April 2017. Meanwhile, with the inauguration of President Trump in January 2017, the U.S. Department of Justice was no longer under the authority of the Obama administration. By February 2017, the Trump administration's Department of Justice dropped the federal lawsuit against the state of North Carolina.

This story highlights several features of today's domestic policymaking environment in the United States. First, it demonstrates the tension that often exists between local governments and state governments. This strain is especially apparent between large cities, which are often progressive in social policy, and state legislatures, which are often more conservative. One thing that is clear, however, is that the state does indeed have the legal authority to void local government rules, as HB2 does, *unless that action by the state itself violates federal law*. In other words, while there are often political disagreements between local and state governments, the tension is almost always resolved in favor of the state. Local governments are created by the state and are therefore subject to the authority of the state. In the last few years, we have seen numerous instances of the tension between local ordinances and state law; indeed, we have seen many cases in which state legislatures voided the actions of local governments. To cite just one example for now: between 2015 and 2016, four counties in Iowa enacted local ordinances that would raise the minimum wage to at least $10 an hour in those counties. By 2017, the Iowa legislature passed a bill to preempt local governments from setting minimum wage above the state minimum wage. The bill was signed into law by the governor, thus voiding the higher minimum wages authorized by the four counties.

Over the past decade, state preemption of local laws has become more prevalent in many states. Some states have been especially active in preempting local laws involving the minimum wage, environmental regulations, immigration, gun control, and civil rights. We will discuss this phenomenon in greater detail in chapter 7.

A second feature is that contemporary policymaking in the United States is often intertwined with partisan and ideological considerations. With a Democratic administration at the national level in 2016, and a Republican state government (the governorship and both chambers of the North Carolina General Assembly were held by Republicans during this period), and with state and national elections to occur later in 2016, the "bathroom bill" issue was quickly politicized. Later, the 2016 election of a Republican president meant that the U.S. Department of Justice dropped its lawsuit against the state of North Carolina. And two years after that, the election of 2018 brought a new policy dynamic to the state, as a Democrat was chosen governor in North Carolina, thus ending unified Republican control of the government.

Finally, the issue became defined as a federalism matter. The state of North Carolina asserted that it had the right to determine whether LGBT individuals should be a protected class, while the national government under the Obama administration claimed that the federal Civil Rights Act is the prevailing authority, arguing that HB2 violates federal law and should not stand. This is far from the only instance in which a state or states have confronted the national government lately. Recent headlines such as "11 States Will Challenge Trump's New Immigration Executive Order in Court"; "Tennessee Set to Sue Federal Government over Refugee Resettlement"; "California Challenges Federal Preemption of Meal and Rest Break Laws"; and "As States Take the Lead to Address Drug Costs, Federal Action Follows"[8] are examples.

On matters of gun control, worker's rights, health care policy, climate change, immigration, abortion, and many other issues, states—at least many states—are increasingly assertive. As a legal scholar has aptly observed, "Federalism today is front-page news."[9]

A vivid illustration is the reaction of some state governments to the passage of the Patient Protection and Affordable Care Act (also known as the ACA, or "Obamacare"), passed by Congress in 2010. Idaho is a case in point. In 2011, the state legislature passed House Bill 117, which stated:

> The Legislature of the state of Idaho, therefore, on behalf of the citizens of this state and to secure the blessings of liberty, hereby asserts its legitimate authority to interpose between said citizens and the federal government, when it has exceeded its constitutional authority and declares that the state shall not participate in and considers void and of no effect the ACA.[10]

Supporters of the Idaho bill contended that states have the authority to nullify laws passed by the national government. This argument for "interposition and nullification" has been around since the adoption of the U.S. Constitution. It is, in effect, an interpretation of federalism that gives primacy to states' rights. While the U.S. Supreme Court has never accepted the "nullification" doctrine, the phrase is resurrected from time to time. In 2011 and 2012, it was in the news often, as "Obamacare" nullification bills were introduced in more than a dozen state legislatures. Attorneys general in twenty-six states filed a lawsuit challenging the law, and three governors vowed to block its implementation in their states.[11] Eventually the U.S. Supreme Court upheld the core component of the law, affirming that the national government did indeed have the authority to enforce the new health care law.[12] But the Court struck down the federal mandate that the states must extend Medicaid health care insurance to their citizens to continue receiving Medicaid funds. As of June 2019, fourteen states still declined to expand their own state programs, constituting a milder form of resistance.[13]

Currently, the degree of political polarization in the United States is at historic levels. The effect on federal–state relations is substantial, leading scholars to coin new terms such as "partisan federalism" and "vertical polarization" in an effort to explain the current intergovernmental environment.

THE "ENDLESS ARGUMENT"

One cannot talk about the role of the states without talking about federalism. Federalism is defined as "a political system in which power and authority are divided between two or more levels of government."[14] That is a pretty imprecise definition because federalism is a pretty imprecise arrangement. What does it mean to say "authority is divided between levels of government?" Divided in what proportion to which level: 50/50, 80/20, 20/80? Is authority divided differently for different policy areas, so that the division is different on transportation policy compared to welfare policy? These and similar questions have been around since the debates over the drafting and adoption of the U.S. Constitution. And here is the key point: the questions are never resolved. As John Donahue wrote in *Disunited States*, "The Framers at Philadelphia launched not only a nation, but an appropriately endless argument over the proper balance between federal and state authority—an argument whose intensity ebbs and flows and whose content evolves, but which is never really settled."[15] One of the reasons it is "never really settled" is that federalism involves political consequences. On many issues, the policy outcome is very much a matter of which level of government—state or federal—is making the policy decision. And since the regime (conservative or liberal) in control at the national level is often the opposite of the regime (liberal or conservative) at the state level, the policy outcome will be different at the national level than at the state level. As one scholar notes, "[F]ederalism plays an essential role as a battleground for all important American political conflicts . . . because it affects who wins and who loses a fight over the use of government power."[16]

Because arguments about federalism—over which level should have governing authority on any particular issue—are usually about policy preferences, both conservatives and progressives will argue for the level of government most consistent with the conservative or progressive policy view at any given point in time. In other words, we argue for states' rights when it is convenient, and we also argue for a more centralized national authority when it is convenient. Principled discussions about the best federal structural arrangements are rare. For so many today, the end justifies the means. Many scholars today refer to this as "fair-weather federalism."[17] Polarized political parties have exacerbated this situation, with the Republican Party staking out policy positions that are strikingly different from those espoused by Democrats.

Federalism is always a complicated arrangement. It is further muddled in the United States because the division or sharing of power involves fifty subnational (regional) units. Whether they are called states, provinces, cantons, or *Länder* (the German word for "lands," in this case meaning states), no other federal system in the world has as many regional units as the United States. Australia has but six; Canada ten. There are thirteen states in Malaysia, while Germany has sixteen, Brazil has twenty-six, and India has twenty-nine.[18] The only countries besides the United States with more than thirty regional governments are Mexico (thirty-one) and Nigeria (thirty-six).

Given the complexity of federal systems, it is no surprise that relatively few countries adopt this arrangement. There are some two hundred sovereign nations in the world today and only about twenty-five of them have a federal system. Federal systems are relatively common among countries with a large geographic size (e.g., Argentina, Australia, Canada, Brazil, India, the United States) or with a large population (e.g., Brazil, Germany, India, Mexico, Nigeria, Pakistan, the United States). Federal systems are found in six of the eight geographically largest and five of the eight most populous countries. The ways that these federal systems operate differ from one another depending on a whole host of variables including size, ethnic and racial diversity, history, and economy. And some are young and not necessarily stable federations at this point.

One recent study maintains that if we impose some conditions such as stability and the presence of truly democratic elections, the number of functioning federal systems is only eleven.[19] Federal systems are difficult to maintain because of the chronic tension between the central (national-level) government and the peripheral (state, regional, provincial) governments. As one federal systems scholar puts it, "Characteristic of federal systems is the simultaneous existence of powerful motives for constituent units to be united (for certain shared purposes) and their deep-rooted desires for self-government (for other purposes)."[20] To put it another way, there are both centrifugal (pulling away from the center) and centripetal (pulling toward the center) tendencies. Such propensities vary across federal systems and over time or by policy area within a particular federal system.

While there are now about twenty-five federal systems worldwide, most emerged only after World War II. According to one authority, there were only four countries with true federal systems of government prior to the twentieth century.[21] The oldest continuous federal system in the world is the United States; inaugurated in 1789, it celebrated its 230th anniversary in 2020. But the federal system in the United States today hardly looks like the federal system of 1789. Of course, the United States itself hardly looks like the country of two centuries ago, as table 2.1 makes clear. We have evolved from a small, rural, and agrarian nation of four million people and thirteen states to a sprawling, urban, and economically complex country with fifty states. The population is almost one hundred times greater; the number of states has quadrupled; the shift from rural to urban and now to suburban locations has been dramatic. The entire population of the United States in 1789 was less than today's population of Oregon. The 1790 census indicated that almost 20 percent of the enumerated population was black (of which 8 percent were free and 92 percent were slaves). The remainder of the enumerated population was almost entirely of European descent.[22] American Indians were not included as a category in the first census, but probably numbered at least six hundred thousand, mostly in the territory beyond the settled borders of the thirteen states.[23]

One quick measure of the magnitude of change is travel time. Consider, for example, a trip from one end of the original country to the other; basically,

Table 2.1. The Evolution of a Federal System

Date	National population	Percent rural population	Population of largest cities	Number of states	Constitutional amendments
1790	4 million	95	33,181 (New York) 28,552 (Philadelphia)	13	1–10 (1791)
1860	31 million	80	813,559 (New York) 565,529 (Philadelphia)	33	13–15 (1865–1870)
1910	92 million	44	3 cities over 1 million*	46	16–19 (1913–1920)
1960	179 million	30	5 cities over 1 million**	50	23–26 (1960–1971)
2020	334 million	19	10 cities over 1 million***	50	None since 1992

*New York, Chicago, Philadelphia (in descending order of population)
**New York, Chicago, Los Angeles, Philadelphia, Detroit
***New York, Los Angeles, Chicago, Houston, Philadelphia, Phoenix, San Antonio, San Diego, Dallas, San Jose
Source: U.S. Census Bureau, various tables.

that would have been from Boston to Savannah (note that Atlanta did not yet exist; it wasn't founded until 1837). Today, by air travel, it is about a two-and-a-half-hour flight between these two cities. In 1789, if a person owned a horse and chose to ride from Savannah to Boston, he could expect the journey to take at least three weeks, if the weather was decent and the roads were passable. The fastest mode of travel would have been by ship, and with luck could be accomplished in five or six days. It would also be quite expensive. Obviously, most people did not travel much at all. Each community, and certainly each state, was something of a world unto itself. This bears no resemblance at all to the world we know today.

Table 2.1 represents five eras in the United States. These roughly half-century intervals were characterized by significant constitutional changes. Indeed, all but six of the amendments to the U.S. Constitution occurred during the periods represented in table 2.1. The federal relationship has changed as well—a theme of much of the rest of this chapter.

THE U.S. CONSTITUTION AND THE ROOTS OF FEDERALISM

Conflict and controversy are endemic to federal systems. Recall that under the Articles of Confederation the states were widely understood to be sovereign and functionally independent of one another. The confederation was little more than a treaty among thirteen sovereign entities. But to say the states were sovereign does not necessarily mean they were effective or powerful. It was their ineffectiveness that led some to call for a formal meeting in Philadelphia to discuss ways to salvage the system. Nonetheless, giving up some portion of their state's sovereignty was not something most did easily. Even with the serious problems the nation experienced under the Articles, there were many citizens and political elites in the states who did not want to relinquish any sovereign power to another, "higher" government.

At the Constitutional Convention there was controversy, disagreement, and different interpretations of the "proper" relationship between the national government and the states. And many of those disagreements and differences of interpretation have never been resolved. This is a core characteristic of American federalism.

The emphasis in contemporary high school history and civics courses is on the debates, the various plans, and the compromises that resulted in the drafting of the Constitution. But we should remember that not all who participated in the Philadelphia convention agreed with those compromises. When it came time to affix their names to the document, three people in the room at Independence Hall refused to sign. All were notables in their day and are still familiar even in our time: George Mason and Edmund Randolph of Virginia and Elbridge Gerry of Massachusetts. At least four delegates left the convention in protest of the proceedings and nine others left early, claiming they were needed at home.

Another twenty-one individuals who were invited to attend declined to show up at all—including the entire Rhode Island delegation. Some were simply unable to attend, but others assuredly boycotted the convention because they were opposed to any effort to reduce the independence of the states. Patrick Henry was among those who was invited but refused to attend, later claiming he declined because "I smelt a rat."[24]

Controversy certainly did not end with the convention's adjournment. While some states, like Delaware, ratified the new form of government almost immediately, others took convincing. Recall that the mechanism for adoption of the new constitution was not the various state legislatures, but ratifying conventions to be held in each state. For our purpose, this is significant for two reasons. First, it was assumed that a number of state legislatures would be opposed to the new government because it clearly diminished the power of the states. And as the key decision-making units in the states under the Articles, the state legislatures would principally be diminished by the new system. Second, under the Articles, the state legislature was in effect the government of the state. In other words, the legislature represented the state as a sovereign entity. In contrast, the ratifying conventions could be thought of as representing the people of the state. For many, this is a crucial distinction.

From the outset, then, there was philosophical disagreement as to whether the Constitution was adopted by the people or by the states.[25] To reiterate, at its core the question comes down to the nature of the ratification assemblies called in the various states to consider and act upon the newly proposed constitution. The Federalist argument was that the delegates to the various ratification assemblies represented the people of the various states, and thus it was the people—the citizens themselves—who chose to discard the government under the Articles of Confederation and to adopt a new government with a more robust national presence.

The Antifederalist argument was that the ratification assemblies represented the sovereign states, not the people directly. Because the states themselves were the sovereign units under the Articles, only the states had the authority to accept, reject, or modify the conditions of the proposed arrangement under the Constitution. In this view, the Constitution was a compact among sovereign states. And because a compact is little more than a voluntary association, any state that agrees to the compact has the right to disassociate when it feels the policies of the compact government—in this case the federal government—are not in the interests of the aggrieved state.

Thus, the conflicting views over whether "the people" or "the sovereign states" are the true adopters of the Constitution and therefore of the new federal arrangement are at the heart of the "states' rights" argument and a key rationale in the argument for "interposition and nullification." Typical of this reasoning is the statement adopted by one state legislature in 1814: "Whenever the national compact is violated, and the citizens of this state are oppressed by cruel and unauthorized laws, this Legislature is bound to interpose its power, and wrest from the oppressor his victim."[26]

While we usually associate such a sentiment with the southern states, this statement is actually from a report of the Massachusetts state legislature in reaction to an embargo placed on American ships by President James Madison. Similar expressions of the right to interposition (and nullification) can be found among other New England states over the embargo and over the efforts to draft state militia during the War of 1812. It is worth pointing out the irony here; these northern states were using the principles of interposition and nullification against the actions of Presidents Thomas Jefferson and James Madison—the authors of the original drafts of the Kentucky and Virginia Resolutions. By late 1814 the dissatisfaction with the embargo and the War of 1812 (1812–1815) led representatives of several New England states to meet to discuss their grievances. This was the Hartford Convention, which met in secret for several weeks during the winter of 1814–1815. Most of the Hartford delegates were members of the Federalist Party, so it is surprising that both nullification and secession were apparently discussed.

Discussion of the idea of nullification usually begins with the Kentucky and Virginia Resolutions (1798–1799), drafted by Thomas Jefferson and James Madison, respectively. The state legislatures of Kentucky and Virginia, controlled by Antifederalists, adopted these statements in response to the Alien and Sedition Acts of 1798, which were passed into law by the Federalist Party–controlled U.S. Congress. These laws were viewed by many as a severe restriction on the right to free speech. Alarmed by what they considered the national government's unconstitutional usurpation of power, the Kentucky and Virginia state legislatures argued they had the authority—indeed, the duty—to resist the repressive tendencies of the national government on behalf of their state's citizens. In other words, a state had the right to "intervene" between its citizens and the national government to protect the rights of its citizens. Kentucky further argued that it had the right to nullify the federal action, while the Virginia resolution did not go quite this far.[27] These sentiments express a thread that runs through the fabric of American history.

The words "interposition" and "nullification" appear in the public discourse surrounding the Kentucky and Virginia Resolutions (1798–1799); the New England resistance (c. 1805–1815); the "nullification crisis" of 1832 involving John C. Calhoun, South Carolina, and the tariff laws; the period immediately prior to the Civil War; the desegregation and civil rights period (c. 1954–1965); and the reaction in some quarters recently to the Real ID Act of 2005 and the Affordable Care Act (2005–present).

Because the terms have reappeared in response to several issues recently, it is worth explaining the terms in their historical context. The terms "interposition" and "nullification" are often used interchangeably, but they do not have the same meaning. As used by Madison and others of his time, "interposition" meant a state should intervene on behalf of its citizens when the national government exceeded its constitutional authority. Basically, this was an oversight function, a calling of attention to an act or policy that deserved resistance or questioning. Moreover, "interposition" was viewed as a collective endeavor, something that several or many states would undertake, and together they might exert sufficient pressure to get the national government to reconsider or amend the policy in question. Within this context, then, interposition is a legitimate action; whether it is successful in getting the egregious act repealed is another matter. It is a procedure by which states can "converse" and perhaps bargain with the national government. Political scientist John Dinan speaks of the "various ways that states can 'talk back' to federal officials," which we think captures the spirit of interposition as conceived by Madison.[28] Thus the Kentucky and Virginia Resolutions called upon other states to join them in resisting the congressional laws. But no other state did.

The act of voiding or rejecting the application of a congressional or presidential act or federal judicial decree within a specific state is "nullification." It is an act of defiance meant to nullify a national policy within the confines of a particular state. Nullification has been consistently rejected by the federal courts as unconstitutional.[29] This does not preclude the term from finding its way into public discourse. One 2015 news story claimed that more than two hundred bills were introduced in state legislatures "aiming to nullify regulations and laws coming out of Washington, D.C."[30] While full "nullification" may not be a realistic option for the states, they do have a handful of other options to divert, blunt, or otherwise circumvent the full letter of the national law.[31]

THE EVOLUTION OF AMERICAN FEDERALISM

While "interposition" and "nullification" are instruments that have been argued over since the Constitution's ratification, we should not lose sight of the fact they are remedial mechanisms designed to correct a perceived transgression on the part of the national government vis-à-vis the state governments. The period surrounding the Constitutional Convention and the ratification process demonstrate considerable resistance by Antifederalists because they feared what they saw as the centralizing tendencies in the document.[32]

A half-century ago, Cecelia Kenyon described the Antifederalists as "men of little faith." She was not referring to their religious attitudes but to the fact that they were, from the outset, distrustful of the constitutional arrangement and were unconvinced that under it the states would be able to hold the national government in check. Their argument rested on "four great pillars of consolidation."[33] The four features of the Constitution that most concerned these defenders of the states were (1) the power of the national government to tax, (2) the power of the national government to raise and maintain a military force, (3) the necessary and proper clause at the end of Article I, Section 8, and (4) the national supremacy clause in Article VI. From the point of view of those who believed that the states were the essential sovereigns and preferred it that way, their fears that the Constitution provided for national consolidation were both real and eventually realized.

For the most part, the centralization process is slow and it is far from complete. Some historical events were instrumental in redefining the relationship between the national and state governments: the Civil War and the Great Depression are the two most obvious. Many other events or trends contributed to the changing relationship over 225 years. A list would include, at a minimum, the following.

1. The Supreme Court's adoption of the implied powers doctrine in 1819

The Antifederalists' concern that the "necessary and proper" clause could be a vehicle for the expansion of the role of the national government seems prescient with the U.S. Supreme Court's 1819 decision in the case of *McCulloch v. Maryland*.[34] As Cecelia Kenyon noted, "This was a clause so sweeping in its possible implications . . . that the Antifederalists could see no logical limit to the powers of the central government."[35]

The issue in *McCulloch* involved the authority of the national government to establish a national bank.[36] Creation of such a bank is not one of the specific enumerated powers of the national government stipulated in Article I, Section 8 of the Constitution; some states therefore argued that the creation of banks was a state power and not a power held by the national government.

Chief Justice John Marshall argued the "general government" (by which he means the national government) is a government of enumerated powers:

> But the question respecting the extent of the powers actually granted is perpetually arising, and will probably continue to arise so long as our system shall exist. In discussing these questions, the conflicting powers of the General and State Governments must be brought into view, and the supremacy of their respective laws, when they are in opposition, must be settled.[37]

Marshall went on to note that the enumerated powers are supported by a variety of actions and means that are not necessarily listed and, he noted, this is one of the ways in which the system established under the Constitution clearly differed from that under the Articles of Confederation:

> Among the enumerated powers, we do not find that of establishing a bank or creating a corporation. But there is no phrase in the instrument which, like the Articles of Confederation, excludes incidental or implied powers and which requires that everything granted shall be expressly and minutely described.[38]
>
> Let the end be legitimate, let it be within the scope of the Constitution, and all means which are appropriate, which are plainly adapted to that end, which are not prohibited, but consist with the letter and spirit of the Constitution, are Constitutional.[39]

The expansion of national powers through the implied powers doctrine did not occur on a grand scale immediately. But the precedent was established with *McCulloch* and this becomes critical almost a century later when one of the enumerated powers—the power to regulate interstate commerce—is broadly interpreted.

2. The Union victory in the Civil War and the passage of the Civil Rights Amendments

The victory of the Union over the Confederacy was essential to the maintenance of the federal system. Virtually by definition, a right to secede would reduce a federal system to a confederation. One immediate result of the Union victory was the nationalization of the rights of former slaves through the adoption of the Thirteenth, Fourteenth, and Fifteenth Amendments between 1865 and 1870. While these amendments were enforced during Reconstruction, the application of the Fourteenth and Fifteenth soon waned. By the end of the nineteenth century, a return to the "dual federalism" of the first half of the century was evident in such cases as *Plessy v. Ferguson* (1896) and *Williams v. Mississippi* (1898). Nonetheless they returned to prominence and became instrumental in redefining the federal relationship in the Civil Rights era of the mid-twentieth century. As one observer notes, "These amendments would become the instruments for a recasting of federal-state relations."[40]

3. The adoption of a broad interpretation of congressional authority to regulate interstate commerce

Since the close of the nineteenth century, one of the most important channels for the expansion of national power has been the interstate commerce clause. Article I, Section 8 of the Constitution says, in part, Congress has the power to regulate commerce "among the several states." Unlike many aspects of the Constitution, this particular power was not contested by Antifederalists.[41] Perhaps this was because they recognized the need for some regulation, given the disastrous situation under the Articles of Confederation.

The pivotal case for our purposes is *Wickard v. Filburn* (1942), in which the U.S. Supreme Court unanimously determined that economic activity that is not ostensibly interstate may nonetheless be regulated by Congress.[42] It marks the beginning of a period in which the Court gave free reign to congressional action in the name of regulating interstate commerce. Indeed, the Court found no limit to congressional authority to regulate via the interstate commerce clause until 1995.[43]

4. The adoption of the Sixteenth Amendment (1913) and the development of fiscal federalism

Earlier, we noted that Antifederalists were concerned about the centralizing effect of granting the national government the right to tax under Article I, Section 8 of the Constitution. Previously, under the Articles, the central government had no authority to tax. Many of the Framers, notably Alexander Hamilton, recognized a need for the new national government to be able to raise revenue on its own.

Although some opponents of the Constitution feared granting the national government such authority, the fact is that the states (and their local governments) exercised most of the taxing authority until well into the twentieth century. With the passage of the Sixteenth Amendment, creating an annual federal income tax, the fiscal dynamics begin to change. In particular, the development of fiscal federalism on a significant scale was not possible until the national government had a substantial and steady source of revenue through the income tax. Later we will discuss fiscal federalism in more detail, but now it is enough to point out that federal grants-in-aid give the national government considerable leverage in the policymaking arena. Some states recognized this early on and voiced concern about where this might lead. One federalism scholar pointed out that in 1947 a declaration by the Indiana state legislature stated that the legislature proposed to raise more revenue in Indiana to avoid the "trap" of federal aid-in-grants, "We propose henceforward to tax ourselves and take care of ourselves. We are fed up with subsidies, doles, and paternalism. We are no one's stepchild. We have grown up. We serve notice that we will resist Washington, D.C. adopting us."[44] That sentiment did not hold; in 2016 Indiana ranked fourteenth among the states in reliance on federal aid;

36 percent of the general revenue in Indiana was federal money transferred to the state.[45]

Federal aid represents about one-third of the general revenue for all states combined. The dependence on such fiscal aid varies by state, however, with some states relying much more on federal aid than others. Over 40 percent of the total state budget comes from federal aid in Mississippi, Louisiana, and New Mexico, while just over 20 percent of the Virginia, Hawaii, and Kansas budgets flow from the federal government.[46]

5. The adoption of the Seventeenth Amendment (1913) and direct primaries

In 2016, the Utah state legislature passed a resolution calling for the repeal of the Seventeenth Amendment.[47] Ratified at the height of the Progressive Reform era, this amendment mandates the direct popular election of U.S. senators. The Constitution originally stated (Article I, Section 3), "The Senate of the United States shall be composed of two Senators from each State, chosen by the Legislature thereof for six Years; and each Senator shall have one Vote." In the context of the role of the states in the new federal system, there are two important components to this provision. The first is that the states have an equal representation in the Senate. As Madison notes in *Federalist* 62, "The equal vote allowed to each State is at once a constitutional recognition of the portion of sovereignty remaining in the individual States, and an instrument for preserving that residuary sovereignty."[48]

The second point is the legislature of each state would select the U.S. senators. The Framers assumed that this would ensure that the states had some influence over Congress because the senators would be accountable to their state legislatures. Once the Seventeenth Amendment was ratified and direct elections of senators were in effect, the power of state legislatures to control their senators was removed.[49] Some see this as being of "transcendent importance to federalism" because it marked the abandonment of one of the key constitutional protections for the states.[50]

The call to repeal the Seventeenth Amendment was especially popular when the "Tea Party" movement emerged within the Republican Party around 2010. One of the key supporting organizations, the American Legislative Exchange Council (ALEC), an organization that drafts and offers conservative "model legislation" to Republican state legislators, declined to support the effort to repeal.[51] And a report by the Heritage Foundation, a bastion of the American conservative movement,[52] concluded that repealing the Seventeenth Amendment would have little real effect.[53] Moreover, direct election of the U.S. senators remains popular among the general public. So despite recent efforts, repeal of the amendment remains "quixotic."[54]

The Seventeenth Amendment was part of the agenda of the Progressive reform movement to weaken the state- and city-based political party organizations, which were seen as corrupt, undemocratic, and controlled by party bosses and machines. Another such reform was the direct primary, instituted in most states by 1915. Primary elections "stripped the parties of a critical source of power: control over nominations."[55] Control over who gets the party's nomination for the general election is an important power; if a small group or a single "boss" controls the nomination phase, they have the opportunity to influence the nominee's behavior once elected. The combined effect of direct primaries and the Seventeenth Amendment was to weaken the linkage between state party organizations and members of Congress.

6. The Great Depression and the development of national social welfare policy

Prior to the 1930s the domestic policy reach of the national government was quite limited. Until that point in time, the activities of the national government and the state governments did not often intersect. The history of U.S. federalism up to the 1930s is often described as "dual federalism" in which the national government had primary authority over foreign affairs and some regulation of economic activity and state governments had primary authority in other policy arenas. This is a generalization and not entirely accurate, but it is not far from the reality of the way things operated. It ended markedly, however, with the crushing effects of the Great Depression.

For those who did not live through the Great Depression of the 1930s, it is difficult to imagine the hardships it imposed. True, the recent "Great Recession" of 2007–2009 and its lingering effects for the next several years was a difficult time for citizens and governments, and is considered the most significant economic downturn in the United States in almost seventy years. But the Great Depression (1929–1939) was much worse. The stock market crash of October 1929 put the American economy into a years-long tailspin. Unemployment rates reached 25 percent (compared to under 10 percent in the recent Great Recession) and the decline in the domestic economy (GDP) was –25 percent (compared to –3.3 percent in the Great Recession). While fewer than one hundred banks failed in the Great Recession, over nine thousand banks went under during the Great Depression. The point is that the Great Depression resulted in economic devastation and social disruption of far greater magnitude than what we recently experienced. By 1931 and early 1932, state and local governments were struggling to cope. States were dramatically slashing their budgets. Illinois, Texas, and Vermont each cut their budgets by 25 percent; Arizona's was cut by an astounding 35 percent. Almost 20 percent of New Jersey's municipalities were bankrupt. Several southern states were on the verge of defaulting on their state debts.[56] Officials in many states were timid and often shortsighted in their response to the crisis, as historian James Patterson describes: "Legislators . . . often compounded problems with factionalism, mindless criticism, and deadly doses of partisan politics. The result before 1933 was a sadly unproductive record."[57]

It is on this basis that we must understand the actions of the national government under Franklin Roosevelt. Public administration scholar Martha Derthick saw this period as one that fundamentally changed the nature of federalism in the United States: "In response to a catastrophic economic collapse . . . [a] new constitutional law emerged after 1937 that swept away previous limits on Congress's power to regulate commerce and solidified its power to tax and spend for any purpose associated with the general welfare."[58] Patterson concurs: "The combination of national policy and depression forever transformed federal-state relations."[59]

7. The Civil Rights/Great Society Era (c. 1954–1968)

It is important to remember that it was just over fifty years ago, in 1963, that George Wallace, in his inaugural address as the newly elected governor of Alabama, said, "I draw the line in the dust and toss the gauntlet before the feet of tyranny and I say segregation now, segregation tomorrow, segregation forever."[60]

This period involved more than civil rights. But it was the drive to desegregate and expand the civil and voting rights of African Americans that led the national government into a more activist role in the domestic affairs of the states, unprecedented since Reconstruction (1865–1877). It is a period in which the Fourteenth and Fifteenth Amendments were rediscovered and reinvigorated. The *Brown v. Topeka Board of Education* (1954) school desegregation case, the use of federal troops by Presidents Eisenhower and Kennedy to enforce this court decision in southern cities such as Little Rock, Tuscaloosa, and Oxford, and the passage of landmark legislation such as the Civil Rights Act (1964) and the Voting Rights Act (1965) demonstrated a strong commitment by all branches of the national government to end the pernicious activities of both private citizens and public entities in the South.

The words "interposition" and "nullification" resurfaced during this time, as politicians in several southern states invoked the right of the state to disregard the actions of the Supreme Court and the Congress.[61] Within two years of the U.S. Supreme Court's decision in *Brown*, eight southern states adopted resolutions invoking interposition and declaring the Court's ruling to have no standing within their specific state.[62]

Beyond the civil rights question, this period found the national government, driven by an activist Congress, developing preemptive policies. As Joseph Zimmerman notes, "A revolution in national-subnational relations commenced in 1965 when the Congress enacted the first minimum standards preemption statute—the Water Quality Act of 1965. . . . Minimum standards statutes regulate private and subnational governmental activities."[63] What this means is that the national government sets standards that all states must meet or exceed; otherwise, the national government will take over the administrative or regulatory control of that policy area from the state. This allows Congress—and the federal bureaucracy to which Congress often delegates power—major policy influence in areas previously left to the states.

This was also a period in which fiscal federalism increased at warp speed. During the decade of the 1960s federal aid tripled, and it continued to grow at a rapid rate in the following decade. It was not just the amount of money distributed to subnational governments but the expansion in functional areas for which the money was intended. In 1960 there were only 132 federal grant programs available to state or local governments. By 1968 there were 387, and by 1978 there were almost five hundred separate and distinct grants.[64] The development of fiscal federalism as both a carrot and a stick to facilitate state compliance with expanding national goals was a defining feature of this period.

At the center of this active period was the U.S. Supreme Court. Writing about its role, Derthick stated, "It emerged as a reformer, and the institutions it chose to change were those of state governments."[65] This is an intriguing statement because it points to the fact that many states were slow to change and adapt to a new political and social environment. Many states were poorly funded and ineffectively administered. As we document in chapters 4 and 5, the capacities of states today are substantially greater than they were in 1960.

The Court, focusing on issues of equality of rights for American citizens, rendered transformative decisions involving school segregation, criminal justice and the rights of the accused, public school prayer, and the "one person, one vote" definition of voting equality. When one looks at the totality of the national effort—the activist role of the U.S. Supreme Court and the efforts on the part of Congress and the president to end segregation, guarantee individual rights, and expand the reach of minimal national standards through statute and fiscal federalism—this period stands out as one in which the fundamental character of federalism in the United States changed more than any other period except the New Deal.

8. The new century

Toward the end of the twentieth century much was being written about a rolling back of the national government's influence—a devolution in the federal relationship. There were certainly some signs pointing in that direction, as indicated by a study published in 1986 by two political scientists titled "The Resurgence of the States."[66]

One of the distinguishing features of Ronald Reagan's presidency (1981–1989) was an effort to slow the growth of federal domestic spending. In part, this effort focused on reducing state and local reliance on federal aid. As a result, federal grants to state and local governments declined as a percentage of GDP and as a percentage of total federal spending and in inflation-adjusted dollars.[67]

The landmark agreement between the GOP Congress and President Bill Clinton that restructured a key component of social welfare policy and shifted more control to states was another such sign. Numerous decisions by the Rehnquist Court that signaled a rethinking of the unfettered use of the interstate commerce clause as a rationale for congressional policymaking in traditionally state arenas is another. The election of a Republican president, George W. Bush—a former governor—coupled with a Republican-controlled Congress, led many to expect an administration sympathetic to a state-oriented version of federalism.

Whatever devolutionary momentum existed was stopped by the events of September 11, 2001. In response to 9/11, President Bush and the Congress pushed for a strong antiterrorism role for the national government in domestic policy. The Patriot Act (2001) and the Real ID Act (2005) were centerpieces of this centralization effort. Additionally, President Bush successfully pushed a major educational reform effort, the No Child Left Behind Act (2001), which broadened national control over what has always been viewed as a state function—public education.[68]

The Great Recession weakened the states further and, as we discuss in chapter 3, led to a substantial increase in the reliance on federal financial assistance for several years. The signature domestic policy of the first Obama administration, the Affordable Care Act, extended national policymaking over health insurance policy in dramatic ways. About half the states challenged the Congress' authority to establish an individual mandate to purchase health insurance. The Supreme Court's decision in this regard was much anticipated. The result, in a complex decision with multiple opinions, was a blow to state sovereign power in that the Court upheld the national government's authority to require such a mandate. The victory was not complete, however, as the Court also ruled that the national government did not have the power to force the states to expand Medicaid coverage. The tug of war still continues, with a different president in the White House, a stronger conservative majority on the U.S. Supreme Court, and a different partisan landscape in many states.

FEDERALISM TODAY

Beyond the health care issue, tension between the national government and the states remains high. Much of it is a result of the ideological polarization that currently exists between the two major political parties. For most of the Obama administration, Congress was gridlocked, unable to reach policy agreements. Over the course of the Obama years, Republicans made great strides in winning state elections and thus gaining control of more and more state legislatures and governorships. Consequently, federalism became viewed as a contest between a Democratic president and Republican-controlled state governments. In this sense, as David Brian Robertson points out, we can think of "American federalism as a political weapon," to be wielded as a call for a national standards or states' rights, depending on the issue and the issue position of the various players.

To put it another way, the tensions inherent in federalism are even greater in times of political polarization, especially so when the forces of polarization have captured different levels of government. When the Republicans control the national government policy apparatus, states with Democratic regimes will resist the policy proposals they view as most egregious. And when the Democrats control the national level, Republican-controlled states will do the same. That is the nature of federalism in a highly politicized and polarized environment. Today, these federal strains are especially evident in conflicts over policy approaches to climate change, poverty, immigration, abortion, and civil rights.

There are other variables in addition to party polarization. In chapter 1, we showed that the number of states with unified government is at a generational high. Meanwhile, at the national level we often experience divided government. Under those circumstances, states are likely to seek to exert greater policy control. This is true not just of governors and legislatures. One of the important stories in today's federalism is the emerging role of the state attorney general.

In 2012, Greg Abbott explained his job as the attorney general of the state of Texas as this: "I go to the office. I sue the federal government. Then I go home."[69] Indeed, between 2009 and 2016, Texas sued the Obama administration at least forty-eight times. Many other Republican state attorneys general also sued the Democratic administration during this time, largely over environmental rules and regulations, banking regulations, "bathroom bills," and the Affordable Care Act. After the election of Donald Trump as president, Democratic state attorneys general began using the same tactic. By mid-2019, California Attorney General Xavier Becerra had filed fifty lawsuits against the Trump administration. Massachusetts' attorney general, Democrat Maura Healey, filed almost as many. Lawsuits filed by coalitions of state attorneys general have grown substantially in number over the last ten years. While such multistate lawsuits are sometimes bipartisan (some Republican and some Democratic state attorneys general join together to present a legal challenge to a federal action), most of them involve the attorneys general from just one party. Recent research points out "the increasingly prominent role of AGs in national policy-making and governance in recent years, noting that AGs' activism has both intensified and become more partisan over time."[70]

The fact that we have experienced divided government at the national level also contributes to this trend. Divided government makes positive congressional action more difficult. Without a legislative majority to work with, presidents may seek to make public policy through executive action, directing an agency to carry out a specific action or issuing waivers.[71] In recent years, both President Obama and President Trump used executive orders to enact sweeping policies without congressional action. Under these circumstances, state attorneys general may test the legal parameters of such orders.

THE INHERENT TENSIONS WITHIN FEDERALISM

The federal system created under the U.S. Constitution is remarkably complex. It fashions a complicated structure with distinct yet overlapping executive, legislative, and judicial powers and two levels of government, each with a claim to sovereignty, or at least partial sovereignty. The structure, as created in Philadelphia, was new to the world. And because it was new and unfamiliar, there was room for competing interpretations. This was true in 1789 and it remains true today. Martha Derthick, an astute analyst of the American form of federalism, noted, "It is, however, a very confusing form of government, with authority widely diffused and obscurely allocated. And it requires much tending. Issues of intergovernmental relations consume a great deal of official attention, including that of the Supreme Court."[72] And, as we argue in chapter 8, it is a system that requires citizens to distinguish between the levels of government in elections—a requirement that some voters today seem to ignore. This is a particularly important point. Recent research shows an increasing "nationalization" of the public perception of government; media attention nowadays focuses mostly on the national government. If people pay attention to politics at all it is at the national level. As Daniel Hopkins recently wrote, "To ignore state and local politics is a costly omission, as it means ignoring the politics that elect the vast majority of officials in the United States as well as the policy areas where state and localities hold sway."[73]

Under the Constitution, the federation seeks to balance a number of values such as national interests and state interests, majority power and minority rights. Larry Gerston points out that two values our federal system constantly struggles to balance are liberty and equality.[74] Liberty is an expression of the freedom to pursue individual self-interest. It was a value emphasized by the Antifederalists, who feared the loss of liberty under a strong national government. Equality, or fairness, is a value best fostered by a central government that can guarantee uniformity of policy across the states. Finding the balance between these values is almost impossible; according to Gerston, "To the extent that government institutions promote liberty, the public policy rules are bound to differ from state to state. And to the extent that government institutions endorse equality, states are disallowed from behaving in ways unique to their individual existences. Therein lies a conundrum of American federalism."[75] The North Carolina "bathroom bill" discussed in the introduction to this chapter is a prime example of this conundrum.

Martha Derthick made a similar point, arguing that the primary tension is between "place-based groups" such as states and communities and the rights of individuals as guaranteed by the national constitution. She concluded that "one type of group—the place-based group that federalism had honored—yielded to groups otherwise defined, as by race, age, disability or orientation to an issue or cause."[76]

It also is, as David Walker noted, a "conflicted" system—one in which both centripetal and centrifugal forces may occur at once: "The system is conflicted insofar as it reflects simultaneously centralizing and decentralizing, cooperative and competitive, co-optive and more discretionary, and activist as well as retrenching tendencies."[77]

This is the case because the operation of federalism may be different in different policy areas at different times. Furthermore, it can be the case because different institutions may pull in different directions or be constrained in different ways during the same time period; for example, Congress and the bureaucracy may seek to expand control through fiscal federalism at a time when the Supreme Court may seek to limit the reach of the national government in certain domestic arenas. It can be the case because, while the general public professes to distrust and dislike the growth of the national government, that same public advocates for the expansion of specific programs funded and administered by the national government. It can also be the case because we focus so much on the formal measures of who is "winning" (the Supreme Court's rulings on federalism, the broadening of congressional statutory authority, the expansion of fiscal federalism) when there are more informal, less obvious trends at work. Relevant in this regard is the argument made by John Nugent that states have learned how to influence national policymakers.[78] In particular, state officials are involved in what Nugent calls "constructive engagement" with members of Congress and federal agencies over (1) the shape of future policy, (2) the conditions associated with federal grants, and (3) the amount and shape of administrative discretion given to the state agencies that often are the primary implementers of federal policies.

While some of this negotiation occurs in a series of single-state to national official interactions, a good deal of it occurs through associations of state officials. These associations essentially serve as interest groups on behalf of the states and their local governments. One group of such organizations is known as "The Big Seven" and is especially active and influential on behalf of state and local governments, each member with a substantial lobbying presence in Washington, DC. The Big Seven are the National Governors Association (NGA), the National Conference of State Legislatures (NCSL), the Council of State Governments (CSG), the U.S. Conference of Mayors (USCM), the National Association of Counties (NACo), the National League of Cities (NLC), and the International City/County Management Association (ICMA). Additional groups representing various other state officials and interests include the National Association of State Budget Officers (NASBO), the National Association of Attorneys General (NAAG), and the National Association of Secretaries of State (NASS). It should be noted, however, that increasing polarization is even affecting the way some of these groups approach their mission. The NGA, for example, has effectively split into two partisan organizations, the Democratic Governors Association and the Republican Governors Association. Political scientist Jennifer Jensen has studied this phenomenon extensively, and she concludes that the two partisan associations of governors are more powerful today, while the more traditional, bipartisan NGA has lost influence.[79]

John Nugent argues that state governments today are far more competent and sophisticated and have dramatically increased their capacity for effective governance. They have, in Nugent's terms, "developed a robust set of institutions to facilitate interstate cooperation and to strengthen their individual and collective hands in dealing with federal officials."[80] This is an important point often overlooked; the states today are not the states as they existed in the middle of the twentieth century. This is a theme we will explore in detail in chapters 4 and 5.

As we trace the historical events and eras that over more than 230 years have led to a more nation-centered federalism, we might despair of the states and their roles. But that would be a mistake. Without a doubt, the role of the national government has grown substantially. But in many respects, so too has the role of the states. It is tempting to think of the federal relationship as a zero-sum game; if the national government expands its power, the states must be losing power. But this assumes that the size of the game itself remains constant—that the sum of all national and state power is a constant. But it is not. Governments at all levels—national, state, and local—are a bigger part of the citizens' lives now than they were in the past. They are certainly a much bigger part of life than any or all government was in 1789. How could it be otherwise in a society as large, complex, and technological as today's? Furthermore, as Joseph Zimmerman notes, while it is clear that the authority of the national government to make policy in the domestic arena has expanded dramatically, such authority is often enacted in such a way as to increase the implementation and regulatory authority of state governments.[81]

It is also the case that states can resist some initiatives of the national government by refusing to accept federal funds for such policies. For example, some states declined funds for "abstinence-only" sex education pressed by the administration of George W. Bush, while more recently others refused to accept hundreds of millions of dollars in federal grants for planning and construction of high-speed rails systems.[82]

Let us be clear on the message here: We are not saying that government *ought* to be as big a presence in citizens' lives as it is. But we are saying that limited government in the way the Founders understood it—in a rural, agrarian society with a relatively small population and few technological advances beyond the printing press and rudimentary steam engines—is not feasible today.

It is also worth keeping in mind that, while the role of the national government in today's American federation is clearly central, it has not eliminated the need for the states. States retain significant policymaking power in most areas of domestic policy, as we discuss in chapter 6. Indeed, states are often ahead of the national government when it comes to innovation. As one analyst has pointed out, "State governments are usually first to act in response to new problems or issues, of which many arise in a time of rapid technological and cultural change."[83] Examples include state laws addressing cybersecurity, regulation of internet service providers (net neutrality), and opioid addiction. These are but a few areas in which the states have moved ahead, "otherwise taking over duties that Congress is too paralyzed to handle," as the *Washington Post* observed.[84] Clearly, the relationship between the national and subnational units are not the same over time. Nor is the relationship the same in all federal systems, as box 2.1 demonstrates.

THE STATE AND LOCAL RELATIONSHIP

Federalism focuses on the relationship between the national government and the states. By now it should be clear that it is a complex relationship, ever changing, inconsistent, and often variable by policy area. It is also clear that today's federalism is different from that of 1789, or even from the federalism of 1930 or 1960. Federalism—here meaning the political and constitutional arrangement between the national and state governments—is just one intergovernmental relationship involving the states. States must also interact with local governments. The difference is that, while states may claim some measure of sovereign authority vis-à-vis the national government—the federal and state governments each have constitutional standing—local governments can make no such claim. They are creatures of the state government—meaning they were created by the state and derive their powers from it. From a legal perspective, local governments in their various incarnations—counties, cities, special districts, school districts, townships, and so on—are entirely dependent on state governments for their policing, regulatory, and taxing authority.[85]

While the local governments are "creatures of the state," they are also "agents of the state" in that they carry out state powers at the local level.[86] They provide services authorized by the state and they regulate behavior as mandated by the state. Precisely how these activities are divided between the state and the local governments is highly variable. For example, in some states, most of the welfare function is carried out at the local—usually county—level, while elsewhere it is centralized at the state level. One study found that the proportion of public services delivered by the state (rather than by the local governments) ranged from almost 80 percent (Vermont) to less than 40 percent (Nevada).[87]

Technically, then, the relationship between the state and its local governments is a unitary system, not a federal one. Local governments are not sovereign; they owe their claim to govern to a grant of authority, called a charter, from the state government. The charter stipulates what local governments can or cannot do and what they are required to do. Some states, either through the state constitution or legislative statute, determine the precise organizational structure that a county or municipality (city) must have. The degree of latitude

Box 2.1 | Federalism Elsewhere

The United States is not the world's only federal system. As noted earlier, of the approximately two hundred sovereign nations in the world, about twenty-five have a federal system. By now it should be evident that there are many gradations of federalism, with some leaning toward a regional- or state-centered system and some more toward a nation-centered federalism. Because each is a product of the culture, history, and specific geographical, political, and economic conditions within a country, each federal system is unique. And even within a single country the federal relationship shifts over time, as we have demonstrated in this chapter.

Any comparison of federal systems leads to the conclusion that there are numerous ways in which the power is distributed between the center and the periphery. On the one hand, some federal systems (e.g., Argentina, Spain, and South Africa) are clearly more centralized than the American federation. On the other hand, a few federations are less centralized and more oriented toward peripheral, regional-level governments, with examples being Canada and Germany.

In Germany, the basis for a federal system was established after World War II and extended with the 1990 reunification of East and West Germany. As one textbook notes, "Its 16 states, or Länder, exercise a great deal of power, far more than states do in the United States. . . . The central government has exclusive authority over foreign affairs, money, immigration and telecommunications. But the Länder retain residual powers over all other matters." This includes education, health and welfare, and civil and criminal law.

Canada is another federal system in which the balance between the center and the periphery is tipped toward the latter. In Canada, it is the regions—the provinces—that enjoy substantial autonomy. Canada is arguably the most periphery-oriented federal system in the world. In part this is because of the mosaic cultures that characterize Canada. The bargain for keeping francophone Quebec in the system is substantial autonomy for provinces on many matters. This includes the fact that the provinces tax and spend at a higher rate than the federal government. Moreover, there is a significant distribution of federal revenues to the provinces but without a heavy burden of national mandates attached to the funds.

Sources: James MacGregor Burns, J. W. Peltason, Thomas Cronin, David Magleby, and David M. O'Brien, *Government by the People* (Upper Saddle River, NJ: Prentice Hall, 2002), 61.

David M. Thomas, "Past Futures: The Development and Evolution of American and Canadian Federalism," in *Canada and the United States: Differences That Count* ,ed. David M. Thomas and Barbara Boyle Torrey, 3rd ed. (Peterborough, ON, Canada: Broadview Press).

offered to local governments by the state authority differs from one state to another and differs over time within each state. In some, local governments are permitted a fair amount of freedom to operate as they see fit (home rule). In others, the state—especially through the state legislature—places strict limits or constraints on the powers and the taxing authority of local governments. Sometimes this brings local governments—especially school districts and cities—into conflict with the state legislature. One particularly salient example is public school funding, a topic discussed in some detail in chapters 3 and 7.

CONCLUSION

Early in this chapter we related the story of the resistance by some states to the controversial health care reform legislation passed by a Democrat-controlled Congress, at the Democratic president's urging, in 2010. Almost all the resistance was from Republican governors and Republican-controlled state legislatures. Partisanship and ideology are often part of the "endless argument" over federalism. In today's highly polarized political environment, federalism is often a political weapon and a rhetorical gambit. It is indeed an endless argument, a contest that is never entirely resolved, but a fight with real consequences for citizens.

It is clear that the role of the national government in domestic policymaking has grown substantially over the centuries. We have outlined a number of trends and events that led to the current configuration. While states have less power today relative to the national government, this does not mean that states are powerless—far from it. As one federalism expert notes, "Political opponents use federalism as a weapon because the states have enormous authority, because they use that authority in different ways, and because they produce different results."[88] In other words, states still matter and they matter in important ways. In many functional areas, states are energetic, imaginative, and primary policymakers, as we will demonstrate in chapter 6. The institutions of state government today are clearly more capable and competent than fifty years ago, as we will demonstrate in chapters 4 and 5.

Furthermore, while states may have less relative power compared to the national government, one can make a case that they have more absolute power than previously—certainly more so than in 1789. Everyday life was fundamentally different then, and the need for regulation and public services was minimal. In today's society of 328 million people, many living in urban environments experiencing rapid technological and social change, government at all levels—including state governments—has a much larger role to play.

Moreover, because of the emphasis on the most visible institutions and most salient issues, we often underappreciate the ability of states to influence federal policies in a meaningful way. Much of this is done through bureaucratic channels.

Finally, we should note that increased concern over the national government's fiscal policies and the growth in the federal debt almost certainly will require a recalibration of the relationship between the national and state governments. As Alice Rivlin observed not long ago, "A thorough rethinking of fiscal federalism is in order. A clearer demarcation of responsibilities between the federal and state levels could improve efficiency, accountability, and performance at both levels."[89] Others have made similar calls for a rethinking of the roles of the national and state governments.[90]

The extent to which these prescriptions are honored or ignored remains to be seen. The next few years will be especially important in determining the role of the states in the federal system. As we show in the following chapters, states are better prepared than ever, despite the growing challenges of governing in our federal system.

3

State Fiscal Systems

States matter because:

* ★ About 10 percent of the average citizen's income goes to pay state and local taxes.
* ★ The way a state puts together its tax system determines which citizens carry more of the tax burden.
* ★ The ability of local governments to tax and spend is controlled by state policymakers.
* ★ Public education in the United States is largely funded by the states and their local governments.
* ★ The sales tax is almost exclusively a state tax.
* ★ Unlike the federal government, states have balanced budget requirements.
* ★ State fiscal systems are pro-cyclical, which magnifies the effects of economic cycles.
* ★ Underfunded public employee pension funds pose a significant future problem in some states.
* ★ State fiscal systems are likely to become more reliant on their own revenue sources in the coming years.

STATE LEGISLATURES PASS A LOT OF BILLS. But the only bills they are actually required to pass are those setting the state budget. Yet, every year there are some states that are unable to pass a budget on time. The number of states with budget problems varies from year to year, but it always seems that a few cannot get their budget done on time. For example, eight states started their new fiscal years without an approved budget in 2015. In 2017, eleven states stalled on the budget, while only five states were late in 2019.

For some states, budget problems are the product of external factors; for example, the precipitous drop in oil prices in 2014 had a major effect on the revenues and budgets in oil-producing states such as Oklahoma, Louisiana, and Alaska the following year. Alaska has continued to struggle because of slumping oil prices, creating a major shortfall in its FY2020 budget and leading the governor to veto over $400 million dollars from the proposed budget. Most notable was a 40 percent decrease ($130 million) in state money for the University of Alaska system.[1]

For other states, the "budget crisis" was more about a clash of political philosophies concerning the role of the state in taxation and government programs. Epic battles occurred in 2015 and 2016 in several states, most notably in Illinois (with a Democratic legislature and a Republican governor) and Pennsylvania (with a Republican legislature and a Democratic governor). An ideological standoff prevented Illinois from producing a full budget for over two years, while Pennsylvania only settled its budget after a nine-month stalemate.[2] During the impasse school districts in Pennsylvania were forced to borrow money from banks to stay open.[3] In Illinois, some social service programs were shut down and a child advocacy group led by the governor's wife was among the organizations that sued to get the state to release promised funds.[4]

In still other states, the budget "crisis" was self-inflicted, largely due to the accumulating effect of personal income tax reductions that did not produce the anticipated increase in state economic growth. Louisiana and Kansas were the prime recent examples of unfulfilled economic growth promises.[5]

Public budgeting is inherently political.[6] This includes state and local budgeting. To a large extent, budgets represent policy preferences with dollar signs attached. Often, they represent compromises between competing policy preferences. They are the product of negotiations and decisions involving the level of taxation, the level of regulation, what services to provide, and the level of those services to be provided. State budgets involve intergovernmental relations in two ways. First, state budgets are affected by the availability and requirements of federal grants. Second, state budgets include state aid to local governments. To appreciate all this, we must examine state and local fiscal systems. There are three broad topics to cover: public budgeting cycles, revenue sources, and expenditures. And as always, there are differences in the way states handle each of these.

A key issue in the future for the states will be their degree of financial independence. This is the central truth about fiscal federalism: when the level of federal aid is high, the independent policymaking authority of the states is low. In contrast, when the level of federal aid is low, the independent policymaking authority of the states is high, but the fiscal capacity of the states to pay for those policies is diminished. In other words, financial dependence is associated with less policymaking independence. The main reason for this relationship is that most federal aid comes "with strings attached"; the state (or local governments) must comply with specific rules and procedures in order to receive the funds.

Over time, the purpose of federal aid has shifted. Nowadays, federal aid is largely directed to entitlements—especially Medicaid at the state level. With health care absorbing more than 60 percent of all federal aid, the states will have to do more of their own heavy lifting in other policy areas. Transportation is a good example; with federal aid for highways and other transportation programs being funded at stagnant levels, states are having to figure out how to fund transportation programs on their own.

It is essential that citizens of each state understand the ways that state and local finances are tied to policy decisions and how the decisions policymakers make affect what state and local governments take (in the form of taxes and fees) and what they provide (in the form of services and protections). These are difficult decisions for which there are no simple solutions. As a Republican West Virginia senator and chair of the State Senate Finance Committee recently noted, "The anti-tax people are convinced there are millions and millions and millions of dollars of government waste that could be squeezed out if there's political will to do it." But, as the senator noted, the "difficulty arises when the discussion moves from cutting spending in general to determining which specific programs are to be cut."[7]

TYPES OF BUDGETS AND BUDGET CYCLES

There are several ways to organize state budgets. One of the most common is a division between operating budgets and capital budgets. For states, most of their expenditures are payments to personnel or to purchase goods or services. These are part of the operating budgets—think of them as the price of ongoing government operations. But some types of expenditures are for long-term projects involving the acquisition of property and the building of something on that property. These are covered in capital budgets, which are about physical items—highways, bridges, university campus buildings, and so on. For the most part, capital budgets involve one-time items—once a building is built, it is no longer in the capital budget. But operating budgets are ongoing. Once a program is started, the personnel have to be paid every year. For states, one of the most important distinctions between operating and capital budgets is that states can only go into debt (i.e., borrow money through government bonding) for capital budgets, not operating budgets. Moreover, in some states the rules for passing operating budgets are different from the rules for approving the capital budget. For example, in most state legislatures a simple majority of votes is required to pass the operating budget. But an extraordinary majority (60 percent or higher) may be required to pass the capital budget. That is because capital budgets are largely funded through bonds (borrowing money).

General Fund and Total Funds Budgets. But when talking about state budgets, there is another important way to distinguish between types of budgets, and it has to do with the control the state has over the way the funds are allocated. There are two of these as well, and in most states they are called the general fund budget and the total budget. The general fund budget typically makes up 35 percent to 50 percent of the total budget. Although it is only one-third to one-half of the total budget, the general fund is the part of the budget that gets most of the media attention. The reason is simple enough: the general fund controls *discretionary* money—meaning it can be spent in a variety of ways, and the state legislature and governor negotiate over its distribution. *Nondiscretionary* funds are monies that are "locked in"—they are required to be spent on specific programs or items and they appear to be a growing proportion of state budgets.[8] The state legislature and governor have no choice in how the money is allocated. It is mandated by the state constitution, state law or court order or, in the case of federal grants-in-aid, by the federal government. For example, in most states, revenue from the state gasoline tax (more formally known as the "motor fuels tax") must go to the state transportation department or state highway department. This money cannot be diverted or reallocated by the legislature or the governor to schools or prisons or something else. Given that there is no discretion, there is no argument over who (what department) gets the money. Figure 3.1 shows an example of a state budget and its component parts.

Discretionary funds can be shifted from one account to another. Consequently, there is almost always an argument in the legislature over who gets what share of general fund money. Thus, the media focuses almost entirely on the fight over the general fund appropriation; it is often characterized as "slices of the (budget) pie," and the story is who is getting a larger or smaller piece. Some types of programs and interests tend to be funded through nondiscretionary funds (e.g., highways), while others (e.g., public education) are mostly financed through discretionary, general funds. From the point of view of program beneficiaries, nondiscretionary funds are more desirable than discretionary funds.

Federal aid—also known as fiscal federalism or federal intergovernmental transfers—is an important component of the nondiscretionary part of the total state budget. Almost all of these funds are accompanied by mandates—rules and regulations on how the money is to be spent. We will say more about fiscal federalism later in the chapter. For now, the key thing to understand is that all states are dependent on federal aid for a significant part of their total budget, although the degree of that dependency differs from one state to another. Figure 3.1 shows that, in fiscal year 2018, Kentucky received 39 percent of its total budget from the federal government. That is a high percentage, one of the highest in the country. One recent analysis found that in four states (Michigan, Mississippi, Montana, and New Mexico) over 40 percent of state spending was from federal aid. In contrast, federal aid comprised less than 20 percent of the state budgets of Connecticut, Hawaii, Massachusetts, Ohio, and Wyoming.[9]

Fiscal Years and Budget Cycles. For most of us, the major annual time referent is the calendar year: it begins January 1 and ends December 31. So when someone makes reference to the year "2021," we take that to mean January 1,

Figure 3.1   A State Budget and Its Component Parts

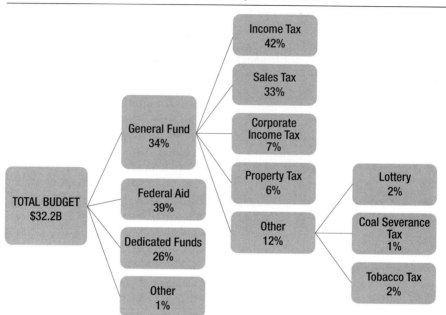

2021, through December 31, 2021. But there are other "years." There is the "academic year," which begins in August or September of one year and ends in May or June of the following year. And then there is the "fiscal year." The fiscal year is when the budget expenditures start anew. Anyone who has served in the military or otherwise been employed by the federal government knows that the federal fiscal year begins October 1. Thus for the federal government, fiscal year (FY) 2021 begins on October 1, 2020, and ends on September 30, 2021.

Almost all states operate on fiscal years that run from July 1 to June 30. For these states, FY 2021 begins July 1, 2020, and ends on June 30, 2021. Only four states do not operate on this calendar. Alabama and Michigan use the same fiscal year as the federal government (beginning October 1), while New York begins the fiscal year on April 1 and Texas begins on September 1.[10] The overlap of fiscal years with the legislative session and the calendar year in a "typical" state is depicted in figure 3.2. Most states have legislative sessions that begin in January and run three or four months. There are, however, numerous exceptions. A few states have legislatures that operate full-time—essentially for the entire year. And a few states meet only every other year or begin their session in March rather than January. But the majority of states operate in the time cycle depicted in figure 3.2.

In terms of the budget process, what this means is that the governor and the legislature are setting the fiscal year 2021 budget in the early part of calendar year 2020. Thus, in January through about March 2020, policymakers

Figure 3.2 Calendar Year, Fiscal Year, and the Appropriations Process in a State Legislature

	Jan	Feb	Mar	Apr	May	Jun	Jul	Aug	Sep	Oct	Nov	Dec
2021 →	2021 Legislature sets FY 2022 budget						FY 2022 begins					
2022 →						FY 2022 ends						

are projecting revenues for a period about sixteen to eighteen months in the future—until June 30, 2021. Because budgets are always forecasts, they are prone to error and are almost never exactly correct. How could they be? State revenues are sensitive to economic trends, and the best that policymakers can do is make an educated guess as to what the condition of the economy will be a year or a year and a half into the future. Recent data shows that on average only 10 percent of budget forecasts are accurate.[11] Usually, forecasts underestimate revenues a bit, but this is variable by changing economic conditions and political considerations. Conservatives may use more pessimistic economic growth forecasts than liberals, for example, while opting for more optimistic forecasts about the economic impacts of tax cuts. For states, the revenue forecasts are especially important because of balanced budget requirements. The important point is that spending is conditioned by revenue forecasts.

When economic conditions change rapidly, state budget processes can become chaotic. A particularly dramatic example of this is the "Great Recession" of 2007 to 2009.[12] The recession began just as most state legislatures were, in early 2008, beginning work on their FY 2009 budgets. And the data they used to make the FY 2009 forecasts were from 2006 and 2007—years of economic growth. Thus, their revenue projections, and the budgets based on those projections, for FY 2009 turned out to be far too optimistic. Of course, this was not apparent for some months. As the National Conference of State Legislatures (NCSL) later reported, "Lawmakers were aware of the slowing economy when drafting their FY 2009 budgets, but none could have foreseen a collapse of the magnitude that has stricken state finances."[13] By the time state legislatures reconvened in early 2009 (halfway through the 2009 fiscal year), they were facing, collectively, a budget shortfall of $110 billion.[14] Some states were hit especially hard; Alabama reported a FY 2009 shortfall amounting to 12 percent, California 14 percent, and Arizona 15 percent. Other states reporting shortfalls amounting to 10 percent or more were Georgia, Nevada, New Hampshire, South Carolina, and Tennessee.[15] The FY 2010 shortfalls turned out to be even worse, approaching $200 billion. The decline in revenues in 2009 and 2010 was unusually large and largely unforeseen. Thus, shortfalls were created.

The situation surrounding the Great Recession required drastic action in some instances. For several fiscal years, California had to cope with budget deficits totaling $100 billion. As one observer noted, some of the spending cuts they had to adopt were "downright breathtaking in size and scope," including eliminating some child care programs, cutting assistance for the elderly, and eliminating $1 billion in appropriations to state universities.[16]

In 2009, *USA Today* ran a story titled "Federal Aid Is Top Revenue for States."[17] In the midst of the "Great Recession," states came to rely more on money transferred from the national government than on any single revenue source of their own. It was the first time this had ever happened. It occurred again in 2010, when federal aid accounted for more than 35 percent of all state revenue.[18] In other words, while state governments rely on numerous sources of revenue for their budgets, in 2009 and 2010 they relied more on federal aid than on their own sales tax, the personal income tax, or any other single revenue source. By 2013 federal aid had declined to 30 percent of state revenue and was no longer the largest single revenue source for most states.

The states' budget situation would have been even more dire if the federal government had not provided close to $800 billion in additional federal assistance as part of the American Recovery and Reinvestment Act (ARRA). These ARRA funds were intended to stimulate state economies and help shore up state education, health care, and unemployment insurance funds. These federal funds were no longer available by 2012, but they were relied upon heavily by some states to help get through the difficult days of the worst economic recession in eighty years. It was also the case that many states were able to soften the budget blow in FY 2009–2011 by transferring money from their "rainy day funds"—basically state government savings accounts. But like the ARRA funds, these state savings accounts were largely depleted by the end of FY 2011. The dramatic economic downturn meant that state policymakers were faced with severely cutting back on program expenditures, raising taxes to make up the shortfall, or some combination of the two approaches. For many states, a key lesson from the Great Recession was the importance of maintaining a rainy day fund to help cushion the effect of economic downturns. States have made building up their reserves a priority since 2010, and the typical state reserve fund has grown from less than 2 percent of general funds to about 7 percent.[19] States, however, have pursued different rainy day funding strategies, and as a result some are much better positioned to help weather any future economic downturn than are others.[20] Overall, it is important to recognize that state budgets have yet to fully recover from the devastation wrought by the Great Recession.[21]

Annual and Biennial Budgets. There is one other budget variation across the states that merits discussion. There are thirty-one states that adopt annual budgets, as the federal government does. The other nineteen states adopt biennial, or two-year, budgets. Of those states, four have state legislative sessions only every other year, but fifteen have annual legislative sessions yet they adopt two-year budgets. The arguments in favor of two-year budgets are that they give state agencies greater budget certainty and an opportunity to engage in long-range decision-making. In addition, state legislatures can spend more time evaluating programs rather than budgeting. The problem, as noted earlier, is that budget forecasts over even one year often prove inaccurate. Annual budgeting allows state legislatures to respond more quickly to changing economic conditions and to operate using more accurate financial data. In practice, however, it is not clear that one budget approach works better than the other.[22]

Balanced Budget Requirements. One of the important ways in which the national government and states differ is their approach to reconciling spending and revenue. The federal government regularly engages in "deficit spending," meaning that the government spends more than the revenue it generates in a fiscal year, but the ability of states to do so is limited.[23] It was not always this way. In the early nineteenth century, states engaged in deficit spending on a regular basis. The problem was severe enough that by 1840 "some states teetered on bankruptcy from excessive debt," and at that point state constitutions were amended to place limits on state spending and debt.[24] Except for Vermont (which only has an informal norm requiring it), all states now require a balanced operating budget, although it should be noted that not all balanced-budget rules are the same. The enforcement mechanism to require a balanced budget is weak in some states and stringent in others.[25] It is less stringent where the governor's proposed budget or the budget the legislature adopts is only forecasted to balance. The most stringent balanced-budget standards require that the budget balance at the end of the fiscal year and that no deficit can be carried forward.[26]

In about half the states, if policymakers cannot agree on a budget on time, a partial shutdown of government functions is required.[27] An example of this occurred in Minnesota in July 2011 (the beginning of the 2012 fiscal year), when many "nonessential" services, such as state parks, road construction, and child care services, were closed for three weeks, until a balanced budget was finally passed.[28] This was the longest state government shutdown since the 1990s, when Connecticut and Pennsylvania each experienced shutdowns over one month long, and California endured a two-month shutdown. For Minnesotans in 2011, it was the second time in five years they had experienced a state government shutdown. But typically, the mere threat of a shutdown is enough to bring state budget makers to some agreement on balancing the budget. Because the consequences of not reaching an agreement can be serious in many states, policymakers have a strong incentive to balance the budget.

Direct Democracy and Fiscal Policy. One of the unique features of some state electoral systems, as described in chapter 8, is the existence of the direct initiative. This is a process by which the public (or some segment thereof) can propose a law or state constitutional amendment to be decided upon by the voters in a subsequent election, effectively bypassing the state legislature. Among the most prevalent types of propositions are tax limits or spending mandates, known collectively as TELs (tax and expenditure limitations). The most famous TEL is California's Proposition 13, which passed in 1978 and put a strict limit on property tax increases. That measure precipitated the tax revolt of the 1980s. Some of these propositions involve a requirement that a certain percentage of the state budget be dedicated to a specific expenditure (such as K–12 public schools). While more than half the states have one or more TELs in place, they are especially prevalent in states that permit the direct initiative. In addition to California, Colorado and Washington are two other such states. States with TELs are constrained in their fiscal policies in ways not found in states without them. There is evidence that TELs and other budget rules such as strict balanced-budget requirements constrain the growth in state government spending and reduce the year-to-year volatility in state expenditures.[29] But they also hamper the choices and actions available to state officials during times of economic stress.

A Note about Variation. State and subnational fiscal systems are complicated because they experience variation in three important ways. First, there is variation *between* levels of government: the revenues and expenditures at the state level look different than the revenue and expenditure patterns at the local government level. Second, there is variation *within* a particular level of government: for example, no two states generate revenue or spend money in precisely the same way. And certainly this is true at the local government level—cities, counties, school and special districts, and townships are all types of local governments but they have different fiscal fingerprints. Finally, there is variation *over time* in the way state and local fiscal systems operate. This is largely because of changes in the supply and demand structure of public fiscal systems: where they get their money (supply) and how they spend it (demand) change over time. With these variations in mind, we turn to an explanation of the revenue structures for state governments. In the following discussion, we occasionally make reference to local government finances as well, because local revenues and expenditures are guided by state government policy. What revenue tools are available to local governments, and what expenditures they are required to make, occur within the parameters set by the state. Remember, local governments are not independent, autonomous units but instead are created by and largely defined by their state governments. Some states hold most of the tax and expenditure responsibilities at the state level; others devolve much of it to their local governments. We will focus more on the public financing of local governments in chapter 7.

STATE REVENUES

For the most part, states must balance their budgets; expenditures cannot exceed revenues. Therefore, government spending is shaped by the revenue generated. And the revenue is generated in many ways. Most of the revenue sources are different types of taxes: personal income tax, general sales tax, tobacco tax, and so on. Lotteries generate revenue. Federal aid is yet another source. Because states need to balance their budgets, their ability to spend money is constrained by the amount of revenue they obtain. During an economic downturn, such as the Great Recession, revenues decline and, as a consequence, expenditures must be cut to keep the budget balanced. The Great

Recession was an extraordinarily difficult period for state and local governments; as noted earlier, many states saw revenues drop by 10 percent or more and, as a result, they were forced to make substantial cutbacks in state spending. As a result, over six hundred thousand state and local employees were lopped off government payrolls.

While most state and local revenue sources are sensitive to economic conditions, some are more so than others. The general sales tax is affected by the economy because when the economy slows, people cut back on discretionary spending; they stop buying expensive items such as jewelry and luxury automobiles and they reduce spending on dining out and weekend getaways. This means that government collects less sales tax money.

The revenue a state can generate through the personal income tax is even more affected by the performance of the economy. During robust economic times, unemployment is low and more people are working, and because of that they are making money and paying state income taxes. And because many states tax higher incomes at a higher rate, the income tax captures a higher percentage of economic activity in good times than in bad times. The sales tax and the personal income tax are key contributors to the general fund budgets of most states. Local governments are also affected. A major source of revenue for cities, counties, and school districts is the property tax. In the recent Great Recession, much of the economic downturn was caused by the collapse of the housing market. As home values declined precipitously in some areas, the property tax revenue fell substantially (although with a time lag) in many cities and counties.

It is these features of state fiscal systems, along with the balanced budget requirement, that make state fiscal systems pro-cyclical. During a recession, when the economy slows, states must either raise taxes or cut programs (or both). Because these actions negatively affect spending and employment, they further slow the economy. Katharine Bradbury, an economist with the Federal Reserve Bank of Boston, sums up the macroeconomic relationship succinctly: "Tax revenues, which are generated by economic activity, tend to move pro-cyclically; as a result, budget-balancing by state and local governments tends to amplify national business cycle swings."[30]

States have an array of revenue sources available to them—as do their local governments. Over time, each state has made decisions about which particular revenue sources to use and how much to rely on each of them. Each state's revenue package is a product of numerous decisions by public officials over many years. Some of these decisions involved hard-fought, well-publicized struggles over the imposition of a particular tax or the raising of a specific tax rate. Other decisions were made incrementally, as short-term adjustments to economic upturns or downturns. Consequently, each state has a unique fiscal fingerprint (see table 3.1 for a summary of the tax rates on various state taxes). We now turn to an examination of the revenue sources that most or all state governments employ. We will briefly mention local revenues as well, a topic to which we will give more attention in chapter 7.

Table 3.1. Various Tax Rates in the States

(1) State	(2) Personal income tax tates (%)	(3) Corporate income tax rates (%)	(4) State sales tax (%)	(5) Average local tax rate	(6) Gasoline tax (cents per gallon)	(7) Tobacco tax ($ per pack of cigarettes)	(8) Total state and local tax rate (%)
AL	2.0–5.0	6.5	4	5.01	18	0.675	9.0
AK	0	0–9.4	0	1.76	8.95	2.00	4.3
AZ	2.59–4.54	4.9	5.6	2.65	19	2.00	9.4
AR	0.9–6.9	1.0–6.5	6.5	2.80	21.8	1.15	10.8
CA	1.0–13.3	8.84	7.25	1.00	47.7	2.87	8.3
CO	4.63	4.63	2.9	4.62	22	0.84	8.9
CT	3.0–6.99	7.5	6.35	0	25	4.35	12.2
DE	2.2–6.6	8.7	0	0	23	2.10	5.6
FL	0	5.5	6.0	0.80	31.4	1.34	8.1
GA	1.0–5.75	6.0	4.0	3.00	27.5	0.37	9.8
HI	1.4–11.0	4.4–6.4	4.0	0.35	16	3.20	11.6
ID	1.6–6.9	6.9	6.0	0.03	33	0.57	8.1
IL	4.95	9.5	6.25	2.39	20.1	1.98	12.6
IN	3.2	5.75	7.0	0	29.0	0.995	11.1
IA	0.33 8.53	6.0–12.0	6.0	0.80	30.5	1.36	10.7
KS	3.1–5.7	4.0–7.0	6.5	2.12	25	1.29	10.6
KY	2.0–5.0	4.0–5.0	6.0	0	26	1.10	11.1
LA	2.0–6.0	4.0–8.0	4.45	4.98	20.125	1.08	10.0

ME	5.8-7.15	3.5-8.93	5.5	0	30	2.00	**9.6**
MD	2.0-5.75	8.25	6.0	0	35.3	2.00	**10.6**
MA	5.1	8.0	6.25	0	24	3.51	**9.3**
MI	4.25	6.0	6.0	0	26.3	2.00	**9.2**
MN	5.35-9.85	9.8	6.875	0.42	28.6	3.04	**9.7**
MS	3.0-5.0	3.0-5.0	7.0	0.07	18.4	0.68	**10.8**
MO	1.5-5.4	6.25	4.225	3.66	17.4	0.17	**9.0**
MT	1.0-6.9	6.75	0	0	31.5	1.70	**7.1**
NE	2.46-6.84	5.58-7.81	5.5	1.39	30.5	0.64	**10.8**
NV	0	0	6.85	1.13	23.805	1.80	**7.6**
NH	0*	7.7	0	0	23.825	1.78	**8.1**
NJ	1.4-10.75	6.5-11.5	6.62	0	41.4	2.70	**10.1**
NM	1.7-4.9	4.8-5.9	5.125	2.43	18.875	1.66	**10.2**
NY	4.0-8.82	6.5	4.0	4.49	25.75	4.35	**12.4**
NC	5.25	2.5	4.75	2.15	36.45	0.45	**9.4**
ND	1.10-2.90	1.4-4.3	5.0	1.787	23	0.44	**8.5**
OH	0-4.99	0	5.75	1.39	28	1.60	**10.7**
OK	0.5-5.0	6.0	4.5	4.32	20	2.03	**10.7**
OR	5.0-9.9	6.6-7.6	0	0	34	1.33	**9.1**
PA	3.07	9.99	6.0	0.34	57.6	2.60	**11.1**
RI	3.75-5.99	7.0	7.0	0	34	4.25	**9.5**
SC	0-7.0	5.0	6.0	1.22	20.75	0.57	**8.1**

Table 3.1. (Continued)

(1) State	(2) Personal income tax rates (%)	(3) Corporate income tax rates (%)	(4) State sales tax (%)	(5) Average local tax rate	(6) Gasoline tax (cents per gallon)	(7) Tobacco tax ($ per pack of cigarettes)	(8) Total state and local tax rate (%)
SD	0	0	4.5	1.89	30	1.53	8.9
TN	0*	6.5	7.0	2.46	26.4	0.62	8.5
TX	0	0	6.25	1.94	20	1.41	9.7
UT	4.95	4.95	4.7	0.81	30.0	1.70	8.2
VT	3.35–8.95	6.0–8.5	6.0	0.18	31.19	3.08	10.1
VA	2.0–5.75	6.0	4.3	0.33	16.2	0.30	9.2
WA	0	0	6.5	2.42	49.4	3.025	11.0
WV	3.0–6.5	6.5	6.0	0.29	35.7	1.20	8.5
WI	4.0–7.65	7.9	5.0	0.42	32.9	2.52	10.1
WY	0	0	4.0	1.40	24	0.60	7.5
						Average	9.9

*New Hampshire and Tennessee (until 2021) tax income on dividends and interest only
Sources for data in each column:

(2) "State Individual Income Taxes" as of January 1, 2019, Federation of Tax Administrators, February 2019 and Tax Foundation, "State Individual Income Tax Rates and Brackets for 2019." Fiscal Facts No. 643. March 2019.

(3) "Range of State Corporate Income Tax Rates" as of January 2019, Federation of Tax Administrators, February 2019.

(4) "State Sales Tax Rates" as of January 2019, Federation of Tax Administrators, January 2019.

(5) "Comparison of State and Local Tax Retail Sales Taxes, 2017." https://www.taxadmin.org/assets/docs/Research/Rates/wa_statelocal_sales_2017.pdf.

(6) "State Motor Fuel Tax Rates" as of January 2019, Federation of Tax Administrators, January 2019.

(7) "State Excise Tax Rates on Cigarettes" as of January 2019, Federation of Tax Administrators, January 2019.

(8) Figures represent the combined income, sales, excise and property tax rates paid by the median taxpayer (middle 20 percent of all nonelderly taxpayers in the state). Calculations are from the Institute on Taxation and Economic Policy, *Who Pays: A Distributional Analysis of the Tax Systems in All 50 States, 6th edition* (October 2018), Appendix A.

Personal Income Tax. Only seven states (Alaska, Florida, Nevada, South Dakota, Texas, Washington, and Wyoming) do not rely at all on a personal income tax. Currently, two states (New Hampshire and Tennessee) tax personal income from interest and dividends, but not from wages, so they are taxed at a much narrower income base—and Tennessee is scheduled to phase out this tax by 2021.[31] For the remaining forty-one states, the personal income tax is an essential source of revenue; in many of them it is the single most important source. But even among these forty-one states, there are substantial differences in how the tax is applied, as box 3.1 demonstrates. A few states tax

| Box 3.1 | **Professional Ball Players Know Why States Matter** |

The March 2019 headline read, "Bryce Harper will save tens of millions in taxes by spurning the Dodgers and Giants." Both the Los Angeles Dodgers and the San Francisco Giants had offered large contracts to Harper, one of the best young baseball players around. Instead, he signed a 13-year, $330-million contract with the Philadelphia Phillies. While there were several reasons why Bryce Harper chose to sign with the Phillies, one of the considerations was the difference in state taxes. California's progressive income tax tops out at a rate of 13.3%. Pennsylvania, on the other hand, has a flat-rate income tax that is just under 3.1%.

One professional baseball agent said, "I've had players in the past say they don't want to go to certain states because they're going to get hammered by taxes." Former NBA basketball player John Wallace pointed out that the amount of money involved in professional sports means many professional athletes recognize how taxes and property values can affect their bottom line. Wallace, a graduate of Syracuse University, said he was taught "to be financially responsible and aware of state taxes, which helped me save thousands of tax dollars over my NBA career. When I played for the New York Knicks, instead of living in New York City and paying a very high state and city tax, I lived in Connecticut, which had a much lower state tax rate."

Indeed, teams in states with low or no income taxes use this information as a recruitment tool. For example, NBA teams in Florida (Miami and Orlando), Texas (San Antonio, Houston, and Dallas), and Tennessee (Memphis) make sure prospective players know that there are no income taxes in those states. In many cases, a player can make more after-tax income with a less lucrative contract than with a larger contract in a high-tax state. As one sports agent pointed out, "You've got to remember the best gross contract might not be the best net contract."

Sources: George Skelton, "Bryce Harper Will Save ..." March 7, 2019, https://www.latimes.com/politics/la-pol-ca-skelton-income-tax-20190307-story.html; Steve Megargee, "Location, Taxes Affect Payoff in Big Deals," Associated Press, Idaho Statesman, July 17, 2017; Harris Solis and Josh Horowitz, "The Influence of State Taxes on NBA Free Agency," June 25, 2017; https://www.slamonline.com/nba/state-taxes-nba-free-agency/.

all personal income at a flat rate (e.g., 3.2 percent in Indiana and 3.07 percent in Pennsylvania); this is known as a "proportional tax" in that everyone pays the same proportion of their income to the state. Other states have a graduated income tax structure, applying a higher tax rate at higher income levels. This system, known as a "progressive tax," means that people who make the most money are paying a higher tax rate than others. For example, New Jersey has six separate tax brackets, beginning at 1.4 percent for those making $20,000 and going up to 10.75 percent for those making over $500,000. (This means people start paying a 10.75 percent tax on each dollar they make above $500,000, not that they pay 10.75 percent on every dollar they earn if they make more than $500,000.)

There are two potential problems with relying on the personal income tax as a primary source of state revenue. First, it can be volatile, surging when economic times are good and receding when they are poor. Second, it can hit wealthier regions of a state much harder than other areas. A recent analysis of California's personal income tax revealed that the San Francisco Bay Area, home of Silicon Valley and the high tech industry, provides 40 percent of the revenue generated by the tax even though it only includes 20 percent of the state's population.[32]

General Sales Tax. Historically, the general sales tax (also known as a "consumption tax") has been an important revenue source for states and, until recently, was a revenue source that was relatively immune to the natural volatility of economic cycles. While the sales tax is not as unpopular as some other taxes, it is an increasingly difficult tax upon which to rely. Most states that impose a general sales tax do so for physical goods (products) but not services. In this sense, a good or product is a tangible item, like a computer. A service is an activity or intangible good, such as legal representation by an attorney. Today the American economy is far more service-oriented than product-oriented. Consequently, over time a particular sales tax rate (say, 5 percent) captures less and less of the overall economic activity as more and more of the economic activity is service-oriented and therefore not subject to the sales tax. The rapid expansion of e-commerce represented another problem for states that rely on the general sales tax. Early in the rise of the internet economy, the United States Supreme Court ruled that states could not impose a sales tax on internet purchases unless the vendor had a physical presence in the state. Thus, as more and more purchases were made online, more and more potential sales tax money was being lost. This changed, however, in June 2018 when the Court reversed course and decided that online purchases would largely be subject to the sales tax of the state in which the purchaser resided.[33] Within a year, most states had plans to implement a state sales tax protocol for internet sales conducted within the state. The anticipated increase in sales tax revenue is dependent on the size of the state and the rate of taxation. In some states the new revenue generated could amount to several million dollars but in large states such as California and New York the anticipated revenue will likely be in the $300 to $600 million range.[34]

For the last half of the twentieth century, the sales tax was the primary revenue source for most states, generating roughly one-third of all state revenue.[35] But as the sales tax became less efficient at capturing revenue as the nature of the economy changed, the personal income tax surpassed the sales tax as the primary revenue source in many states. As one analyst notes, absent any dramatic change in state tax systems, "public finance experts generally believe that personal income tax revenue will continue to grow as a percentage of state tax revenue, while sales tax revenue will continue to decline."[36] It is, however, the case that income tax rates have been reduced recently in some Republican-controlled states. Kansas was particularly aggressive on this score, but significant income tax reductions also occurred in Wisconsin, Maine, Ohio, and North Carolina between 2012 and 2014.[37] Moreover, after the federal tax reform of 2017, another seven states made modest reductions to their state personal income tax rates.

The sales tax tends to be a regressive tax, meaning the tax burden falls disproportionately on people at lower income levels. This is because poorer people must spend virtually their entire income on food, clothing, and other items that are subject to the sales tax, while people at higher incomes can save or invest some of their income and those funds are not captured by the sales tax. High-income earners are also more likely to spend money on services, which are usually not subject to the sales tax.

In other words, the sales tax is actually a tax on spending rather than on income, and it is an inefficient tax on spending because it usually only captures one type of spending—goods, not services. A few states (Alaska, Delaware, Montana, New Hampshire, and Oregon) do not have a general sales tax at all. For the other states, a general sales tax between 5 percent and 6.5 percent is typical. But there are substantial differences from state to state in this regard; over a dozen states impose an income tax of 4 percent or less. Meanwhile, at least four states have a state income tax of 7 percent or higher. This is just the state sales tax; many states permit local governments to also charge their own sales tax (a topic discussed in chapter 7), and in some, notably Alaska, the local sales tax rate can be high. In order to lessen the sting of regressivity, most states exempt purchases of prescription drugs from the sales tax, and about half the states exempt food purchases as well.

Excise Taxes. Also known as "product taxes" and sometimes called "sin taxes," excise taxes are sales taxes on specific items or goods (thus "excise" taxes are distinguishable from a "general sales" tax). The most common excise taxes are the motor fuels (gasoline) tax, the tobacco tax, and various alcohol (beer, wine, distilled spirits) taxes. In many states, these taxes are "earmarked," or dedicated, for specific expenditure funds; gasoline taxes are usually set aside for the highway or transportation department. Therefore, the contribution of these revenues to the state general fund may be limited. Moreover, the tax rate is highly variable by state. For example, in 2019 the gasoline tax was 8.95 cents per gallon in Alaska but 57.6 cents per gallon in Pennsylvania. The state-by-state disparity in the tobacco excise tax rate is even greater: 17 cents per pack of cigarettes in Missouri to $4.35 per pack in New York and Connecticut.[38] With the rise of vaping, states have begun to institute taxes on it as well; by mid-2019 seventeen states had done so.[39]

A recent development is the imposition of an excise tax on the sale of recreational marijuana in those states that have legalized marijuana for personal use. Colorado is a case in point. The state imposes a 15 percent excise tax at the point of first sale (from wholesaler to retailer). Then there is a 10 percent sales tax when the product is sold by the retailer to the consumer. This sales tax surcharge is in addition to the standard 2.9 percent general sales tax. Overall, then, there is a 25 percent tax on the sale of recreational marijuana, in addition to the regular sales tax. In 2019, Colorado announced that it had raised $1.02 billion in tax revenue from marijuana sales since it was legalized in the state in 2014.[40] One might be tempted to say that the tax is a blunt instrument to improve Colorado's budget situation, generating more money than the long-established tax on liquor.[41] Meanwhile, the state of Washington, where the sale of marijuana for personal use is also legal, was expected to generate more than $150 million from a 37 percent sales tax surcharge in 2016.[42] It turns out that the estimate was too low; the state has been generating over $300 million a year in revenue from recreational marijuana sales, also exceeding what the state raised from its various alcohol taxes.[43] As of August 2019, eleven states had legalized recreational marijuana, and given the potential revenue bonanza more states will likely be considering the issue in 2020 and beyond.[44]

Corporate Income Tax. There are forty-four states that impose income taxes on corporations that do business in the state. Another four states—Nevada, Ohio, Texas, and Washington—impose a gross receipts tax on businesses. Both a gross receipts tax and a corporate income tax are applied in Delaware and Virginia. Only South Dakota and Wyoming fail to impose either a corporate income tax or a gross receipts tax.

In the case of the corporate income tax, more states use a flat rate rather than a graduated (progressive) structure. A typical flat rate is around 6 percent, but it is as low as 2.5 percent (North Carolina) and as high as 9.8 percent (Minnesota) and 9.99 percent (Pennsylvania). A minority of states have graduated corporate income taxes. Iowa actually imposes the highest rate, 12 percent on income above $250,000.[45] In recent years, many states have reduced their corporate income tax rates as a tactic to attract new enterprises or retain existing business.[46] Consequently, corporate income taxes have declined as a percent of total state revenue for most states.[47]

Severance Tax. This is a tax on the extraction or depletion of a non-renewable natural resource, usually a resource associated with energy production. A few states—Alaska and Texas are the obvious examples—have substantial underground reserves of oil or natural gas. Coal is another such resource. States that have such resources tax the "producer"—the coal or oil company—for extracting the resource from the state. The producer, of course, will eventually pass this tax on to the consumer as part of the total cost of the good.[48]

States that rely heavily on resource-based severance taxes are at budgetary risk because state revenues are closely tied to fluctuations in resource markets that are outside the state's control. For example, the severance tax on oil and natural gas generates the majority of budget revenue in Alaska, so much so that Alaska does not have a state general sales tax or a personal income tax. But a plunge in oil prices and the drop in oil production in the state created a $4 billion hole in the state's 2017 fiscal year budget, leaving the governor lamenting, "We've lost 80 percent of our income in about a year and a half."[49] Or take the case of North Dakota: between 2005 and 2014, almost half of the North Dakota general fund budget came from the severance tax on its newly developed "western oil patch." As we noted before, this recent "oil boom" meant that North Dakota was the only state that consistently had a budget surplus during the otherwise lean recession years. But when U.S. crude oil prices dropped from a high of $104 a barrel in 2014 to a mere $27 a barrel in January 2016, budgetary havoc ensued.[50] Recently, state officials in North Dakota estimated that every dollar increase or decrease in the price of a barrel of oil translates to a $33 million impact on the revenue of the state of North Dakota.[51]

Alaska (43.9 percent of state-generated revenue), North Dakota (47.3 percent), and Wyoming (39.4 percent) are heavily dependent on severance taxes. To a lesser yet still important extent, Louisiana, Montana, New Mexico, Oklahoma, Texas, and West Virginia are somewhat reliant on severance taxes, and thus are vulnerable to tax volatility based on the market for oil, natural gas, or coal.[52] But for the vast majority of states, the severance tax generates little revenue.

Charges and Miscellaneous Revenue. User fees, license fees, and fines are often lumped together under this category. These sources tend to be regressive because they are usually a flat amount ($50 for vehicle registration, for example) rather than a percentage of income. But there are exceptions: some states charge a higher license or registration fee for luxury cars, for example. Moreover, the states vary a lot in what they charge. In Mississippi, vehicle registration and title fees can be as low as $21.75, while in Montana it can cost up to $229 to register the same vehicle—almost ten times as much.[53] The same is true of fines: failure to wear a seatbelt can cost the driver $127.50 in Iowa but only $10 in neighboring Wisconsin.[54] User fees include highway or bridge tolls, camping fees at state parks, tuition at state colleges and universities, and a host of other charges. Following the 2008–2009 recession, many states increased user fees to help close their budget gaps.[55] As we will see in chapter 7, charges and miscellaneous revenues are an important part of the budgets in some types of local governments.

Lotteries, Gambling, and Other Revenue Sources. State-authorized lotteries were common in the nineteenth century but became increasingly contaminated by fraud and corruption. Interstate lotteries were outlawed by Congress and most states banned lotteries within their borders. By 1900 there were no state lotteries. This remained the case until 1964, when New Hampshire authorized a state lottery. Once New Hampshire opened the door, other states followed—New York in 1966 and New Jersey in 1970. By 1975, fifteen states had reintroduced lotteries. The modern-day adoption of state lotteries basically followed a regional pattern; once one state in a region introduced a lottery the neighboring states created their own lotteries within a few years. In 2019, Mississippi became the forty-fifth state to establish a lottery.[56] Lotteries do not generate nearly as much revenue for the states as sales and income taxes—about 1 percent of state revenues, but almost all states have adopted them, in part to capture these gambling dollars for the state.[57] If a state does not sponsor its own lottery, its citizens who are attracted to this type of gaming may simply take their dollars across the border to a neighboring state with a lottery. A vivid example of this phenomenon occurred in the intermountain region of the United States. Prior to 2014, neither Wyoming nor Utah had a lottery, but Idaho did. The stores with the highest volume of lottery sales in Idaho were in the sparsely populated southeast corner of the state—close to the Utah and Wyoming borders. One analysis found that Utahans bought almost 20 percent of traditional lottery tickets purchased in Idaho.[58]

Among the states that do maintain a lottery, there is a lot of variation in the way the lotteries are administered. Typically, about 62 percent of the ticket sales are returned as prize money, about 5 percent goes to administering and advertising the lottery games, and 33 percent is retained as revenue for the state. Overall, the states netted a total of about $18 billion on sales of $53 billion.[59] But there are big differences in the payout margin by state. Massachusetts (76 percent) and Minnesota (73 percent) return the highest percentages of total sales as prizes, while Louisiana, North Dakota, and Oklahoma return less than 55 percent. In other words, if you are inclined to play a state lottery, it is a better deal to play in East Grand Forks, Minnesota, than across the river in Grand Forks, North Dakota. Of course, by paying out more, Massachusetts and Minnesota retain a relatively low percentage of the revenue from lottery sales for the state coffers (around 20 percent), while Oklahoma keeps over 40 percent.

The absence of a state lottery should not be taken as a signal that a state is necessarily opposed to gambling. One of the five states that do not allow a state lottery is Nevada, where a lottery is prohibited by the state constitution.

A related source of state revenue that has gained in popularity in recent years is casino gambling, which generates money for states from licenses and taxes on the profits. For many years, gambling was illegal in every state except Nevada (which legalized it in 1931). In 1976, New Jersey legalized gambling in Atlantic City as part of an effort to revive the downtrodden resort community. In 1989, Iowa responded to budgetary problems by permitting gambling on riverboats plying the rivers along the state's borders. Riverboat gambling quickly became adopted by several other states along the Mississippi as they too searched for new revenue streams. By 2019, twenty-five states had legalized commercial casino gambling, generating about $25.5 billion in tax revenue.[60] In addition, twenty-eight states have agreements allowing American Indians to operate casinos on tribal lands, generating another $15.2 billion in tax revenue and tribal revenue share.[61] Only Hawaii and Utah do not allow any form of wagering, thereby forswearing that potential source of state revenue.

In 2018, the U.S. Supreme Court handed down a decision, based in part on the Tenth Amendment that, the federal government could not prevent states from legalizing and taxing gambling on sporting events (sports betting).[62] Almost immediately, states began passing laws to take advantage of this potential revenue source. Within six months of the Court decision, Delaware, Mississippi, New Jersey, Pennsylvania, and West Virginia legalized sports betting and set up mechanisms to tax the winnings. By mid-2019 ten states had legalized sports betting and other seven states had passed laws that will allow them to pursue it.[63] But the early revenue gains are disappointing; most states estimate they will generate only between $5 million and $25 million per year.[64]

The states have miscellaneous other revenue sources. In seventeen states the state government controls the wholesale market for alcohol.[65] North Dakota owns its own state bank, and has done so profitably for one hundred years.[66] For the most part, these are not major revenue generators and the funds they produce are usually earmarked for specific expenditure accounts (and therefore are not part of the discretionary general fund account).

Federal Aid. For generations now, federal grants-in-aid to states and, to a lesser extent, to local governments have been an important part of the total subnational revenue package. The first significant transfer of funds from the national to subnational governments began during the Great Depression of the 1930s.[67] As table 3.2 shows, the proportion of federal aid to state and local governments has increased over time, but not in a monotonic manner. In 1960, 14.3 percent of the funds spent by state and local governments came from the national government as federal aid. This figure steadily increased during the 1960s and 1970s, first under Lyndon Johnson's "Great Society" and then Richard Nixon's "New Federalism." By the time Ronald Reagan became president, state and local governments relied on federal aid for over 27 percent of their expenditures. In other words, state/local dependence on federal aid basically doubled between 1960 and 1980. Under the Reagan administration, there was an effort to roll back the magnitude of the reliance on fiscal federal dollars—in part because of the president's desire to reverse the growing state dependence on the federal government and in part because of growing concerns over the size of the federal deficit. This effort was largely successful and by 1990 the state/local reliance on federal aid had declined.

But by 2000 the figure crept back up a bit, largely due to an ever-expanding Medicaid program. The Great Recession and the active role of the Obama

Table 3.2.   Federal Grants-in-Aid as a Percentage of State and Local Expenditures

Year	Percentage
1960	14.3
1970	19.6
1980	27.3
1990	18.7
2000	21.8
2010	26.4
2017	23.0

Source: U.S. Office of Management and Budget.

administration in providing additional assistance to states and local entities is reflected in the 2010 figure, 26.4 percent. By 2017, that figure had receded to 23 percent. Recall that these figures represent the percentage of federal aid for state and local governments combined, and that most federal aid is directed to states rather than local governments. Consequently, the proportion of just state spending received from federal assistance is higher—about 31 percent.

CHANGES IN THE STATE REVENUE STRUCTURE

State fiscal systems are not static. They change over time as they adapt, albeit often somewhat slowly, to changing economic circumstances. For example, look at table 3.3, which shows the adoption of various taxes and lotteries by the states over time. Almost all states quickly adopted the gasoline tax between 1910 and 1929, as the automobile became more and more prevalent and the demand for paved roads became stronger. The personal income tax became a primary revenue source in the early decades of the twentieth century; thirty-two states adopted the income tax between 1900 and 1939. Adoption of the general sales tax occurred slightly later; forty-four states adopted the sales tax between 1930 and 1969. Finally, lotteries became a common revenue source in the later part of the twentieth century as thirty-seven states established state-authorized lotteries between 1960 and 1999.[68]

One of the reasons that states seek new or altered revenue sources is because the revenue generation capacity of some older sources declines over time. A case in point is the general sales tax. As noted earlier, most states tax sales on goods (products) but not on services. This worked when most of the economic activity in the United States was goods-oriented. But over the last half-century, the economy has increasingly shifted toward the service sector. This means that less and less of the overall economic activity is captured by the goods-oriented sales tax. This is one of the reasons that so many states have increased the sales tax rate over time—to make up for the revenue "lost" to

Table 3.3. The Number of States Adopting Revenue Sources in Each Decade

Decade	Income tax	General sales tax	Gasoline tax	Lottery	Recreational marijuana excise tax
1900–1909	1	—	—	—	—
1910–1919	9	—	4	—	—
1920–1929	5	—	44	—	—
1930–1939	17	23	1	—	—
1940–1949	1	5	1	—	—
1950–1959	—	5	—	—	—
1960–1969	7	11	—	2	—
1970–1979	4	—	—	11	—
1980–1989	—	—	—	18	—
1990–1999	—	—	—	6	—
2000–2009	—	—	—	6	—
2010–2019	—	—	—	1	11

Source: Calculations by authors.

the service sector. As a result of all of these changes, the relative impact of the general sales tax as a revenue source has declined over the past quarter-century. In 1977, this tax accounted for 31 percent of all state general revenue. By 2016, it accounted for 23 percent. During that same period, corporate income taxes declined from about 5.5 percent to 2 percent. Meanwhile, reliance on charges and miscellaneous revenues increased from about 12 percent to 19 percent.[69] Clearly, the relative contribution of various revenue streams changes over time. As we shall see later, the same can be said on the expenditure side—over time, spending changes. Both the supply and demand sides of state fiscal systems are in constant flux.

THE REGRESSIVE CHARACTER OF STATE AND LOCAL TAX SYSTEMS

As mentioned earlier, the way a state structures its overall tax system—and that of its local governments—defines several fiscal consequences. How the tax burden is spread among the citizens of the state is one of these. As noted earlier, tax structures may be progressive, proportional, or regressive. A progressive tax is one that takes a larger percentage as income rises, a proportional tax takes the same percentage from all income levels, and one that is regressive taxes people with lower incomes at a higher rate than wealthier people. The focus here is on rate, or percentage, not on the total amount the tax generates. Even a regressive tax will often mean a wealthier person is paying a greater amount than a poor person, even if the wealthy person is paying a lower percentage. For example, if Person A makes $100,000 and pays 5 percent toward taxes and Person B makes only $10,000 but pays 15 percent toward taxes, A pays $5,000 while B pays $1,500. Person A paid more in actual dollars ($5,000 to $1,500) but considerably less as a percentage of his or her income (5 percent compared to 15 percent for B). Nonetheless, the discussion about the regressive, proportional, or progressive nature of the tax structure is a common one because it is ultimately a discussion about what "share" of one's income goes to taxes and what amounts to a "fair share" across various income levels. To illustrate how the tax structures of states can affect the citizens, consider table 3.4. Notice that the states designated as "most regressive" are Washington, Texas, Florida, South Dakota, and Nevada (they rank 1 through 5 in regressivity). All five are states without a personal income tax, meaning they must rely more heavily on sales taxes, excise taxes, and fees and licenses—all of which tend to put a greater relative tax burden on the poorer citizens.

A particularly interesting contrast in state taxing approaches occurs in the Pacific Northwest. Oregon and Washington are neighboring states that many people consider to be alike in policies and political cultures. But their state tax structures are diametrically opposed and as a consequence they place different tax burdens on different economic groups within their state. Oregon has a personal income tax but no general sales tax, creating a system that is basically proportional, with all income groups paying taxes between 8.8 percent and 10.1 percent. In contrast, Washington has no personal income tax but instead relies heavily on sales taxes, excise taxes, and fees, creating a tax system that puts a much greater relative burden on the poorest one-fifth (the lowest quintile). That group pays almost 18 percent of their income in state taxes in Washington, while the highest quintile pays only 6.4 percent. Washington's is a dramatically regressive tax structure.

The fact is that almost all state and local tax structures are at least mildly regressive. The reason, as mentioned previously, is that most excise taxes, licenses and user fees, and sales taxes are regressive. For example, a $100 per year automobile registration fee is a larger percent of the income of someone making $5,000 a year than it is of someone making $50,000 a year. A sales tax is also regressive because it is based on the purchase of goods (consumption) rather than income. Most state and local governments rely heavily on fees, sales taxes, and excise taxes. For the most part, the only tax that can be designed as truly proportional or even progressive is the individual income tax. Thus, the degree of regressivity of a state and local tax structure is largely a matter of how much that state relies on a progressive individual income tax structure instead of a general sales tax or user fees. While most states have a tax structure that is at least somewhat regressive, a few have tax structures that approach proportionality: Oregon, Delaware, Minnesota, and Vermont are currently the best examples.

Table 3.4. State Tax Burdens for Different Income Groups

State	Tax burden for LOWEST quintile (lowest 20% in state)	Tax burden for MIDDLE quintile (middle 20% in state)	Tax burden for HIGHEST quintile (highest 20% in state)	Regressivity ranking (1 = most regressive)
AL	9.9	9.0	6.6	18
AK	7.0	4.3	2.7	26
AZ	13.0	9.4	7.3	11
AR	11.3	10.8	8.9	20
CA	10.5	8.3	9.7	50
CO	8.7	8.9	7.3	35
CT	11.5	12.2	10.6	29
DE	5.5	5.6	6.2	48
FL	12.7	8.1	5.2	3
GA	10.7	9.8	8.4	27
HI	15.0	11.6	9.3	15
ID	9.2	8.1	7.6	38
IL	14.4	12.6	10.5	8
IN	12.8	11.1	8.1	12
IA	12.4	10.7	9.4	21
KS	11.4	10.6	9.5	23
KY	9.5	11.1	9.3	25
LA	11.9	10.0	7.8	14
ME	8.7	9.6	9.8	45
MD	9.8	10.6	10.3	42
MA	10.0	9.3	8.3	30
MI	10.4	9.2	8.3	22
MN	8.7	9.7	9.5	47
MS	10.2	10.8	7.7	24
MO	9.9	9.0	8.4	28
MT	7.9	7.1	6.7	43
NE	11.1	10.8	9.2	36
NV	10.2	7.6	4.9	5
NH	9.1	8.1	5.3	16
NJ	8.7	10.1	10.0	46

Table 3.4. (Continued)

State	Tax burden for LOWEST quintile (lowest 20% in state)	Tax burden for MIDDLE quintile (middle 20% in state)	Tax burden for HIGHEST quintile (highest 20% in state)	**Regressivity ranking (1 = most regressive)**
NM	10.6	10.2	8.3	**19**
NY	11.4	12.4	12.3	**44**
NC	9.5	9.4	8.1	**31**
ND	10.3	8.5	5.6	**17**
OH	12.3	10.7	9.3	**13**
OK	13.2	10.7	8.2	**9**
OR	10.1	9.1	8.8	**41**
PA	13.8	11.1	9.0	**7**
RI	12.1	9.5	9.0	**32**
SC	8.3	8.1	7.9	**39**
SD	11.2	8.9	5.3	**4**
TN	10.5	8.5	5.3	**6**
TX	13.0	9.7	6.8	**2**
UT	7.5	8.2	7.7	**40**
VT	8.7	10.1	10.3	**49**
VA	9.8	9.2	8.4	**33**
WA	17.8	11.0	6.4	**1**
WV	9.4	8.5	8.4	**37**
WI	10.1	10.1	9.6	**34**
WY	9.6	7.5	4.7	**10**
Mean	11.4	9.9	8.8	

Source: Institute on Taxation and Economic Policy, "Who Pays? A 50-State Report, 6th edition" 2019, http://www.itep.org/whopays/full_report.php. Figures represent state and local tax rates. Regressivity rank calculated by ITEP.

FISCAL FEDERALISM: FEDERAL AID TO STATES (AND LOCALITIES)

Fiscal federalism is a sensitive subject for the states. On the one hand, state officials (especially state elected officials) assert the independence and sovereignty and innovation capacity of their state. On the other hand, the same officials are willing to accept federal financial assistance, particularly during tough times.

As mentioned earlier in this chapter, the American Recovery and Reinvestment Act (ARRA) of 2009 provided a generous infusion of federal funds to help the states weather the worst of the Great Recession. These federal "stimulus" funds totaled about $500 billion to the states for FYs 2009, 2010, and 2011 combined.[70] They were used by the states in many different ways, but principal among them was to help the states pay their share of Medicaid costs and to extend unemployment benefits for longer periods than usual.[71] ARRA funds also helped many states avoid cuts (or avoid deeper cuts) in K–12 and higher education funding and continue or start a number of infrastructure construction projects (e.g., road building and other "shovel-ready" projects). Without this additional assistance from the federal government, there is little doubt that state and local governments would have suffered even greater program cuts than they did. Of course, there was the requisite partisan posturing first. Several governors, among them Republicans Bobby Jindal of Louisiana and Mark Sanford of South Carolina, announced that their states would not accept some of the "bailout" funds. Ultimately, however, the legislatures in both states passed bills that accepted virtually all the money available to them.[72] It is hard for a state to walk away from federal money, particularly during times of great fiscal stress.[73]

Unlike the ARRA, most federal aid is ongoing, composed of annual transfers of money from the federal government to state or local governments with specific conditions and guidelines ("strings attached") for the use of those funds. Federal grants, therefore, are not part of the state "general fund" budget but rather are part of the nondiscretionary part of the budget over which states have little control. Moreover, most federal grant-in-aid programs require that states share in the cost by using some state funds to pay for part of the program, as with the Medicaid and TANF programs discussed in chapter 5. This is known as the "match" or "cost-share" that a state must contribute. As Marilyn Rubin and Katherine Willoughby observe, "Federal funds often come with matching requirements that states must contribute a certain percentage of total funding for specified programs and particular services. Given that states must balance their budgets, if they decide to accept the federal money, they must make trade-offs between spending money for federally funded programs and other state spending priorities."[74]

Some of the programs mandated by the federal government (perhaps especially environmental and health care programs) might go unfunded in some states without the federal mandate. Overall, of the money state and local governments spend, over the last several generations a larger proportion of it has come from the federal government. And if the money comes from the federal government, it almost always comes with conditions. Accordingly, there is a reduction in state control over policy (the federal "strings" require states or local governments to do certain things). It is certainly possible that some types of federal aid to the states will diminish. If reductions do come to pass, they will pose additional challenges for the states and their local governments, as the programs currently funded in part by federal grants will have to be pared back, eliminated altogether, or funded by an increase in state revenues, likely necessitating an increase in state taxes. None of these are politically attractive alternatives.

Looking back to table 3.2, we find that it shows that the proportion of state and local revenues received through federal aid has increased, then decreased, and then increased again over recent decades. But what table 3.2 does not show is how the nature of that aid has changed. At one time, the largest federal aid program was physical infrastructure needs—especially the construction of the interstate highway system. Over time, the emphasis shifted from infrastructure to social programs, especially health care in the form of Medicaid, as shown in table 3.5.

In 1960, there was no Medicaid program (health care, largely for lower-income groups) at all. At that time highway grants were the largest federal aid program (accounting for 43 percent of federal aid), followed by income security ("welfare," primarily Aid to Families with Dependent Children at 38 percent) and education and unemployment (8 percent). Those three functional areas accounted for almost nine out of every ten dollars of federal aid.

By 1980, federal aid flowed to the four functional areas of health care, welfare, education/unemployment, and transportation in a roughly equal manner, and it was increasing modestly for all four functional areas. This trend changed dramatically by 1990. Medicaid, which had been created in 1965, had become the driving force behind the increase in federal aid, and by 2019 it accounted for well over half of all federal aid.

Table 3.5. Federal Grants to State and Local Governments, by Selected Policy Areas

	Health (%)	Income security (%)	Education and social service (%)	Transportation (%)	Community development (%)
2019	60.5	15.2	8.9	9.0	2.9
2010	47.7	18.9	16.0	10.0	3.1
2000	43.7	23.8	12.6	11.2	3.3
1990	32.6	26.7	15.6	14.1	4.0
1980	17.7	20.2	24.0	14.3	7.0
1970	16.0	24.1	26.7	19.2	7.4
1960	3.0	38.0	7.4	42.9	7.6

Source: Congressional Research Grants, Federal Grants to State and Local Governments, May 22, 2019, https://fas.org/sgp/crs/misc/R40638.pdf.

To look at this point from another angle, consider that most grant money goes to one of two purposes: costs to provide for individuals and costs to build or maintain physical infrastructure. In 1960, about half of all federal aid was for "physical capital" (i.e., infrastructure).[75] By 2019, infrastructure costs accounted for only 10 percent. Today, federal aid to individuals accounts for over three-quarters of all federal aid. In a half-century the broader purpose behind federal assistance to the states and their local governments had shifted from infrastructure to social services. What this suggests is that any reduction in federal aid will likely have a human face attached to it—meaning that the decisions about what the state should do about these programs will directly impact some number of citizens of the state.

While federal aid is important in all states, it is far more central in some states than in others. The Tax Foundation reports that the median state receives about 33 percent of its "general revenue" from federal aid. Note that this figure is just for state revenue and does not include federal aid to local governments. By this reckoning, state reliance on federal aid ranges from about 21 percent (Virginia) to 43 percent (Mississippi). There are currently six states that rely on federal aid for at least 40 percent of their general revenues: Arizona, Kentucky, Louisiana, Mississippi, Montana, and New Mexico.[76]

STATE EXPENDITURES

The first point we want to emphasize is that the services and regulatory actions performed at the local level—by cities, counties, and so on—are ultimately the responsibility of the state government. States delegate some of their governmental responsibilities to local governments because it makes sense to do so. But exactly which responsibilities they delegate and to which local governments and to what extent they are delegated are questions that are answered differently by each state. We will discuss this topic in greater detail in chapter 7. It is a complex situation. We will try to simplify it by using the term "subnational" to refer to actions of both the state and local governments, when appropriate. Public education, for example, is largely a subnational responsibility—one shared and largely funded by both state and local governments. While K–12 education is delivered at the local government level, state constitutions generally hold the state government responsible for providing primary and secondary education.

Table 3.6 shows the proportion of state spending devoted to various functions, and it reports these percentages in two ways. The first column shows the percentage of total spending for various functions and includes both federal aid and state own-source spending. The third column shows the spending just from own-source state spending (i.e., does not include federal aid). Clearly, the two largest expenditure categories are Medicaid and education. Note the relative positions of those two categories depending on whether we look at the first column (with federal aid) or the third column (without federal aid). The conclusion to draw is that states receive a great deal of federal help for Medicaid spending,

Table 3.6. State Spending by Functional Area (all states combined)

Total spending by states (including federal aid) (%)	Functional area	Total spending by states from own source funds only (%)
29.7	Medicaid	17.1
19.6	K–12 education	25.1
10.1	Higher Education	13.2
8.0	Transportation	7.7
3.1	Corrections	4.5
29.6	Other (transfers to local governments, contributions to pension funds, etc.)	32.6

Source: National Association of State Budget Officers, "Summary: NASBO State Expenditure Report." November 15, 2018, https://higherlogicdownload.s3.amazonaws.com/NASBO/9d2d2db1-c943-4f1b-b750-0fca152d64c2/UploadedImages/Issue%20Briefs%20/2018_State_Expenditure_Report_Summary.pdf.

but much less for education. The "other" category in table 3.6 includes transfers to local governments, which is a major source of expenditures in some states. This is a topic we will discuss in greater detail in chapter 8.

Exploding health care costs are a major concern, especially for state-level officials. The reason is that Medicaid costs continue to command an ever-increasing share of the state budget.[77] Medicaid costs to the states have increased an average of 7 percent per year over the past decade—that means the costs basically doubled in ten years, prompting one New Mexico legislator to describe Medicaid costs as a "runaway train."[78] Moreover, Medicaid costs increase during an economic downturn, because as more people become unemployed and lose job-related health care insurance, they become eligible for health care benefits through Medicaid. So, the demand for Medicaid benefits increases but the supply of state revenue to fund those benefits decreases (because the unemployed pay less in taxes). It is, in other words, a pro-cyclical effect. For example, the Medicaid caseload in Colorado grew by 19 percent as the Great Recession took effect.[79]

Another increasingly significant expenditure for subnational governments is their contribution to public employee pension funds. In 2011, a report from the Congressional Budget Office made the dire observation that, "The recent financial crisis and economic recession have left many states and localities with extraordinary budgetary difficulties for the next few years, but structural shortfalls in their pension plans pose a problem that is likely to endure for much longer."[80] That forecast has largely been proven correct. Historically, retirement packages for many state and local employees included "defined benefit" plans, meaning that the recipient would receive a specific, defined, annual retirement benefit based on their years of service and the salaries they earned. These benefits (pensions) are paid from funds state and local governments maintain. In most instances, retirement funds rely on income from three sources: contributions from the public employee, direct appropriations from the state or local government budget, and revenue generated by investments of pension funds. Today, many of these pension funds are underfunded; they do not contain enough money to meet their projected obligations as "baby boomer" public employees begin to retire. This problem was caused in part by the Great Recession, which caused pension fund investments to perform poorly. But it is also the case that many states opted to skip their required contributions, using that money instead to fund other priorities.[81]

The public employee pension problem is especially acute in Illinois, Kentucky, and New Jersey, but several other states are also seriously underfunded.[82] The Pew Center on the States has referred to this on the aggregated level as "the trillion dollar gap," and it is a looming demand side (expenditure) problem for many states. According to their 2019 analysis,

> Overall in 2017, states had 69 percent of the assets they needed to fully fund their pension liabilities—ranging from 34 percent in Kentucky to 103 percent in Wisconsin. In addition to Kentucky, four other states—Colorado, Connecticut, Illinois, and New Jersey—were less than 50 percent funded, and another 15 had less than two-thirds of the assets they needed to pay their pension obligations. Only Idaho, Nebraska, New York, North Carolina, South Dakota, Tennessee, and Utah joined Wisconsin in being at least 90 percent funded.[83]

Kentucky in particular has made some efforts recently to begin to address its pension crisis, but it will take many years to adequately address the problem. Even a prolonged bull stock market has proven insufficient to fill the pension coffers in the states with the biggest funding gaps.[84]

One result of this situation is a movement to change the way public employee pensions are going to be funded in the future. According to a recent analysis, "Among the most frequent reforms are reduced benefit levels, longer vesting periods, increased age and service requirements, limited cost-of-living adjustments, and increased employer and employee contributions."[85] Many states are also instituting "defined contribution" plans for the newly hired, in which the employee and employer both contribute to a retirement account that the employee controls. Once the state makes its contribution, however, it is no longer on the financial hook in the manner it is with a traditional "defined benefit" plan. The financial risk is transferred completely onto the employee. Some states have developed "hybrid" pension plans that combine features of both defined contribution and defined benefit plans and share the risks.[86]

CONCLUSION

In this chapter we have discussed a number of variables that, in combination, bode ill for state fiscal systems in the future. Balanced budget rules and heavy reliance on income and general sales taxes as revenue sources mean that state fiscal systems tend to be pro-cyclical. To exacerbate the situation, economic downturns trigger a higher demand for state social services (unemployment benefits, health care, and the like). Furthermore, federal aid to the states may diminish in the future as the national government grapples with its own daunting fiscal challenges. As two public finance experts note, "While the federal government has recently provided antirecession assistance to states and localities in the short term, escalating deficits in the short and long term will sap the flexibility and capacity of the federal government to play its time-honored role as the equalizer in public finance."[87] Meanwhile, many states have gravely underfunded public employee pension plans at the same time that their baby boomer workers are beginning to retire.

Compounding this situation, many states have infrastructure systems that are rapidly deteriorating. Recently, the American Society of Civil Engineers graded the quality of American infrastructure—roads, highways, bridges, and levees, and so on—as "D+."[88] Much of the responsibility for dealing with the sorry state of the infrastructure—estimated to cost some $4 trillion over the next decade—will likely fall to the states. As one report states, "Over the last two years state and local governments have come to realize that the federal government isn't coming to the rescue. The cavalry isn't coming."[89]

Interestingly, some Republican governors and legislators—usually extremely reticent to discuss tax hikes—have pushed to raise gasoline taxes or automobile license fees as a way to generate money for road and highway upgrades.[90] Notably in 2015, Republicans in Iowa and Washington agreed to gas tax increases to fund transportation projects. But in 2016, Republicans in other states—Oklahoma and Kansas are prime examples—opted to raid their transportation budgets to plug budget shortfalls in the general budget. By 2019, many states seem to have reconciled themselves to the fact that, despite the rhetoric from Washington, DC, they were largely going to have to address the infrastructure problem on their own. On July 1, 2019 (the first day of FY 2020 in most states), thirteen states raised their gasoline taxes, including a 10 cents per gallon increase in Ohio and a whopping 19 cents per gallon increase in Illinois. As one energy service analyst observed, "I don't ever recall these many states raising gas taxes on the same day."[91] Necessity forced the states to take the politically risky act.

More generally, a 2018 report by the federal Government Accountability Office stated, "Since 2007, GAO has published simulations of long-term fiscal trends in the state and local government sector, which have consistently shown that the sector faces long-term fiscal pressures."[92] This means that it will be necessary for states to tackle their fiscal issues head-on. "States' rights" also means "states' responsibilities." It may also mean "opportunities for the states." Given the prospects of chronic federal deficits and given that most federal aid now and in the future will have to be spent on health care, now is the time for states to contemplate their roles and responsibilities in the various policy arenas in which they are involved. This includes the way in which states allow their local governments to address problems at the community level.

A report from the Urban Institute notes that any balance between state revenues and expenditures is increasingly tenuous and some of the problems facing the states—such as increased Medicaid costs, aging populations, and potential cutbacks in many federal aid programs—do not lend themselves to simple solutions. As two political scientists recently described it, state and local governments are facing a "fiscal ice age" in which "a given level of tax revenue purchases a considerably lower level of current services."[93] States will face painful decisions. As the report states,

> This challenge is not new. What is new is the unwillingness to acknowledge the dilemma that leads to recurring budget showdowns even as the economy recovers. Eight states could not agree on a budget by the time their fiscal year started in July 2015. Many of them were in the same position last year and are likely to be in the same position next year.[94]

Indeed, as the headlines at the beginning of this chapter demonstrate, the problem has not gone away. And it may become a chronic feature of American political life.

4

The Policymaking Environment in the States

States matter because:

* State government structures are distinctive from those of the national government.
* State legislatures are different one from another and operate with a variety of structures and resource levels.
* Governors have become powerful political actors, with great influence over the policymaking process.
* Bureaucracies have evolved to handle the policy burdens required by the states.
* State courts operate with different structures and different methods of selection to the bench.

IT IS EASY TO THINK of the fifty state governments as being smaller, less powerful versions of the federal government. In this view, the governors are simply minor league versions of the president, state legislatures a pale imitation of the Congress, and state courts the institutions left to handle traffic violations and minor property disputes while the federal courts tackle the heavy legal issues. But such a perspective is fundamentally misguided; as discussed in chapter 1 state governments make a host of significant policy decisions. They have their own histories and have developed their own governing structures, none of which exactly mirror the federal experience. Moreover, as discussed in chapter 2, the lines of policy authority separating the federal and state governments have never been clear and are continually shifting. Thus, it is critical to understand how the state governments we have today have come to be as they are and how their decision-making power over the endless number of policy decisions that shape our daily lives has developed, because it is not self-evident from understanding government at the national level.

In this chapter we trace the development of the policymaking environment in the states. We discuss why over time state legislatures came to lose power, while governors and state courts increased their influence over policymaking. We then discuss why these changes matter and what difference they make to the policymaking process. Finally, we turn to an examination of which policies the states dominate and how the mix of policies over which they govern has changed over time.

DESIGNING GOVERNMENTS

It is essential to appreciate that the original thirteen states were governing entities before any national government was established. When the first states emerged during the early movement toward independence, they had to create ruling structures to replace the colonial structures against which they were rebelling without having any national model to emulate. The initial governing device employed in most of the emerging states was called the provincial congress. These bodies were representative assemblies that assumed legislative, executive, and, to a much lesser extent, judicial functions. They governed from roughly 1774 through early to mid-1776, when the newly written state constitutions began taking effect.[1]

In designing new governing structures, those who wrote these constitutions wanted systems that functioned more effectively than the provincial congresses had. Indeed, in the preamble to New York's 1777 constitution, the authors admitted, "And whereas many and great inconveniences attend the said mode of government by congress and committees, as of necessity, in many instances, legislative, judicial, and executive powers have been vested therein." Thus, the new governments were created with the now familiar idea of separate legislative, executive, and judicial branches. But in reality, this initial separation of powers was fuzzy and uneven. What was actually created in the first states was a system where the legislative branch clearly dominated the other two branches. Policymaking effectively rested entirely in the hands of each state's lawmakers, establishing legislative supremacy.

THE RISE, FALL, AND RESURRECTION OF THE STATE LEGISLATURES

Explicit references to a separation of powers were present in about half of the original state constitutions. But only in New York and Massachusetts was the notion given much attention, and even in these constitutions clear lines dividing the branches were not to be found. The muddled nature of separation of power greatly bothered James Madison, who later complained in *Federalist* 47:

> If we look into the constitutions of the several States we find that, not with-standing the emphatical and, in some instances, the unqualified terms in which this axiom has been laid down, there is not a single instance in which the several departments of power have been kept absolutely separate and distinct.[2]

In designing the new federal government, Madison and his colleagues made a conscious effort to establish a more clearly defined and balanced distribution of power among the three branches.

In particular, those who wrote the federal constitution were concerned that in the state constitutions too much power had been concentrated in the hands of state legislatures. There was considerable evidence to support their apprehensions. In eight of the new states, the legislature elected the governor. And in a slightly different set of eight states, the legislature selected judges. This meant that in a majority of the new states the governor and the judges were directly beholden to the legislature for their positions. Not surprisingly, legislatures used their dominant position to bully the other branches to do their bidding. In a celebrated 1786 legal case, *Trevett v. Weeden*, Rhode Island's Supreme Court issued a decision declaring a measure passed by the legislature to be unconstitutional, the first time any state court had done so. Lawmakers responded by demanding that the justices appear before them to justify their decision. The justices' arguments were not persuasive and when their terms expired the following year, legislators voted to replace all of those who had supported the decision.

But the era of legislative supremacy did not last long in most states. As early as the 1780s efforts were made to rein in legislatures, in part by taking away their control over gubernatorial selection and also by giving the judiciary greater independence.[3] When the original states replaced their initial constitutions, the newer documents included provisions that constrained lawmakers; when new states were admitted to the Union, their constitutions limited legislative power from the start. As will be discussed shortly, these changes unyoked governors and judges from legislative dominance. And constitutions also came to place explicit limits on the kinds of laws the legislature could pass. Article IV, Section 27 of the 1865 Missouri constitution, for example, contained specific prohibitions against the legislature "establishing, locating, altering the course, or affecting the construction of roads, or the building or repairing of bridges; or establishing, altering, or vacating any street, avenue, or alley in any city or town" and "extending the time for the assessment or collection of taxes, or otherwise relieving any assessor or collector of taxes from the due performance of his official duties." Similar sorts of detailed limitations appeared in most nineteenth-century state constitutions.[4]

Arguably, the most prominent among the constitutional restraints imposed were provisions allowing legislatures to meet only once every other year. In the original states, legislatures were required to meet each year because it was thought frequent meetings promoted closer ties between representatives and the represented and also afforded the legislature greater control over the executive.[5] When legislative supremacy began to fall out of favor, the rationale behind legislative sessions shifted. Because it was thought that legislatures had abused their powers, holding sessions only every other year came to be preferred because it was calculated that lawmakers would be able to cause less trouble, the system of laws would become more stable, and the cost of running the legislature would be reduced.[6] As documented in table 4.1, the trend over the course of the nineteenth century was unmistakable. At the beginning of the century, almost every state had annual sessions. By the end of the century, almost every state had biennial sessions. In 1901, Alabama even went so far as to institute quadrennial sessions. As we will discuss later, governors were the main beneficiaries of the trend toward having legislature meet less often. In essence, a power vacuum was created and the executive filled it.

The trend toward less frequent legislative sessions reversed course in the twentieth century, as public pressure on the states to perform better began to build. As more demands were made of state government, it seemed prudent to have the legislature meet annually. It was also thought that, echoing ideas in the original constitutions, annual sessions would help rein in gubernatorial power.[7] As table 4.1 documents, by 2019 only four states (Montana, Nevada, North Dakota, and Texas) still meet every other year; the rest have annual sessions.

State legislatures, of course, underwent other important changes during the twentieth century, as will be detailed in chapter 5. Most important, as they came to meet annually, their sessions also became longer and they met for more days. Because legislative service became more demanding, legislative compensation

Table 4.1. The Rise, Fall, and Resurrection of Legislative Power, 1777 to 2019

Year	Number of states	Number of states with:		
		Annual sessions	Biennial sessions	Quadrennial sessions
1777	13	13	—	—
1832	24	21	3	—
1861	33	15	18	—
1889	38	6	32	—
1931	48	6	41	1
1960	50	19	31	—
1999	50	43	7	—
2019	50	46	4	—

Source: Adapted from Peverill Squire, *The Evolution of American Legislatures: Colonies, Territories, and States, 1619-2009,* Ann Arbor: University of Michigan Press, 2012, pages 243-49, 270-73.

and benefits improved. Staff also increased, giving lawmakers a greater ability to generate and evaluate information needed to make decisions. Facilities generally improved as well; members usually came to have private offices and access to computers and other technological innovations that improved their capacity to do their job. All of these changes are subsumed under the concept of legislative professionalization. The idea driving these changes was to make the legislatures more competitive with the governor and the executive branch in the policymaking process. Thus, during the American federal experience, state legislatures have traveled from being the dominant governing institution to being weakened to the point of near irrelevancy to being rehabilitated to once again be important players in policymaking.

THE INCREASING POWER OF THE GOVERNOR

The American colonies had governors who were, in all but Connecticut and Rhode Island, appointed and imbued with impressive formal powers. But in reality, their ability to exercise those powers was greatly constricted by the fact that control over taxing and spending came to be asserted by the colonial assemblies. As noted earlier, when the new states wrote their constitutions, they opted to make the legislatures powerful and the governors (called presidents in several states) weak. Indeed, New Hampshire chose to go without any chief executive at all until its 1784 constitution! As James Madison noted during the Constitutional Convention, "The executives of the states are in general little more than ciphers; the legislatures omnipotent."[8] The original governors' lack of power can be documented in two ways, as shown in table 4.2. First, in eight of the states the governor was elected by the legislature. This method of election put the executive under the legislature's thumb. Governors who wanted to retain office had to appease lawmakers. Second, in nine of the states the governor was given only a one-year term, leaving them little time to accomplish any significant policy goals. Election by the legislature and short terms of office were adopted to ensure that all significant policy decisions were made by the legislature.

The flaws of this institutional design became apparent relatively quickly. Those who wrote the federal constitution, for example, decided against having Congress elect the president and gave the office a four-year term. In the states, as legislatures came to be seen as be abusing their exalted position, power was taken from them and given largely to the executive.[9] By 1833, only four of the twenty-four governors were still elected by the legislature, meaning most of them were put into office by the voters. Indeed, every state that entered the union following the first thirteen states required its governor to be elected by the people. By 1889, all governors were directly elected, with South Carolina being the last state to give way on this score in 1866. Being directly elected gave governors an independent political base, which in turn could be leveraged to increase their ability to influence policy decisions.

Table 4.2. Gubernatorial Terms of Office over Time

Year	Number of states	Length of gubernatorial term by states							
		1 years		2 years		3 years		4 years	
1776–77	13[a]	9	CT, **GA**, **MD**, MA, **NJ**, **NC**, **PA**, RI, **VA**	1	**SC**	2	**DE**, NY	0	
1789	13	8	CT, **MD**, MA, NH, NJ, NC, **PA**, RI	1	**SC**	4	**DE**, **GA**, NY, **VA**	0	
1833	24	9	CT, ME, **MD**, MA, NH, **NJ**, **NC**, RI, VT	6	AL, GA, MS, NY, OH, **SC**	3	IN, PA, **VA**	6	DE, IL, KY, LA, MO, TN
1889	42	2	MA, RI	20	AL, AR, CO, CT, GA, IA, KS, ME, MI, MN, NE, NH, ND, OH, SC, SD, TN, TX, VT, WI	2	NJ, NY	18	CA, DE, FL, IL, IN, KY, LA, MD, MS, MO, MT, NV, NC, OR, PA, VA, WA, WV
1933	48	0		24	AZ, AR, CO, CT, GA, ID, IA, KS, ME, MA, MI, MN, NE, NH, NY, NM, ND, OH, RI, SD, TN, TX, VT, WI	1	NJ	23	AL, CA, DE, FL, IL, IN, KY, LA, MD, MS, MO, MT, NV, NC, OK, OR, PA, SC, UT, VA, WA, WV, WY

Table 4.2. (Continued)

Year	Number of states	Length of gubernatorial term by states				
		1 years	2 years	3 years		4 years
1989	50	0	3 NH, RI, VT	0	47	AL, AK, AZ, AR, CA, CO, CT, DE, FL, GA, HI, ID, IL, IN, IA, KS, KY, LA, ME, MD, MA, MI, MN, MS, MO, MT, NE, NV, NJ, NM, NY, NC, ND, OH, OK, OR, PA, SC, SD, TN, TX, UT, VA, WA, WV, WI, WY
2019	50	0	2 NH, VT	0	48	AL, AK, AZ, AR, CA, CO, CT, DE, FL, GA, HI, ID, IL, IN, IA, KS, KY, LA, ME, MD, MA, MI, MN, MS, MO, MT, NE, NV, NJ, NM, NY, NC, ND, OH, OK, OR, PA, RI, SC, SD, TN, TX, UT, VA, WA, WV, WI, WY

Note: States in bold indicate executive was elected by the legislature.
Source: Gathered by the authors from state constitutions.
[a]New Hampshire did not have a formal executive until 1784. Pennsylvania operated with a Supreme Executive Council headed by a president until 1790. Massachusetts did not adopt its constitution until 1780.

Governors also came to enjoy longer terms, affording them more time to accomplish their objectives. In 1833, fewer than half the states still retained one-year terms, while a quarter of them allowed their governor four years in office. A century later, no state had one-year terms; half had two-year terms and the other half either three- or four-year terms. The trend toward longer terms has continued. Currently only two states (New Hampshire and Vermont) have two-year terms; the rest have four-year terms. Governors now have more time to pursue their agendas, and lawmakers and others in the political process have to take that fact into account.

The second way it can be shown that governors have increased their powers is through the veto. Today, every governor enjoys some variant of a veto—the power to prevent legislation that has passed the legislature from becoming law.[10] The veto gives the executive the ability to greatly influence the legislative process. Most colonial governors had exercised an absolute veto, one that the assemblies had no ability to override. In reaction, in the majority of the new states the writers of their constitutions shied away from endowing the governor with any veto power. South Carolina's governor briefly enjoyed a veto of the sort his colonial predecessors had, but that was taken away completely within two years. In New York, the veto power was exercised collectively by the governor jointly with the council and the court. The only state with a veto that would be familiar today was Massachusetts, whose veto power was the model for the veto given the president in the U.S. Constitution.

Relatively quickly, however, most governors acquired a veto power, as voters came to fear legislative overreach more than arbitrary decisions by a monarchial chief executive. Among the original thirteen states, most gave their governor a veto as soon as they replaced their first constitutions. A few of them, however, lagged, most notably North Carolina, which did not grant its governor a veto until 1996. Among the states admitted after the original thirteen, almost all of them gave their governor a veto in their initial constitutions. Thus, all governors today have some capacity to veto measures passed by their legislatures, giving them significant leverage in the legislative process.

But, of course, not all vetoes are created equal. A line-item veto gives an executive the ability to pick and choose which provisions of a bill to accept and which to block. The original veto power in the Massachusetts constitution (and the one still in the U.S. Constitution) is a package veto; an all or nothing proposition in which the chief executive either accepts an entire measure or rejects it all. A line-item veto gives a governor even greater leverage over the legislature by allowing him or her to threaten specific provisions that matter greatly to lawmakers without risking losing things that he or she wants.

The line-item veto first appeared in American politics in, of all places, the Confederate constitution.[11] Georgia put one into its 1861 Confederate constitution twelve days later.[12] The line-item veto proved to be of sufficient interest that by the end of the nineteenth century a majority of states had given their governor a version of it, as shown in table 4.3. Maine was the most recent to institute a line-item veto in 1995.

Table 4.3. The Adoption of the Line-Item Veto

Century line-item veto adopted	Number of states	States (year adopted)
1800–1899	28	GA (1861), TX (1866), WV (1872), PA (1873), AR (1874), NY (1874), AL (1875), FL (1875), MO (1875), NE (1875), NJ (1875), CO (1876), MN (1876), CA (1879), LA (1879), IL (1884), ND (1889), MT (1889), SD (1889), WA (1889), ID (1890), MS (1890), WY (1890), KY (1891), MD (1891)[a], SC (1895), UT (1896), DE (1897)
1900–1999	16	VA (1902), OH (1903), KS (1904), MI (1905), OK (1907), AZ (1912), NM (1912), OR (1916), MA (1918), CT (1924); WI (1930), TN (1953), AK (1959), HI (1959), IA (1968), ME (1995)
No line-item veto	6	IN, NC, NH, NV, RI, VT

Sources: Rui J. P. de Figueredo Jr., "Budget Institutions and Political Insulation: Why States Adopt the Item Veto," Journal of Public Economics 87 (2003): 2677–701; John A. Fairlie, "The Veto Power of the Governor," American Political Science Review 11 (1917):473–93; National Conference of State Legislatures, Inside the Legislative Process, Table 98-6.10, http://www.ncsl.org/documents/legismgt/ILP/98Tab6Pt3.pdf, various state constitutions.

[a]Maryland's line-item veto is limited and rarely employed. Some consider the state as having no line-item veto.

Governors in forty-four states now enjoy some ability to pick and choose provisions of legislation they wish to sign into law. Of course, within line-item vetoes some are more powerful than others—Wisconsin's "partial" veto is thought to be the most powerful.[13] Even with its reach whittled down over the last few decades, Wisconsin's governor can still strike entire words and individual digits from appropriations bills, and appropriated sums may be stricken with lower sums substituted. With creative use the partial veto can be employed to increase spending and to change legislative intent.[14] In contrast, Maryland's line-item veto is the most limited. It applies only to projects in the capital budget and not to appropriations in the larger general operating budget.[15]

The power behind a governor's veto hinges on the ability of the state legislature to override it. All gubernatorial vetoes are subject to being overridden. The question is how many votes are required to do so. Gubernatorial veto power is strongest where a higher percentage of lawmakers have to agree to an override. The most stringent override requirement is three-quarters of the membership on appropriations bills in Alaska. The weakest requirement is a majority of the elected membership, which is found in seven states.[16] When in 2013 the Alabama Constitutional Revision Commission contemplated increasing the vote required to override a gubernatorial veto to three-fifths from a simple majority, the Republican governor appeared in person to complain that only a few states had a veto as weak as Alabama's. But Republican legislators sitting on the commission rejected the proposal, saying the lower threshold allows them to protect their constituents' interests.[17] More likely, they were concerned with protecting the legislature's power relative to the governor.

Being directly elected to longer terms and armed with veto powers makes governors today much more powerful than their predecessors. But as is always the case with the states, some governors are granted greater formal powers than are others. Along with their veto powers, governors also vary in the degree to which they can influence the budget process and in their appointment powers. In addition, while some governors can serve for an unlimited number of terms, most can only hold the post for two terms, and Virginia's governor is limited to a single four-year term.[18] Thus, the role a governor can play in his or her state's policymaking process will vary across the states.

Given that governors have increased their powers over time, it is worth pointing out that states have two mechanisms by which they can remove them from power before the scheduled end of their term in office. As discussed in box 4.1, like the federal government, almost every state allows the

Box 4.1	**Impeachment Processes in the States**

Impeachment is an English procedure brought to America during the colonial era. It is a mechanism that allows the legislature to remove government officials from office. Most prominently, it provides a way to dismiss a chief executive before his or her term expires. Under the U.S. Constitution, the House of Representatives is given the right to impeach (or to bring charges) on a majority vote, while the Senate is authorized to try the impeachment. Upon conviction by a two-thirds vote in the Senate, an impeached official is removed from office.

As is true with many procedures, impeachment at the state level does not always follow the same set of rules, as shown in the table below. First, note that not every state allows for impeachment: Oregon's constitution does not provide for such a process. Second, not every state follows the national model by having the lower house impeach and the upper house try that impeachment. In both Alaska and Oklahoma, the state senate brings the impeachment charges. And, of course, Nebraska has only one chamber. Third, the vote required to impeach varies. In thirty-three lower houses, the Oklahoma senate, and the Nebraska unicameral, impeachment only requires a majority vote. In thirteen lower houses and the Alaska senate, a two-thirds vote is needed to impeach, establishing a higher standard.

The procedures to conduct impeachment trials also vary across the states. In forty-two states the state senate tries the impeachment and conviction requires a two-thirds vote, the same process as at the national level. In Alaska, the lower house conducts the impeachment trial, but it too requires a two-thirds vote to convict. In Alabama, Iowa, Massachusetts, and New Hampshire, while the state senate conducts the impeachment trial, conviction can be attained with a simple majority vote.

The three remaining states that allow impeachment employ entirely different trial procedures. In Oklahoma, the state senate and house of representatives sit jointly and a two-thirds vote of all the members is required for conviction. To try the governor on impeachment charges in

(Continued)

Missouri, the state senate is required to appoint seven "eminent judges" to conduct the trial, and conviction needs the votes of five of those seven judges. Nebraska turns over its impeachment trial to its state supreme court and conviction requires a two-thirds vote of the justices.

Impeachment processes in the states					
Power to impeach:		Body that conducts impeachment trial:			
House		Senate		House	
By majority vote (33 states)	By 2/3 vote (13 states)	By majority vote (4 states)	By 2/3 vote (41 states)	By 2/3 vote (1 state)	Other (3 states)
AL, AZ, AR, CAª, CO, CT, GAª, IA, KSª, KYª, ME, MD, MA, MI, MN, MS, MOª, NV, NHª, NJ, NM, NY, ND, OH, PAª, SD, TN, TX, VA, WA, WV, WI, WY	DE, FL, HI, ID, IL, IN, LA, MT, NC, RI, SC, UT, VT	AL, IA, MAª, NHª,	AZ, AR, CA, CO, CT, DE, FL, GA, HI, ID, IL, IN, KS, KY, LA, ME, MD, MI, MN, MS, MT, NV, NJ, NM, NY, NC, ND, OH, PA, RI, SC, SD, TN, TX, UT, VT, VA, WA, WV, WI, WY	AK	MO (7 eminent judges, by 5/7 vote) NE (State Supreme Court, by 2/3 vote) OK (House and Senate jointly, by 2/3 vote)
Senate					
By majority vote (1 state)	By 2/3 vote (1 state)				
OK	AK				
Unicameral (1 state)					
NE (by majority vote)					
No impeachment process (1 state):					
OR					

Source: Adapted from *Book of the States*, 2018 edition (Lexington: Council of State Governments, 2018), 120–21.
ªNo specific provision, leaving assumption of a majority rule.

legislature to impeach the governor and upon conviction on that impeachment, to remove him or her from office. The second mechanism is the recall and it is a power only found at the state level, and then in less than a majority of the states. Recall allows dissatisfied voters to gather a specified number of signatures to put the question of whether the governor should remain in office before the state's voters. If they opt to remove the governor, he or she is replaced.

Impeachment or recall of a governor are both rare events. As shown in table 4.4, in American history only fifteen governors have been impeached, and of those only eight were convicted and removed from office. (One of the seven who did not advance to trial resigned to preempt the effort.) A slight majority of all of the impeachment efforts took place in the 1860s and 1870s. Since then relatively few impeachments have been pursued, although almost all of those that have been have resulted in the governor's conviction and removal from office.

Recall is even more rare. Only three gubernatorial recalls have gotten to the point where they have been put to the voters for a decision. Two of those

Table 4.4. Impeachment and Recall of Governors

Governor impeached but not convicted and removed	Governor impeached, convicted, and removed	Recall election held, governor not recalled	Governor recalled
Charles Robinson (KS, 1862)	William W. Holden (NC, 1871)	Scott Walker (WI, 2012)	Lynn Frazier (ND, 1921)
Powell Clayton (AR, 1871)	David Butler (NE, 1871)		Gray Davis (CA, 2003)
Harrison Reed (FL, 1872)	William Sulzer (NY, 1913)		
Henry C. Warmoth (LA, 1872)[a]	James Ferguson (TX, 1917)[c]		
Adelbert Ames (MS, 1876)[b]	John Walton (OK, 1923)		
William P. Kellogg (LA, 1876)	Henry Johnston (OK, 1929)		
Huey Long (LA, 1929)	Evan Meacham (AZ, 1988)		
	Rod Blagojevich (IL, 2009)		

Source: Compiled by the authors.
[a]Term of office ended before trial could be held
[b]Resigned before trial
[c]Resigned before conviction, impeachment sustained and prohibited from holding office again

occurred in this century. In 2003, California governor Gray Davis was recalled from office and replaced by Arnold Schwarzenegger. In 2012, Wisconsin governor Scott Walker survived a recall election. Although neither impeachments nor recalls are frequent occurrences, the fact that they are options may help keep state chief executives from engaging in personal or political misbehavior.

THE INCREASING IMPORTANCE OF THE STATE GOVERNMENT BUREAUCRACY

Another reason that governors today exercise considerable power is because they each sit atop a large bureaucracy. As noted in earlier chapters, government at all levels did relatively little when the country was young. Thus, state bureaucracies were almost nonexistent. But as state populations increased and as their economies grew and diversified, more demands were made on government. The bureaucracy grew in response as, over time, more agencies were created to administer the new programs demanded by voters.

The early growth of the bureaucracy can be demonstrated by the changes in New York between 1800 and 1925. At the beginning of the nineteenth century, New York had just ten state agencies. By 1850, another ten agencies had been added. At that point, state government growth accelerated: by 1900 there were eighty-one agencies, and another eighty agencies were established by 1925. This dramatic increase was driven by changes in society. As education came to be seen as an important governmental function, for example, New York responded by creating a superintendent of public instruction in 1854. The state started agencies to regulate banking in 1829, insurance in 1859, and public utilities in 1882. As the Industrial Revolution took hold, a commissioner of statistics of labor was established in 1883. Urbanization raised sanitation issues and a public health department was fashioned in 1880. Environmental issues also surfaced and in response game and fish protectors were created in 1880, followed by a forest commission in 1885, a fisheries commission in 1892, and a state water commission in 1905. All were eventually swept into a single conservation department in 1926. Similar growth trajectories driven by similar social trends were found in other states.[19]

Indeed, the growth of state government continued unabated over the rest of the twentieth century and into the twenty-first century, as documented in table 4.5. Again, state agencies were added as new problems appeared on the public agenda. In 1959, there were fifty-one agencies that existed in at least thirty-eight (or three-quarters) of the states. These were units devoted to what most would agree were core governmental activities, such as corrections, education, and highways. As fresh issues emerged, states responded by creating bureaucracies to deal with them. Thus, among the twelve agencies initiated in most of the states in the 1960s were ones devoted to air quality, economic development, and highway safety. The 1970s saw a significant increase in the

Table 4.5. Growth in State Agencies, 1959–2019

Year	Number of state administrative agencies present in 38 or more states	Notable examples
1959	51	Corrections Education Highways

Year	Number of new state administrative agencies created in 38 or more states during previous decade	Notable examples
1969	12	Air Quality Economic Development Highway Safety
1979	29	Civil Rights Consumer Affairs Mass Transit
1989	8	Ground Water Management Hazardous Waste Underground Storage Tanks
1999	8	Lotteries Mining Reclamation Public Broadcasting Systems
2009	7	Campaign Finance Recycling State Data Center
2019	6	General Services Information Systems Purchasing

Sources: Adapted from Cynthia J. Bowling and Deil S. Wright, "Public Administration in the Fifty States: A Half-Century Administrative Revolution," *State & Local Government Review* 30 (1998): 52–64; and various editions of *The Book of the States*.

size of government; in addition to agencies overseeing civil rights, consumer affairs, and mass transit, arts councils, energy departments, and women's commissions were also added. Growth rates subsided in the 1980s and 1990s, but state governments still created agencies to oversee ground water management, hazardous waste, lotteries, mining reclamation, public broadcasting systems, and underground storage tanks. Over the two most recent decades, agencies for campaign finance, recycling, state data centers, general services, information systems, and purchasing were added.

At the same time, states have on occasion sought to reform and streamline their bureaucratic structures. In 2019, for example, the Arkansas legislature approved the governor's plan to reduce the number of cabinet-level agencies to fifteen from the existing forty-two, almost entirely through mergers. The managerial rationale for this reorganization was straightforward. As a Republican state legislator explained, under the existing bloated configuration, "the governor cannot effectively reach into those agencies and get thousands of employees going where he wants to go." But Arkansas also provides an object lesson in the dynamics of government agency growth. In 1971, another Arkansas governor had reduced the count of state agencies to thirteen from sixty. Between 1971 and 2019 the number crept back up to forty-two, mostly because new agencies were created (or recreated) in response to demands from the political environment.[20] This sort of thing happens because the easiest way for a governor or state legislature to demonstrate that they are responding to an emerging problem is by creating an agency they can point to that will be given the responsibility to solve it.

Because of this dynamic, by 2019, state government bureaucracies touched on an extraordinary array of policy areas. Consider the list compiled by the Council of State Governments of *selected* state agencies found in almost every state: administration, agriculture, auditor, banking, budget, civil rights, commerce, community affairs, comptroller, consumer affairs, corrections, economic development, education, election administration, emergency management, employment services, energy, environmental protection, finance, fish and wildlife, general services, health, higher education, highways, information systems, insurance, labor, licensing, mental health and developmental disabilities, natural resources, parks and recreation, personnel, planning, post audit, pre-audit, public library development, public utility regulation, purchasing, revenue, social services, solid waste management, state police, tourism, transportation, and welfare.[21] In one way or another, state governments are now involved with almost every aspect of Americans' daily life. As the state's chief executive, this reality makes the governor role in governing even more central today than it was in the past.

But it is again important to appreciate that although states all have departments, agencies, and bureaus devoted to most of the same policy issues, those bureaucracies can be configured differently, which can have important implications for way they carry out their missions.[22] In New Jersey, for example, the governor appoints the heads of most agencies, in some cases with the approval of the state senate. Occasionally, an agency head is allowed to make the appointment of subsidiary bureau leaders, but of course, the agency head is a gubernatorial appointee. Thus in New Jersey the state bureaucracy is under the governor's direct control. In contrast, in North Dakota a large number of agency heads are elected by the voters, giving each of them independent political standing. Accordingly, where the New Jersey Commissioner of Education is nominated by the governor, subject to state senate confirmation, and serves at the governor's discretion, the North Dakota Superintendent of Public Instruction is elected by the voters, leaving one officeholder to boast on his

Table 4.6. Method of Selection for State Attorney General

Method of selection (number of states using)	States using method
Elected by the voters (43 states)	AL, AZ, AR, CA, CO, CT, DE, FL, GA, ID, IL, IN, IA, KS, KY, LA, MD, MA, MI, MN, MS, MO, MT, NE, NV, NM, NY, NC, ND, OH, OK, OR, PA, RI, SC, SD, TX, UT, VT, VA, WA, WV, WI
Appointed by the governor (5 states)	AK, HI, NH, NJ, WY
Elected by the legislature (1 state)	ME
Appointed by the state Supreme Court (1 state)	TN

website that as "an extremely popular public official, Dr. Sanstead received more votes in his 1988 reelection than any other candidate for any office in the history of North Dakota."[23] Clearly, New Jersey's education leader has to be responsive to the governor's wishes in a way that North Dakota's educational leader does not.

As this comparison would suggest, states have developed a number of different ways of selecting statewide officials. Take, for instance, the state attorney general. As noted in chapter 2, over the last several decades, state attorneys general have come to play prominent roles in both state and national politics.[24] They are, however, put in office through different mechanisms across the states, as shown in table 4.6. The voters in the vast majority of states elect the attorney general. But governors appoint them in five states, among them New Jersey, as noted earlier. In Maine, the legislature elects the attorney general. Finally, in Tennessee, the attorney general is selected by the justices of the state supreme court. Obviously, elected attorneys general will enjoy greater independence than their counterparts who are appointed by the governor or elected by the legislature. And these elected attorneys general are the ones who, when faced with a president or Congress controlled by the other party, are more likely to challenge federal actions.

THE COURTS AS A PARALLEL DIMENSION OF FEDERALISM

Perhaps nowhere is the American federal system of government more easily discerned than in the judicial system. American courts operate on parallel tracks, one federal and the other state. Similarities between the two are largely superficial. Although the U.S. Constitution's supremacy clause means that any conflict between federal and state law will be resolved in the former's favor, the designs of the two systems differ, and the laws before them and the interpretation of those laws also vary.

Courts existed during the colonial era, but what we take today to be exclusively judicial powers were actually shared among different governing institutions. Legislatures, for example, often heard legal cases and rendered decisions on them. Indeed, the archaic name still used by the state legislatures in Massachusetts and New Hampshire, the General Court, harkens back to this reality. The first state constitutions did little to give the newly created state courts clearly defined jurisdictions. Indeed, as with the drafting of the U.S. Constitution a decade later, the design of the court system was treated as something of an afterthought. Thus under New Jersey's original constitution, the governor and his council functioned as the state's court of last resort. Final judicial authority was not granted to a separate court of last resort (or state supreme court) until the constitution of 1844. Similar final authority power was only granted to every state's court of last resort in the middle of the nineteenth century.[25]

The separation of trial courts from appellate courts was also slow in developing in the states. Initially, appellate court judges also served as trial court judges, devoting part of their time each year to riding their circuit, moving from town to town in their district along with lawyers and court clerks, in something of a legal road show. The burden this system placed on judges proved great. But the system really changed only in response to the increased demands made on a state's legal system as populations and economies grew. Thus, during the nineteenth century, trial courts and appellate courts eventually became distinct operations, and later appellate courts usually split into a court of last resort with some subsidiary court of appeals, all to accommodate the increased demands being made on the legal system.[26]

As state judicial systems have continued to evolve, they have come to look different from the federal system and often from each other. In simplified form, the current federal court system consists of three levels, with district (or trial) courts, courts of appeal, and the Supreme Court (or court of last resort). Similar unified court systems, where trial courts handle all matter of civil and criminal cases, are only found in six states: California, Illinois, Iowa, Minnesota, New Hampshire, and South Dakota. The other states have constructed more complicated systems.[27] New York has two general jurisdiction courts (Supreme Courts and County Courts) and eight limited jurisdiction courts, with different systems for New York City (separate civil and criminal courts), and the rest of the state (District Courts, City Courts, and close to thirteen hundred Town and Village Courts), along with specialized Family Courts, Courts of Claims, and Surrogate's Courts. Such complexity is not unusual. There are separate civil and criminal courts of last resort in Oklahoma and Texas. Water Courts were established in Colorado and Montana in the late 1960s and early 1970s to handle special issues involving water rights in those states. Vermont's Superior (or trial) Court has an Environmental Division that "hears appeals from state land use permit decisions . . . from state environmental permits and other decisions of the Agency of Natural Resources, and from municipal land use zoning and planning decisions."[28] Some states have separate courts that try cases involving taxes, workers' compensation, and probate matters. In terms of structures, then, each state has largely devised its own system to handle legal cases. These structures continue to evolve. In 2010, for example, Vermont completely reorganized and simplified its court structure, while New Hampshire streamlined its circuit courts in 2011.[29]

Another structural difference is the membership size of the state courts of last resort. They vary from five judges (seventeen courts of last resort), to seven judges (twenty-eight courts), to nine judges (seven courts).[30] Note that all have odd-numbered memberships, which is important because they make decisions collectively by voting. What happens when a vacancy leaves a state appellate court with an even number of judges? When the U.S. Supreme Court was left with only eight members in 2016, it handed down a number of tied decisions on four to four votes. This meant that in those cases the Court set no legal precedents. If lower courts had reached conflicting decisions on the case in question, different regions of the country were left to live under different interpretations of the law. Supreme courts in sixteen states operate like the U.S. Supreme Court and hand down tied votes in such circumstances. The remaining thirty-four state courts of last resort employ procedures whereby a temporary judge is appointed, allowing any ties to be broken. The particular selection procedures used to appoint the temporary member vary—in Louisiana the court clerk "plucks [judges] names from a plastic Halloween Jack-o'-Lantern," while North Dakota and Utah take the first lower court judge who volunteers—but they all allow those courts to avoid the predicament in which the U.S. Supreme Court found itself.[31]

In recent years, a number of states have debated whether to expand or contract the size of their courts of last resort. In 2016, Arizona expanded its court of last resort to seven members from five members, while Georgia went to nine members from seven members. Ostensibly, these debates have centered on the workload and the number of judges needed to manage it. In most cases, however, partisan politics was the real motivator, with each side angling to have a court composed of the number of judges it calculated was more likely to produce the decisions it prefers.[32]

State courts vary in the way they reach decisions. The U.S. Supreme Court makes all decisions by majority vote. While all state courts of last resort have the right to overturn state laws, those in Nebraska and North Dakota require a supermajority vote instead of a simple majority vote to do so.[33] When in 2015 the Nebraska Supreme Court voted 4–3 to overturn a state law allowing construction of the controversial Keystone XL pipeline, a simple majority was not sufficient. Under the Nebraska constitution, the court needed five out of the seven votes to do so.[34] State trial courts also do not have to have a unanimous jury verdict for criminal convictions. Federal trial courts and those in forty-nine states require all jurors to agree. But juries in Oregon can convict on an 11–1 vote for any offense except first-degree murder (which requires a unanimous vote).[35] (Louisiana juries could convict on a 10–2 vote until voters passed a constitutional amendment to require unanimous verdicts in 2018.)[36]

States have also developed a range of approaches to judicial selection. Even the original thirteen states split in the way they put judges on the bench, as shown in table 4.7. In five states, governors appointed judges with the consent of the council; in the other eight states they were elected by the legislature. As noted earlier, legislative election made judges beholden to lawmakers to gain and retain their position. In contrast, gubernatorial appointment hinted at greater judicial independence. The Framers of the U.S. Constitution opted for this latter approach, allowing the president to nominate and the Senate to confirm federal judges to life terms. The idea that judges should enjoy independence from the political branches of government never gained complete favor in the states. By 1833, roughly half the states used gubernatorial appointment, but, with one exception, the rest employed legislative election.

That one exception proved enormously important. In its 1832 constitution, Mississippi became the first state to have its judges elected by the voters. New York followed suit in 1846, and by 1889 the vast majority of states elected their judges. The move to judicial elections was triggered in large part by dissatisfaction with the performance of the judicial branch, which many voters thought catered too much to elite and moneyed interests. They preferred to make the courts more responsive to the interests of the voters. Thus, instead of promoting judicial independence, the states opted for elections in order to accentuate judicial accountability. Judges would have to defend their decisions to the public to retain their place on the bench.

Judicial elections proved popular, and every state that entered the Union between 1846 and 1912 required them in their constitutions. But a backlash against the use of elections to name judges developed over the second half of the nineteenth century. The concern was that elected judges were little more than another cog in the political machines that dominated state politics. It was feared that judges were beholden to party bosses and therefore susceptible to corruption.

An altogether new approach to naming judges was proposed in 1914 by Albert Kales, a Northwestern University law professor. Kales devised a system that placed great value on merit. Under his plan, a governor would fill a judgeship by naming one of the people suggested by a panel of lawyers and laypersons who would evaluate the qualifications of candidates who applied. The people selected to be a judge would serve for a year or two and then face the voters in a retention election, a contest in which the voters would only decide whether or not they wanted that judge to serve a full term. The idea behind this system was that it would improve the legal qualifications of the people named as judges, while still giving the voters, but not the political parties, a say in whether they would stay on the bench. It was also reasoned that judges would be able to focus on the law and not have to devote time and effort to campaigning.

Table 4.7. State Judicial Selection Procedures over Time

Year	Number of states	Selection procedure for court of last resort:					
		Gubernatorial appointment		Legislative election		Popular election	
1789	13	5	MD, MA, NY, PA[a], NH	8	CT, DE, GA, NJ, NC, RI, SC, VA	0	
1833	24	11	DE, IN, KY, LA, ME, MD, MA, MO, NH, NY, PA	12	AL, CT, GA, IL, NJ, NC, OH, RI, SC, TN, VT, VA	1	MS
1889	42	7	CT, DE, ME, MA, MS, NH, NJ	6	GA, LA, RI, SC, VT, VA	29	AL, AZ, AR, CA, CO, FL, IL, IN, IA, KS, KY, MD, MI, MN, MO, MT, NE, NY, NC, ND, OH, OR, PA, SD, TN, TX, WA, WV, WI
1933	48	6	CT, DE, ME, MA, NH, NJ	4	RI, SC, VT, VA	38	AL, AZ, AR, CA, CO, FL, GA, ID, IL, IN, IA, KS, KY, LA, MD, MI, MN, MS, MO, MT, NE, NV, NM, NY, NC, ND, OH, OK, OR, PA, SD, TN, TX, UT, WA, WV, WI, WY
1989	50	24	AK, AZ, CA, CO, CT, DE, FL, HI, IN, IA, KS, ME, MD, MA, MO, NE, NH, NJ, NY, OK, SD, UT, VT, WY	3	RI, SC, VA	23	AL, AR, GA, ID, IL, KY, LA, MI, MN, MS, MT, NV, NM, NC, ND, OH, OR, PA, TN, TX, WA, WV, WI
2019	50	26	AK, AZ, CA, CO, CT, DE, FL, HI, IN, IA, KS, ME, MD, MA, MO, NE, NH, NJ, NY, OK, RI, SD, TN, UT, VT, WY	2	SC, VA	22	AL, AR, GA, ID, IL, KY, LA, MI, MN, MS, MT, NV, NM, NC, ND, OH, OR, PA, TX, WA, WV, WI

Source: Data gathered by authors from http://www.judicialselection.us/.

[a]In Pennsylvania, judges were appointed by executive council. In the other states the council consented to gubernatorial selections.

It took a quarter century before any state opted to implement a variant of what came to be called the "merit plan." In 1940, Missouri became the first state to adopt a version of it. No state followed suit until 1958, and then over the next two decades nineteen states adopted what was now becoming referred to as the "Missouri Plan." By 1989, roughly half the states selected their judges through some merit system.

Today, the variation in state judicial selection procedures is substantial, as shown in table 4.8.[37] Looking just at the court of last resort, the governor nominates judges, usually through a merit system, in twenty-six states. In twelve of those states the governor's selection is final. In the others, the governor's choice must be approved by a judicial commission or executive council, or by the legislature, either jointly or by the senate alone. Legislative election is

Table 4.8. Current Procedures for Selection of Court of Last Resort Justices

Procedure	Number of states using procedure	States using procedure
Gubernatorial appointment from nominating commission	12	AK, AZ, CO, FL, IN, IA, KS, MO, NE, OK, SD, WY
Gubernatorial appointment, confirmation by commission on judicial appointments	1	CA
Gubernatorial appointment, approval of governor's or executive council	2	MA, NH
Gubernatorial appointment from nominating commission, state senate confirmation	8	DE, HI, ME, MD, NJ, NY, UT, VT
Gubernatorial nomination from nominating committee, state senate and house confirmation	3	CT, RI, TN
Nonpartisan election	13	AR, GA, ID, KY, MN, MS, MT, NV, ND, OR, WA, WV, WI
Partisan election	7	AL, IL, LA, NM, NC, PA, TX
Partisan nomination, nonpartisan election	1	MI
Partisan primary, nonpartisan election	1	OH
Elected by the legislature	2	SC, VA

Source: Data gathered by authors from http://www.judicialselection.us/.

still used to put judges on the bench in South Carolina and Virginia. The voters elect judges in the rest of the states; partisan contests are held in seven states, nonpartisan elections are employed in thirteen states, and in a curious hybrid approach, judicial candidates in Michigan and Ohio are nominated through partisan mechanisms but elected in nonpartisan elections. It is important to realize that with the provision of simple information about the candidates, nonpartisan judicial elections are easily turned into partisan contests.[38] This happened in West Virginia's 2016 election for a state supreme court judgeship. The contest was the first nonpartisan race under a law passed in 2014. But the infusion of more than $3 million to one of the candidates from the Republican State Leadership Committee thwarted the law's objective.[39] To further complicate selection procedures, some states use one system to select judges for the court of last resort and another system to select lower court judges. Even in Missouri, the "Missouri Plan" is only used to select lower court judges in a handful of the largest counties; in the rest partisan elections are held.

There are two main points to take away from this discussion. First, few of the states follow the federal model of judicial selection in any significant way. Second, state selection procedures place greater weight on judicial accountability, whereas the federal system places greater weight on judicial independence.

Major take away

There are two additional differences at the state level that accentuate judicial accountability rather than independence. How judges stay on the bench is the first difference. Only Rhode Island judges enjoy lifetime appointments like their federal counterparts do; those in Massachusetts and New Hampshire continue to serve until they reach age seventy. In the rest of the states, judges serve for a specific term. To stay in office, most of them must face the voters in an election, be it partisan, nonpartisan, or retention. In Connecticut, Maine, New Jersey, and New York, the governor reappoints judges, while in Hawaii a judicial nominating commission makes that decision. And in South Carolina, Vermont, and Virginia, the state legislature decides whether to reappoint them, a process that can influence the decisions judges make.[40]

The second difference it more subtle. It revolves around the ability of the legislature to use compensation as a lever with which to exert influence on the courts. Article III, Section 1 of the U.S. Constitution says that the salaries of federal judges "shall not be diminished during their Continuance in Office." Only twenty-nine states have similar provisions in their state constitutions. In North Dakota, only judges on the state supreme court enjoy such protection, while lower court judges do not. Constitutional provisions in five states—Alaska, Hawaii, Kansas, Michigan, and Pennsylvania—allow for judicial salaries to be reduced at the same rate as reductions imposed on other state officers. Constitutions in the remaining sixteen states either do not address the question or have ambiguous provisions, leaving their judges potentially vulnerable to such pressure.[41] And some lawmakers are not averse to trying to financially squeeze judges. In 2019, the Judiciary Committee in the West Virginia House of Delegates adopted an amendment stating that until the Supreme Court of

Appeals overturned a decision that many lawmakers disliked, "the legislature shall not fund the retirement system for judges or justices as set out in this article."[42]

What, then, about the decisions that judges make? As noted in chapter 1, laws vary across the states. The way judges treat those laws also varies to some extent. In significant ways, states have developed their own approaches to applying and interpreting their laws. Perhaps the most significant development in the last half-century has been the appearance of the "New Judicial Federalism." Starting in the 1970s, state courts began looking to state constitutions rather than the federal constitution to drive their decisions on a number of questions involving civil liberties.[43] It was a dramatic development: "From 1950 to 1969, in only ten cases did state judges rely on state guarantees of rights to afford greater protection than was available under the federal constitution. However, from 1970 to 2000, they did so in more than 1,000 cases."[44] Under this new perspective, the federal constitution and the way the U.S. Supreme Court interprets its provisions establishes a floor, or minimum standard, for civil liberties, while state courts interpreting state constitutional provisions have the opportunity expand and strengthen those liberties.[45] Thus, in 2019 the Supreme Court of Georgia relied on that state's constitutional protection against self-incrimination to hold that prosecutors could not use a driver's refusal to submit to a breath test as evidence in drunk driving cases, while the Kansas Supreme Court looked to its state constitution's provision on the "right of personal autonomy," to uphold access to abortion.[46]

The new judicial federalism has been the source of some momentous policy changes in recent American history. In granting same-sex couples the right to marry in 2004, the Supreme Judicial Court of Massachusetts did so by finding that the ban against it violated provisions of the state constitution. There have, of course, been backlashes against such decisions, and it is critical to understand that state courts operate in a context in which their decisions can be resisted in ways that decisions by federal courts largely cannot. First, voters in some states can put measures on the ballot to overturn state court decisions. When the Supreme Court of California held same-sex marriage to be constitutional under that state's constitution in early 2008, opponents of the decision quickly launched a successful effort to overturn it at the ballot box. (An effort to allow the voters to overturn the Massachusetts court's decision failed because under that state's rules only the legislature could place such a measure on the ballot and lawmakers resisted calls to do so. In California, voters could gather signatures to get the measure put on the ballot.) Second, as noted earlier, voters in many states get to pass judgment on judges in elections. Thus, after the Iowa Supreme Court found a ban against same-sex marriage to be unconstitutional under the state constitution in 2009, a majority of Iowans vented their displeasure by voting against retaining three of the judges when their names appeared on the ballot in 2010. (Iowa voters could not, as California voters could, place the decision itself on the ballot. As in Massachusetts, only lawmakers could do so, and Iowa legislators never did. And in Massachusetts, judges do not go before the voters, leaving them insulated from any voter displeasure.) Of course, the U.S. Supreme Court's 2015 decision legalizing same-sex marriage in all fifty states demonstrated the power of the Constitution's supremacy clause in the federal system. Although some states resisted, their efforts to override the Supreme Court's decision proved futile.[47]

THE DESIGN OF STATE GOVERNMENTS

As they have evolved, the structures of state governments have come to look much like the federal government, with three separate branches. But as noted, upon closer inspection, there are notable differences, both between the federal government and the state governments, and across the state governments themselves. Indeed, the notion of separation of powers means something slightly different in each state. In Rhode Island, for example, only since voters passed a constitutional amendment in 2004 has the era of legislative supremacy ended. Prior to the amendment's passage, the legislature dominated the executive branch through lawmakers' control over appointments to regulatory agencies.[48]

This leads to one final point that needs to be emphasized. Each state government is, in some fashion, unique. They operate under somewhat different sets of rules, with somewhat different structures. Thus, the policy decisions they make are the products of different governmental arrangements and procedures.

STATE GOVERNMENTS AND POLICY DOMAINS OVER TIME

When they were first established, state governments did relatively little. But by their fifth decade, their involvement in various aspects of the economy and society was beginning to expand. Take, for example, the sorts of state laws passed in Georgia between 1819 and 1829.[49] Much legislative time in the state during this time period was devoted to public education, both at the primary and higher levels. Transportation issues, mostly dealing with ferries and roads, were important. Writing and refining criminal law consumed time, as did the creation and maintenance of a judicial system to administer it. Overseeing the conduct of elections was important. Regulation of the economy commanded attention. The legislature determined "the mode of granting a license to" physicians, while individual lawyers were "authorized to plead and practice." Banks and corporations were chartered. The state was also involved with gaming issues, authorizing a large number of lotteries, while determining the "punishment for keeping gambling-houses, tables, or rooms." A public health officer was authorized for Savannah.

What is of particular interest about these policy areas is that two centuries later they are still central to the policy jurisdictions of the states. As noted in the discussion on federalism in chapter 2, although the U.S. Constitution established a federal system, and in some instances allocated specific powers to each governmental level, there is sufficient ambiguity in the overall design that there has been an ongoing resorting of policy powers. The federal government has, over time, become more intimately involved in most of these areas. But as we assess the roster of policies that we still look to the states to deliver—education, transportation, the administration of justice, public health, and economic development—we find the same basic set that the states took responsibility for when they were first established.

5

The Policymaking Capacity of State Governments

States matter because:

- ★ The policymaking capacity of state governments has increased markedly in the past two generations.
- ★ The training and preparation of elected officials today is far advanced over past generations.
- ★ The ability of governors to affect policymaking is substantial; many politicians think being governor is "the best job in politics."
- ★ Despite the deleterious effect of term limit laws in some states, today's legislatures are more capable partners in the policymaking process.
- ★ The standards for ethical behavior of elected officials appear to vary by state.

OVER RECENT DECADES, an increasing number of policy decisions have been turned over to state governments to handle, as we have documented in earlier chapters. And as we have argued, in many regards this trend is positive. But one important question has been left unanswered. As more and more policy decisions are pushed onto state governments, do they enjoy sufficient capacity to make competent decisions? By capacity, we mean the organizational resources to generate and analyze the information needed to make knowledgeable policy choices.

In this chapter, we assess the policymaking capacities of the four governmental institutions intimately involved in the policymaking process: the governor's office, the executive branch, the state legislature, and the state courts.

Each is charged with making important policy decisions. The question to address is whether each institution has sufficient capacity to handle all that is now asked of it.

Before directly addressing these questions, we note a related development. Today, there are numerous professional organizations that assist state officials. Examples include the Council of State Governments and the National Association of State Budget Officers. Some of these organizations, such as the National Governors Association, have been around for more than a century. Others, notably the National Conference of State Legislatures and the National Legislative Leaders Foundation, have existed for only a few decades. Regardless of when they were founded, all have become active in providing services, information, and training to state officials. Most are nonprofit organizations that the general public has never heard of and knows nothing about. But they are important support organizations that have helped state governments increase their capacity to govern. In addition, there are university-affiliated entities, such as the Carl Vinson Institute of Government (University of Georgia) and the Hubert Humphrey School of Public Affairs (University of Minnesota) that devote many hours to the training and education of state and local officials. These and other university-housed institutes and organizations have also contributed to the capacity-building efforts of state governments.

GUBERNATORIAL CAPACITY

In the not so distant past, state governors were denigrated as being "good-time Charlies."[1] In 1962, for example, James Reston, an influential political columnist for the *New York Times*, lamented that "it is difficult to make a political swing around America these days without coming to the conclusion that the governors of the states, taken as a whole, are a poor lot."[2] Indeed, they often appeared to be less than engaged in the policymaking process. A reporter covering a National Governors Conference in 1970 noted with some hyperbole, "Most of the governors snored through dozens of 'policy statements.'"[3] Such characterizations suggested many governors were, at best, political hacks, interested more in the rough and tumble of elections than in the nitty-gritty of policymaking.

Over the following decade, that image began to improve. By the late 1970s, governors were seen as serious policymakers, focused on improving their state's lot. It is this latter image that appears to dominate today. In a recent treatise on governors, Alan Rosenthal chronicled the growth in policymaking influence of the governors over the past generation.[4] Interviews with numerous former governors led him to conclude that the governorship "according to nearly all of those who have held it, is now 'the best office in American politics.'"[5] For the most part, this is because state problems are more manageable than those at the national level and governors tend to have the resources necessary to address at least some of them. A particularly telling comparison comes from those who have served as both state governor and U.S. senator. Rosenthal claims that of the dozen members of the U.S. Senate in 2010 who were former governors, all but one "preferred their job as governor to their job as senator."[6]

Indeed, as former governors Jimmy Carter, Ronald Reagan, Bill Clinton, and George W. Bush intimated, in many regards governors today may be better able to influence state policies than the president is able to influence national policies. There are three reasons why this might be the case. First, governors dominate state media. Between January 1, 2019, and July 1, 2019, for example, a search of the *New York Times* reveals 261 news stories mentioning New York governor Andrew Cuomo compared to only 48 stories mentioning the state house speaker, Carl Heastie. Governors can exploit their media advantage to set their state's policy agenda, leaving legislators and others to only be in a position to react.

Second, governors enjoy a significant information advantage over their state legislatures. The governor's job is, of course, a full-time position. And as will be discussed later in this chapter, governors typically have large staffs to assist them, and they can draw on the state bureaucracy's expertise as well. In contrast, legislatures in most states are part-time and many have relatively meager staff resources. Any disparity in information resources gives governors the upper hand in policy debates that turn on facts and analyses. When in 2016 Kansas had to make significant cuts to balance its budget, the legislature allowed the governor to impose most of them. Their reasoning was explained by the vice chair of the state senate budget committee. He admitted,

> We're a citizen Legislature. . . . We don't know the details of the agencies. The agency cabinet members, they work with the governor every day, so we just left it up to him and them to decide what they can do within their agencies.[7]

Third, as noted in chapter 4, most governors enjoy a powerful veto, one that in most states gives them great leverage over the legislature. Unlike the president, who must take or leave an entire bill, many governors can pick and choose provisions that they wish to keep. Knowing that a governor can veto specific provisions forces lawmakers to be more accommodating to the governor's preferences. A veto threat provides governors considerable leverage in any legislative negotiations.

Thus, the evidence suggests that governors today are powerful. The question then becomes whether they are serious and capable policymakers. In table 5.1, we examine two personal characteristics of governors serving in 2019 that act as indicators of their capacity as policymakers. The first indicator is a governor's level of educational attainment. The idea behind this measure is simple: higher levels of educational attainment suggest that a governor has the academic training to critically analyze the vast amounts of information available on policy issues. Not surprisingly, as table 5.1 reveals, governors today are well educated. In 2019, almost all of them had at least

Table 5.1.   Capacity Indicators for Governors, 2019

Capacity indicator	Number of governors with indicator
Minimum educational attainment	
Some college	2
BA, BS, or other undergraduate degree	48
Postgraduate degrees	
MA or MS	6
JD	16
MBA	8
MPA	2
MD	1
PhD	2
Previous Elective Office Experience	
School board	1
City council, county supervisor	6
Mayor, county executive	1
State legislature	18
State attorney general	6
Other statewide office	12
Lt. Governor	13
U.S. House of Representatives	9
U.S. Senate	1
No elective office experience	9

Source: Compiled by the authors.

an undergraduate degree. The two who did not—Gary Herbert (R-UT) and Mike Parson (R-MO)—attended college but left without graduating. Overall, a much higher percentage of state chief executives graduated from college than did the general public.

Perhaps even more impressively, over 58 percent of governors had a graduate degree of some sort. As might be anticipated, a third of them had a law degree. Another 16 percent had MBAs and 4 percent held MPAs. Some held other graduate degrees, among them Ralph Northam (D-VA), an MD and Tom Wolf (D-PA), a PhD in political science. These varied educational backgrounds indicate that governors have the intellectual training to tackle the complex policy problems confronting state governments.

The second indicator of policymaking capacity is political experience as measured by other elective offices held previously. The notion that governors who have held other elective offices may be better positioned to navigate the complexities of policymaking in a governmental system characterized by the separation of powers is reasonably well accepted. Previous office holding, for example, is embedded in a widely used measure of gubernatorial power.[8] Governmental experience provides a governor with exposure to policy questions and a measure of expertise on some aspects of them, as well as a network of connections both within and outside of government that can be drawn upon to assist in policy development and evaluation. A legislative background can be especially helpful. A former Vermont governor who had also served as a state representative remarked,

> Legislative experience was a plus . . . lawmakers knew I had some of the same experiences they were having. I was familiar with the protocols and the committee process. I could relate to their problems, and they knew they couldn't snow me, either.[9]

Not surprisingly, the vast majority of governors—82 percent in 2019—had previous elective office experience. Some had served in local government; for example, Gavin Newsom (D-CA) was mayor of San Francisco. A number of others had served in the state legislature or in a statewide office. Governor Mike DeWine (R-OH) had a particularly varied political résumé. He began his political career by being elected county prosecutor in Greene County. DeWine then served in the Ohio state senate and the U.S. House of Representatives. After that he was elected lieutenant governor, U.S. senator, and Ohio attorney general. Such experiences provide governors with extensive knowledge of the policy problems, policymaking processes, and policymakers in their states, as discussed in box 5.1.

In 2019, nine governors were political neophytes in that they had not previously held elected office. Experience reveals that the tenures of political newcomers do not always go smoothly. Before he served as the governor of Illinois between 2015 and 2019, Bruce Rauner, a Republican, had enjoyed great success in finance, becoming extraordinarily wealthy in the process. But once in office he quickly learned that government does not operate like the private sector. A lengthy budget impasse with the Democrat-controlled legislature led even his GOP predecessors as governor to publicly criticize him. One observed that Rauner

> does not come from government. . . . He doesn't really come from mainstream business. He comes from (being an) entrepreneur where you buy a business, you tear it apart and you sell it. . . . I don't think you're going to tear apart the state and sell it. He might want to, but you can't do that.[10]

| Box 5.1 | Jerry Brown's Reflections on Governing |

Jerry Brown has had an extraordinary life in politics. The son of a California governor, he began his political career in 1969 by being elected to the Los Angeles Community College Board of Trustees. Brown's next move was to a statewide office, California secretary of state, in 1971, and then he served as the state's governor from 1975 to 1983. He lost a race for the U.S. Senate in 1982 (and failed to win the Democratic Party's presidential nominations in 1976, 1980, and 1992) and did not return to elective office until 1999, when he was elected as the mayor of Oakland. After serving two terms in that office, Brown got elected California attorney general in 2006. He won the governorship again in 2010—thirty-five years after first winning it—and was reelected in 2014.

As he left office in 2019, Brown reflected on what he had learned after serving in so many elective offices across so many years. He offered a number of insights on serving as a governor in modern American politics.

On the value of having served as the mayor of Oakland before his second stint as governor:

> After I had been in Oakland, I got a good sense of how things worked, a more concrete sense. . . . I learned that from my own experience, which you don't get from going directly from secretary of state to governor [as he had in the mid-1970s].

On working with the state legislature as governor:

> We have more lawmaking than in any time in human history. . . . Many of the laws are stupid. Many of them are not warranted. But in order to get along with the legislature, you've got to sign bills that aren't needed. And you have to sign bills that you'd prefer not even to have.

On using the governor's veto power:

> What's hard is when you are in conflict [with the legislature], and you know if you say "no," maybe next time they'll say "no" to you. So this is a give-and-take business. Just like I ask them to do something they don't want, they get to ask me to do something I don't want.

On the economy and gubernatorial popularity:

> I think I've been a good governor. Most people believe that. And I do attribute a lot of that success to the business cycle and the fact that I've had continuous growth every year that I've been governor. The total of three million new jobs, the $800 billion in new gross domestic product is incredible. So that's a [fortunate] platform, to say the least, on which to launch my governorship. Yes, I think my experience, practice makes perfect. The force was with me. And we'll see how it works when you ride into that recession—Gray (Davis) ran into that, (Arnold) Schwarzenegger ran into that. And (George)

(Continued)

Deukmejian, by the way, who made the colossal mistake of overbuilding the prison system, he enjoyed great popularity. And I always wondered why was he so popular, you know he wasn't that dramatic or charismatic, but the economy grew virtually during his entire governorship and then just collapsed when (Pete) Wilson got there. He had that eight-year growth cycle and I've had the eight-year growth cycle. And both of us, if you look at the surveys, are the two most popular governors. Even (Ronald) Reagan was below 50% and a lot of it is the vagaries of the business cycle.

On anticipating problems:

Well, I would say a nice methodology in political management is to imagine what could go wrong and what could go wrong in the worst way possible. And after you imagine that, then take careful steps to avoid it. You got to think not about all your little pet programs, of which there'll be plenty, but what are the things that could go awry. And there are big things that can go awry. You can have scandals. You can have a major earthquake. We had the fires. They're a huge disaster. But you've got to stand back and try to look over the horizon and say, OK, what are the things that might not go right? How do we correct that? How do we deal with it ahead of time? And then what is most important? And also, I would say, what can you really do? Because you might don't want to be chasing rainbows and turn up with an empty hand.

On the limits of serving the people as governor:

Not only can't you make them all happy, but you can't solve all problems—otherwise, you'd be dead. . . . As long as you're alive, you've got new issues for tomorrow and next week and next year.

Sources: Calbuzz, "Exit Interview: Jerry Brown Stresses Elder Wisdom," January 6, 2019; "Jerry Brown's Exit Interview: Don't Say He Didn't Warn You," NPR.org, December 11, 2018; John Wildermuth, "What Jerry Brown Has Learned," *San Francisco Chronicle,* January 4, 2019.

Another counseled, "running government is not like running a business."[11] Legislative Democrats rebelled as well, with one representative complaining the governor "doesn't understand how the Legislature works. We're not his middle management. He is not the boss of Illinois government."[12] In 2018, Rauner lost his reelection bid by sixteen percentage points.

There is another potential problem with executives who move into government directly from the private sector. Those who continue to own businesses may not be able or willing to devote themselves to the governorship. In 2019, there were complaints that West Virginia governor Jim Justice spent too much time running his many mines, farms, and resorts, and too little time dealing with all the tasks expected him as the state's chief executive. Justice, who was elected as a Democrat but then switched to the Republicans, was criticized by a Democratic leader in the state senate who said that "He seems like he doesn't have his whole heart in it. . . . You either want to be governor or you want to run your business. You're going to have to choose one or the other." A Republican colleague agreed, noting that the governorship is "a big job and you can't put it on autopilot."[13]

Moreover, there are several reasons why business acumen may not transfer to the public sector. First, although a governor is routinely referred to as a state's chief executive, that does not mean the same thing as being a chief executive officer in the private sector. State government agencies operate in a world with multiple masters. That is, while agencies need to be responsive to the governor, it is the legislature that creates them, the legislature that funds them, and it is the legislature that can abolish them. Lawmakers can expand agency missions, contract agency missions, or change agency missions. Thus, bureaucrats have to be responsive to legislators as well as to the governor. Second, private sector organizations are built around generating a profit, a goal that, even with the complexities of accounting rules, is measured in a manner most people understand and accept. Consequently, we can usually tell the degree to which a business is successful. The same is not true with government. Government agencies perform a range of diverse activities and there is little agreement about their goals and whether they have achieved them or not. Finally, businesses usually enjoy the ability to make decisions out of public view. In contrast, government decisions are almost always debated with the media and interested parties watching and commenting. This complicates decision-making.

It must be pointed out, of course, that previous governing experience does not guarantee success in office or that having only a business background dooms a governor to failure. In North Dakota, John Hoeven had spent his career in banking prior to winning the governorship in 2000. During his ten years in office he was enormously popular, in large part because of the state's strong economic performance. When Hoeven left the governorship, he was elected to the U.S. Senate by a comfortable margin and then was reelected six years later. In contrast, Illinois governor Rod Blagojevich brought impressive political credentials into office in 2003, having served both in the Illinois House of Representatives and the U.S. House of Representatives. But by 2012 he was serving in the Federal Correctional Institution in Englewood, Colorado. As noted in chapter 4, in 2009 Blagojevich was impeached and removed from office by a legislature controlled by his fellow Democrats and he was later convicted in federal court on corruption charges. But despite such aberrations, political experience is, on average, beneficial.[14]

It is often particularly useful to look at the experience immediately prior to ascending to the governorship. Here we find an interesting temporal trend. As Margaret Ferguson shows, the proportion of governors who held some other statewide office prior to taking office has grown from about 20 percent in the period from 1900 to 1980 to 29 percent in the period from 1981 to 2015.[15] Thus not only do governors today have more experience, but the quality of that experience is higher. Even more telling is the fact that in the earlier period, from 1900 to 1980, less than 10 percent of governors were former members of Congress. During the most recent period, from 1981 to 2015, that number jumped to 17 percent. Almost one of every five governors chose to leave federal office in order to "come home" and serve as governor. If we accept that politicians are progressively ambitious beings, then one implication of this move from federal office to state office is clear: states matter and may be where many politicians now think they can make a greater impact.[16]

Interestingly, the apparent attraction over the last several decades of better qualified people serving as governor has not been driven by the salaries paid to them. In 1959, the mean gubernatorial salary was $18,980, which is the equivalent of $164,741 in 2019. The mean salary actually paid governors in 2019 was $139,827. Gubernatorial salaries failed to keep pace with inflation in thirty-three states over that time period, with the biggest losers being governors in some of the largest states: New York, California, and Pennsylvania. Governors reaping the greatest real increases since 1959 are in mostly moderate-sized states: Tennessee, Vermont, and Arkansas.[17]

Today, governors make far less than a number of other state employees. In 2017, more than twenty-seven hundred Michigan state employees were paid more than the state's governor.[18] A similar situation obtained in South Carolina in 2019, with almost three thousand state employees making more than the governor.[19] At its most extreme the pay differential can be absurd; in 2019 the University of Alabama's head football coach was paid 72.3 times as much as the state's governor.[20] Governors are often not even the highest-paid members of their own offices. Again in 2019, Georgia Governor Brian Kemp was paid $175,000, while six of his staff members earned at least $190,000.[21] That same year, Iowa Governor Kim Reynolds had three staff members who earned more than her salary.[22]

At the lowest end of the gubernatorial wage scale, Maine's governor is paid only $70,000, a figure that is unchanged since 1987. In 2016, the then governor's wife took a tourist season job waiting tables, telling a reporter, "Oh honey, it's all about the money; it's all about the money. . . . I want to buy a car this summer."[23] After he left office, the former governor, a Republican, counselled, "Maine deserves a governor with executive leadership experience who is in the prime of their career. Leaders who would make excellent governors have told me that they won't consider running because of the pay cut. Competitive compensation is good public policy."[24] Similar concerns motivated Utah to recently raise its governor's salary to $150,000 from $109,900. Lawmakers there worried that the relatively low salary they had been offering would make it hard to attract and keep talented leaders. After the legislature voted to increase the governor's salary, a Republican member confessed, "We want to be conservative, but we don't want to appear cheap. . . . Right now we look a little cheap on those executive offices."[25] One final comparison is instructive on this score: in 2019 the median salary paid to the CEOs of S&P 500 companies was

$12.4 million.[26] Adding all of their salaries together, the fifty state governors collectively were paid just under $7 million. It seems clear that salary has not contributed to the improvement in the quality of state governors.

One positive change that has occurred over the last few decades is an expansion in the pool of potential candidates for the governorship. By the end of the 1960s, only three women had ever served as governor, each of them filling in, in one fashion or another, for her husband. Starting in the 1970s with Ella Grasso in Connecticut and Dixie Lee Ray in Washington, women who had worked their way up through the political ranks began winning the governorship on the basis of their own credentials, as documented in table 5.2.

Table 5.2. Women Serving as Governor and Their Path to Office

Name	State	Party	Years in office	Path to governor's office
Nellie Tayloe Ross	WY	D	1925–1927	Special election to replace deceased husband
Miriam "Ma" Ferguson	TX	D	1925–1927 1933–1935	Elected as surrogate for husband who had been impeached and prohibited from holding elective office
Lurleen Wallace	AL	D	1967–1968	Elected as surrogate for husband who could not succeed himself
Ella Grasso	CT	D	1975–1980	Elected in her own right
Dixy Lee Ray	WA	D	1977–1981	Elected in her own right
Vesta Roy	NH	R	1982–1983	Elevated when incumbent died
Martha Layne Collins	KY	D	1983–1987	Elected in her own right
Madeleine Kunin	VT	D	1985–1991	Elected in her own right
Kay Orr	NE	R	1987–1991	Elected in her own right
Rose Mofford	AZ	D	1988–1991	Elevated when incumbent was impeached and removed from office
Joan Finney	KS	D	1991–1995	Elected in her own right
Ann Richards	TX	D	1991–1995	Elected in her own right
Barbara Roberts	OR	D	1991–1995	Elected in her own right
Christine Todd Whitman	NJ	R	1994–2001	Elected in her own right

Table 5.2. (Continued)

Name	State	Party	Years in office	Path to governor's office
Jane Dee Hull	AZ	R	1997–2003	Elevated when incumbent resigned, later elected in her own right
Jeanne Shaheen	NH	D	1997–2003	Elected in her own right
Nancy Hollister	OH	R	1998–1999	Elevated when incumbent resigned
Jane Swift	MA	R	2001–2003	Elevated when incumbent resigned
Judy Martz	MT	R	2001–2005	Elected in her own right
Ruth Ann Minner	DE	D	2001–2009	Elected in her own right
Linda Lingle	HI	R	2002–2010	Elected in her own right
Olene Walker	UT	R	2003–2005	Elevated when incumbent resigned
Janet Napolitano	AZ	D	2003–2009	Elected in her own right
Kathleen Sebelius	KS	D	2003–2009	Elected in her own right
Jennifer M. Granholm	MI	D	2003–2011	Elected in her own right
Kathleen Blanco	LA	D	2004–2008	Elected in her own right
M. Jodi Rell	CT	R	2004–2011	Elevated when incumbent resigned, later elected in her own right
Christine Gregoire	WA	D	2005–2013	Elected in her own right
Sarah Palin	AK	R	2007–2009	Elected in her own right
Beverly M. Perdue	NC	D	2009–2013	Elected in her own right
Jan Brewer	AZ	R	2009–2015	Elevated when incumbent resigned, later elected in her own right
Nikki Haley	SC	R	2011–2017	Elected in her own right
Mary Fallin	OK	R	2011–2019	Elected in her own right
Susana Martinez	NM	R	2011–2019	Elected in her own right

Table 5.2. (Continued)

Name	State	Party	Years in office	Path to governor's office
Maggie Hassan	NH	D	2013–2017	Elected in her own right
Kate Brown	OR	D	2015–	Elevated when incumbent resigned, later elected in her own right
Gina Raimondo	RI	D	2015–	Elected in her own right
Kay Ivey	AL	R	2017–	Elevated when incumbent resigned, later elected in her own right
Kim Reynolds	IA	R	2017–	Elevated when incumbent resigned, later elected in her own right
Laura Kelly	KS	D	2019–	Elected in her own right
Michelle Lujan Grisham	NM	D	2019–	Elected in her own right
Janet Mills	ME	D	2019–	Elected in her own right
Kristi Noem	SD	R	2019–	Elected in her own right
Gretchen Whitmer	MI	D	2019–	Elected in her own right

Source: Compiled by the authors.

Similarly, by the 1980s, minority politicians in several states found the governorship open to them, further expanding the pool of possible contenders for the office. As shown in table 5.3, African Americans, Latino Americans, and Asian Americans have been elected governor in a number of different states. They have also represented both major parties.

Members of other previously excluded groups have also been elected recently. In 2018, Jared Polis became the first openly gay man to be elected governor when he won in Colorado. A Princeton University graduate, Polis became a multimillionaire after founding several successful internet businesses and had served in the U.S. House before winning the governorship. That same year Kate Brown was elected to serve a full term as Oregon's governor, becoming the first openly bisexual person in the country's history to win that office. She holds a law degree from Lewis & Clark College and had served in both houses of the state legislature and as Oregon's secretary of state before assuming the governorship.

Allowing women and members of other underrepresented groups to hold the governorship dramatically increases the prospects for electing high-quality candidates. Among other recent examples are Michelle Lujan Grisham (governor of New Mexico, law degree from University of New Mexico, former

Table 5.3. Minorities Serving as Governor

African American governors

Name	State	Party	Years in office
P. B. S. Pinchback	Louisiana	Republican	1872–1873[a]
Douglas Wilder	Virginia	Democrat	1990–1994
Deval Patrick	Massachusetts	Democrat	2007–2015
David Patterson	New York	Democrat	2008–2010[a]

Latino American governors

Name	State	Party	Years in office
Romualdo Pacheco	California	Republican	1875[a]
Ezequiel Cabeza De Baca	New Mexico	Democrat	1917
Octaviano Larrazolo	New Mexico	Republican	1919–1921
Jerry Apodaca	New Mexico	Democrat	1975–1979
Raúl Castro	Arizona	Democrat	1975–1977
Toney Anaya	New Mexico	Democrat	1983–1987
Bill Richardson	New Mexico	Democrat	2003–2011
Susanna Martinez	New Mexico	Republican	2011–2019
Brian Sandoval	Nevada	Republican	2011–2019
Michelle Lujan Grisham	New Mexico	Democrat	2019–

Asian American governors

Name	State	Party	Years in office
George Ariyoshi	Hawaii	Democrat	1973–1986[a]
John Waihee	Hawaii	Democrat	1986–1994
Ben Cayetano	Hawaii	Democrat	1994–2002
Gary Locke	Washington	Democrat	1997–2005
Bobby Jindal	Louisiana	Republican	2008–2016
Nikki Haley	South Carolina	Republican	2011–2017
David Ige	Hawaii	Democrat	2014–

Source: Compiled by the authors.
[a]Elevated from lieutenant governorship when governorship became vacant

U.S. representative), David Ige (governor of Hawaii, MBA from the University of Hawaii, former member of both houses of the state legislature), and Gina Raimondo (governor of Rhode Island, DPhil from Oxford and a law degree from Yale, former state treasurer).

There are two other noteworthy developments that have improved the average policymaking capacity of governors. As noted in chapter 3, gubernatorial terms of office have changed over time. Currently, all but two states—New Hampshire and Vermont—have shifted their governors to four-year terms of office. The move to four-year terms was motivated by a desire to spare the governor from perpetual campaigning and to allow for sufficient time to learn the job and to pursue complex policy agendas.

In many states, however, there are limits on the number of terms governors may serve. At the most extreme, the Virginia governor may serve only a single four-year term. Such a stringent limit makes it more difficult for a governor to fulfill his or her campaign pledges. The reason is that a one-term governor is quickly deemed a lame duck—an officeholder whose political power is weakened because his or her time in office is coming to an end. Because legislators and other government officials know that the governor cannot run for reelection, they have less incentive to cooperate with the governor's office. Most states sidestep this problem—or at least push it off for a few more years—by adopting a two-term limit. Currently, thirty-five states mimic the Twenty-Second Amendment of the U.S. Constitution and limit their governor to two four-year terms. (A handful of these states do allow a term-limited governor to run for office again after a specified period of time out of office. California instituted its two-term lifetime limit in 1990. Jerry Brown was able to serve two additional terms after then because his earlier service had been completed before the limits were imposed.)

No limits on how many terms a governor may serve are found in fourteen states, although among these states, a few have an informal norm that limits service to two terms. In recent decades, several Midwestern states have had governors serve for more than two four-year terms. In Iowa, Terry Branstad, a Republican, held the office from 1983 to 1999 and then was elected again by the voters in 2010 and 2014. In December 2015, he became the longest-serving governor in American history.[27] (Branstad left the governorship in 2017 to become U.S. ambassador to China.) Such lengthy service affords a governor the best chance to leave his or her mark on a state.

Another significant development over the last few decades is that governors have come to sit atop a growing bureaucracy devoted exclusively to serving the governorship.[28] Staff is important, as will be argued again in discussing legislatures and the courts, because it expands an officeholder's reach. In this case, the more people the governor has working for him or her, the more information he or she has to use in making policy. In 1980, gubernatorial staffs ranged in size from just four in Texas to eighty-two in California. The mean size of gubernatorial staffs was twenty-eight. By 2019, staff sizes ranged from nine in Nebraska to 277 in Texas, with the mean being fifty-six.[29] These numbers, however, are often supplemented by additional staff members commandeered by governors from state agencies on whose payrolls the staffers continue to appear.[30] The important point is that governors now have larger numbers of policy experts and other assistants on whom they can rely to help them in making public policy, thereby increasing their policymaking capacity.

BUREAUCRATIC CAPACITY

Has state bureaucratic capacity kept up with the policy demands being made on it? Over the last half-century, state governments have grown terrifically in size. There are, of course, a number of different ways to document this expansion.

The first and most obvious measure to examine is the number of people employed by state governments. Over the past seven decades, every state government has increased its number of full-time equivalent positions (FTEs). In 1953, the aggregate number of state FTEs was 966,000. By 2018 that number had exploded to 4,386,219.[31]

There are two things driving this growth. The first may be somewhat underappreciated. In 1953, there were about 160 million people in the United States. By 2018, the estimate was close to 328 million residents, the population having doubled in roughly sixty years. Obviously, states are now providing governmental services to far more residents, requiring some increase in the number of FTEs.

The second driving force in the growth of state government is, perhaps, more obvious: state government is being asked to do more than it was asked to do in the past. Evidence for this is provided by the dramatic expansion of state bureaucracies over the last half-century, not just in the sheer number of agencies but, more importantly, in the scope of their activities. As noted in chapter 4, in the 1960s, twelve additional agencies were present in thirty-eight or more states that had not been present the decade before. Among the agencies added were ones devoted to then-emerging policy issues, such as air quality, community affairs, highway safety, and natural resources.[32] The next decade witnessed the emergence of twenty-nine more agencies appearing in most of the states, dealing with a series of new problems confronting state governments, including alcohol and drug abuse, historic preservation, Medicaid, occupational health and safety, and women's commissions. The 1980s and 1990s saw fewer new agencies being established across most of the states—a total of sixteen across the two decades—but again those that were created allowed government to respond to new policy concerns, for instance ground water management, hazardous waste, lotteries, mining reclamation, and crime victim compensation. The most recent decades saw several more agencies established in most of the states. In the context of the discussion here, the addition of these new bureaucracies represents a significant increase in the capacity of state governments, giving them the ability to respond to a wider range of issues.

The real capacity of government agencies, however, rests on the abilities of the people working within them. Importantly, the educational credentials of the top state bureaucrats have improved significantly over the last half-century.[33] In 1964, 14 percent of top state administrators had only a high school degree or less. By 2008, only 1 percent had such limited education. At the other extreme, in 2008, 75 percent had a graduate degree or had done graduate work, substantially above the 40 percent who had done so in 1964. Thus, the educational credentials of the people running state agencies have improved dramatically since the 1960s.

Current top administrators are also drawn from a substantially larger pool of potential candidates. In 1964, 98 percent of top state administrators were male and 98 percent were white. By 2008, 29 percent of leaders were female and 10 percent were minorities. Their experience levels have also improved. In 2008, administrative leaders averaged eighteen years in state government, and 44 percent of them had worked their way up through the ranks of the agency they led. In contrast, forty-four years earlier, top administrators averaged eleven years in state government and only 28 percent had held a subordinate position in their agency. Thus, administrators today are drawn from a larger pool of potential candidates and have more agency experience than their predecessors several decades ago.

As we might expect, however, states vary on many of these dimensions. The percentage of women who head state agencies differs dramatically. Averaging data from 2012 to 2014, nationally a third of all state agencies were headed by women. But while women led 41 percent or more of state agencies in Arizona, Oregon, North Dakota, and Alaska, they were in charge of 23 percent or less of agencies in Ohio, Texas, and Georgia. Comparable disparities are found across other groups.[34]

One significant capacity concern currently facing state bureaucracies is the so-called silver tsunami, the impending retirement of a large number of their workers. In 2019, the youngest baby boomers turned fifty-five years old. That year, in California, 23 percent of the permanent state workforce was age fifty-five or older, as was 28 percent of all managers and supervisors.[35] This means that many California state employees are nearing retirement. The same is true elsewhere. It is forecasted that a quarter of the Connecticut state workforce will be eligible to retire in 2022.[36] Nationally, state governments experienced more employee retirements than the year before in both 2018 and 2019, and the expectation is that there will continue to be a surge in workers leaving.[37]

Replacing baby boomer employees and their experience and expertise is proving to be a challenge for state governments.[38] Recruiting new state workers is more difficult than in the past. Between 2013 and 2017, state job postings increased 11 percent, while the number of applicants declined by 24 percent. In a national survey, almost half of state administrators said that attracting new employees had become a significant problem. The biggest obstacle they faced was offering competitive wages, a problem 85 percent of state managers cited. Over half of them also noted that a "negative perception" of government work hindered their recruitment efforts.[39] As a result, over half of administrators had turned to the "gig economy" to hire at least some temporary workers, particularly to provide office and administrative support and accounting services.[40]

There is ample evidence to substantiate administrators' compensation concerns. Some 42 percent of state government workers earn $50,000 or less, with 4 percent being paid $30,000 or less.[41] Taking into account differences in the cost of living across the country, the best-paid state workers were in California, with an adjusted annual average annual salary of $73,835, while the lowest paid were in Missouri at only $41,223.[42] As a result, in 2019 almost twenty states passed pay and benefits increases in an effort to improve their prospects for attracting and retaining talented workers.[43]

Because state government salaries often lag behind those in the private sector, administrators fear that state government workforces face a growing skills gap.[44] In 2019, for example, Oregon passed a law requiring that child welfare case workers need only an associate's degree to be hired instead of the bachelor's degree that was previously mandated. While part of the motivation for the easing of the job requirement was to increase workforce diversity, it was also the case that it would make it easier to fill vacant positions.[45]

Another concern that may weigh on prospective state workers is a diminishment of job security. With the rise of civil service protections more than a century ago, state workers generally enjoyed protections against job losses, particularly those associated with a change in partisan control of state government. But, as some states have moved to give governors and administrators greater control over the state workforce, those protections have been weakened. In Kansas, for example, in 2015 there were 12,460 classified state employees, meaning those enjoying civil service protections, and 5,963 unclassified or "at will" employees who were more easily fired. By the end of 2018 those numbers had reversed; there were 6,277 classified employees and 11,546 unclassified employees.[46] The prospects of relatively low pay and limited job security make it harder to recruit people to work for state governments.

Even in the face of these current problems, most evidence shows that state bureaucratic capacity has increased impressively over the last half-century. States today generally have highly qualified people working in a wider array of specialized agencies making and implementing policies than in the past. Administrative leaders are better educated and more experienced than were their predecessors. All of this indicates that states are currently well prepared to implement the policies assigned to them, although there are serious concerns about their ability to maintain a high-quality workforce going forward.

LEGISLATIVE CAPACITY

State legislatures play a central role in developing state policies. Thus, it is important to measure their capacity to make policy. Perhaps even more to the point, it is necessary to assess whether state legislators and the institutions in which they serve have improved their policymaking capacity at a time when the federal government has devolved more policies to state control.

Given the trends that are already evident from the examinations of governors and top state bureaucrats, it should come as no surprise that state legislators today are, on average, better educated than were their predecessors a generation or two ago. Today, 73 percent of state legislators have graduated from college and 40 percent have earned a master's degree or higher. Sixty years ago, far more state legislators had only a high school degree and a few had not even attained that level of education.[47] State legislators today also are drawn from a much larger pool of potential candidates. In 1971, only 5 percent of the nation's state legislators were women; in 2019 the figure was 28.9 percent.[48] Similarly, the number of state legislators from various minority groups has increased substantially in recent decades.[49]

Legislators have also become considerably more experienced over the last century. Legislative experience is typically measured by the turnover rate, the percentage of new members coming into a legislative chamber. A high turnover rate translates into many inexperienced lawmakers and an increased likelihood that the legislature is not a powerful policymaking force. Longer-serving legislators gain a better understanding of the complexities and nuances of policymaking. At the institutional level, a legislature with experienced members is better able to compete in policymaking with the governor, the governor's staff, and the state bureaucracy.

There has been a noteworthy decline in the average turnover rate across state legislatures over the last century. In the 1930s, turnover each session averaged over 50 percent in state senates and almost 60 percent in state lower houses. But over the next five decades, there was a steady decrease in turnover rates. Just prior to the reapportionment revolution in the 1960s, the aggregate figures had declined to 34 percent—admittedly still troubling, but not as high as in the 1930s. In some states, however, the turnover rate was still extraordinary: 52 percent in Maine, 57 percent in Maryland, 58 percent in Tennessee, 59 percent in Alabama, 61 percent in Utah, and an astounding 67 percent in Kentucky.[50] But by the end of the 1980s, turnover averaged 22 percent in state senates and 24 percent in lower houses. Turnover in some states, notably Arkansas, California, Delaware, Illinois, New York, and Pennsylvania, averaged 15 percent or less for each electoral cycle in the decade, figures comparable to those found in the U.S. Congress.[51]

The implementation of term limits in fifteen states, beginning in the 1990s, has led to two very distinct patterns in turnover. On the whole, the states that impose legislative term limits have much higher turnover rates than those without them. While there is certainly some variation caused by other variables and by year-to-year electoral swings, the term-limited states generally experience turnover in the range of 35 percent. In some instances, it is much higher; the Michigan House of Representatives had turnover of more than 50 percent in 2010 and it is not unusual to see turnover of 40 percent or more in term-limited states. Meanwhile, the states without legislative term limits experience turnover that averages around 20 percent, although again this figure varies by state and circumstances. For the states that limit legislative service, the benefits experience generates in terms of increased policymaking capacity are sacrificed.[52] Furthermore, term limits heighten partisanship in the legislature and suppress collaboration across the aisle. By limiting the time legislators can stay in the institution, the incentive for bipartisan compromise is not as strong, exacerbating polarization.[53]

The effect of term limits is conditioned by several factors. One of the most important is the severity of the term limit law. There is a significant difference between a six-year lifetime term limit, such as exists for the Michigan House of Representatives, and a twelve-year consecutive limit allowing for legislators to return after sitting out for a term like the Louisiana House of Representatives limit.[54] In chambers with more restrictive limits, the effects on the institution may be substantial. Increased turnover also appears to accelerate the heightened partisanship evident in many legislatures and to aggravate incivility and an inability to compromise.[55] Such behavioral effects can have important policy consequences; for example, over time states with strict legislative term limits receive lower bond ratings.[56] So while state legislatures as a group are certainly more capable policymaking institutions than they were a few decades ago, not all legislatures have progressed at the same rate, and some may have even regressed a bit.

The evidence presented here shows that state legislators today are better educated, more experienced, and drawn from a larger segment of the population than were their predecessors. This indicates that lawmakers as individuals are now better prepared to act as policymakers. The question then turns to whether the institutions in which they serve are also better prepared. The informational capacity of a legislature is usually measured by its level of professionalization.[57] Professionalization has three components: the salary paid to legislators, the number of days the legislature meets in session each year, and the staff provided. Legislatures that pay members well, meet for extended periods, and have adequate staff resources are more professional, meaning that they have a greater capacity to generate and process the information needed to make policy. More professional legislatures are also better equipped to compete with the governor and bureaucracy in the policymaking process.

How, then, do contemporary state legislatures compare to legislatures several decades ago on the components of professionalization? Table 5.4 compares state legislatures in 2019 with state legislatures in 1979 on each of the three dimensions. It must be pointed out that 1979 was a point in time when the significant advances made in professionalization during the 1960s and 1970s had begun to stall.[58] Perhaps it is a bit surprising that in terms of constant dollars, legislative salaries have lost ground over the last four decades. The mean salary has dropped by $2,931, while the median salary is lower by $4,174. Both the

Table 5.4. **Professionalization Components for State Legislatures, 1979 and 2019**

Indicator	1979	2019	Change from 1979 to 2019
Mean Member Salary	$34,223[a]	$31,292	−$2,931
Median Member Salary	$28,282[a]	$24,108	−$4,174
Mean Days in Session	62.4	74.3[b]	+11.9
Median Days in Session	58.5	61.8[b]	+3.3
Mean Staff per Member	3.7	4.5[c]	+0.8
Median Staff per Member	2.7	3.3[c]	+0.6

Source: Calculated by authors from data in various editions of *Book of the States* and http://www.ncsl.org/research/about-state-legislatures/staff-change-chart-1979-1988-1996-2003-2009.aspx.
[a]1979 salary calculated in 2018 dollars
[b]Data are for 2013–2014 sessions
[c]Data are for 2015

mean and median salaries for 2019 are modest sums, well under the national median household income of $61,372. These numbers, of course, mask the great range in legislative salaries across the states. California lawmakers, for example, earned $110,459, a sum that actually represented a drop from the $116,098 they were paid until late in 2009 when the commission that governs their salaries dropped them in response to state budget problems brought on by the Great Recession. In contrast, New Hampshire legislators were paid the same $100 a year the state has paid since 1889. New Mexico lawmakers are not paid a salary, only a per diem. Overall, in most states legislative compensation does not appear adequate to attract the best policymaking talent.

There has been an increase in the number of days state legislatures meet in session over the last four decades. The mean number of days in session in 2016 was 74.3, while the median was 61.8. The difference between the two numbers reveals that a few state legislatures meet for many days, thereby greatly increasing the overall mean. Indeed, that is the case. The National Conference of State Legislatures considers four state legislatures to be full-time institutions like the U.S. Congress: California, Michigan, New York, and Pennsylvania. On the other end of the spectrum are a handful of legislatures that demand considerably less time from their members: Montana, New Hampshire, North Dakota, South Dakota, Utah, and Wyoming. Most state legislatures fall somewhere in between the two extremes, with sessions that last four or five months each year. Such sessions allow legislatures to play a role in the policymaking process, but it makes it more difficult for them to challenge the governor and the executive branch, both of which are, of course, year-round institutions. Indeed, the challenge to keep up with the rest of the government is even more acute in the four states (Montana, Nevada, North Dakota, and Texas) that allow their legislatures to meet only every other year.

Perhaps the only hopeful sign for the increased policymaking capacity of state legislatures is found in the area of staff support. Both the mean and median number of staff per state legislator have increased since 1979. Again, some legislatures, such as California, afford their legislators considerable staff, while others, notably New Hampshire, provide very little. Staff is important because it greatly increases the informational capacity of a legislator to make policy by allowing them to generate and analyze much more data than they could hope to do on their own. Research shows that more legislatures with more staff are better able to monitor and review the actions of state agencies to ensure the agencies comply with legislative intent. In other words, legislative oversight of the agencies is stronger in more professionalized legislatures, just as we would expect.[59]

One saving grace for less professionalized legislatures may be the resources made available to them through the National Conference of State Legislatures and the Council of State Governments, both of which provide access to non-partisan and detailed information about policies being developed across the nation. Other national organizations offer more ideological assistance. When asked about the American Legislative Exchange Council (ALEC), an organization that offers pro-business and conservative "model legislation" to state legislators to introduce, an Oregon senator said the group was a great resource, noting that "we have such limited staff that this helps us look at things and consider them."[60] Indeed, studies have found that part-time legislatures with limited staff and information resources are especially likely to adopt the "model legislation" produced by outside groups.[61]

Overall, state legislators appear to be increasingly capable to make policy, but the institutions in which they serve may lag a bit in that regard. This is, of course, in contrast to the increased capacities exhibited by the governor and the executive branch, both of which have made significant progress over the last several decades. Any inability of state legislatures to keep up may signal a potential problem with shifting policymaking demands back to the states.

JUDICIAL CAPACITY

The bulk of the legal activity and judicial system in the United States is at the state level. While there are about twelve hundred judges in the entire federal judicial system, there are more than twenty-seven thousand judges in the state systems.[62] More judges are required at the state level because state judicial systems handle far more cases than does the federal court system. In 2016, approximately 1.2 million cases were filed with U.S. District Courts, U.S. Bankruptcy Courts, and U.S. Appellate Courts. In comparison, that same year more than 84 million cases were filed in state courts. Although large, the latter figure actually represents a substantial decline since 2008 when 106 million cases were filed.[63] If a person comes in contact with the American judicial system, it is far more likely to be at the state level than at the federal level.

Although controversy occasionally surrounds state courts and their legal decisions, most scholars accept the reality that they are, at least in part, policy-making institutions, particularly at the appellate level. But courts differ from other policymakers in at least one important regard: They cannot act as policy entrepreneurs surveying the political landscape for problems to solve, as legislators and executives can. Instead the courts are inherently reactive, only solving problems that are brought to them. This means that they typically get involved with policies that the other governmental institutions have failed to adequately resolve, leaving some aggrieved party or parties to take their complaints to them.

The courts also differ in that the public has always assumed (if not actually required) that their members have attained a certain level of education. In the nineteenth century, this typically meant that aspiring lawyers had "read" the law and been trained by established attorneys. By the twentieth century, formal law schools had taken over the education of new lawyers.[64] And of course, although it was not always spelled out in early constitutions (including the U.S. Constitution), the expectation was that judges would have the appropriate legal training. So, from an educational perspective, state courts have always had the capacity to render legal decisions because judges were expected to have attained a high level of education prior to being put on the bench. Thus, for example, while less than 50 percent of New Hampshire's state legislators have college degrees, all of their state judges have both bachelor's and law degrees. Today almost every current state constitution requires some number of years as a state bar association member before becoming a state judge.[65] Thus, state judges are expected to have both legal training and experience as a lawyer before gaining the bench.

The next question is whether states are willing to offer salaries sufficient to attract top legal talent. Here again the contrast with state legislatures is dramatic. As shown in table 5.5, in 2019, judges on state courts of last resort were paid a mean salary of $176,714 and a median of $172,716. The range of salaries was from Maine's $136,000 to California's $253,189. Even general (or trial) court judicial salaries are high relative to legislative salaries: in 2019 the mean salary was $158,748 and the median was $168,059, with a range from a low of $125,499 in Kansas to a high of $208,000 in New York.[66] Thus even the lowest-paid state trial court judge is paid more than the highest-paid state legislator. States are much more willing to invest in their judges than they are to invest in their state legislators. The most extreme example of this is New Hampshire. As noted earlier, New Hampshire state legislators are paid $100 a year, with no per diems. That means each year the state pays its 424 state lawmakers a total of $42,400 in salary. The five members of the New Hampshire Supreme Court each make $175,837, thereby costing the state $879,185 in salary.[67] This is not to claim, of course, that judicial salaries are necessarily sufficient to attract and keep the best legal minds. State judges are almost always paid less than their federal counterparts and less than what top lawyers in their

Table 5.5. Judicial Salaries, 2019

Level	Mean salary	Median salary	Highest salary	Lowest salary
State court of last resort justice	$176,714	$172,716	$253,189 (California)	$136,000 (Maine)
State trial court judge	$158,748	$168,059	$208,000 (New York)	$125,499 (Kansas)

	Salary			
US Supreme Court justice	$258,900			
US trial court judge	$210,900			

Sources: State judge salaries from National Center for State Courts, "Survey of Judicial Salaries," January 2019; federal judge salaries from https://www.uscourts.gov/judges-judgeships/judicial-compensation.

state make, and those comparisons enter into a prospective judge's calculations about whether to take a state judgeship.[68] And there are ongoing battles in many states over judicial pay, with judges decrying stagnant wages.[69] Still, there is evidence that current salaries attract and maintain competent jurists.[70]

Like governors and bureaucrats—and unlike most state legislators—almost all state judges, and all appellate court judges, hold full-time positions. As argued earlier, this time commitment enhances their policymaking capacity. State appellate judges also benefit from staff assistance, most importantly in the form of law clerks. Typically, clerks are relatively recent law school graduates with distinguished academic records. Their contributions greatly increase the judiciary's capacity. At the state court of last resort level, the number of clerks varies, from fewer than one clerk per justice in Alabama to more than five clerks per justice in Pennsylvania. Once again, most states are far more willing to invest in assistance for judges than in assistance for lawmakers. In New Hampshire, for example, supreme court justices are each allowed two clerks. In contrast, each of the state's legislators enjoys only half of a staff member (including clerical support). Trial court judges in many states also have law clerks.[71]

As with the other institutions of state government, state courts now draw on a larger pool of potential judges than in the past. Over time, more women and minorities have entered law school. In recent years, this has translated into more of them making it onto the state bench. In 2018, women held 33 percent of state judgeships, with a high of 44 percent in Minnesota and a low of 15 percent in Arkansas. They held 33 percent of all state court of last resort positions, which actually represented a slight decrease from a few years before.[72]

Minorities have slowly increased their numbers. In 2010, a few states, such as New Hampshire, had no minorities on the bench, but other states, notably Florida and Maryland, had large contingents.[73] By 2016, no state had achieved population parity with either women or minority judges: Hawaii, Oregon, and New Mexico came the closest to doing so, while West Virginia, Alaska, and Utah had the furthest to go.[74] But some progress has been made. With the 2016 appointment of Anne McKeig, a descendant of the White Earth Nation, as a justice, the Minnesota Supreme Court gained a female majority.[75] And in 2018 Melody Stewart became the first African American woman elected to the Supreme Court of Ohio, while in 2019 Cheri Beasley became the first black woman named as chief justice of the Supreme Court of North Carolina.[76] Still, a 2019 report revealed that "people of color compose nearly 40 percent of the U.S. population, but hold only 15 percent of state supreme court seats. . . . Women make up roughly half the U.S. population but hold only 36 percent of state supreme court seats. White men make up less than a third of the U.S. population, but they constitute 56 percent of today's supreme court justices."[77]

Overall, state courts are full-time institutions, populated by well-educated judges who in turn are assisted by capable law clerks. Salaries appear sufficient to attract and keep qualified people on the bench. All of this suggests that in terms of judicial capacity, state courts are currently well positioned to handle the tasks given them. There is evidence to support this assertion. Over the course of the twentieth century, state courts of last resort greatly reformed, restructuring to allow them to gain greater control over the cases they decided.[78] When modern state courts of last resort are compared to the U.S. Supreme Court, they stack up well. Indeed, state courts of last resort in California and Pennsylvania are on the same level as the U.S. Supreme Court in terms of salary and the provision of law clerks. Overall, the typical state court of last resort is much more like the U.S. Supreme Court in terms of its capacity than any state legislature is like the U.S. Congress.[79] Consequently, it is not surprising to learn that because of its importance in the corporate world, Delaware has made sure its court of last resort is capable of meeting the unusual demands on it. According to a law professor, "Academics regard [the court's justices] as among the most scholarly bench to be found anywhere. Corporate lawyers know them by name and temperament in much the same way that others know the justices of the U.S. Supreme Court. Their published opinions and academic articles are influential in other states and with the federal judiciary."[80]

This brings us to one final question about state court capacity: Are there enough state judges to meet the demand for their services? Given 1.2 million federal cases each year—the bulk of which are bankruptcies—each federal judge handles approximately one thousand cases. The twenty-seven thousand state court judges tackle eighty-four million cases annually—over half of which are traffic violations—or about 3,111 cases per judge. These are, of course, crude calculations. Many of these cases get settled outside the courtroom. But there is little to suggest that state courts are overwhelmed. There is a tendency for smaller population states to enjoy a lower ratio of residents (and therefore likely cases) per judge. This is to be expected because in the American federal system, most legal cases fall under state law, requiring each state to create an extensive judicial system. Consequently, even small population states have to have the same basic court structures that larger states have.[81] In any event, the indications are that state courts are capable institutions.

CONCLUSION

Much is now demanded of state governments. The pressure on them has come from two directions. First, the public expects them to be involved in a much wider range of policy areas than in the past. Second, over the last few decades the federal government has devolved many policy decisions to the states. The question we have tried to address is whether state governments are up to the tasks assigned them. By and large, we find that state government capacity has increased as more is being asked of it. Governors are better educated, more experienced, and supplemented with more staff than in the past. State bureaucracies are led by better educated and more experienced people drawn from a wider pool of applicants. State courts also appear to have increased their capacity.

Perhaps the only concerns are with the capacities of state legislatures. Lawmakers are, like their counterparts in the rest of the government, better educated than in the past. Increases in member experience, however, have been forcibly truncated in the fifteen states with term limits. There are also doubts that the salaries offered in many states are sufficient to recruit the best and brightest to service; indeed, they have fallen behind in most states over the last few decades. But the most troubling limitation involves staff support. Legislators are asked to respond to policy questions across a wide range of issues, taxing their own abilities to be competent in developing appropriate responses. Staff support is necessary to allow lawmakers to generate and digest the vast amounts of information they need to consume to make good public policy. Unfortunately, in a number of states, legislators are not provided the assistance they need, leaving them to look to other parts of the government or to people and groups outside of government to give them the information they need. As an eminent legislative scholar said of state legislatures, "They are probably the most unappreciated institutions in the country."[82]

Of course, legislatures and all other state government institutions must have more than policymaking capacity to effectively serve the public. Institutional capacity does not guarantee proper individual behavior. Recently, there have been a few spectacular examples of state officials failing to meet expected standards. Between 2013 and 2019, the Speaker of the House—the highest legislative office in the state house of representatives—resigned amid scandal in at least seven states (Kentucky, Missouri, New York, Ohio, Rhode Island, Tennessee, and South Carolina). In Alabama a few years ago, the chief justice of the state supreme court was suspended, the governor was facing impeachment, and the house speaker was convicted on corruption charges—all at the same time. An

Illinois legislator admitted to taking a bribe, a longtime California lawmaker was sent to prison for racketeering and money laundering, and a Michigan member was convicted for shooting his ex-wife's Mercedes. Since 2015, the governors of Alabama, Missouri, and Oregon have resigned over various scandals. These are, to say the least, disheartening signs. In chapter 9, we will have more to say about these and similar events, and why it is more important than ever that citizens become knowledgeable about state politics.

In this chapter we have focused on the policymaking capacity of state officials. But we cannot leave this topic without noting that most policies also involve funding. And, as discussed in chapter 3, the funding, or fiscal capacity, of states is another matter entirely. It is clear that the chronic federal budget problems will impact states. This impact will be twofold. First, a reduction in federal aid to state and local governments (outside health care) is likely. Second, the national government's "policy footprint" may shrink as the national budget is increasingly constrained. If so, then the states will have to decide which programs to fund and how to fund them on their own. Developing the fiscal and analytical capacity to do so is emerging as one of the major challenges for state officials.

6

Public Policy and the Role of the States in a Changing Federal System

States matter because:

- ★ Significant issues are addressed in state legislative sessions every year.
- ★ Innovative policy often begins with a single state and later gets adopted by other states and/or by the national government.
- ★ States are the "default" setting of policymaking.
- ★ Gridlock at the national level increases the opportunity for state-based policymaking.
- ★ Concerns over the federal deficit will increase the opportunity for state-based policymaking.

THE TITLE OF THIS CHAPTER can be read two ways. It can be read retrospectively, as a comment on the past, as in "because of the centralizing tendencies of the changes in the federal system the role of the states has changed." Or it can be read prospectively, as a prediction of the future, as in "fiscal exigencies at the federal level are going to require a recalibration of the federal relationship." We intend that it be read both ways because federalism is indeed a dynamic relationship, ever changing, and citizens of every state need to be aware of that reality.

There are those who see the states today as mere administrative outposts of the federal government.[1] In some policy areas that may in fact be close to the truth. But in most domestic policy arenas, states retain a fair amount of discretion. And in other areas, they are the dominant crafters of public policy.

If states were not important actors, why would there be such interest and anticipation at the beginning of each new state legislative session? Every year, in just about every state, one can find news stories about the issues to watch. Take, for example, this sample of headlines from early 2019, as many state legislatures were about to convene (with key issues in parentheses):

- *AL.com:* "9 Issues to Watch During the 2019 Alabama Legislative Session" (gas tax, prisons, lottery, distracted driving, teacher and state employee pay raises).[2]
- *The Gazette:* "6 Issues to Watch in the 2019 Iowa Legislature" (traffic cameras, Iowa Public Employees Retirement System, sexual harassment, medical cannabis).[3]
- *Spokesman-Review:* "Washington Legislative Preview: Issues to Watch in the Coming Months" (education, mental health, environment, guns).[4]
- *Vermont Public Radio:* "6 Issues to Watch During the 2019 Vermont Legislative Session" (paid family leave, $15 minimum wage, clean water funding, forced school district mergers).[5]

National publications such as *Governing* identified the key 2019 state legislative issues across the country as Medicaid, tax reform, paid sick leave, marijuana, education funding, minimum wage, and environmental regulations, among others.[6] None of these issues is trivial. Moreover, as Martha Derthick noted, absent concerted national action, "the states are the 'default setting' of the American federal system. To the extent that other levels of government lack the resources to act—authority, revenue, will power, political consensus, institutional capacity—the states have the job."[7]

In the previous chapter, we showed how state governmental institutions, which were denigrated for decades, have become much more capable over the past two generations. Today, state policymakers across the country are far more likely to share information and experiences about issues and how each state is addressing specific problems than their counterparts were in the past. But this does not mean that the states follow the same policy paths—far from it. The policy variation across them is considerable. In many important respects, the states continue to be the "laboratories of democracy," as U.S. Supreme Court Justice Louis Brandeis once characterized them.[8] Different states have taken the lead on a range of policy innovations: Minnesota (the first state to experiment with charter schools), Oregon (the first to permit physician-assisted suicide for terminally ill patients), Florida (the first to require drug testing to qualify for public assistance), California (the first to create a carbon trading market), Washington (the first to ban texting while driving), and Texas (the first to pass an in-state resident tuition policy for undocumented immigrant students). Sometimes the novel policies adopted by states seem idiosyncratic; in 2019, California became the first state to bar fur trapping, Maine the first state to ban Styrofoam food containers, New York the first state to prohibit cat declawing, and Washington the first state to allow the composting of human remains.[9] But some groundbreaking state laws have had big national impacts;

it was a Wisconsin policy requiring welfare recipients to be enrolled in school or training for a job (workfare) that became an integral part of the federal welfare law in 1995, and the Massachusetts health insurance program was the model on which the federal Affordable Care Act law was based in 2010.

States approach policy problems in different ways. Variables such as a state's political culture and economic resources lead to policy variations. Dramatic shifts in policy are often evident when a state changes control from one political party to the other. Examples from recent years include the enactment of policies by Republican-dominated governments to weaken unions in Wisconsin and Michigan, places where labor had traditionally been strong. But partisanship is not always the driver of innovation. In 2016, both Connecticut, under unified Democratic Party control, and South Carolina, under GOP leadership, adopted trial "pay for success" programs. "Pay for success" is a novel approach to funding social programs, one where funding organizations only get promised public monies once their approach has proven successful.[10] A federal version was subsequently included in the Bipartisan Budget Act of 2018.[11]

In this chapter, we discuss some of the important ways in which policies vary from state to state. As a team of political scientists recently put it, "Although the states share cultural and historical similarities, the political, economic, and demographic heterogeneity at the state level is enormous."[12] Some of these variables, such as political party control, are obvious. Others are less so, among them are the level of competition between the two parties; the policymaking capacity of the legislative, executive, and judicial branches of state government; interest group balance and strength within a state; public opinion; and the presence or absence of instruments of direct democracy such as the initiative process.

Public opinion and ideology appear to be important in the sort of policymaking that has come to be called "morality policy."[13] Morality policy is characterized by an underlying appeal to "core values." Typically, it does not have significant economic impacts. The policy discussion surrounding morality policy is less technical and more about "right" and "wrong" than is the case in most other policy areas. It is often highly salient and emotional. Because at least one side of the policy debate views the issue as about core values, there is little room for negotiation and compromise. Religiosity is often strongly related to public opinion on morality policy.

Physical and socioeconomic characteristics are important because, as Virginia Gray points out, "These factors structure a government's problems and affect a state government's ability to deal with them."[14] State demographics are an example; the size and structure of the population are often important in determining the context in which problems are defined. For instance, in Utah a larger proportion of the population is under eighteen years old than in any other state. This puts a special burden on the state's public education system. Other states, notably Arizona and California, have substantial numbers of primary and secondary school students who are from immigrant families with limited English-speaking skills. This places a different burden on the state's public education system.

A state's physical characteristics define some policy problems and solutions. Montana is a geographically large state with a small population, which means road and highway expenditures per capita are higher than in most other states. The differences in terrain and climate from one state to another help define the role of such diverse economic sectors as agriculture and tourism. The presence of nonrenewable natural resources such as oil, natural gas, or coal and renewable ones such as hydro, solar, and wind affect the nature of economic activity and the types of environmental concerns in a state. Sometimes the economic future and the state budget outlook can change rapidly because of the discovery of oil or some other resource. Just look at recent developments in North Dakota. Between 1930 and 2000 North Dakota had a net population loss of forty thousand people—an extraordinary statistic when one realizes that the overall population of the United States more than doubled during that time period. But over the last eighteen years the state has experienced something of a population boom, adding almost 130,000 residents. Why this sudden change? It was driven by the development of the oil- and shale-rich Bakken Formation in the western part of the state. North Dakota is now the second-largest oil producer behind Texas and as a result its per capita income ranking leaped from thirty-eighth to sixth among the states between 2000 and 2018. The financial benefits to the state government have been substantial: North Dakota was the only state to enjoy a budget surplus every year during the Great Recession and its immediate aftermath.

State economies play a critical role in state policymaking. First, the relative wealth or poverty in a state is a major variable in social welfare costs and the capacity to finance the service and regulatory activities of the state government. Second, the nature of the economy—agricultural, industrial, service, resource extraction—has a significant impact on the nature of a state's interest group system and its ability to adjust to changing economic realities. Once the price of a barrel of oil declined dramatically in between 2014 and 2016, for example, North Dakota and other states that rely heavily on revenue from oil extraction faced budget shortfalls. When oil prices began to recover, so did the states' revenues.

While many policies vary from state to state, it is also true that states learn from one another. A good contemporary example is cell phone use while driving. In 2001, New York became the first state to ban talking on a cell phone while driving. By 2019, eighteen additional states had done so, but thirty-one states had not followed New York's lead. Some states have banned texting but not talking; still others have prohibited talking for young drivers (under age eighteen) only.[15] Within the field of comparative state politics, there is a remarkably rich literature on policy innovation and diffusion.[16] Often policies begin in one state and are incrementally adopted by a few other states. A larger group of states then may adopt them in rapid succession, while some states may never implement them. In these types of cases, if one were to graph the policy adoption by states over time, typically an "s-curve" pattern would emerge.

At other times, one state develops a policy that then "breaks outs" and experiences "rapid and sudden adoption" across states.[17] "Amber Alert" laws are an example; first adopted in Texas, every state in the United States passed such a law within six years. The pattern of innovation diffusion depends in part on the type of policy being addressed. Some are highly salient to the public and the media, others are not. Some policy problems (and their potential solutions) are complex, others are simpler. The interplay between issue salience and complexity helps define the degree and manner to which other states adopt the policy.[18]

There is also evidence that some states are consistently more likely to be innovators (policy leaders) and that innovation often comes in "waves"—periods in which many states are adopting new policies.[19] Among the states identified as innovation leaders are California, Colorado, Florida, Illinois, Minnesota, and North Carolina. Furthermore, we have been experiencing an "innovation wave" for the past quarter-century just as we might anticipate, given the growing capacity of state governments. Keeping in mind the political, physical, and socioeconomic variables and how they define the context of policymaking and how policies diffuse across states, we now turn to an examination of some of the most important policy areas for the states.

PUBLIC EDUCATION AND THE STATES

Education has long been considered the primary responsibility of the states and their local governments. Almost all state constitutions contain provisions to that effect, although their specific language varies. Consider, for example, the mandates in the following state constitutions:

- New York: "The legislature shall provide for the maintenance and support of a system of free common schools, wherein all the children of this state may be educated."
- Oklahoma: "The Legislature shall establish and maintain a system of free public schools wherein all the children of the State may be educated."
- Illinois: "The State shall provide for an efficient system of high quality public educational institutions and services."
- Minnesota: "It is the duty of the legislature to establish a general and uniform system of public schools. The legislature shall make such provisions by taxation or otherwise as will secure a thorough and efficient system of public schools throughout the state."[20]

The last two constitutional clauses appear to hold Minnesota and Illinois to a higher standard in the provision of public education than do the comparable clauses in the Oklahoma and New York constitutions. This is not a casual observation; most states (in particular the state legislatures) have been sued at one time or another for failing to maintain their public school systems at state constitutional standards. Whether the state constitution simply requires "a system of free public schools" or "a thorough and efficient system of high quality public educational institutions" may determine how these lawsuits are decided by state courts. There are many ways in which states matter in setting education policy. Here we will emphasize four: funding patterns, curriculum content, school choice, and higher education.

School funding. K–12 education funding is the single largest expenditure for the states (although health care is challenging that position), accounting for about one-quarter of a typical state's general fund budget. It varies depending on how a particular state divides up the funding responsibility with its local school districts. (As another example of how states differ, Hawaii does not have school districts; the state department of education oversees all of its public schools.[21]) Some states require most of the K–12 school funding to be generated at the local level, which means the primary funding source is the local property tax. Because of its heavy reliance on local school districts, only 33 percent of public school funding in Nebraska comes from the state. In contrast, in Vermont very little of the K–12 money arises from the local governments, and the state undertakes the primary responsibility through a state property tax, covering more than 90 percent of the total cost from the state budget. The consequence, therefore, is that public schools account for a much larger state expenditure in Vermont (33 percent of the entire state budget) than in Nebraska (14 percent).[22]

Regardless of how a state divides this revenue and spending function with its local governments, public education is ultimately the state's responsibility. The amount of total state and local spending on K–12 per student varies substantially, as shown in table 6.1. Utah spends the lowest amount per student ($7,179), while at the high end New York spends three times as much ($23,091).[23] Some of the variation can be accounted for by differences in state wealth, the cost of living, the magnitude of the school-age population relative to total state population, and average class size. Education is a personnel-intensive endeavor, so most (about 75 percent) of the K–12 funding is spent on personnel—teacher and staff salaries and benefit packages. The fact that there are a large number of education personnel in each state means that educators can bring considerable pressure on state lawmakers. Massive teacher protests in 2018 in Arizona, North Carolina, Oklahoma and West Virginia forced their legislatures to substantially increase state funding for primary and secondary education.[24]

The level of funding matters because, as one analysis reports,

> The recent quasi-experimental literature that relates school spending to student outcomes overwhelmingly support a causal relationship between increased school spending and student outcomes. All but one of the several multi-state studies find a strong link between spending and outcomes–indicating that money matters on average.[25]

Table 6.1. Spending per Pupil in Public Elementary-Secondary Schools, Fiscal Year 2017

Alabama	$9,511
Alaska	$17,838
Arizona	$8,003
Arkansas	$9,967
California	$12,143
Colorado	$9,809
Connecticut	$19,322
Delaware	$15,302
Florida	$9,075
Georgia	$10,205
Hawaii	$14,322
Idaho	$7,486
Illinois	$15,337
Indiana	$10,045
Iowa	$11,461
Kansas	$10,961
Kentucky	$10,121
Louisiana	$11,199
Maine	$13,690
Maryland	$14,848
Massachusetts	$16,197
Michigan	$11,907
Minnesota	$12,647
Mississippi	$8,771
Missouri	$10,589
Montana	$11,443
Nebraska	$12,579
Nevada	$9,320
New Hampshire	$15,683
New Jersey	$18,920
New Mexico	$9,881
New York	$23,091

Table 6.1. (Continued)

North Carolina	$9,072
North Dakota	$13,760
Ohio	$12,645
Oklahoma	$7,940
Oregon	$11,264
Pennsylvania	$15,798
Rhode Island	$15,943
South Carolina	$10,590
South Dakota	$9,939
Tennessee	$9,184
Texas	$9,375
Utah	$7,179
Vermont	$18,290
Virginia	$11,886
Washington	$11,989
West Virginia	$11,554
Wisconsin	$11,968
Wyoming	$16,537
United States	$12,201

Source: https://www.census.gov/data/tables/2017/econ/school-finances/secondary-education-finance.html.

The relationship is far from perfect; there are many variables that are important in determining the overall quality of education from one state to another, including the number of students for whom English is a second language. Nonetheless, on average, the states that spend more on education see better student performance. Consequently, lawsuits by citizens to force states to spend more on K–12 education are reasonably common.

The policy consequences of those lawsuits differ from one state to another. First, remember that most of these lawsuits are settled at the state supreme court level based on state laws and state constitutional provisions and not by federal courts relying on federal laws. With certain exceptions, the U.S. Supreme Court has determined that K–12 school funding is a state function. So while both the level and formula used to fund public schools in some states has been upheld, in others the courts have required dramatic revisions. One recent study finds that from 1973 to 2018, lawsuits based on education adequacy liability have been decided in forty-four states, and in twenty-two of those states the decision went against the state, with mixed decisions in five other states.[26] In most of those instances, "the funding systems were completely or partially overturned."[27] Kentucky and Michigan were two such cases, and in both significant changes were made to the state education system, including the manner in which they were funded. In Kansas, the state legislature and the state supreme court engaged in a heated battle over K–12 funding for more than nine years.[28] In 2016, the court forced the state legislature to revise its K–12 funding allocation process, but it took until 2019 for the justices to finally approve a legislative plan to do so.[29]

States, therefore, are intimately involved in the funding of K–12 education. They continue to grapple with school funding issues—both in terms of how schools are funded and the level at which they are funded. Lawsuits continue to be filed. This remains a key policy issue for states because they are a large funder of public schools. Taking all states together, the source of funding for public schools is equally derived from state and local sources—47 percent from the state government and 45 percent from local school districts. From 1995 until 2013, states were supplying a slightly larger share overall than the local districts (about 47 to 50 percent depending on the year), but many states cut their funding to local schools during the Great Recession, and their contributions have only recently begun to rebound to their earlier levels. The federal government provides only about 8 to 13 percent of public school funding, depending on the year, with the most recent figure being on the low end of that range.[30] These percentages, of course, vary considerably by state. Wealthier states (Connecticut, Massachusetts, and New Jersey at less than 5 percent) rely little on federal funds, while poorer states (Mississippi and New Mexico at 14 percent or higher) are more dependent on federal money.[31]

Curriculum. High school graduation rates diverge by state more than one might imagine. The most recent report of the adjusted cohort graduation rate showed New Mexico (71 percent) and Oregon (77 percent) at the low end, while Iowa (91 percent) and New Jersey (91 percent) had the highest rates.[32] There are many reasons for differences in graduation rates, among them the percentage of students for whom English is not their native language.

Different states also have different curriculum requirements. While there remains a voluntary but politically controversial effort among the states to develop a "common core" of subjects and classes—by 2019 they were adopted in forty-one states—there is still considerable variation in what each state requires.[33] For example, at the high school level only nine states require a full year of American government, thirty states require only a half-year, and eleven have no requirement.[34] In 2015, eight states—Arizona, Idaho, Louisiana, North Dakota, South Carolina, Tennessee, Utah, and Wisconsin—adopted laws requiring high school students to pass a citizenship test along the lines of those taken by people seeking to become naturalized citizens in order to graduate.[35] By 2019, thirty-one states mandated that their students pass such an exam.[36] More generally, mapping course content requirements in about a dozen states at several different grade levels, scholars recently found only moderate alignment of curriculum content requirements from one state to another, with minimal alignment between some states' requirements in certain subjects.[37] Meanwhile, controversies erupted in some states over the curricular content of a variety of school subjects. In Texas, there was a heated debate over material covered in high school history textbooks and who has the authority to review such materials.[38] Lawmakers and school districts in Arizona battled over Mexican American studies courses.[39] In 2020, four states (California, Colorado, Illinois, and New Jersey) required that LGBT contributions be taught as part of the history curriculum, while six states (Alabama, Louisiana, Mississippi, Oklahoma, South Carolina, and Texas) had laws that prohibited the "promotion of homosexuality."[40]

One of the more contentious issues in regard to curriculum is the teaching of evolution and creationism in science classes. Most people are at least vaguely familiar with the "Scopes Monkey Trial," a 1925 case involving a prohibition against teaching evolution in Tennessee public schools. Fewer people know that Tennessee was not the first state to pass "anti-Darwin" legislation. Oklahoma was the first in 1923, followed by Florida. Mississippi and Arkansas also passed such laws soon after Tennessee. The issue reemerged toward the end of the twentieth century. In Kansas, where the state board of education is an elected body, religious conservatives won six seats on the ten-member board in 2005 and the new majority voted to change the way evolution was addressed in the school curriculum. They required evolution be presented as a flawed theory and permitted "intelligent design" to be taught as an alternative theory.[41] By 2007, several of the conservatives on the state board had been defeated, resulting in a more moderate majority. The board subsequently repealed the 2005 policy. That action did not, however, end the controversy. In 2012, Tennessee passed a law that permits teachers to discuss alternatives to evolution in science class, claiming an "academic freedom" right to do so. Louisiana had passed a similar law in 2008.[42] In recent years, a handful of other states legislatures have considered comparable measures, while other states have specifically rejected such policies.[43]

The issue of teaching evolution and alternative theories in public schools is interesting because it is tied, in a broad sense, to state political culture and public opinion. Polls find that, while a solid majority of respondents believe evolution should be taught in science classes, a majority also believes that creationism should be taught.[44] The belief that creationism should be part of the curriculum is especially strong among Evangelical Christians, a group that is prevalent in the South.[45] Many (but not all) of the states in which the public school curriculum provides an alternative to evolution in science classes or at least a challenge to evolution are, indeed, southern states. As one report on this topic notes, "State evolution standards are strongly influenced by public opinion, which is itself strongly related to the number of Evangelicals and the number of advanced degree holders in the state."[46]

Another example of political culture influencing curriculum is sex education. As of 2019, twenty-four states required their public schools to teach sex education. Almost all of these states mandate HIV education as well. When provided, sex education or HIV education are required to be medically accurate in thirteen states. At the same time, three states (Arizona, Nevada, and Utah) require parental consent before a child can receive any sex education instruction, and thirty-seven states allow parents to opt out of such instruction on behalf of their children. Abstinence must be stressed in sex education instruction in twenty-seven states and covered as a topic in ten other states; thirteen states have no requirements on the teaching of abstinence.[47] Consequently, the sort of sex education children get varies across the states.

School choice. One of the biggest educational movements in the past three decades has been the effort to allow parents and children more choice in the public schools they attend. By far the largest component of this program is the charter school movement. The first state to authorize charter schools was Minnesota in 1991. According to the Minnesota Legislative Reference Library, "The basic charter concept is simple: a group of teachers or other would-be educators apply for permission to open a school. The school operates under a charter, a contract with the local school board or state."[48] A charter school is exempt from most of the regulations required of traditional public school and is authorized to experiment with different types of curriculum or learning techniques. Students must still meet traditional graduation requirements, and the school must demonstrate that it has accomplished the learning objectives stipulated in the charter. If the school has not met those objectives, it may lose its charter to operate. The idea is to introduce more innovation into the public school system. The key, and the source of much of the initial resistance to charter schools in many quarters, is that the charter schools receive state tax dollars, generally in the same amount as traditional public schools. In addition, some charter schools are created and managed by private companies—another reason for resistance to them from some quarters.

Since the first charter schools were authorized three decades ago, the system has expanded rapidly. Today, there are over seven thousand charter schools enrolling more than 3.2 million students in forty-four states. Even with this rapid growth, however, charter schools remain a small part of the overall public school system, comprising just over 7 percent of all public schools and enrolling just over 5 percent of all public school students, although in a few cities such as New Orleans, Camden, and Newark, more than 30 percent of public school students attend public charter schools.[49] Only 7 percent of charter schools are in rural areas; 57 percent are in urban locals and the rest are in the suburbs.[50]

The success of the charter school movement appears uneven. Research comparing outcomes between charter school and traditional school students is mixed and inconclusive.[51] Some schools have had their charters revoked for failure to meet state graduation standards or for mismanaging public funds. But others are innovative, popular, and successful, with long waiting lists of prospective students desiring to attend. Over half of the charter schools are in urban areas, and many serve minority communities for whom the public school system has not succeeded. There is some evidence that charter schools often outperform traditional public schools in these settings.[52] It is clear, however, that charter schools are not a panacea for all the ills of the public school system. But at their best, they offer the potential to experiment with learning strategies that, in the long run, may provide "best practices" that will advance the larger education system in many states.

While the overall assessment of charter schools' success remains open, the concept of them appears to be accepted by a plurality of the American public. A 2018 poll found that 44 percent of respondents favored the idea of charter schools, with greater support being found among Republicans (57 percent) than among Democrats (36 percent). But the cleavages among voting groups on the topic can be unusual. An analysis of Washington's 2012 school charter initiative, for example, found a "coalition of strange bedfellows: minority voters and high-income Eastside suburbanite voters on one hand, against Seattle liberals and Eastern Washington rural residents on the other hand."[53]

The public also splits on the concept of using publicly funded vouchers to help pay for a student to attend private schools. Vouchers take the idea of school choice a step further. The idea is that under certain circumstances students may take all or a significant portion of their public education tax dollars with them as they move from public schools to private schools. Because most private schools in the United States are church-affiliated, many people are reluctant to see taxpayer funds used in this way.[54] These are not just opinions held about an abstract concept. After the Utah legislature passed a statewide universal school voucher program in 2007, opponents of the measure gathered enough signatures to put the matter on the ballot, where voters rejected it, 62 percent against to 38 percent in favor.

Today, only fifteen states offer any sort of voucher programs.[55] Both Maine (1873) and Vermont (1869) have actually had targeted voucher programs in place for over 140 years. In each state they are granted to students living in towns that do not operate public schools. Other sorts of voucher programs exist in only a handful of states. Currently, eleven states offer them to students with certain disabilities to attend private schools.[56] A few other states make them available to students from failing schools or from low-income families, and several states allow both students with disabilities or from low-income families to use them. Even in these states such programs are limited in use. For example, Wisconsin initially permitted students in two cities (Milwaukee and Racine) to use vouchers (in 2019–2020, the maximum voucher amounts in Milwaukee were $7,954 for grades K–8 and $8,600 for grades 9–12) to attend a private school. In 2013, it added the Parental Choice Program, allowing parents living outside of Milwaukee and Racine and who meet certain income qualifications to use a voucher to send their children to private schools.

In the 2018–2019 school year, only 7,140 students used the vouchers in the statewide program. The earlier targeted programs are more popular; in 2018–2019, 28,917 students in Milwaukee and 3,324 in Racine received vouchers.[57] Other states, such as Louisiana, only allow students to make use of vouchers if they (1) meet certain income eligibility requirements and (2) attended a public school that was poorly performing on the state school assessment report, which again constrains their use. Its use peaked in 2014–2015 and has declined a bit since then.[58]

Perhaps because of public resistance to the idea that government funds should be transferred to private schools through a voucher system, some states have instead moved toward a "tax credit" program. Such programs allow taxpayers to reduce their tax liability by "donating" money to private schools for scholarships, similar to a tax credit for charitable contributions. But because the taxpayer (i.e., the parent) can specify the scholarship recipient (their child) in some states, this program can become a "backdoor voucher" system. Ultimately, tax revenue that would have gone to the state is transferred to a private school as part of the private school tuition. Currently, eighteen states have some sort of tuition tax credit program.[59] The first state to authorize such tax credits was Arizona in 1997. The U.S. Supreme Court upheld Arizona's law in 2011, and several states (most notably Florida and Georgia) have adopted an expanded version of it.[60]

Education savings accounts are another school choice option available in some states. These accounts "allow parents to withdraw their children from public district or charter schools and receive a deposit of public funds into government-authorized savings accounts. Those funds can cover private school tuition and fees, online learning programs, private tutoring, educational therapies" among other costs. Only five states—Arizona, Florida, Mississippi, North Carolina, and Tennessee—currently offer such programs. Nevada has passed legislation to create such accounts, but its program has been entangled in litigation and has not gone into effect.[61]

The final alternative to traditional K–12 schools is homeschooling, a phenomenon that was growing rapidly but has since plateaued. In 2012, 1,773,000 students were homeschooled. That number constituted 3.4 percent of all K–12 school-age children in the United States. But by 2016, 1,690,000 students were homeschooled, representing 3.3 percent of all primary and secondary students.[62] Generally, it is up to the state legislature, the state board of education, or the state department of education to set standards for homeschooling. As one might expect, these standards differ from one state to another. According to the Home School Legal Defense Association, five states (all in the northeast) are "high regulation" states, requiring parents of homeschooled students to supply the state with achievement test scores, an approved curriculum, and the teacher qualifications of the parent, and allowing home visits by state officials. At the other extreme are eleven states (scattered across the country but concentrated in the Midwest) that have no requirements. In these states, parents neither have to notify the state that they intend to homeschool their child nor show any evidence of the students' academic progress. The rest of the states, mostly in the South and West, are categorized as having moderate or low requirements.[63]

The issue of school choice will remain a difficult one, as many states wrestle with issues of underperforming schools, the costs of public education, and the need to adapt to new technologies and circumstances. Like Minnesota (charter schools) and Wisconsin (vouchers), some states will be at the forefront of new, intriguing educational ideas. Different states will likely try different things; some will succeed and others will not. This is the essence of states as "the laboratories of democracy."

Higher education. Unlike many other federal countries, there are no national universities (with the exception of the service academies) in the United States. Instead, the nation relies on state universities. For them, the direct support of teaching is provided mostly through an appropriation from the state budget and student tuition, while more than half of their research funding comes from the national government.[64] Table 6.2 shows the tuition cost for in-state students in 2018–2019 at the flagship public university in each state. The differences are substantial, ranging from a low of $5,400 at the University of Wyoming to a high of $18,499 at the University of New Hampshire. There are a number of reasons for the variations. An obvious one is labor (faculty and staff) costs. These tend to vary by region, with the costs being higher on the east and west coasts and lower in the Midwest and the South. The state appropriation to higher education is another variable. If State A appropriates a larger share of the total higher education budget than State B, then, all other things being equal, tuition should be lower in State A. Of course, all other things are not usually equal from one state to another. Other variables that affect tuition costs include the amount of state financial aid awarded to students and the number of private colleges and universities in a state.[65]

Public universities are funded by a combination of sources: appropriations from the state budget, student tuition and fees, research grants and contracts, donations (gifts and endowments), and licensing and merchandising fees. The relative importance of these revenue streams to the public higher education system will diverge from state to state, and this makes generalizations difficult. But today most state flagship universities appear to receive between 20 percent and 30 percent of their total budgets from state appropriations, although in some cases it is as low as 6 percent.[66] Over time, state appropriations have not kept pace with the cost of higher education, leading to some dramatic shifts in who shoulders the financial burden. According to the University of Michigan at Ann Arbor, appropriated state support for its academic programs dropped from 78 percent of the university budget in 1960 to a mere 14 percent in 2020.[67] As a proportion of total funds, the particularly sharp decline in state support over the past generation has shifted more of the costs onto students. In 1993, students contributed 30.7 percent of public higher education total

Table 6.2. In-State Tuition and Fees at State Public "Flagship" University, 2018–2019, and Five-Year Percentage Change

State and campus	2018–2019 tuition and fees	Percentage change in tuition, 2013–2014
University of Alaska Fairbanks	$8,087	25%
University of Alabama	$10,780	6%
University of Arkansas	$9,130	8%
University of Arizona	$12,487	11%
University of California: Berkeley	$14,184	2%
University of Colorado at Boulder	$12,532	10%
University of Connecticut	$15,730	21%
University of Delaware	$13,680	5%
University of Florida	$6,381	-6%
University of Georgia	$11,830	7%
University of Hawaii at Manoa	$11,970	12%
University of Iowa	$9,267	7%
University of Idaho	$7,864	12%
University of Illinois at Urbana-Champaign	$16,004	1%
Indiana University Bloomington	$10,681	-3%
University of Kansas	$11,148	2%
University of Kentucky	$12,245	14%
Louisiana State University and Agricultural and Mechanical College	$11,950	41%
University of Massachusetts Amherst	$15,887	10%
University of Maryland: College Park	$10,595	7%
University of Maine	$11,170	-2%
University of Michigan	$15,262	8%
University of Minnesota: Twin Cities	$14,693	0%
University of Missouri: Columbia	$9,880	-3%
University of Mississippi	$8,660	19%
University of Montana	$7,244	11%
University of North Carolina at Chapel Hill	$8,987	0%
University of North Dakota	$8,695	7%

Table 6.2. (Continued)

State and campus	2018–2019 tuition and fees	Percentage change in tuition, 2013–2014
University of Nebraska - Lincoln	$9,154	5%
University of New Hampshire	$18,499	4%
Rutgers, The State University of New Jersey: New Brunswick/Piscataway Campus	$14,974	3%
University of New Mexico	$7,322	5%
University of Nevada: Reno	$7,764	9%
State University of New York at Buffalo	$10,099	11%
Ohio State University: Columbus Campus	$10,726	–1%
University of Oklahoma	$11,763	22%
University of Oregon	$11,898	13%
Penn State University Park	$18,454	1%
University of Rhode Island	$14,138	5%
University of South Carolina	$12,616	8%
University of South Dakota	$9,061	5%
University of Tennessee: Knoxville	$13,006	8%
University of Texas at Austin	$10,622	1%
University of Utah	$9,222	15%
University of Virginia	$16,520	23%
University of Vermont	$18,276	8%
University of Washington	$11,207	–16%
University of Wisconsin-Madison	$10,555	–6%
West Virginia University	$8,856	27%
University of Wyoming	$5,400	14%

Source: https://trends.collegeboard.org/college-pricing/figures-tables/tuition-fees-flagship-universities-over-time.

education revenue through tuition and fees. That figure hit a high of 47.7 percent in 2013 as states slowly began to recover from the Great Recession before dropping slightly to 46.6 by 2018.[68] Higher education budgets took a major hit in most states during the 2008 to 2012 period as the effects of the Great Recession caused many lawmakers to cut back on appropriations. During economic downturns, when state finances suffer, higher education budgets are usually among the first casualties because budget writers in the state legislatures know that universities can soften the financial blow by raising tuition. Thus between 2007 and 2012, tuition and fees doubled in Arizona, California, Florida, and Hawaii.[69] Increases have generally slowed some since then, but as shown in table 6.2, in some states tuition and fees have still continued to escalate at a dramatic pace. In large part this is because state support for higher education has, ten years since the start of the Great Recession, "only halfway recovered."[70] Unfortunately, the public is not aware of this; a 2019 survey found that "most Americans believe state spending for public universities and colleges has, in fact, increased or at least held steady over the last 10 years."[71]

The cost of a college education is a topic on the agenda of many state officials today, including governors, state legislatures, and university governing boards. Because of this states are experimenting with a host of innovative education systems, among them online delivery of instructional materials, the use of massive open online courses (MOOCs), curricular changes, and the reformation of graduation requirements to squeeze four-year degrees into three years. One of the most popular reforms is performance-based funding, which ties state appropriations to objective measures of educational outcomes, such as graduate rates[72] By 2018, twenty-nine states employed such funding mechanisms for their state universities, with another four states in the process of developing such programs. But it is not clear whether performance-based funding is effective in actually producing the outcomes those states wish to encourage.[73] In any event, given chronic state budget problems, public universities and colleges will likely operate under financial pressures for the foreseeable future, and, as a result, they will have to continue experimenting with new ways of doing business.

THE POLICE POWER OF THE STATES: PUBLIC SAFETY, CRIME, AND CORRECTIONS

Despite the role of the federal government in ensuring due process and the rights of the accused, and in interpreting the "cruel and unusual punishment" clause of the Eighth Amendment, states retain substantial police powers. This includes state discretion in determining criminal definitions and penalties. States matter on a wide range of criminal justice issues, from texting while driving laws to capital punishment.

Gun control laws are often a major topic of conversation. As debate over the regulation of firearms continues at the national level, it is worth noting that a few states have adopted much more restrictive gun laws than others. At the beginning of 2019, seven states were considered to have comparatively strict gun control laws: California, Connecticut, Hawaii, Maryland, Massachusetts, New Jersey, and New York. In contrast, twenty-two states, mostly in the South, the Midwest, and the Mountain West, had the fewest restrictions.[74] In part, this pattern largely tracks with the political cultures of the states. But traumatic events can lead to the adoption of gun control laws, even in states that usually resist them. Following the 2018 mass shooting at Marjory Stoneman Douglas High School in Parkland, Florida, passed a significant array of gun control laws, among them an extreme risk protection (or red flag) law, a higher minimum age for buying firearms, and stronger waiting period regulations.[75]

Florida's response was not unusual. Other tragic incidents had prompted the states in which they had occurred to strengthen their gun laws. Following a series of mass shootings in Colorado, the legislature in 2013 passed laws limiting the size of ammunition magazines and requiring universal background checks on all gun purchases. The 2012 Newtown massacre had similarly pressured Connecticut to adopt stringent gun control laws.[76] But during that same time period the responses in other states differed. One study found that between 1989 and 2014, "A mass shooting increases the number of enacted laws that *loosen* gun restrictions by 75% in states with Republican-controlled legislatures."[77]

It is critical to recognize that gun laws are far from static in the American federal system. In the aftermath of the 2018 Parkland shootings, for example, voters in Washington passed an initiative to tighten their state's gun laws and legislatures in Florida and twenty-five other states did so as well.[78] And extreme risk protection (or red flag) laws to temporarily remove firearms from people thought to be threats have recently passed in a number of states, often with bipartisan support.[79] Again, however, it should be emphasized that between 2012 and 2018 more than 660 new gun laws were passed by the states and roughly two-thirds of them expanded gun rights.[80]

Indeed, the most notable development over the last quarter-century has been the spread of laws allowing people the right to carry a concealed weapon. State government officials were given discretion over the issuance of concealed carry permits ("may issue" laws) in another twenty-six states, essentially allowing them to give permits only to applicants who could demonstrate a need. Officials were compelled to give permits to applicants ("shall issue" laws) in only eight states. Vermont was in its own category, allowing anyone to carry a concealed weapon without any permit or license. Through a sustained campaign spearheaded by the National Rifle Association, over time resistance to concealed carry laws dissipated. In 2013, Illinois became the final state to allow it. But concealed carry law provisions vary in important ways. By 2019, fourteen states allowed anyone to carry a concealed weapon without restriction. Laws in only eight states fell into the "may issue" category, meaning the government retained some discretion over who is issued a permit. The much less restrictive "shall issue" or a "no discretion to deny" mandate applied in the other twenty-eight states.[81] A "shall issue" or "no discretion to deny" directive really does mean that virtually every permit request is granted. In the first two years following Iowa's switch to "shall issue" rules, 99.6 percent of permit requests were approved.[82] Thus with the recent changes in the law across the states, far more people today have the right to carry a concealed weapon than was the case just a generation ago. The biggest issue left unresolved involves reciprocity. California, Connecticut, Illinois, Maryland, Massachusetts, New Jersey, and New York do not honor concealed carry permits issued by other states, while twenty other states recognize all concealed carry permits issued in the United States.[83] Some gun-rights supporters have sought a national solution to this regulatory patchwork quilt, and in 2017 a measure to force all states to recognize any concealed carry permit passed the U.S. House of Representatives, but it never gained any traction in the U.S. Senate.[84]

Another area in which there has been some agreement on gun control involves domestic abusers. Over the last decade, twenty-nine states have passed legislation making it more difficult for at least some of those convicted for domestic violence to have access to guns. Even several states dominated by Republicans, notably South Carolina and South Dakota, have passed such measures. State laws in this area are generally thought to be stronger than the federal laws.[85]

A related shift in state laws over the last few years has been in so-called "castle" and "stand your ground" laws. Castle laws, referred to initially as "make my day" laws, essentially allow a person to do whatever he or she deems necessary, including using deadly force, to protect themselves in and around their home. By 2019 such laws were on the books in thirty-three states.[86] Stand your ground laws, first passed in Florida in 2005, expand that right to any place a person feels threatened. By 2019 thirty states had some variant of stand your ground laws. Such laws usually remove any personal duty to retreat and also remove any civil liability attached to one's actions. They are most common in the South and the Mountain West.[87] Consequently, in a majority of states today people are allowed to legally take actions against another person that they were not allowed to take a generation ago. But the movement toward adoption of such bills is not inexorable, even in the South. In 2019, a stand your ground measure failed in the GOP-controlled Arkansas state legislature.[88]

Dynamism and differentiation in the American federal system also surface in state laws governing police powers. Take, for example, marijuana laws, which, as suggested by the opening vignette in chapter 1, also vary both across the states and over time. In 2012, two states—Colorado and Washington—legalized possession of marijuana in small amounts. They were the first states to permit the use of marijuana for recreational use, although at that time eighteen states had already legalized use of marijuana for medical reasons.[89] While all of these provisions contradicted current federal law in regard to marijuana use, the Obama administration announced it did not intend to pursue the conflict. Both the Colorado and Washington laws were the product of the initiative process in which the voters approved the measures in a direct vote. In 2014, voters in Alaska and Oregon used the same mechanism to legalize marijuana in their states, as did those in California, Maine, Massachusetts, and Nevada in 2016 and Michigan in 2018. Legislatures in Vermont (2018) and Illinois

(2019) passed legislation legalizing recreational marijuana in those states. It is often the case that a few states innovate a policy and other states take a "wait-and-see" position to see how the new policy is received. It is a common pattern for policy innovations to diffuse slowly across the states, often on a region-by-region basis. Thus, medical marijuana, having first been adopted by California voters in 1996, is an older policy innovation, and consequently it has been approved in more states—thirty-four by mid-2019—than had recreational marijuana to that point in time.[90]

Another case of policy diffusion is a ban on tobacco smoking in public places (worksites, restaurants, and bars). In 1995, only Utah banned smoking in restaurants (but not elsewhere). In 2000, Delaware became the first state to pass a comprehensive ban on smoking in three public places (offices, restaurants, and bars). By 2005, four additional states (Massachusetts, New York, Rhode Island, and Washington) had passed comprehensive bans. By 2019, twenty-seven states had such laws. None were southern states, where traditionally almost all the tobacco in the United States has been grown. Several of them, however, had banned smoking in two of the three public places. But there were thirteen states in which there was no statewide ban on smoking in any of the public sites listed earlier.[91]

The minimum age at which tobacco products can be purchased is an emerging case of policy diffusion. In 2015, Hawaii raised the legal age to purchase tobacco products to twenty-one, followed the next year by California. By 2019, sixteen other states had also raised their minimum age to 21.[92] And further changes may be in store. In 2019, a member of the Hawaii House of Representatives (and who is also a physician) introduced a bill to raise the age to buy tobacco in that state to thirty in 2020, forty in 2021, fifty in 2022, and one hundred in 2024, which, of course, would effectively end legal tobacco in that state.[93]

The prison dilemma. One problem faced by all states over the past generation is prison overcrowding. Public concern with the rise in crime rates in the 1960s and 1970s resulted in "get tough" policies being put in place across the states by the 1980s. This was manifested in harsher sentencing laws, including mandatory and determinate sentencing. In particular, tougher mandatory sentences were imposed for nonviolent crimes such as illegal drug possession. A consequence of this policy decision was a dramatic rise in both the number of people incarcerated and the resulting cost of housing prisoners.[94] Today, the United States has the highest incarceration rate of any country in the world.[95] Most of those prisoners are housed in state prisons, not federal prisons, or county or city jails. State prisons house 61 percent of all incarcerated individuals in the country, with local jails accounting for 29 percent and federal prisons 10 percent.[96] Approximately 1.31 million people are currently in state prison systems. Incarceration rates vary considerably by state; Louisiana has an incarceration rate (719 per 100,000 residents) that is six times higher than Massachusetts' (120 per 100,000 residents).[97]

Virtually all states experienced a dramatic increase in the number of prisoners they housed over the last four decades. In 1980, state prisons collectively held 305,500 prisoners. By 2009, that number had exploded to 1,407,400. At that point, five states were spending as much or more on their prisons than they were on higher education.[98]

As mentioned above, there were several reasons for this dramatic increase. The biggest contributor was the change in penalties for drug convictions. A second reason was an increase in the length of sentences. The consequences of these policy changes were substantial. State corrections budgets grew dramatically, straining state budgets. But states made different decisions on how punitive to be. Although all states became more punitive between 1983 and 2013, some were considerably more so than others. Crime was the most severely punished in Mississippi and Idaho and the least severely punished in Washington and Maine.[99]

Since 2010, however, the number of prisoners has declined nationally, in part because of state decisions to supervise some nonviolent offenders in their home communities rather than in prisons.[100] States vary widely in how they choose to supervise their correctional populations. In 2016, in Rhode Island, 95 percent of the correctional population was under community supervision, usually on probation or parole. At the other end of the spectrum, Nevada and Oklahoma had only 48 percent of their correctional populations under community supervision.[101]

In the last few years criminal justice reform has emerged as an important political issue. Much of the public's attention has been directed to reforms at the national level, because in 2018 Congress passed and the president signed an initial step toward reforming the federal criminal justice system. But, as noted above, only about 10 percent of those incarcerated are held in federal prisons. Most prisoners are housed in state or local facilities. Consequently, it is only at the state level that significant changes can take place. And some notable steps have been taken by the states. In 2018, for example, California, Florida, Michigan, Mississippi, and Oklahoma passed laws reforming their sentencing practices with an eye toward reducing the number of people held in prison in their states.[102]

Related to this trend is a reassessment of the "Three Strikes and You're Out" (TSAYO) laws that were first passed in the mid-1990s. These measures were adopted by some states in reaction to a particularly heinous crime in California committed by an individual who had been released after serving time for several violent felony crimes. But the first state to adopt such a law was actually Washington in 1993. California quickly followed in 1994, with a law passed by the legislature and subsequently confirmed by the public through the initiative process with over 72 percent of the voters approving it. Significantly, the California law made no distinction between violent and nonviolent felony offenses. A total of twelve states passed TSAYO laws in 1994 and another nine followed suit the next year. In a three-year period, almost half the states passed such laws, but only Arizona (2006) and Massachusetts (2012) have done so since.

The details of these laws diverge. In most of the states that passed TSAYO laws, considerable discretion was left to prosecutors to determine whether or not to pursue penalties under the TSAYO provision. As a result, TSAYO laws did not dramatically alter incarceration rates in most states that adopted them. The case of California, however, was another matter entirely. Its TSAYO law severely curbed the discretion available to prosecutors and judges to consider mitigating circumstances, such as the nature of the "third strike" crime. Furthermore, the law allowed some crimes such as shoplifting, which is usually a misdemeanor, to be considered a felony if it was the third offense. Thus, California's law led to lengthy prison sentences for some "three-time losers" even if their third conviction was for a minor or nonviolent crime. The law also mandated lengthier sentences for "second strike" offenders. Reviewing the impact of the law a decade after its passage, the California Legislative Analyst's Office estimated the additional costs directly attributable to the TSAYO law to be about $500 million per year, which was actually less than the original projection that had been made when TSAYO passed in 1994.[103] However, one unanticipated consequence of the law is that TSAYO has contributed to an aging of the prison population. In 2012, half of the TSAYO prisoners in California were over fifty years of age.[104] The cost of housing aged prisoners is much higher than for most other prisoners, largely because of increased health care costs. There is also an analysis that suggests that while the deterrent effect of the policy was real and a significant number of career criminals actively sought to avoid committing a third offense, those who did commit them committed more violent acts because they calculated they had little to lose. And California's strict law may have encouraged many of its career criminals to relocate to neighboring states where they did not face any additional sanctions, thus only shifting the problem.[105]

In 2012, again through the initiative process, California amended its TSAYO law to allow consideration of the nature of the third strike offense to be taken into account, a decision that permits minor crimes or nonviolent offenses committed by third-time offenders to be treated less harshly than under the original California TSAYO measure. By 2014, 1,613 inmates sentenced to life for nonviolent crimes under TSAYO had been released. They have had a remarkably low recidivism rate.[106] Nationally, TSAYO laws remain popular in the states that passed them and none have been fully repealed, although roughly half have, like California, passed measures to soften them.[107]

States differ considerably on sentencing philosophies, with some states taking stronger "get tough" stances while others emphasize rehabilitation. Based on whether a state has adopted such policies as mandatory sentencing, the abolition of parole, TSAYO laws, and a required minimum prison term for six offender groups, an index of "sentencing policy toughness" has been constructed.[108] By this measure, the states with the toughest sentencing policies are

California, Florida, Idaho, and Indiana. The states at the other end of the scale are New Mexico, Massachusetts, Kentucky, and Kansas. Generally speaking, "policy-liberal states tend to have more lenient sentencing practices and lower incarceration rates."[109] But the correlation is far from perfect, and a few states, such as California and New York, which are generally considered to be liberal in policy outlook, have tough sentencing requirements. But, again, as states pursue sentencing reforms, these relationships are apt to change.

Further examples of how states vary in the application of their police powers include the institution of a death penalty and the willingness to turn over some corrections functions to "for-profit" corporations. Capital punishment is not imposed in twenty-one states, most in the Midwest and the Northeast. The trend in recent years has been to abolish the death penalty.[110] Since 2009, legislatures in New Mexico (2009), Illinois (2011), Connecticut (2012), Maryland (2013), and New Hampshire (2019) have passed laws abolishing the death penalty. The Nebraska legislature also did so in 2015, even overriding the governor's veto. But through a referendum, the state's voters reinstated the law in 2016. That same year California voters not only decided to keep the death penalty but also opted to allow the legal process governing it to be expedited. Still, there is a growing movement among conservative state lawmakers to reassess the death penalty, if only because of its costs. In 2019, for example, bills to end it were introduced by Republican legislators in Kansas, Kentucky, Missouri, Montana, and Wyoming.[111]

Many states in the South, however, have demonstrated little reluctance to impose and carry out death sentences. Of the ten states with the most executions since 1976, seven are southern states, and two others—Missouri and Oklahoma—border the South. As of July 2019, Texas (561 executions), Virginia (113), and Oklahoma (112) had executed the most prisoners over the last thirty-three years. Nationally, the number of executions each year has steadily declined over the last two decades, from ninety-eight in 1999 to twenty in 2016, before rising slightly to twenty-five in 2018.[112]

"Prison privatization" also has a distinct regional flavor. While only 8 percent of all state prisoners are currently housed in correctional facilities run by "for-profit" companies such as CoreCivic (formerly Corrections Corporation of America) and the Geo Group (the two largest such companies), twenty-one states have no prisoners in such facilities and several others make only minimal use of them. Some states have laws specifically prohibiting such privatization. In contrast, over a quarter of the state prison populations in Montana (38 percent of state prisoners), Hawaii (28 percent), Tennessee (26 percent), and Oklahoma (26 percent) are incarcerated in for-profit facilities.[113] (New Mexico did not report its data for 2017; in 2016, 43 percent of its prisoners were held in privately operated facilities.[114]) As private prisons have become big business in many states, particularly in the South and the Mountain West, they have become energetic in lobbying state officials and making contributions to candidates for public office.[115] Scandals associated with the way some private prisons have been operated have forced a few states to retake control of them. In 2014, for example, Idaho resumed running one of its major correctional facilities following falsified staffing records by the private company that had been in charge.[116]

THE STATES AND SOCIAL ISSUES

The states have traditionally controlled policies lumped together under the label of "social issues" or "morality issues." In recent years the most prominent and controversial of these have involved gay rights, particularly in regard to same-sex marriage, and abortion. Over time, the states have arrived at a number of different policies on these matters, with the federal courts playing a central role in establishing the boundaries of their actions.

Laws regarding marriage have largely been left to the states and there have always been differences across them on who can marry. Today, for example, nine states recognize common law marriages—where a couple lives together for some extended period and consider themselves as married—and another five states have laws that grandfather such marriages for those who formally registered before a certain date. The rest of the states do not recognize common law marriages.[117] There have been many other differences. Well into the twentieth century many states enforced laws banning miscegenation, or marriage between people from different racial or ethnic groups. A handful of states in the Northeast and the upper Midwest never had anti-miscegenation laws, and several others in those regions repealed the laws they had during the nineteenth century. But the largest movement to overturn anti-miscegenation bans was initiated by a California Supreme Court decision, *Perez v. Sharp* (1948), which declared unconstitutional that state's law preventing blacks and whites from marrying.[118] Over the following two decades, other states in the West followed California's lead and swept aside their anti-miscegenation laws. But it took the U.S. Supreme Court's decision in *Loving v. Virginia* (1967) declaring such laws to be unconstitutional to force southern and Border States to allow such marriages.[119]

In recent years, controversy surrounded the question of state laws governing same-sex marriage. Serious political debate on the question first surfaced in 1993 when the Hawaii Supreme Court ruled that unless the state demonstrated that it had a compelling reason for denying same-sex couples the right to marry, the practice would be held to violate the state constitution. This led to a protracted political struggle over the issue. In 1998, Hawaii voters overwhelmingly passed Constitutional Amendment 2, granting the state legislature the power to limit marriage to only opposite-sex couples. The Hawaii Supreme Court subsequently dismissed the original lawsuit as being moot because of the voter-approved state constitutional amendment.

The decision reached by Hawaii mattered for the rest of the states because had that state recognized a right for gays and lesbians to marry in the mid-1990s, those marriages might have had to be recognized in the other forty-nine states because the U.S. Constitution (Article IV, Section 1) requires that "full faith and credit shall be given in each state to the public acts, records and judicial proceedings of every other state." This clause can be read to mean that marriages performed in one state must be recognized as legal in other states. In response to the possibility of same-sex marriages being allowed in Hawaii, Utah passed a law in 1995 that denied recognition to all out-of-state marriages that did not conform to Utah law. This approach was essentially taken national in 1996 when Congress passed the Defense of Marriage Act (DOMA). The measure, which was signed into law by President Bill Clinton, barred federal recognition of same-sex marriages and permitted states to take no legal notice of same-sex marriages performed in other states where they might be allowed. How DOMA squared with the U.S. Constitution's full faith and credit clause was left for the courts to decide.

Although Hawaii did not pursue same-sex marriage, debate on the issue percolated across the states. Hawaii created domestic partnerships in 1997, a policy that gave same-sex couples limited rights. A few years later Vermont became the first state to pass legislation allowing same-sex partners to establish a civil union, providing them many of the same legal rights granted to married couples under state (but not federal) law. The prospect of legislation creating civil unions led the Massachusetts state senate in 2003 to seek an advisory opinion from the state's Supreme Judicial Court as to whether such unions would be legal under the Massachusetts constitution. The court's advisory opinion, handed down in February 2004, held that any law that fell short of allowing same-sex marriage would be unconstitutional because it would be discriminatory. The advisory opinion set the stage for allowing same-sex marriage in Massachusetts. The decision in Massachusetts pushed the issue of same-sex marriage back onto center stage in national politics.

The same day the Massachusetts opinion was handed down, President George W. Bush asked Congress to "promptly pass, and to send to the states for ratification, an amendment to our Constitution defining and protecting marriage as a union of man and woman as husband and wife." Although he was unequivocally opposed to same-sex marriage, the president recognized the federal dimension of American government by leaving open the possibility of accepting civil unions, saying that state legislatures should be left "free to make their own choices in defining legal arrangements other than marriage."[120] Although President Bush and many members of Congress backed the Federal Marriage Amendment, it never came close to passing. Same-sex marriage opponents enjoyed much greater success at the state level, with bans passing in all thirteen states where they appeared on the ballot in 2004, and two more states in 2005. But while bans passed in another seven additional states in 2006, the first cracks in opposition to same-sex marriage appeared that year when voters in Arizona rejected such a measure.

By 2008, forty-four states had either constitutional provisions or statutory laws on the books that prevented same-sex marriages. Only in Massachusetts and California were such marriages legal, and voters in the latter passed a state constitutional amendment to ban them that November. But public views about same-sex relationships had begun to shift and that change started to show up in state laws. Civil unions had become more accepted after encountering some initial resistance. Connecticut had established them in 2005, followed by New Jersey in 2007, and Oregon and New Hampshire in 2008. Another five states adopted them by 2013.

The biggest change, however, came in same-sex marriage laws. State court decisions forced their acceptance in Connecticut and Iowa. Starting in 2009, state legislatures passed laws allowing same-sex marriage on their own initiative, with such measures being adopted in Vermont, Maine, and New Hampshire. But in a referendum Maine voters soon repealed the law passed by the legislature. Legislatures in Maryland, New York, and Washington, however, passed measures allowing same-sex marriage. In 2012, Maryland and Washington voters upheld their measures in referenda, while voters in Maine reversed their earlier decision by passing a ballot proposition allowing same-sex marriage. The political tide that initially rolled so heavily against government recognition of same-sex relationships had clearly begun to recede.

By June 2015, the nation was living under a mishmash of marriage laws, as shown in table 6.3. State legislatures had passed statutes allowing same-sex marriage in eleven states and voters had done likewise in Maine. State courts had established same-sex marriage in five states, while federal courts had done so in nineteen states. There were no provisions allowing same-sex marriage in fourteen states. At that point the U.S. Supreme Court handed down its decision in *Obergefell v. Hodges*, declaring laws prohibiting same-sex marriage to be unconstitutional because they violated the Fourteenth Amendment's due process and equal protection clauses.[121] Thus rights guaranteed by the federal constitution as interpreted by the U.S. Supreme Court trumped state laws.

The decision legalizing same-sex marriage met resistance in some states. Alabama's state supreme court, for example, only ended the battle over the matter in that state in 2016.[122] Even after that decision, the court's chief justice had to be suspended from his position for ordering state probate judges to ignore the U.S. Supreme Court's decision and to refuse to issue marriage licenses to same-sex couples.[123] The final vestige of resistance in Alabama came in the form of a law passed in 2019 to end the issuance of state marriage licenses, replacing them with an official recording of the union in the county in which the nuptials took place. This was done so that county officials who disapprove of same-sex marriages would not have to certify them by signing a license. But under the new law they are required to officially record them.[124]

Most of the defiance in other states has been somewhat less overt, emerging mostly in the form of "religious freedom" bills.[125] In 2015, even before the U.S. Supreme Court decision, Indiana adopted a measure that opponents

Table 6.3. Status of State Same-Sex Marriage Laws at the Time of 2015 U.S. Supreme Court Ruling

State legislature passed law allowing same-sex marriage	Voter ballot measure passed allowing same-sex marriage	State court decision establishing same-sex marriage	Federal court decision establishing same-sex marriage	No state provision allowing same-sex marriage
11 States	1 State	5 States	20 States	13 States
Connecticut	Maine	California	Alabama	Arkansas
Delaware		Iowa	Alaska	Georgia
Hawaii		Massachusetts	Arizona	Kentucky
Illinois		New Jersey	Colorado	Louisiana
Maryland		New Mexico	Florida	Michigan
Minnesota			Idaho	Mississippi
New			Indiana	Missouri
Hampshire			Kansas	Nebraska
New York			Montana	North
Rhode Island			Nevada	Dakota
Vermont			North Carolina	Ohio
Washington			Oklahoma	South
			Oregon	Dakota
			Pennsylvania	Tennessee
			South Carolina	Texas
			Utah	
			Virginia	
			West Virginia	
			Wisconsin	
			Wyoming	

Source: Derived by authors from http://www.ncsl.org/research/human-services/same-sex-marriage-laws.aspx.

decried as legalizing discrimination against gays and lesbians. A broad public outcry against the measure forced the legislature to quickly amend the new law, assuring that commercial businesses could not discriminate.[126] The most significant religious freedom bill passed in 2016 was in Mississippi. According to the senator who offered the measure to her chamber,

> This is presenting a solution to the crossroads we find ourselves in today as a result of Obergefell v. Hodges. . . . Ministers, florists, photographers, people along those lines—this bill would allow them to refuse to provide marriage-related business services without fear of government discrimination.[127]

A similar measure was vetoed by Georgia's governor, while a number of like bills foundered in other state legislatures.[128] Mississippi's law was quickly challenged in federal court and a judge struck it down.[129] Eventually, in 2017 the court of appeals allowed the law to go into effect because it held that those who had brought the suit could not demonstrate that they had been harmed by it, and therefore they did not enjoy legal standing. That decision was put on hold by the U.S. Supreme Court pending more litigation. But by that point in time many Mississippi businesses no longer evidenced much support for the policy. And its most visible impact has been to prevent the Stony Brook University baseball team from traveling to an away series against Southern Mississippi University because the state of New York has banned nonessential government travel to states with discriminatory laws of this sort and Stony Brook University is a state school.[130]

Even with the same-sex marriage matter settled, the states still vary in how they treat members of the LGBTQ community and there are a number of contentious issues left unresolved. In 2019, for example, twenty-one states had laws that prohibit discrimination based on sexual orientation and gender identity, while Wisconsin only prohibits discrimination on sexual orientation. Another seven states do not permit discrimination against public employees based on sexual orientation and gender identity, and four others only forbid discrimination against public employees on the first score.[131] The other states do not have laws protecting the LGBTQ community from facing discrimination. Conversion therapy is another issue on which the states diverge. As of 2019, mental health practitioners in eighteen states were prohibited from trying to change the sexual orientation or gender identity of minors.[132] No law prevents such efforts in the other states.

Another social issue that continues to vex state politics is abortion. Since the U.S. Supreme Court handed down its decision in *Roe v. Wade* (1973), the landmark ruling that made abortion legal during the first trimester of pregnancy but recognized the "legitimate" right of the government to impose restrictions beyond that point, initially to protect the mother's health and later at viability to protect the life of the unborn child, controversy and passion have driven the debate over abortion policies at the state level.[133] Through a seemingly endless series of legislative and legal battles, the states have greatly reconfigured their approaches to regulating abortions. What is less appreciated is that even before the Court's decision in *Roe*, the states had already begun to diverge in the ways they handled the issue.

During the course of the nineteenth century, states passed laws that outlawed abortions. Those laws largely carried over until the 1960s. In 1962, the American Law Institute's Model Penal Code recommended allowing abortions to protect the mental and physical health of the mother and when there was a risk of birth defects. Colorado became the first state to liberalize its abortion laws along the lines of the American Law Institute model in 1967, followed shortly thereafter by California, North Carolina, and Oregon. By 1970, several other states pushed abortion rights even further, with Hawaii allowing the abortion of nonviable fetuses as long as the procedure was done in a hospital. That same year, New York adopted a law allowing all abortions during the first twenty-four weeks of pregnancy. Similar laws were passed in Alaska and Washington.[134]

By the time the Court decided *Roe*, abortion laws actually varied a great deal across the states. Abortions for any reason were allowed in four states, thirteen states permitted them to protect the physical and mental health of the mother, and twenty-nine states to preserve the life of the mother. Women in Mississippi could get an abortion to preserve their life or if they had been raped. All abortions were banned in Louisiana, New Hampshire, and Pennsylvania.[135] Thus the Court's decision in *Roe* only forced most, not all, of the states to revise their laws.

In the more than forty years since abortion was largely legalized, a number of states have pursued policies that have narrowed the conditions under which one can be obtained. For the most part, these states have operated in the space granted by *Roe* and later decisions, notably in *Planned Parenthood v. Casey* (1992), to limit abortions toward the end of pregnancy.[136] A 2019 analysis of recent trends in abortion laws documents a remarkable divergence in approaches across the states. Over the preceding few years laws aimed at imposing stricter regulations on abortions had been passed in twenty-three states and laws easing restrictions in thirteen states, with the remaining fourteen states leaving their laws unchanged.[137]

Over the last decade a few states have opted to push even harder on limiting abortions. In 2013, Arkansas passed a law to prohibit abortion after twelve weeks, and North Dakota followed by adopting a measure to outlaw the procedure after six weeks, the point at which a fetal heartbeat can usually be detected. When he signed the North Dakota six-week bill into law, the governor admitted as much, saying, "Although the likelihood of this measure surviving a court challenge remains in question, this bill is nevertheless a legitimate attempt by a state legislature to discover the boundaries of Roe v. Wade."[138] His trepidations proved correct; the North Dakota law was struck down by the federal courts, as was the Arkansas law.[139]

The courts have also been heavily involved in determining whether the nineteen states that have forbidden so-called partial birth abortions have gone too far; the laws in a majority of these states have been enjoined by the courts, preventing them from going into effect. And there have been other efforts to restrict abortion. North Dakota tried to outlaw abortion altogether by putting a "personhood measure" on the 2014 ballot. Among other things, the proposal would have banned abortions under any circumstances. The voters rejected the measure, with 64 percent voting no. In 2016, lawmakers in nine states introduced bills to effectively outlaw abortion, with Oklahoma's actually making it to the governor's desk. She vetoed it.[140]

But it was in 2019 that a large number states passed legislation that posed serious challenges to abortion rights, making it arguably the most active legislative year on the topic since *Roe* was handed down.[141] The most extreme law was adopted in Alabama. It prohibits abortion at any stage and makes performing one a crime punishable by up to life in prison. Other bills banning abortions after a detectable heartbeat (approximately six to eight weeks into a pregnancy) passed in Kentucky, Louisiana, Mississippi and Ohio. Missouri lawmakers approved legislation prohibiting abortion after eight weeks, with no exceptions for rape or incest. Why were so many lawmakers willing to vote for such laws? One commentator characterized them as "a dare," asserting that:

> The State legislators who are passing these bills know they will be challenged in court. They also know they will probably lose. But . . . [w]ith a solidly conservative majority on the [U.S.] Supreme Court, anti-abortion advocates are eager to seed the challenge that could one day take down *Roe v. Wade* . . .[142]

A Tennessee state senator admitted that was his goal, saying in regard to a fetal heart-beat bill that while he assumed it would be blocked by the courts if it were to be signed into law, "We want a vehicle to lead the Supreme Court to consider, I hope, overturning or at least chipping away at Roe v. Wade."[143]

What would happen if the U.S. Supreme Court returned control of abortion rights back to the states? Currently, ten states protect abortion rights under their state constitutions, while another nine states have laws on their books that do so.[144] Thus, in just under half the states the right to an abortion would likely be maintained. On the other side of the ledger, nine states still retain their pre-*Roe* prohibitions in their statutes, while six states have passed legislation indicating their intent to forbid abortion if the Court permits them to do so. Several other states have similarly signaled a desire to prohibit abortions to the "maximum extent permitted."[145] Thus, if the decision is turned over to them, the states will have widely different abortion laws.

Beyond seeking the outright prohibition of abortion, many states have imposed regulations on the procedure, with the intent of making one more difficult to obtain. Health officials in states that wish to limit access to abortions have seized on the government's regulatory powers to try to close abortion facilities.[146] There are many regulations imposed on facilities that perform abortions, and on the personnel providing the service. Failure to abide by these rules leaves abortion providers vulnerable to losing their licenses.

Counseling, for example, is mandated before the procedure can be performed in eighteen states. In five of those states, those seeking abortions must be told of a possible link between the procedure and breast cancer (although such a linkage has not been established scientifically), thirteen states require that they must be told that the fetus could feel pain, and eight states mandate that negative psychological effects must be discussed. Over half the states require a waiting period before an abortion can be performed, most setting it at twenty-four hours, but Missouri, North Carolina, Oklahoma, South Dakota, and Utah impose a seventy-two-hour wait in most cases. Parental involvement is required for minors getting an abortion in thirty-seven states, with roughly a third of them demanding only that notice be given and the rest mandating that a parent, or in some states both parents, give consent. Another political flashpoint has been over public funding. Public funds can be used for medically necessary abortions in sixteen states, while such funds are limited to situations in which the mother's life is endangered or the pregnancy is the result of rape or incest in thirty-four states. Private health insurance coverage of abortions is limited by law in twelve states.[147] Another route a number of states took to limit access to abortions was the imposition of laws requiring doctors performing abortions to obtain admitting privileges at a local hospital (ten states) and abortion clinics to meet the standards expected of ambulatory surgical centers (seventeen states).[148] A 2016 U.S. Supreme Court decision struck down those laws in Texas, and it was expected to lead to similar laws also being declared an unconstitutional burden on the right of women to have access to abortions. But in 2018 a court of appeals decision upheld a similar law in Louisiana, leaving the question of hospital admitting privileges and abortion unsettled.[149]

Thus the obstacles a woman must overcome to secure a legal abortion vary significantly across the states. In North Carolina, for example, an abortion must be performed by a licensed physician and, after twenty weeks, the procedure must be done at a hospital and not a clinic. More important, any abortion after twenty weeks is only allowed if necessary to save the life or health of the mother. Additionally, any woman wishing to have an abortion in North Carolina is required to wait for seventy-two hours following required counseling and she must be told of possible negative psychological effects. In contrast, a woman in New Hampshire seeking an abortion faces few hurdles. She would not be required to have counseling or to wait, and the procedure could be performed at a clinic by a clinician. These two cases not only highlight the substantial differences in an important social policy across the states, but they also reveal the dynamism of state politics and policies. When *Roe* became the law of the land more than four decades ago, New Hampshire was one of the few states where all abortions were outlawed. In contrast, North Carolina had been one of the states that had pioneered liberalizing abortion laws. Now, their relative positions are reversed.

HEALTH AND PUBLIC WELFARE POLICIES IN THE STATES

Traditionally, states have also controlled health and public welfare policies. But as noted in earlier chapters, over time the federal government has come to play a larger role in these areas. This is perhaps most obvious in the way government provides health care.

Currently, questions about government's role in health care are centered on the implications of the Patient Protection and Affordable Care Act, a measure signed into law by President Obama in 2010 and more commonly referred to as "Obamacare." Among the many provisions in this law are requirements that businesses with more than fifty employees provide them with health care coverage or pay a penalty, that individuals have health care coverage or again pay a penalty—the so-called individual mandate—and that the states either set up and operate their own health care exchanges or have the federal government operate one on their behalf or jointly with them.

Each of these provisions is controversial and there is a widespread perception that they represent radical change. But each policy is rooted in programs that were already employed in some states. Indeed, people fail to appreciate the diversity of health care laws that were in place across the country prior to the adoption of the Affordable Care Act. For instance, under a 1974 state law employers in Hawaii have to provide health care coverage for all employees who work at least twenty hours a week, a requirement that has greatly lowered the number of uninsured people over the years.[150] Health care exchanges already operated in Massachusetts and Utah; in both states they had been pushed into law by Republican governors.[151] And of course, the Affordable Care Act's individual mandate was modeled on a similar provision in the health care law adopted by Massachusetts in 2006. As a consequence of its mandate and health care exchange, Massachusetts had the lowest percentage of uninsured people among the fifty states.[152]

Although it had proven successful in Massachusetts, the individual mandate associated with the Affordable Care Act at the national level was politically unpopular. As a consequence, Congress effectively removed it, starting in 2019.[153] That decision potentially impacted state insurance markets. But as can happen in a federal system, some states opted to impose their own individual mandates. Massachusetts kept the one they had in place and by 2020 California, New Jersey, Rhode Island, and Vermont also had mandates for their state residents.[154]

The federal government's involvement with health care did not begin with the Affordable Care Act. It started playing a prominent role with the passage of the law creating Medicare and Medicaid in 1965. Medicaid was designed to allow the federal government to assist the states in providing care for eligible needy people. It is a complicated program; the federal government establishes national guidelines, but eligibility and service standards are set by the states. Costs are split. Overall, the federal government covers at least half of the expense for Medicaid in each state, but the amount of money it contributes varies based on a state's per capita income. The wealthiest states receive the statutory minimum of 50 percent, leaving the other 50 percent of the program's cost for the state to cover. The federal government covers a greater share of the cost of the program for poorer states. In fiscal year 2020, fourteen states received the minimum 50 percent federal match, while Mississippi, the poorest state, received a match of 77 percent, leaving it to pay for only 23 percent of the program's cost.[155]

The Affordable Care Act provides financial incentives for the states to expand their Medicaid programs. The U.S. Supreme Court's decision that found the Affordable Care Act to be constitutional allowed the states the option of whether or not to accept the incentives. The expansion decision has proven to be contentious and different states have arrived at different conclusions. As of August 2019, thirty-six states had expanded their Medicaid programs, while the other fourteen had not done so.[156] These decisions were largely driven by ideology, with conservative state legislators resisting expansion.[157] The different choices made means residents in some states are much more likely to have health care insurance coverage than are residents of other states.[158] In 2018, the percent of residents uncovered by health insurance ranged from a low of 2.8 percent in Massachusetts, a state that has expanded Medicaid, to a high of 17.7 percent in Texas, a state that has not expanded Medicaid.[159]

Given their control over Medicaid eligibility and service standards and whether to expand the program or not, it should come as no surprise that the program's details vary considerably across the states. As of 2019, thirty-two states have Medicaid eligibility levels for parents and other adults set at 138 percent of the federal poverty level (FPL), as required by the Affordable Healthcare Act's Medicaid expansion provision. (Three other states have adopted Medicaid expansion but not yet implemented it.) Another state, Connecticut (155 percent), has adopted an even higher threshold. Among states that have not expanded their Medicaid coverage, three have thresholds below 25 percent FPL: Missouri (21 percent), Alabama (18 percent), and Texas (17 percent). Thus parents in a family of three in Connecticut with an annual income under $33,061 qualify for Medicaid, while in Texas that same family of three would only qualify with an income of less than $3,626. Childless adults in sixteen states do not get any Medicaid coverage at all.[160]

Medicaid and Children's Health Insurance Program (CHIP) coverage for children is uniformly more generous. Again, as of 2019, forty-nine states cover children with family incomes above 200 percent FPL, with the median being 255 percent FPL. The two states below the 200 percent FPL are Idaho (190 percent) and North Dakota (175 percent). The highest coverage is extended in New York at 405 percent FPL, or incomes up to $85,320 for a family of three. Coverage for pregnant women is also extended in most states, with thirty-four states covering women at levels at or above 200 percent FPL.[161]

States have also arrived at different decisions in regard to whether they wish to establish their own state health care exchange under the Affordable Care Act, partner with the federal government in creating one, or rely entirely on using an exchange built and run by the federal government. The question revolves around state control versus federal control. Michigan's governor, a Republican, calculated it this way: "The state exchange is something I'd ultimately prefer because, otherwise, if you have a federal exchange, you're going to have people at the federal government taking care of Michigan citizens and my preference is to have Michiganders helping Michiganders in terms of customer service."[162] Despite the governor's clear preference, the GOP-dominated state legislature initially refused to allow the state to partner with the federal government, leaving Michigan to use the federal facilitated exchange. Ultimately, the state implemented a state partnership marketplace, allowing the state to take over some consumer assistance functions, while leaving the rest to the federal government. The same trend was found across much of the rest of the country; generally, states controlled by the Republicans opted to have the federal government run their exchanges, while states under Democratic control either chose to partner with the federal government or to create their own exchanges. As of 2019, in addition to Michigan, another five states have state partnership marketplaces. There are eleven states that operate their own state-run marketplaces and five states that have federally supported state-based marketplaces, in which the federal government supplies the site's information technology and the state does the rest. The remaining twenty-eight states direct their residents to the federal facilitated exchange where consumers enroll through the healthcare.gov website.[163]

Perhaps the most significant instance of decentralization of power to the states from the federal government occurred in 1996, when Congress passed the Personal Responsibility and Work Opportunity Reconciliation Act. This legislation reformed welfare and created the Temporary Assistance for Needy Families (TANF) program, over which the states gained primary responsibility. Like Medicaid, TANF is funded jointly by the federal government and the states have considerable leeway over eligibility standards for receiving benefits from the program. As a result, the stringency of eligibility standards varies. In 2017, for example, a family with one parent and two dependent children could make, at most, in their thirteenth month receiving the benefit, $268 a month to be eligible in Alabama, while in Minnesota that same family could earn $2,243 a month and still be eligible. Benefits also vary. A family of three with no income would receive $215 a month in TANF benefits in Alabama, but $1,021 a month in New Hampshire. The median monthly benefit across the states was $432.[164]

There are, of course, other important differences in TANF programs across the states. A central component of the program is an effort to move recipients into jobs. Indeed, most of those who receive TANF must participate in "work activities." States have devised a number of different approaches to fulfilling this requirement.[165] Occasionally, states adopt TANF policies that risk running afoul of federal regulations. Since 2011, at least fifteen states have passed laws requiring drug testing or screening of public assistance applicants or recipients. As mentioned at the beginning of the chapter, Florida adopted a measure requiring all TANF applicants to submit to a drug test. Under the law the applicant is required to pay for the test. If the test turns out to be negative, the applicant is reimbursed through a higher TANF benefit. A positive drug result makes the applicant ineligible for benefits for one year or for six months after the completion of a substance abuse treatment program. An injunction permanently preventing the program from going into effect was granted by a federal judge and upheld by a federal appeals court. The program adopted in Missouri requires a drug test only of those applicants about whom there is reasonable suspicion of drug use. That approach appears to pass judicial scrutiny.[166]

Health and welfare benefits vary across the states. But they do not always do so in the ways we might predict. A few decades ago, health and welfare benefits largely tracked each other, with states that were generous on one policy also being generous on the other policy. Today, that relationship has broken down. Wisconsin, for example, ranks high on the amount of money it spends per TANF recipient but low on money per Medicaid recipient. Additionally, there are no real regional differences in benefits. The only apparent relationship between health and welfare benefits and state characteristics is with state wealth: wealthier states tend to provide better benefits. Surprisingly, wealth is a much stronger predictor of benefits than is the prevailing political ideology of a state.[167]

THE RESPONSIVENESS OF STATE POLICYMAKING

One of the underappreciated aspects of the American federal system is that states can, on their own initiative, respond to emerging issues. Indeed, with the federal government's policymaking capacity appearing in recent years to be paralyzed, states have had to fill the governing vacuum. Take, for example, paid family and medical leave insurance laws to allow people to take care of new children or sick family members. There are now eight states—California (originally adopted in 2002), New Jersey (2008), Rhode Island (2013), New York (2016), Washington (2017), Massachusetts (2018), Connecticut (2019), and Oregon (2019)—that have put in place such measures.[168] In the area of environmental regulations, twenty-nine states have adopted renewable energy standards, forcing their utilities to secure more power from wind, solar, and other renewable sources.[169] Roughly half of the growth in renewable electricity generation since 2000 is attributable to the imposition of state standards.[170] All of these actions have come largely in advance of federal laws or regulations.

It should be added that not all state efforts meet with immediate success. Because nearly half of all working Americans do not have an employment-based retirement plan, several states have passed laws to create automatic individual retirement accounts for those workers who are not offered such a plan by their employer. The first such law was adopted by California in 2012, and since then variations on it have been adopted by Connecticut, Illinois, Massachusetts, Maryland, and Oregon. But, in part because of resistance from the federal government as well as "numerous legal and cost concerns, as of mid-2019 none of these plans have been implemented or become operational."[171] Such programs promise to save states money, mostly through lowering Medicaid costs.[172]

Still, the states have been proactive on a wide range of emerging issues. As discussed in box 6.1, sometimes the push from these developments comes from unexpected sources. The result is often that one state innovates and the others monitor the response to the new policy. Since Georgia passed an anti-bullying law in 1999, every state has followed suit, with Montana being the last to do

| Box 6.1 | **Students and Excused Mental Health Days Legislation** |

In 2019, Oregon adopted a law allowing primary and secondary students to have excused absences for behavioral or mental health related personal issues. Previously, excuses were only allowed for physical maladies. The "mental health day" legislation received considerable national attention, although it should be noted that Utah had adopted a similar law the previous year.

Although the topic at issue in the new law generated considerable public interest, what really merited attention was the means by which it had been put on the agenda and pushed through the legislative process. Unlike most issues debated by state legislatures, this measure did not have a legion of well-heeled lobbyists backing it. Instead, it was developed and supported by a group of high school students.

One of those students, Hailey Hardcastle, had attended a summer program for the Oregon Association of Student Councils, and while there she participated in a workshop on mental health issues facing the state. Motivated by learning that suicide was the second-leading cause of death among fifteen- to thirty-four-year-old Oregonians, the students in the workshop generated the ideas behind the mental health days proposal.

Taking on the role of a policy entrepreneur, Hardcastle and several of her high school colleagues got a bill introduced in the Oregon legislature and then lobbied on the legislation's behalf. They were inspired by the student activism provoked by a 2018 Florida school shooting: "We were inspired by Parkland in the sense that they showed us that young people can totally change the political conversation. . . . Just like those movements, this bill is something completely coming from the youth." Although lobbying lawmakers can seem intimidating, Hardcastle observed, "When I went down [to the Capitol] I saw people who looked just like me walking around and trying to make a difference so it really made me realize that if you believe in something, you can do something about it, no matter how old you are or where you come from or what you already know about politics."

The students succeeded in getting their mental health day law passed. They did not achieve everything they might have hoped; bills they backed on gun control legislation and to lower the voting age were rebuffed. But what they accomplished will allow young people who are struggling to seek help without being penalized for doing so by their schools.

Sources: Dani Matias, "Feeling Blue? Oregon Students Allowed to Take 'Mental Health Days,'" NPR.org, July 22, 2019; Sarah Zimmerman, "Teen Activists Win Excused Mental Health Days for Oregon Students," *Oregonian*, July 22, 2019.

so in 2015. The laws passed have differed; some focused on cyberbullying, while others have centered on behavior in school.[173] But as bullying rose on the national agenda, the states responded. And as Congress and the White House fumbled their way toward passing legislation to deal with the opioid abuse crises sweeping parts of the country, states again took the initiative. In 2016, Massachusetts, for example, passed what was hailed as the most comprehensive legislation on the problem.[174] By October 2018, at least thirty-three states had passed legislation responding to the public health emergency.[175]

Technological innovations often force states to make policies in the absence of congressional leadership. As the prospects for autonomous or self-driving cars move closer to reality, a majority of states have passed legislation addressing it. Nevada was the first to move, passing a law authorizing their operation in 2011. Since then, legislatures in twenty-eight other states have also passed laws governing self-driving vehicles, while governors in another seven states have signed executive orders covering the topic.[176] As drones have gained popularity, state governments have responded with legislation to regulate their use. By 2016, laws had been passed in ten states. Idaho, for example, "prohibits the use of UAS [unmanned aircraft systems] for hunting, molesting or locating game animals, game birds and furbearing animals," while Kansas expanded its law prohibiting stalking to include the use of drones in such illegal behavior.[177] Just two years later, forty-one states had passed drone laws.[178] By mid-2019, eight states had passed laws allowing personal delivery robots to operate legally on public sidewalks. Washington governor Jay Inslee even had the bill allowing their use in his state delivered to him in his office by an autonomous delivery robot.[179]

Complexity, however, can hinder quick legislative responses to emerging issues. In 2018, California passed the first consumer data privacy legislation governing the collection and control of private information. Only a few states have followed its lead, in part because in 2019 California had to revisit its law to fix several problems with it. By mid-2019, only Vermont (2018), Illinois (2019), Maine (2019), and Nevada (2019) had passed their own consumer data privacy laws, although roughly half of the remaining states had at least considered bills on the topic and a handful of them have established task forces to investigate their policy options.[180]

States often devise policies to protect what they identify as their economic interests. In 2018, Missouri adopted a law to prohibit products not "derived from harvested production livestock or poultry," from being labeled and sold as meat. The policy was pushed by the state's cattle industry because it feared growing competition from plant-based or lab-grown foods. The idea caught on quickly and the following year similar bills were introduced and adopted in several other states.[181] The economic motive driving them was clear. The Nebraska lawmaker who authored a deceptive meat labeling bill (and who is herself a vegetarian), said "I don't make laws for me, I make laws for Nebraskans, and part of what I have to do is protect our No. 1 industry, and that's cattle in Nebraska."[182]

Likewise, the author of a similar measure in Arkansas admitted that his bill was introduced to "protect the agricultural producers in this state."[183]

But there is a second motivation behind such bills. In 2019, Louisiana passed its own "truth in labeling" law that "broadly bans the use of the terms 'meat,' 'rice' or 'sugar' on food products derived from non-traditional sources, such as plant-based or cell-derived 'meats' and cauliflower 'rice.'"[184] The legislation was designed to protect several state industries, but it was also an effort to prod the federal government to develop national labeling standards. Louisiana's Commissioner of Agriculture complained,

> When you buy beef or you buy crawfish or you buy rice, it's my responsibility to make sure that you're getting beef, crawfish or rice. . . . If you look under the USDA definitions of food products, there are more than 80 pages of specific definitions. . . . But they never went in and defined meat or beef or pork or chicken because we always assumed that would be commonly understood.[185]

In the absence of federal action, states often feel obligated to devise their own policies.

It is important, however, to keep in mind that taking action does not always mean that the states are moving in the same direction on an issue. As noted earlier, in the wake of a number of horrific mass shootings in recent years, states have responded by pursuing completely opposed policy paths.[186] Similarly, states have pursued contrasting approaches on abortions. The same is true on environmental policies, with some state aggressively pushing more stringent standards than the federal government.[187] The important point for the discussion here is that the states can often respond more expeditiously on policy matters than can the federal government. As a lobbyist noted admiringly, "In the states things can happen very quickly."[188]

Of course, government does not always move quickly, whether at the national, state, or local level. And, as noted earlier, when they do act the states' responses are apt to be varied. One observer recently noted that across many policy fronts, "the states are pushing in diametrically opposed ways. Some are tugging hard to the right. Others are pulling strongly to the left. . . . the states are riding off in different directions."[189] Occasionally the measures particular states pursue can even seem extreme. Following Arizona's adoption of several controversial bills, comedian Jon Stewart jokingly referred to the state as "the meth lab of democracy."[190] But through the passage of a variety of different approaches to solving problems, states can begin to identify which among them are successful and which are not.

CONCLUSION

Although Americans tend to think that all policies flow from Washington, DC, the reality is that there is vast space in the federal system for the states to adopt different and distinctive approaches to solving problems. Moreover, policies often move from the states to Washington. During the summer of 2016, for example, Congress frantically worked on a bill requiring food manufacturers to label products containing genetically modified organisms (GMOs). The reason Congress spent time on the issue was because in 2014 Vermont had passed a stringent labeling law that went into effect in July 2016. Many members of Congress and the food industry wanted a less demanding law that would apply nationally rather than having to meet Vermont's tougher standard.[191] The importance of this story for our purposes here is to point out that Congress (and food manufacturers) had to respond to an innovative policy developed by a state, in this case the state with the smallest state economy.

A major theme that runs through this book is that where you live makes a difference. Our attention in this chapter has been on large policy questions. But keep in mind that these differences also appear on small matters. Take state laws on noodling. Noodling, or hand fishing, is an activity largely pursued in the rural South, where people use their hands to explore nooks and crannies in and around river banks to extract fish—usually catfish—from their hiding places. In recent years, a few states, most recently West Virginia, have opted to make noodling legal. Other states, notably Missouri, have decided to keep noodling illegal in order to protect catfish populations from being overharvested.[192] These decisions matter because states that prohibit noodling enforce the law, as Davenport, Iowa's "Fish Guy" recently learned to his dismay.[193] So which state you live in will not only determine what sort of educational and health care options you enjoy or the conditions under which you can get an abortion or carry a gun, but it will also dictate whether you can legally noodle.

7

States and Their Local Governments

States matter because:

★ Local government powers and structures are determined by the state.

★ How these powers are distributed among local governments differs from one state to another.

★ The ways in which local governments generate revenue is determined by the state.

★ Certain types of local governments receive a large percentage of their revenue from state transfers.

★ States can and do mandate that local governments undertake certain responsibilities.

★ States can forbid local governments from undertaking certain policies through preemption.

THE LOCAL GOVERNMENT SYSTEM in the United States is complicated, extensive, and dynamic, and it is almost entirely a product of the states. Local governments are not mentioned in the U.S. Constitution, but they are defined and discussed in every state constitution. The role of local governments has grown substantially as the country has urbanized. As one report observes,

> The collective local government sector in the United States is a system of highly diverse entities working in and across thousands of jurisdictions. Its scale and complexity make it unique among the world's nation-states. It is common for citizens to be simultaneously served by multiple forms of local governments.[1]

When the U.S. Constitution was ratified and a new political system formed, it featured a nascent national government, thirteen state governments, and relatively few local governments. The new country was largely rural, with only a few "cities." As we noted in earlier chapters, the most urban place was New York City with 33,000 inhabitants, followed by Philadelphia (28,500 residents), Boston (18,000), Charleston (16,000), and Baltimore (13,500). No other city in the country had as many as 10,000 people.[2]

While there were only a handful of urban settlements worthy of the name "city," there were many less populated jurisdictions called towns, or in some states, townships. In fact, along with counties, towns and townships were probably the most important type of local government in colonial America, as they were often created by charter by the British crown or through the colony's corporate or religious authority. Once the colonies transformed into states, the state legislatures became the authority for granting municipal charters. Aside from providing public safety (and education, in a few New England states), town responsibilities were few, and they were funded through a small annual tax on the "head" of each person (hence, the term "head tax," also known in early days as a poll tax).[3]

Counties also existed in almost all the colonies and they were a primary form of local government as the colonies transformed into states. The 1790 census counted a total of 292 counties in the United States.[4] Often, as the states grew and territory expanded, more counties were added. Georgia provides an example; in 1800 there were twenty-four counties, but much of the territory in the state was not subject to state authority because it was Cherokee and Creek tribal lands. By the 1830s, the state of Georgia exerted authority over all those tribal lands and encouraged their occupation by the growing population of white settlers. To that end, the former tribal lands were divided into more and more counties over time. By 1832, the state had eighty-nine counties. Today, the number stands at 159.[5]

Two of the most common types of local governments today—special districts and independent school districts—were almost unknown in 1790. The few examples of special districts by 1800 were found in the form of toll road authorities or canal corporations. The point is that local governments—at least some types of local government—did exist in 1790. But their functions were limited. In addition, the role of the new national government was uncertain. As one scholar notes, "From 1790 to the 1840s, state governments were the most active level of government."[6]

Over time, of course, the relationship between the national, the state, and the local governments changed. For one thing, there are many more local governments today, about ninety thousand of them. As the population steadily grew and eventually transformed from a rural to an urban and suburban population, local governments took on new forms and functions. Local governments often must contend with immediate and important issues. Sometimes they are the first level of government to address these problems, and they exercise government powers far beyond what the Founders might have imagined as ever necessary.

In many respects local governments are more immediately responsive to public problems and preferences. They often have to address the effect of new products or technologies more immediately than the state or national government can. For example, local governments were the first to feel the effects of the opioid epidemic and some of the first to sue the pharmaceutical companies, beginning with a suit filed by the city of Chicago in 2014. Cities were the first governments to seek regulation of short-term rental agreements in private homes and among the first to regulate ridesharing companies. Eventually, some of these local government actions were enhanced, amended, or overturned by the state legislature or state courts. Although they may act first, what local governments do and how they do it is ultimately determined by the state.

TYPES OF LOCAL GOVERNMENTS

There are five basic forms of local governments in modern America. The first three are referred to as "general-purpose governments" because they have multiple functions, as defined by state law; the other two are "single-purpose governments." The precise nature of these functions for the general-purpose governments differs from state to state. The number of each of these types of local governments at several points in time is shown in table 7.1.

County government. Counties are one of the oldest forms of local government. When the country was primarily rural, counties were usually the local unit charged with administering state laws and functions, and this heritage continues today in most states. For example, many of the responsibilities of the Office of Secretary of State, such as election administration and maintenance of civil records like deed transfers or marriage licenses, are handled by an official of county government—usually the county clerk. The relative significance of counties as administrative and political units varies by region of the

Table 7.1. Number of Local Governments in United States, over Time

	1942	1957	2007	2017
Counties	3,050	3,047	3,033	3,031
Municipalities	16,228	17,153	19,492	19,495
Townships	18,919	17,196	16,519	16,253
School Districts	108,579	50,446	13,051	12,754
Special Districts	8,299	14,405	37,381	38,542
TOTAL	**155,116**	**102,328**	**89,476**	**90,075**

Source: United States Census Bureau, Census of Governments.

country; they play a central governing role in the Southern and the Western states. In Louisiana, counties are called "parishes," but they function in the same manner as counties elsewhere. In a few other states there are notable differences. In Alaska, "boroughs" are similar to county government elsewhere, but because of the vast expanses of Alaska with few or no inhabitants, boroughs do not cover the entire land mass of the state. In two other states—Connecticut and Rhode Island—counties have no political or administrative functions; they are simply place designations, not governments.

The authority for county operations is defined by state legislative statute, state constitutional provisions, and state judicial rulings. For example, in Tennessee, Article VII, Section 1 of the state constitution specifies the county officers to be elected and the term of office for each. Many legislative statues relevant to county governance appear in the Tennessee Code, the body of law passed by the legislature. Title 5 pertains to counties' organization and powers. It is further divided into more than twenty subsections, called chapters, that explain the structure, functions, and procedures of county government in Tennessee. For example, Title 5, Chapter 5 describes the laws by which county legislative bodies (known as boards of commissioners) operate in Tennessee, while Title 5, Chapter 12 describes the procedures for county budgeting. Furthermore, over the years, numerous Tennessee State Supreme Court cases determined the precise limits of county powers.[7]

Because they function as local administrative units of the state, counties cover the entire territory of the state. This is true in almost all states, but there are exceptions. There are a few instances where the county boundary ends and a municipal (city) boundary begins. For example, Baltimore exists outside the area of the adjacent neighboring counties.[8] In Missouri, St. Louis is an independent city and is not part of any county (not even St. Louis County).[9] San Francisco is both a city and a county, operating with a mayor and a county board of supervisors.[10]

The precise mix of services and regulatory activities required or authorized will not necessarily be the same from one state to another, but for most the responsibilities include health regulations, law enforcement, local court administration, welfare services, election administration, tax collection, and record-keeping associated with the secretary of state's requirements. It should be obvious that the level of services provided depends on both the state requirements and the size of the population served. Contrast, for example, the different levels of service and regulation encountered in two California counties: Alpine County (with a total population of 1,162 and no official towns) and Los Angeles County (population of over 10 million, and at least eighty-seven incorporated cities within its limits).[11] Both Alpine and Los Angeles are counties and have the same legal status within the state of California. But they are remarkably different entities. California is a state with large contrasts across its counties and their governance footprint; six different California counties have fewer than nineteen thousand residents each, while nine counties each contain populations of more than one million residents. Texas is another state where the magnitude of the county administrative responsibilities can be quite different: Harris County (Houston area) administers to a population of 4.6 million, while Loving County has a population of 134.[12]

Municipal government. Cities are municipal corporations, created by the state to provide additional public service and regulation beyond what the county provides. Generally, this need arises because of the scale of human settlement. When people live in closer proximity, additional infrastructure (e.g., sidewalks, water and sewer lines, parks), land use regulation (e.g., zoning and building codes), and services (e.g., health inspection, police and fire protection) are required. A city (municipal corporation) is granted a charter by the state to provide these enhancements for people in a geographically defined area. The organization, authority, and finances of these municipalities are stipulated in the state constitution and statutes passed by the state legislature. For example, the West Virginia Code includes a lengthy chapter (Chapter 8) describing municipalities. The chapter includes, among other items, articles on how a city can amend its municipal charter (Article 1), how officials are elected (Article 5), the procedures for a city to annex additional land (Article 6), taxation and financing of city operations (Article 13), and numerous other subjects.

Because they usually provide a higher level of service and regulation than in rural areas, municipalities must generate more revenue. Incorporation simply provides the legal authority to operate as a city, but the scale of that government operation is different from one municipality to another. In Texas, four cities (Austin, Dallas, Houston, and San Antonio) are large municipalities with one million or more residents in each. In contrast, the 2010 census listed the Texas towns of Abbott (population 356), Christoval (163), and Eustace (991) as official municipalities. In the middle there are more than fifty cities in Texas with populations between fifty thousand and three hundred thousand.

Township governments. In some ways, townships are a mysterious category of local government. For one thing, the term "town" has multiple meanings. In everyday usage "town" simply denotes a small community. There is no precise definition for this use of the term; it is a colloquial term used in casual communication to indicate "a community smaller than a city." But another meaning is a more formal one: in some states a "town" or "township" has a precise legal definition; it is an administrative and political subdivision of a county. And exactly what that subdivision looks like differs from state to state. In New England and a couple of Midwestern states, they are called "towns," and historically are most associated with the "town meeting" form of governance. In New England, the town was the fundamental form of local government, and undertook most of the responsibilities associated with county government in other states.

Elsewhere, this type of local government is called a "township." Here, we will follow the convention of the U.S. Bureau of the Census and use the term "township" rather than "town." Exactly how these local governments work varies by state. In most states, township jurisdiction exists only outside the boundaries of any incorporated cities. In some states, townships have very limited functions. In Ohio, the township responsibilities are "cemetery maintenance, trash collection, road upkeep and snow removal."[13]

But in a few states, they are a robust local form of local government. In Michigan, for example, townships are authorized to provide a range of services, many of which are performed by special districts or counties in other states. According to the Michigan Township Association, "Virtually all townships provide fire protection and many also offer law enforcement as well. Parks and recreation programs, public water and sewer services, trash collection and recycling programs, sidewalks and trails, and cemeteries are other common township functions."[14]

In contrast, townships in New Jersey and Pennsylvania are, in legal terms, municipal corporations and are virtually indistinguishable from "regular" cities. Furthermore, most states in the South and the West never established townships as a type of local government at all. And in a few other states, townships are disappearing as they are absorbed into cities (municipalities) as urbanization expands the city boundaries outward. This phenomenon is evident in table 7.1. In 1942 there were 18,919 townships in the United States, but by 2017 the number had dwindled to 16,253. The number of township governments declined by almost twenty-seven hundred in a seventy-five-year period.

School district governments. The U.S. Census Bureau defines school district governments as:

> Organized local entities providing public elementary, secondary, and for higher education which, under state law, have sufficient administration and fiscal autonomy to qualify as separate governments. Excludes dependent public school systems of county, municipal, township, or state governments.[15]

In other words, "school districts" here refers to "independent school districts," which are a local unit of government outside the control of another local government such as a county or city. In some states, such as Maryland, public schools are the responsibility of county government or, in the case of Baltimore, a city government. In New York City, the public schools are run by the New York City Department of Education. In a few states, some townships still have responsibility for public education. In several states, there is a mix, with independent school districts in some areas and dependent school districts (i.e., run by the county or a municipality) in other areas. In Hawaii, the public schools are administered directly by the state. But the great majority (perhaps 85 to 90 percent) of K–12 public schools in the United States today are operated by independent school districts. These districts are most often governed by a locally elected school board, but with some state government oversight.

As shown in table 7.1, there has been a dramatic decrease in the number of school districts in the United States since 1942. Historically, school districts were small geographic units, often administering a single school. Around the middle of the twentieth century, a movement to consolidate school districts occurred in most states. Primarily, this was a cost-saving device, allowing school districts to merge and thereby achieve economy of scale. The consolidation movement met with considerable resistance in many communities, but ultimately the number of school districts was reduced by almost 90 percent. At the same time, the number of students in the K–12 system grew substantially as the U.S. population more than doubled. While public schools are administered by one or another local government (except Hawaii), ultimately public education is the responsibility of the state. As pointed out in chapter 6, the obligation of the state to fund and ensure public education is enshrined in the state constitution. This means that even "independent school districts" are not truly "independent." They receive a considerable portion of their governing mandate, and a considerable share of their funding, from the state government.

Special district governments. The Census Bureau defines special districts as local entities other than counties, municipalities, townships, or school districts "authorized by state law to provide only one or a limited number of designated functions, and with sufficient administrative and fiscal autonomy to qualify as separate governments." They are known by a variety of different titles, including districts, authorities, boards, and commissions.[16] In some states special districts are known as "public authorities." The vast majority of special districts are single-purpose governments, meaning that they have only one function. Examples are a Parks and Recreation District, Fire Protection District, Auditorium District, Irrigation District, Hospital District, or many others. The Census Bureau identifies a "partial list" of possible special districts that describes twenty-two separate functional types. The types of special districts allowed varies by state. Some permit a long list of different types of special districts; others allow only a few types. Special districts are typically governed by a board of commissioners, as defined by state law. State statutes also define how commissioners are selected, their term of office, their responsibilities, and their salary (if any). For example, the Iowa State Code, Title IX, subtitle 2, Chapters 357 and 358, describes thirteen different types of special districts authorized in the state, and delineates the functions, operations, finances, and officers for each of them.

Counties, municipalities, and townships are known as "general-purpose governments" because they provide multiple functions, and they have been in existence for centuries. All three types of general-purpose governments existed in some or all of the states in 1790. But "single-purpose" governments—special districts and independent school districts—came much later, with the exception of toll roads and canal companies, which came into being around 1800. Independent school districts are really just one form of special district, but they are so numerous and have such an important history in the United States that they are almost always treated as a separate category. Most local government units today are single purpose; about 60 percent of all local governments fall into that category. When the country was formed, almost no single-purpose governments existed.

In Illinois, the state legislature authorized the creation of three park districts in Chicago in 1869.[17] In California, the state legislature established irrigation districts as a local government authority by 1887. But, for the most part, special districts were not a common type of local government until well into the twentieth century. Special districts are a response to an increasingly complex society. In 1900, the population of the United States was about 76 million, and mostly rural (60 percent of the population lived in rural areas, according to the U.S. Census). By 1950, the population had doubled to 152 million, and the spatial distribution was now 40 percent rural and 60 percent urban. In a fifty-year span, the urban population grew from about 30 million to 90 million. By 2010, the population reached 309 million, with 80 percent of that population living in urban areas. In other words, the urban population was about 247 million—almost three times as large as it was in 1950 and over eight times larger than in 1900. American communities were much larger and far more complex, with multiple local governments and a much greater need for both regulatory activity and service provision.[18]

The remarkable growth in special districts is documented in table 7.1. In 1942 there were about eighty-three hundred special districts distributed across the forty-eight states (Alaska and Hawaii were not yet admitted into the Union). By 1957 the number of special districts had almost doubled. In 2017 special districts numbered over thirty-eight thousand. They are now, by far, the most numerous type of local government authority in the country. Because special districts can be created to address a specific need in a specific community, they are well adapted for a rapidly urbanizing society. It is also true, of course, that more special districts contribute to the complexity of state and local governance. In particular, they add to the fragmented nature of local government. This is especially the case in metropolitan areas, where there may be hundreds of local government units. The Chicago metro area, for example, consists of more than fifteen hundred local units of government. The metro areas incorporating Pittsburgh, St. Louis, and New York City are also highly fragmented.[19]

The relative importance of each type of local government unit varies by state. As mentioned previously, counties have stronger powers in certain regions of the country than in others. In some places, townships remain an important component of local governance; in others townships as governing bodies do not exist at all. And, of course, the total number of local governments varies by state, as table 7.2 shows. The average number of local governments per state is about 770, but that figure belies large differences. The number ranges from Hawaii with a total of only twenty-one local governments in the entire state, to Illinois with 6,919 local governments. Fourteen states have fewer than eight hundred local governments each. This list includes Arizona and Virginia, two states with relatively large populations and land areas. In contrast, there are eleven states with more than three thousand units of local government each.

Box 7.1	Municipal Madness in New Jersey

New Jersey is known as "The Garden State." Apparently, it is especially prolific at growing municipalities. One recent article claimed that "New Jersey has more municipalities per capita than any other state in the Union." This is not actually true; for example, Arkansas has one-third the population of New Jersey but almost as many municipalities. But it SEEMS as if New Jersey leads the nation in municipal governments, perhaps because there are 565 municipalities packed into a very small space; New Jersey is the fourth-smallest state by square miles. One could fit fourteen New Jerseys into the state of Arkansas. So, indeed, there are a lot of municipalities in New Jersey. What makes this especially confusing is that in the Garden State all types of municipalities—boroughs, cities, towns, and townships—have the same municipal duties. Basically, there is no difference between them other than how the officials are chosen.

In most states, boroughs, towns, and townships have fewer functions and powers than cities because they represent smaller communities. But, as New Jersey transformed from a rural, agricultural state to a suburban area between the large cities of New York and Philadelphia, the distinction between townships, boroughs, and units faded away. This trend was probably facilitated in New Jersey because it is truly a *suburban* state without a large urban center. In a state with a population of almost 9 million residents, the largest city (Newark) has fewer than three hundred thousand residents. But there are thirty-seven municipalities each with a population of at least fifty thousand. It is a state full of midsize communities, almost all of which grew from small agricultural villages.

Today, so many municipal units in so small a space leads to some odd situations. There are SIX communities in New Jersey with the name Washington. There is a Washington Township in Gloucester County. There is also a Washington Township in Morris County. And another Washington Township in Bergen County. And one in Warren County and one in Burlington County.

In Warren County there is both a Washington Borough and a Washington Township (yes, they are separate municipalities). Morris County has two municipalities named Chatham (the Borough of Chatham and the Township of Chatham). In that same county there is a Chester Borough and a Chester Township, a Mendham Borough and a Mendham Township, and a Rockaway Borough and a Rockaway Township. All are municipal governments of equal standing.

The municipality of Metuchen is completely surrounded by the municipality of Edison. Start in Metuchen and drive in any direction and you will wind up in Edison.

Then there are the Brunswicks. New Brunswick is the largest and the home of Rutgers University and several pharmaceutical firms. North

(Continued)

Brunswick is south of New Brunswick. East Brunswick is also south of New Brunswick. As one reporter (and New Jersey native) lamented, "How anyone navigated this godforsaken state before GPS is beyond me."

Let us not lose sight of the fact that all of these municipalities were authorized by the state legislature at some point. Today, the New Jersey State League of Municipalities represents more than 250 boroughs, 50 cities, 240 townships, and 15 towns in the state—all with equal standing. One local government scholar notes that a feature of local government structure in many states "is fragmented and multi-layered," with overlapping and intersecting boundaries, and that "one outcome of this fragmentation is confusion for citizens." Given the local government fragmentation in their state, we can excuse New Jersey residents if they are confused.

Sources: Megan Mullin, "Local Boundaries," in Donald Haider-Markel, ed. *The Oxford Handbook of State and Local Governement* (New York: Oxford University Press, 2014), p. 397.

New Jersey League of Municipalities, https://www.njlm.org/.

Michael V. Pettigano, "Here's Why Bergen County Has So Many Towns," NorthJersey.com, February 1, 2018, https://www.northjersey.com/story/news/bergen/2018/01/31/boroughitis-bergen-county-nj-70-towns/1080349001/.

Sergio Bichao, "NJ Has So Many Municipalities, 75 of Them Have to Share the Same Names," New Jersey 101.5, August 6, 2016, https://nj1015.com/nj-has-so-many-municipalities-75-of-them-have-to-share-the-same-names/.

Bobby Olivier, "NJ Has Too Many Damn Towns: Here Are 25 That Need to Go." NJ.com, https://www.nj.com/entertainment/2018/03/nj_has_way_too_many_towns_here_are_25_we_definitel.html.

As we might expect, most of these are larger population states (e.g., California, New York, Texas, and Pennsylvania). But half of them are midsize states in the Midwest. In other words, the number of local governments in a state is a product of numerous variables—notably geographic size, population size, and region.

The specific mix of local government types in a state appears to be even more idiosyncratic. We can get a sense of this from table 7.3, in which we show the relative mix of local governments in three large states: Georgia, Illinois, and Washington. These states are similar in terms of population and geographic size (square miles), but they differ in the way they distribute units of local government. Illinois stands out because of its sheer number of governmental units, which includes many special districts and townships. In contrast, Georgia and Washington do not have any townships at all. Georgia has many counties (second-most among all the states, after Texas), while Washington has relatively few counties.

Table 7.2.   Number of Local Governments, by State

Alabama	1,196
Alaska	180
Arizona	659
Arkansas	1,542
California	4,445
Colorado	3,142
Connecticut	626
Delaware	335
Florida	1,713
Georgia	1,381
Hawaii	22
Idaho	1,171
Illinois	6,919
Indiana	2,639
Iowa	1,942
Kansas	3,793
Kentucky	1,323
Louisiana	517
Maine	835
Maryland	345
Massachusetts	859
Michigan	2,864
Minnesota	3,644
Mississippi	970
Missouri	3,769
Montana	1,227
Nebraska	2,539
Nevada	190
New Hampshire	542
New Jersey	1,339
New Mexico	1,014
New York	3,451
North Carolina	971

Table 7.2. (Continued)

North Dakota	2,665
Ohio	3,898
Oklahoma	1,831
Oregon	1,511
Pennsylvania	4,831
Rhode Island	130
South Carolina	672
South Dakota	1,917
Tennessee	907
Texas	5,344
Utah	620
Vermont	730
Virginia	518
Washington	1,901
West Virginia	652
Wisconsin	3,097

Source: United States Census Bureau, Census of Governments.

Table 7.3. Number of Local Governments, Selected States

	High-population states			Low-population states		
	Georgia	Illinois	Washington	Delaware	Hawaii	Vermont
County	152	102	39	3	3	14
Municipality	537	1,297	281	57	1	42
Township	0	1,429	0	0	0	237
School District	180	886	295	19	0	277
Special District	511	3,204	1,285	255	17	159
TOTAL	**1,380**	**6,918**	**1,900**	**334**	**21**	**729**

Source: United States Census Bureau, Census of Governments.
Georgia, Illinois, and Washington have 2019 population estimates in the range of 7.5 million 12.7 million, and they rank eighth, sixth, and thirteenth, respectively, in terms of population. They are also similar in land size (square miles), ranging from 55,500 to 66,500 square miles and ranking twenty-first, twenty-fourth, and twentieth, respectively, in square miles. Delaware, Hawaii, and Vermont population estimates are between 0.6 million and 1.4 million, and they rank forty-fifth, forty-first, and forty-ninth, respectively, in population.They are also small in geographic size; all of them are below the ten-thousand-square-mile level and they rank, respectively, forty-ninth, forty-seventh, and forty-third in land mass.

We also show the mix of local units for three small states: Delaware, Hawaii, and Vermont. These have smaller populations and are geographically tiny. It makes sense that they would have a more limited number of counties and municipalities. But Vermont, true to its New England heritage, has quite a few townships, while Delaware and Hawaii have none. Over 75 percent of all local governments in Delaware are special districts. Hawaii has its own system: few local governments, with most services provided at the state level. The only incorporated city is Honolulu, which is a consolidated city and county.[20]

Tables 7.2 and 7.3 demonstrate that the local government arrangements are different from state to state. And, again, it is important to recognize that these differences result from the fact that local governments are products of state governmental decisions. States have authority over local governments and the way they choose to allocate that authority among them varies.

LOCAL GOVERNMENTS AND PUBLIC FINANCE

Across the United States, the amount of revenue generated by the states is roughly equal to the amount of revenue generated by local governments. But all of these funds—whether collected at the local or state level—are authorized by the states. States determine what taxes and other revenue sources their local governments may use, the types of expenditures for which their local governments are responsible, and the relative mix of state revenues to local revenues and expenditures. Different states handle this in different ways. In some states, the bulk of the revenue and expenditures are processed at the state level. In 2016 in Vermont, 81 percent of the funds generated were state revenues. At least 75 percent of the state and local revenues were provided by the state in Arkansas, Delaware, Hawaii, and Vermont. Given the information presented in table 7.3, this is not a surprise. Recall that Delaware, Hawaii, and Vermont are all states with few local governments, so it makes sense that the state would be the primary public financing agent in those places.

In contrast, there are some states where more than half of the revenue is generated at the local level, including Florida (55 percent), New York State (53 percent), and Texas (52 percent). In other words, the relative fiscal magnitude of state governments to their local governments varies from one state to another.[21] This is why it is important to look at total state and local tax rates—not just the state tax rate—when comparing tax burdens across the country.

The ability of local governments to generate their own funds depends on what revenue tools the state allows them. Moreover, different types of local governments within a state may have different revenue sources. In some states, counties may be allowed to impose a local sales tax but cities may not. School districts may be permitted to tax property at a higher rate than special districts. Consequently, where the figures reported are averaged for all types of local governments in all states, remember that there is quite a bit of variation from state to state and type of local government.

Generally, the largest revenue streams for local governments are the property tax, miscellaneous revenue (charges, user fees, licenses, fines), and intergovernmental transfers (direct state aid, some direct federal aid, and federal aid passed to local governments from state governments).[22] Overall, these revenue streams account for 90 percent of local funds nationwide, but, again, there are large variations in these figures from state to state. For example, 60.1 percent of the total local revenues in Vermont are from intergovernmental transfers, while only 14.6 percent in Hawaii are from state and federal aid accounts.[23] There are also big differences by type of local government. In most states, about half of all school district funds come from state aid—money appropriated by the state legislature and sent to local school districts. But less state aid is sent to special districts and to cities or counties.

Intergovernmental transfers. Overall, intergovernmental transfers are the single largest source of revenue for all local governments combined. According to the Tax Policy Center, 36 percent of local government revenue comes from such transfers.[24] Most transfers are from states directly to local governmental units (primarily school districts), although a fair amount is federal grant money passed through the state to local governments.

Local governments that are heavily dependent on state aid (transfers) are susceptible to budget problems when state revenue does not meet expectations. Again, the Great Recession provides examples. As state revenues fell short in FY 2009, seventeen states reduced their aid to local governments, and in 2010 twenty states did so. Local governmental units in Arizona and Ohio were hit especially hard, experiencing state aid reductions of 24 percent and 19 percent, respectively.[25] Many states continued this practice when their own budgets struggled to recover; sixteen states reduced aid to local governments in FY 2011, and seventeen did so in FY 2012. By 2014, most state economies and budgets had recovered. Consequently, only two states reduced aid to local governments that year.[26] Nonetheless, in many states the earlier reduction in aid was never fully restored even after the recession ended.[27] In other words, some local governments, especially cities, received less state aid in 2017 than they had gotten in 2007.

Local governments have multiple revenue streams aside from intergovernmental aid. For most local governments, much of their revenue comes from their own sources. Because of the wide array of state and local fiscal practices, the following discussion is based on general arrangements and trends. The situation in specific individual states will likely vary.

Property taxes. For most local governments in most states, the property tax is by far the largest own-source revenue generator, accounting for about 30 percent of total local revenues. All types of local governments—school districts, special districts, townships, counties, and cities—make use of the property tax. The degree to which they use the property tax is determined by the state. This usually means that the state sets a maximum percentage that a particular type of local government can impose.

The actual amount of property tax paid is determined by two things: the property tax rate and the assessed value of the property. Using data on the median property tax paid on owner-occupied homes and the median home value, it is estimated that in 2019 the typical effective property tax rate ranged from lows of 0.27 percent (Hawaii) and 0.43 percent (Alabama) to a high of 2.30 percent (Illinois) and 2.35 percent (New Jersey).[28] By this particular metric, property owners in some states are paying property tax rates eight or nine times higher than property owners in some other states.

Local governments were hit hard in the Great Recession because of their reliance on the property tax. One of the primary causes of the recent economic recession was the collapse of the housing market, causing property values to plummet in many areas. Nationwide, home prices dropped about 20 percent, but in states such as Nevada and Arizona the plunge was even more precipitous. The decline in property values resulted in a significant drop in the revenue produced by the property tax. By 2010, property tax collections had suffered their largest decline in thirty years.[29] In many states, local government finances suffered for several subsequent years. By 2019, property values had returned to their prerecession levels (or even higher) in most places.

Charges and miscellaneous revenues. Just as states make use of fees, charges, and fines, they often permit their local governments to do so as well. Charges and fees account for almost one-quarter of all local revenues, but a much larger percentage for some types of local governments than for others. Cities and special districts, in particular, often rely heavily on such fees. In Pennsylvania, for instance, such charges account for about 45 percent of all the revenue generated by cities.[30] Many special districts (also known as special purpose districts) rely primarily on fees and charges. Common examples include airport districts and public utility districts like water and sewer districts. Perhaps the most curious such district is found in Washington. State law allows for the creation of "Television Reception Improvement Districts," which may be financed by the imposition of an annual fee of up to $60 per television on households and hotels/motels. There is at least one such district in operation, in the municipality of Okanogan.[31] More generally, during the Great Recession, many subnational governments increased various user fees to help fill the budget holes created by declining property tax revenues.[32]

In some places, fees and fines have become a major part of the revenue structure. This is particularly the case in some smaller communities where property tax revenue is stagnant, or where state aid transfers to local government have dwindled. One recent analysis finds that many such communities have come to rely heavily on fines for traffic violations and other misdemeanors, "sometimes accounting for more than half of their revenues."[33] In the case of two small Louisiana cities, over 90 percent of their general fund revenues were generated from fines and fees. Several states, notably Georgia, Maryland, Missouri, and Texas, have recently passed legislation capping the percentage of local government revenues that can be generated through fines.[34]

Local option taxes. While these are called "local option" taxes, they must be first authorized by the state. In other words, some states permit their local governments (if the local government so chooses) to impose such taxes, but other states do not allow them. Nationwide, these local option taxes represent a relatively small proportion of total local revenues. But in some states, they may account for a large proportion of local revenue—especially for cities or counties. According to the Tax Foundation, thirty-eight states allow for local option sales taxes.[35] A much smaller number of states permit local option income or payroll taxes. Where such taxes are permissible, they are usually collected at the county level, although in some states they may be imposed by municipalities (cities). Where these taxes are permitted, they may become a significant source of revenue. Looking back at chapter 3 for a moment, compare, columns 4 and 5 in table 3.1. Column 4 reports state sales tax rates, while column 5 shows the average rate for local option sales tax, where allowed. In Alabama, the sales tax jumps from 4 percent (state) to almost 9 percent when we include the local option sales tax. Similar increases occur in Colorado, Georgia, Louisiana, Missouri, New York, and Oklahoma—suggesting a heavy reliance on local option taxes in these states.

STATES AND THEIR LOCAL GOVERNMENTS

It is clear that local governments are defined by their state. The system for distributing authority from the state to local governments is set by a combination of state legislative actions, state constitutional mandates, and state court interpretations.[36] The organizational structure of a local government, its finances, powers, and responsibilities all exist within parameters set by the state government. In some states, the parameters allow local governments, or at least certain types of local governments, great latitude to operate. In other states, the constraints placed on local governments are much tighter.

Charters and the Division of Authority

Any understanding of the relationship between states and their local governments begins with a principle known as "Dillon's rule." From 1860 until the end of the century, John F. Dillon served on the Iowa Supreme Court, the Eighth U.S. Circuit Court of Appeals, and the law faculties at Columbia University and Yale University. In his numerous court decisions and academic writings, Dillon elaborated a principle on the relative powers and limits of municipalities. The principle is that municipalities and other local governments derive their power exclusively from the state, and especially from the state legislature. The legislature can authorize local powers, and it can withdraw those powers.[37] Importantly, this means that the authority and powers of a local government must be clearly defined by the state in order for the local government to exercise those powers. If there is a reasonable doubt as to whether the city or other local government has authority in a specific instance, then such local government likely does not have that authority. Over time, the principle of Dillon's rule has prevailed most of the time in most of the states; one analysis contends that almost 80 percent of the states clearly operate under the principle of Dillon's rule.[38]

There are numerous consequences to this principle, but two that are especially important are, first, local units, especially cities, are likely to find themselves in litigation whenever an action is not clearly established under the state constitution or statutes, and second, local governments spend considerable time lobbying the legislature to protect and sometimes extend their authority. As one frustrated local official in Virginia complained, "We have to go to the General Assembly for pretty much everything except to brush our teeth in the morning."[39]

In every state there are organizations that represent local governments. For example, in Idaho there is the Association of Idaho Cities, Idaho Association of Counties, Idaho Association of Highway Districts, Idaho School Board Association (representing school districts), and Idaho Water Users Association (representing two types of special districts, irrigation districts and groundwater districts). Each of these organizations has at least one person registered as a lobbyist. Recent reports show that in Pennsylvania, the County Commissioners Association of Pennsylvania had six registered lobbyists, while the Pennsylvania School Board Association and the Pennsylvania Association of Township Supervisors each had four lobbyists.[40]

The legal document that defines the organization and powers of a local government is called a charter. A municipal charter allows a broader exercise of power than what is usually found in a rural county or township. There are several types of charters. They range from the most restrictive (special act charter) to the least restrictive (home rule charter). But even "home rule" does not approach true independence for the local government. As the National League of Cities explains, "Home rule is a delegation of power from the state to its subunits of governments (including counties, municipalities, towns or townships or villages). That power is limited to specific fields, and subject to constant judicial interpretation, but home rule creates local autonomy and limits the degree of state interference in local affairs."[41] At one time, many states adopted a "special act" charter system wherein a separate charter was created for each city; each municipal charter pertained to just one local government. This system meant individual cities were dependent on the goodwill of the legislature (or, more likely on the goodwill of a specific committee in the legislature that had the authority to create and amend local charters). Most states have moved to a city classification chartering system, or some manner of home rule charters. Some states have a mix. For example, Tennessee switched from a special act (called "private-act") system to a general law system in 1953, but cities incorporated prior to 1953 maintain their private act status.[42] Other chartering categories include a "general charter" that applies to all municipalities equally, and a "classification charter" system in which municipalities are divided into three or four groups by population, and each population group is subject to a charter tailored for that size community. For our purposes here, the main point remains that local governments are under the aegis of their state government, and the degree of autonomy and authority the state chooses to grant to its local governments is not the same in all states, or even within a state.

Mandates, Polarization, and Preemption

In recent years much has been written about the regulatory tension between some states and their local governments. As one intergovernmental relations text notes,

> Because states have vast legal powers over local governments, a state may order its local units to do all sorts of things: regulate private activities, provide services, refrain from using some types of taxes, limit tax rates, utilize a particular personnel system—the possibilities are enormous.[43]

The usual term for this phenomenon is "mandate." The state mandates that a local government perform a certain service or activity. A state may, for example, require that counties provide certain programs for prisoners housed in county jails. In some cases these mandates are federal mandates passed from the state to the local governments. In either situation, this is generally not a major problem as long as the higher-level government (federal or state) provides full funding to the local government for the mandated program. But, states often mandate a specific local government action but do not provide the full funding to carry it out. This is called a "partially unfunded mandate." Sometimes the state requires local action but provides none of the funding (a fully unfunded mandate). Obviously, if the state (or federal) government does not provide the funding for a mandate, the local government must find a way to pay for it out of its own-source revenues. This is a source of tremendous frustration for local governments, especially those that rely heavily on property taxes for their own-source revenues. As one Illinois elected official noted, "Illinois residents pay the highest property taxes in the nation. Much of this can be attributed to the fact that we have the most units of government, and an ever-increasing number of state unfunded mandates."[44]

Because county governments historically are administrative arms of the state, they seem more likely to feel the brunt of unfunded or partially funded mandates. A recent report from the New York State Association of Counties lamented "the large number of state programs must administer and fund with local resources. . . . The State partially reimburses counties for administering and paying for these mandated services, but the shortfall is made up by county property taxpayers."[45] In Texas, one organization reported that while counties are mandated to provide a legal defense for indigent defendants, the state only reimburses $37 million for a mandate that cost the counties $260 million in attorney fees.[46] What makes this especially exasperating for local officials is that many state legislatures have passed laws to prevent the state (including the legislature) from passing unfunded mandates. But these laws are often ignored. The state of Washington is one that does, even though unfunded mandates were banned through popular initiatives passed in 1979 and 1993. Yet, such mandates still occur. For example, in 2018 the Washington legislature passed a bill allowing same-day voter registration, a law that would impact election officials at the county level, but the legislature provided no funds for its implementation. The director of the Washington Association of Counties expressed his frustration; "We're managing on the edge of risk. I think [the counties] feel backed into a corner with no option at this point."[47] By June 2019, the counties announced that they were likely to file a lawsuit against the state in hopes of putting a stop to the unfunded mandate problem.[48]

Unfunded or underfunded mandates are a source of annoyance for many local governments. But, recently, another cause of strain is the increasing use of legislative preemption by states against local governments. Preemption prohibits a local government from undertaking a specific action. The tension can be especially acute between a state legislature and the larger cities and more urban counties within the state. As one legal scholar notes, "recent years have seen a sharp increase in express preemption of local policy."[49] She attributes this increase to two things: the polarized politics and interest group lobbying. One recent study confirms that "politically conservative states are the most likely to use preemption," although other variables are also at play.[50]

In recent years, most state legislatures have been in the hands of Republican majorities and therefore pursued conservative policies. At the same time many urban areas have elected liberal officeholders who pursue a progressive political agenda, in part because cities tend to have a younger and better educated population compared to the rest of the state.[51] The potential for conflict is clear, and recent examples abound. Since 2012, for example, forty-six cities and counties have passed legislation raising their minimum wage above the federal level.[52] But in some instances state legislatures have blocked these efforts. When Birmingham, Alabama, adopted such a measure, the GOP-controlled state legislature passed a bill barring any local government from passing a law raising its minimum wage above that set at the state level. A Republican state representative conceded, "While we say we want local control of certain things, I don't believe the minimum wage is one of those. . . . No one ever envisioned that cities would do this."[53]

Republican-controlled state legislatures have also passed preemption laws to curb local governments (usually cities) from enacting plastic bag bans, firearms restrictions, paid sick leave mandates, and occupational licensing requirements. Some states have prevented local governments from banning or regulating Uber drivers or the use of e-cigarettes. In 2015, Oklahoma passed a measure preventing local governments from barring hydraulic fracturing (fracking). Texas did the same after the city of Denton passed an anti-fracking ordinance. In 2019, several states moved to preempt their local governments from passing restrictive ordinances on vacation rentals.

One new development in the ongoing battle over preemption laws is that state governments under Democratic control have begun to deploy them. In 2019, for example, both Illinois and New Mexico adopted measures blocking local governments in their states from passing right-to-work measures.[54] And Colorado repealed a state law that had prohibited local governments from setting a higher minimum wage.[55] Of course, governors can also play a role in this fight. In 2019 the Florida legislature passed a bill limiting the ability of cities in the state to ban plastic straws, but the Republican governor vetoed the attempted preemption measure.[56]

It is usually clear that states have the legal authority to pass preemption laws. As we might expect, however, local government officials bristle at them. When Columbia, Missouri, considered a measure to ban the use of plastic bags in stores, the Republican-dominated state legislature passed a bill blocking any such efforts in the state. A city council member who had been a Republican candidate for the legislature responded, "While I'm opposed to local governments, or anyone, banning useful products, I am even more opposed to our state representatives getting involved in our local issues."[57] Similar sentiments were expressed by local government officials in North Carolina in the aftermath of the "bathroom bill" controversy. Greensboro's mayor fumed, "It's frustrating when you have a legislature, who instead of taking care of their business, is sticking their nose in our business."[58] Some voters appear to agree. A Missouri farmer unhappy that the state legislature had passed a bill prohibiting county officials from adopting more stringent rules regulating concentrated animal feeding operations (CAFO) than the state standards, observed "It's kind of ironic. The state doesn't want the federal government telling them what to do. Well then, why would the state want to tell the locals what to do?"[59] A Republican legislator in North Carolina countered such claims by arguing, "The state government is the government that's closest to the people. . . . If you don't like it, run for state government and try and change it."[60]

Finally, we should reemphasize that states not only sometimes preempt what local governments can do in making certain local policies, but states can pass mandates for local governments. In other words, for the most part states can tell their local governments what they are *forbidden* to do, but—just as importantly—states can tell local governments what they *must* do.[61] For local governments, local government officials, and local citizens, state governments and state-elected officials really do matter.

8

Elections and Political Parties

States matter because:

- ★ All elections in the United States, including the presidential election, are conducted at the *state* or local level.
- ★ Almost all electoral rules of candidacy, qualifications, timing, and so on are *state* rules.
- ★ Congressional districts are drawn by *state* officials.
- ★ Candidates for federal (national) office often are former *state* elected officials.
- ★ Most *state* judges are elected, whereas no federal judge is elected.
- ★ Instruments of direct democracy—the initiative, the referendum, and the recall—exist in many *states* but not at the national level, and these instruments have an important effect on public policy.
- ★ The presidential nominees are chosen by delegates in a series of fifty separate *state* events.
- ★ The mechanism by which we choose the president is the Electoral College, which is a *state*-based system.
- ★ Political parties build their base at the *state* electoral level.

IN THE SUMMER OF 2019, a renowned scholar of American politics was quoted as conceding, "The state legislatures are probably just as important as the presidency. In a lot of ways, they're the whole ballgame."[1]

In our view, she is correct. Electoral laws in the United States are largely produced at the state level. This includes the rules defining the procedures for registering to vote, how elections are conducted, whether electoral districts are drawn to advantage one political party over the other, and even how winners are determined. States, and especially state legislatures and state courts, have central roles in this process. But, until recently, few people recognized that, indeed, state elections are often crucially important in determining the direction of the nation.

THE IMPORTANCE OF STATE ELECTIONS IN THE AMERICAN FEDERAL SYSTEM

Arguably, the oddest fact about the American electoral system is that there are no truly nationwide elections; none. In the United States, all elections are conducted by the states. For example, the president is not elected in a nationwide popular vote but in a series of fifty-one elections (the fifty *states* plus the District of Columbia), all of which now happen on the same day. The purpose of these fifty-one separate elections is to choose a total of 538 individuals (called "electors") who, a month later, cast the actual votes for president. This is the procedure known as the Electoral College. The manner in which these "electors" are chosen is a matter for each state to decide. Thus, the president is not selected through a national popular vote but by a group of intermediaries who are chosen through a series of state elections.

What about the U.S. Congress—the legislative branch? The 435 members of the U.S. House of Representatives are elected in 435 separate districts apportioned by *state*. And surprisingly, the rules for election are not the same in all 435 districts. This is because most of the rules for administering them are determined by each state, not the national government. And of course, each *state* elects two individuals to represent it in the U.S. Senate. And again, the rules by which each state chooses its two U.S. senators are not necessarily the same.

To illustrate this point, consider the 2018 U.S. Senate election in California. Since 2010 California has employed a "top-two" primary system in which all candidates, regardless of party affiliation, run in the same primary election. The top two vote-getters, again regardless of party affiliation, face one another in the November general election. A total of thirty-two candidates entered the contest (ten Democrats, eleven Republicans, nine Independents, one Libertarian, and one from the Peace and Freedom Party). The top two vote-getters ended up being the Democratic incumbent Diane Feinstein with 44 percent of the vote, and Democrat Kevin De Leon, with 12 percent of the vote. The highest-polling Republican was James Brady with 8 percent of the primary vote. Thus, the November 2018, U.S. Senate race in California was between two Democrats, and in that election the Democrat Feinstein defeated the Democrat De Leon, 6 million votes to 5.1 million votes.[2]

The larger point is that the electoral rules of California (a state) defined the vote choice for a U.S. Senate (national) office. In fact, the same phenomenon happened in four more races for federal office in California in 2018. Because of the top-two primary rules in California, three U.S. House races in that state featured a Democrat against a Democrat in the November general election, while another one pitted a Republican against another Republican.

Another election in 2018, this time in Maine, provides an additional example of how state rules can affect the outcome of a federal office. In 2016, voters in Maine approved a ballot initiative to develop a new voting method in certain elective offices. This includes elections for Maine's congressional delegation. The new system went into effect in 2018 and had an immediate impact in the election in Maine's second congressional district. As shown in table 8.1, there were four candidates in the general election: the incumbent congressman Republican Bruce Poliquin, the Democrat Jared Golden, and two Independent candidates, Tiffany Bond and William Hoar.

The new system goes by several names, but in Maine it is called "ranked-choice voting" (RCV).[3] Under RCV the voter ranks the candidates by her preference, so that her most preferred candidate is ranked "1," her next preferred candidate is ranked "2," and so on. If no candidate receives a majority of "first-place" votes, the candidates with the fewest votes are eliminated but the "second-choice" votes on those ballots are "transferred" to the remaining candidates. This process continues until one candidate has a majority of votes. The idea is that this system facilitates the election of someone who is "acceptable" to a majority of voters.

In the Maine Congressional District 2 general election in November 2018, the incumbent Bruce Poliquin received more first preference votes than anyone else; he had 134,184 votes, while the runner-up, Jared Golden, had 132,013 first preference votes. The two independent candidates received 16,552 (Bond) and 6,875 (Hoar) votes, totaling 23,427 first preference votes between them. In terms of percentages, Poliquin received 46.3 percent, Golden 45.6 percent, and the two Independents received a total of about 8 percent combined. Under the "plurality wins" rule used in most places in the United States, the incumbent Poliquin would have been declared the winner. But, because Poliquin failed to get a majority under the new RCV rules, the independent candidates were

Table 8.1. Ranked Choice Voting in Maine's 2nd Congressional District, 2018

Candidate	First ballot count		Transfers	Second ballot count	
	Votes	Percentage		Votes	Percentage
T. Bond	16,552	5.7	−16,552	0	—
W. Hoar	6,875	2.4	−6,875	0	—
J. Golden	132,013	45.6	+10,427	142,440	50.6
B. Poliquin	134,184	46.3	+ 4,747	138,931	49.4

dropped and their second-preference votes were transferred to the remaining candidates. As table 8.1 shows, among the voters who originally chose Bond or Hoar, many more of them preferred Golden (10,427 second preference votes) as their second choice than preferred Poliquin (4,727 second preference votes). Thus, Golden received 132,013 first-place votes plus 10,427 second-place votes, giving him 142,440 total votes; Poliquin tallied 134,184 first-place votes plus 4,747 second-place votes, giving him 138,931 total votes.[4] Under RCV rules, Golden was declared the winner of the Maine Second Congressional District race. The point, again, is that state electoral rules determine winners of federal offices. And not all states use the same electoral rules.

While the California and Maine examples show how the state rules can affect a general election, state rules also affect party primary nomination races. In Texas, candidates seeking the party nomination for U.S. Senate, U.S. House, statewide races, and state legislative races must win a majority of the votes cast. If there is no majority winner in the primary, the top two vote-getters face each other in a runoff election. In the 2012 Republican primary for U.S. senator, this rule became crucial.

The primary was held in May. The major candidates in the race were lieutenant governor of Texas David Dewhurst and Tea Party favorite Ted Cruz, making his first run for office.[5] A well-known and longtime elected official in Texas, Dewhurst was the overwhelming favorite and he received 145,000 more votes than second-place finisher Cruz. Dewhurst won over 44 percent of the vote compared to Cruz's 34 percent, with the rest of the vote being split among seven other candidates.

But the electoral rule in Texas primaries is that a candidate must receive a majority of the total vote to win the nomination—and 44 percent is not a majority. In the runoff election held nine weeks later, Cruz turned the tables and won by a substantial margin. He went on to defeat his Democratic opponent in the general election, and a few years later became a player in the Republican presidential campaign in 2016. If Texas did not have a majoritarian rule for its state primaries, Ted Cruz would not have been elected to the U.S. Senate in 2012. Clearly, state electoral rules do indeed matter.

NATIONAL POLITICAL FIGURES OFTEN COME FROM THE STATES

Elected officials at the state level are sometimes characterized as the "farm teams" for national office. After all, about half of all members of Congress are former state legislators (since 2005 the percentage has consistently ranged between 45 and 51 percent). Since 1975, four of the seven presidents (Carter, Reagan, Clinton, and George W. Bush) were former governors and another (Obama) had been a state senator. In other words, the president of the United States was a former state elected official in all but eight years in a forty-five-year period. During that time only Presidents George H. W. Bush and Donald Trump had never served in any state office. Throughout American history most presidents have;

indeed, more former governors (eighteen) have served in the office than have U.S. senators (sixteen).[6]

Despite the anomalous 2016 presidential race—both the major party candidates had never served in state government, although for many years Hillary Clinton was Arkansas' first lady—the United States has a long history of choosing candidates for national office who have state political experience. This is not the case in all federal systems. In Canada, for example, provincial and national political careers are largely separate tracks; only a small proportion of the Canadian Parliament previously served in the provincial legislative assemblies.[7] And in Germany, the flow of personnel often runs the other direction; state parliamentary leaders are drawn from the ranks of the national parliament.[8] But in the United States, states provide both a "farm system" and a place for the out party to rebuild its strength. And sometimes, as in 2010, the out party can rebuild very quickly. The Republican Party lost its congressional majority in 2006, the presidency in 2008, and over five hundred state legislative seats in 2006 and 2008 combined. But in 2010, they gained some seven hundred state legislative seats nationally, as well as regaining control of the U.S. House of Representatives. The point here is that these gains were made through elections at the state level.

But the flow of talent in the United States is not just in one direction. At the start of 2020, nine of the fifty governors were former members of the U.S. Congress. As noted in chapter 5, the proportion of governors with congressional experience is higher now than it used to be. This is an important point because it highlights the political significance of the states. Strategic politicians do not voluntarily give up a seat in Congress to run for governor "back home" unless they perceive that being governor is a more meaningful position.[9] In other words, they recognize that states matter.

STATE PARTY AND ELECTORAL SYSTEMS

In this chapter, we discuss state electoral structures and state political party systems and how they influence federal politics. Electoral laws and party systems are separate but related topics. The electoral structure affects the nature of the party system.

Because both the media and education establishments in the United States place heavy emphasis on the role of the national government, many people are unaware of the variation in electoral laws and political party strength across the states. Far more than most people realize, state electoral laws differ. Here we will focus on four of these differences: electoral rules, redistricting, direct democracy, and term limits.

We will also look at political party systems at the state level and note how the state party systems interface with the national parties. Political parties are not equally competitive in all states. We will explore the consequences of this fact, from recruitment to policy impacts.

Finally, we discuss the ways in which national elective office in the United States is heavily influenced by state-based politics. This is clearly true in Congress, by virtue of the fact that its members are chosen from the states. It is also true because of that unique American mechanism known as the Electoral College. Born of a new federal system of government more than two centuries ago, the Electoral College is an important illustration that even national offices are heavily influenced by state politics—as was intended by the Founders. Indeed, an Electoral College–type mechanism was first devised by Maryland to elect members of its state senate.

To emphasize the state-based nature of the national electoral system, we can point to the recent movement to repeal the Seventeenth Amendment to the Constitution—a movement especially embraced by "Tea Party" enthusiasts. As we discussed in chapter 2, originally the Constitution stipulated that U.S. senators were to be chosen by their own states' legislature. Obviously, this provision empowered state legislatures and it remained in effect for 125 years. But corruption in some state legislatures in the late nineteenth century, coupled with the drive toward greater participatory democracy as embodied in the Progressive reform era, led to a widespread movement to have senators directly elected by the voters rather than chosen by state legislatures. This was achieved with the ratification of the Seventeenth Amendment in 1913.

Today, some political activists contend that the states would be better served by repealing the Seventeenth Amendment and reverting to a system whereby state legislatures would choose senators. Their argument centers on the notion that senators would be more sensitive to state interests rather than national interests if they were selected by state legislators. It is unlikely that such a movement will succeed for many reasons. In any event, our point remains that U.S. senators are chosen through mechanisms that are located in the states. And, again, that there are no national elections.

But it is also the case, perhaps increasingly so, that the national partisan and electoral system affects the states. Today, candidates running for *state* office often run by campaigning for or against *national* elected officials. There also is abundant evidence that many voters choose state officials on the basis of national issues or politics. It seems some voters do not appreciate the difference between state issues and national issues, or state candidates and national candidates. The blurring of national issues or officials with elections for state offices makes it more difficult for voters to hold elected state officials accountable. This is a key observation, and one that is will be discussed in more detail later in this chapter.

STATE ELECTORAL RULES

Sometimes it takes an outside perspective to truly grasp how different the American system is and how important the states are in it. The venerable British newsmagazine *The Economist*, with proper British spelling and syntax, recently reported, "America organises its democracy differently from other rich countries. Each state writes its own voting laws, there is no national register of eligible voters and no form of ID that is both acceptable in all polling booths and held by everyone."[10] It is, in other words, a crazy quilt system of electoral laws, one largely constructed by the states but with substantial impact on elections for the national offices—the president and vice president, the U.S. House of Representatives, and the U.S. Senate.

As improbable as it may seem, there are more than five hundred thousand elected government officials in the United States.[11] And 99.9 percent of them are officials elected by rules established in the states. As noted earlier, even the 537 elected federal offices are influenced by state electoral laws—laws that define the way primary elections operate, for example. And state electoral laws vary in many ways, among them voter eligibility, ballot structure, district magnitude, and timing of elections. Here we focus on five important ways that states matter when it comes to electoral rules.

1. The prevalence of single-member districts using plurality rules

For legislative bodies in a representative democracy, there are many ways to translate votes into seats. While there are a number of crucial decisions that go into creating an electoral system for translating votes to seats, two are paramount. The first is district magnitude: How many officials will be elected from each district? The choice ranges from one (a single-member district) to two or more representatives being elected in each district (multimember district) to the entire legislature being elected at large.

The second key decision is the allocation formula: On what basis do we decide who wins a seat? The choices are plurality, majority, and proportional (seats are allocated proportionate to the total votes received) or some combination thereof. This is not the place for a lengthy discussion of the variety of electoral systems that have evolved around the world based on these two key decisions.[12] But it is important to recognize there are consequences to the way an electoral system is structured—consequences for the party system, for the nature of campaigning, and even for the way we think about the job of the representative.[13]

In the United States, the most common method employed is single-member, plurality (SMP) elections—known in many places as "first past the post." Under this system, one person is elected per district. The person elected is the one who received more votes than any other candidate. Like all electoral systems, SMP has certain characteristics. It is generally thought to be a system that reinforces a two-party political system, creates a substantial degree of incumbent stability, and fosters a direct link between constituents and their elected legislator. All of these features have implications for politics.

The SMP system is so prevalent in the modern United States that we might mistakenly think it is the only one used. But there are some American states that use other systems, at least for a few offices. For example, South Dakota requires that a nominee receive a majority (not just a plurality) of votes cast in the primary elections for governor, U.S. senator, and U.S. representative. Several other states, mostly in the South, have similar rules: Alabama, Arkansas, Georgia, Mississippi, Oklahoma, South Carolina, and Texas.[14] If no candidate receives a majority in the first election, a runoff between the top two vote-getters is held several weeks later.

Some states use multimember districts (MMDs) for state legislative seats.[15] Fifty years ago, over forty states used MMDs for at least some of their legislative seats.[16] That number has declined dramatically over the years. Currently, only ten states use MMDs for all or some house legislative districts, while two states (Vermont and West Virginia) use them for their state senate.[17] The most common form is a two-member plurality district. Each voter casts two votes, and the two candidates with the most votes win. But in New Hampshire, as many as eleven members are chosen from a single district, and in Vermont, as many as six state senators are chosen from a single district. At one time, some states used multimember districts to choose their members of Congress, but that practice ended by 1967.[18]

Single-member districts are usually smaller geographic units with fewer constituents per district. Multimember districts are typically larger with more people contained in each district, especially if there are four or more officials per district. In terms of representational theory, there are advantages and disadvantages to each system. Single-member districts are smaller and easier to gerrymander (a process which will be discussed later in this chapter). Consequently, some argue, they are likely to lead to more safe seats in which one party dominates. This in turn can accentuate polarization because many legislators will represent districts that are overwhelmingly Republican, while others will represent districts that are overwhelmingly Democratic.[19] There is an appealing logic to the argument that single-member districts facilitate safe seats and therefore exacerbate polarization. But there is little evidence that multimember districts would by themselves eliminate polarization.[20]

It is also important to note that Georgia and Louisiana require a majority vote in the general election to win (at least for some offices). The "top-two" primary system used in California and Washington also forces a majoritarian requirement in the general election (because there can only be two contestants in the general election). And, as previously discussed, the ranked-choice vote (RCV) system in use for certain offices in Maine is another way to produce a majority vote. Some people favor RCV because it allows voters' preferences to continue to be considered even if no one candidate receives a majority on the first ballot. Some think this system discourages the election of ideologically extreme candidates and therefore may help dampen polarization.[21]

Obscure provisions of Mississippi's constitution (Article 5, Sections 140 and 141) impose yet another form of a majority vote rule to win statewide offices in that state. Not only does a winner need to get a majority of the popular vote, but he or she must also win the vote in 62 of the state's 122 state House of Representatives districts. If no candidate succeeds on both scores, the election is decided by the members of the state House of Representatives who are limited to choosing between the top two candidates but are not bound to vote as their districts voted. This variant of an electoral college system was imposed when the state adopted its current constitution in 1890 to ensure that whites would control statewide election outcomes. A legal challenge to this provision was filed in federal court in 2019, claiming that it discriminates against minority voters.[22]

As discussed in chapter 7, state law also applies to local governments, of course. And some states allow their local governmental units considerable latitude in electoral design. Unusual (by American standards) voting systems such as the cumulative vote, limited vote, and ranked choice vote are used in some local jurisdictions in the United States. But again, it is important to emphasize that this is all a matter of *state* law and that local governments cannot establish electoral systems that are not permissible under state law, as the cities of Austin, Texas, and Vancouver, Washington, discovered. Both cities adopted ranked-choice voting for municipal elections but were prevented from employing it because state law in both Texas and Washington prohibits such voting systems.[23] The RCV system is, however, allowed for municipal elections in a few other states, notably California (used in Berkeley, Oakland, San Francisco, and San Leandro), Colorado (Basalt and Telluride), Maine (Portland), Maryland (Takoma Park), Minnesota (Minneapolis, Saint Paul, and St. Louis Park), and New Mexico (Las Cruces and Santa Fe).[24]

2. The election schedule

Not all elections are held concurrently with the presidential contest. In fact, most states hold elections for their governors and other statewide officials (such as attorney general) in a year other than the presidential election year. The reason is obvious: the presidential contest commands much time, media focus, and campaign resources. Within the last half-century, most states moved the election for their own chief executives (the governors) to what is known as the "off-year"—the even numbered years in which the presidency is not on the ballot. Thus, while presidential elections are scheduled in 2020, 2024, 2028, and so on, thirty-four states will hold gubernatorial and other statewide elections in 2022, 2026, and so on. Granted, there are still congressional contests in those years, but these are really state elections, even though taken collectively they usually have national implications. Additionally, a few states such as New Jersey, Virginia, Louisiana, and Mississippi go even further and hold their state elections in odd-numbered years, when there are no presidential *or* congressional races at all. Perhaps the strangest arrangement is Kentucky's; the Bluegrass State holds its election for governor and other executive officers (secretary of state, etc.) in an odd-numbered year (2019, 2023) but its state legislative races in an even-numbered year (2020, 2022, 2024).

Focusing on statewide elections for governor, then, we find the following arrangements: two states (New Hampshire and Vermont) elect their governor every two years in even numbered years, thirty-four states hold their governor's election every four years in the even-numbered nonpresidential years, and five states hold governor's elections in odd-numbered years.[25] Only nine states are on the same gubernatorial electoral cycle as the presidential electoral cycle. That is, nine states have four-year electoral cycles that are held at the same time as the presidential election. But because New Hampshire and Vermont have elections every two years, there are actually eleven states holding gubernatorial elections during the presidential election year.

3. Judicial elections

A major difference between the states and the federal government, as noted in chapter 4, is that while no federal judge is elected, *most* state judges must win election in some way or another.[26] This includes state courts of last resort judges in over forty states.

Most state judges are chosen through one of three types of elections: partisan, nonpartisan, or retention. The most common is a retention election, a procedure whereby judges who are initially selected by the governor for an initial term of office must eventually stand for election for a full term, with the question being whether they should be retained on the bench or not.

The financing of judicial campaigns is currently a major topic of discussion in a number of states. A recent example is the 2019 election for the Wisconsin Supreme Court. While the election of the Supreme Court is a nonpartisan election in Wisconsin, the last decade has witnessed a clear ideological divide on the Wisconsin Court. When incumbent Justice Shirley Abrahamson decided to retire, the election to replace her was fraught with ideological implications. Over six million dollars was spent on the campaign; about half by the candidates themselves and about half by outside groups with an ideological stake in the outcome.[27] It was not an isolated episode. In 2016, over $3 million was spent on another Wisconsin Supreme Court race. Most of that money was not spent by the candidates but by independent groups.[28] Even more dramatic was the level of independent spending outside the candidates' control; the Chamber of Commerce spent over $5 million in support of one of the candidates.[29] In 2008, two candidates for the Michigan Supreme Court spent $2.5 million between them, and interest groups allied with one or the other candidates spent another $3.8 million.[30] In Alabama, a 2008 supreme court race cost over $4 million.[31]

Even retention races have become expensive. As mentioned in chapter 3, in Iowa in 2010, three Supreme Court justices were voted out because of their decision in support of gay marriage. Interestingly, most of the money spent on the campaign to oust the justices came from out of state.[32] This too has become commonplace. A similar story unfolded in 2016 in Kansas, where the Republican-dominated legislature and the state supreme court continued their long-standing clash over public education funding. Up for retention were five of the nine justices, and the campaigns for and against them totaled over $2 million. As a veteran observer of Kansas politics noted, "Without a doubt, we are going to see a tremendous amount of money spent on judicial elections—retention elections—in Kansas."[33] The issue here is not just that judicial elections are expensive, but that some of the donors to the candidates, and virtually all of the groups engaging in independent spending, appear before the courts in one or more cases.

4. Primary election rules

One of the most obvious ways in which state electoral laws affect national politics is through the rules for nominating candidates—that is, deciding which candidate will represent each political party in the general election. The rules are complex, involving (1) who can vote in the primary, (2) when the primary is held, and (3) what determines a winner in the primary. Moreover, the rules may not be the same for each party in the same state, particularly in regard to who can vote. Finally, the rules may differ within a state between presidential nominations and other nominations. Indeed, the presidential and nonpresidential nomination systems within a state are different enough that we will discuss the presidential system by itself in a later section. For now, we concentrate on the nomination system for offices other than president.

Each state decides when to hold its primary election. The primary calendar for 2020 is shown in table 8.2. States decide for themselves when to hold their nominating events (primary elections, conventions, etc.). Note that this is the primary calendar for the nomination of candidates for state office, not the presidential primary in each state. Some states hold their presidential primary at the same time, but most do not. In 2020, over thirty states held their primaries for state offices at a different date than their presidential primaries. For example, the Arizona state primary was scheduled for August 4, but the state held its presidential primary on March 17—four months earlier.

In 2020, state primary elections were spread over a seven-month span, from March 3 (Alabama, California, North Carolina, and Texas) to September 15 (Delaware, Massachusetts, and Rhode Island). The most popular months for primary elections were June (twelve states) and August (fourteen states). Seven states held primaries in March and another seven held theirs in May. Meanwhile, the presidential primary or caucus dates for each state were generally earlier on the calendar, running from February to June. Most states (twenty-nine) held their presidential primaries in March.

Each state (or state party) decides who can vote in the primary election. Primary elections (or conventions in a few states) determine the party nominees for the general election. One of the issues each state must address, therefore, is who should be allowed to vote in the primary election: anyone who is

Table 8.2. Calendar of Primary Elections for State Offices, 2020

March	April	May	June	July	August	September
Alabama	Maryland	Georgia	Colorado		Alaska	Delaware
Arkansas	Pennsylvania	Idaho	Iowa		Arizona	Massachusetts
California		Indiana	Maine		Connecticut	N. Hampshire
Illinois		Kentucky	Montana		Florida	Rhode Island
N. Carolina		Nebraska	Nevada		Hawaii	
Ohio		Oregon	New York		Kansas	
Texas		W.Virginia	N. Mexico		Michigan	
			N. Dakota		Minnesota	
			Oklahoma		Missouri	
			S. Carolina		Tennessee	
			S. Dakota		Vermont	
			Utah		Washington	
					Wisconsin	
					Wyoming	

Note: Louisiana, Mississippi, New Jersey, and Virginia hold congressional and some local elections in 2020, but state office elections are held in odd years.

Source: National Conference of State Legislatures.

registered to vote in the general election or only those who are registered as members of the political party. The parties themselves usually argue that only those who are registered members of the party should be able to determine who the party nominees will be. State parties see this as a matter of the "right of association." Others, however, argue that the choices available in the general election are determined by the results of the primary election; therefore, everyone who is interested should have the right to help make those choices. These two arguments represent the philosophies behind the closed primary and the open primary.

In truth, there are several shades of open and closed; in some states the primary is closed only to registered members of the other party but not to independent or unaffiliated voters. One authoritative source determines that twenty-one states are truly open and nine states are truly closed (see table 8.3). The remaining states reflect considerable variation. Semi-open systems require that a voter publicly declare which party primary ballot he or she wishes to vote. To further complicate this process, the two major parties within a state may use different systems. In Alaska, for example, only those who are registered Republicans, nonpartisans, or undeclared can vote in the GOP primary, while all registered voters can vote in the Democratic primary.[34]

Finally, there are a few states that use a system called a "top-two" primary (also known as a "Cajun Primary" because Louisiana was the first state to adopt it). In a "top-two" system, all the candidates for a particular office are listed together on the ballot, regardless of party affiliation. The two highest vote-getters, even if they are from the same party, face each other in the general election. Thus, as noted at the beginning of this chapter, it is possible to have two Republicans (or two Democrats) run against one another in the general election. All registered voters, regardless of party affiliation, are permitted to vote in a "top-two" primary.

There are practical effects to the distinction between open and closed primaries. Among those states that conduct truly open primaries for both parties, there is no reason to require voters to register by party. As a consequence, in these states, parties, interest groups, and candidates find it more difficult to target specific voters.[35] While they may have a list of who voted in previous primaries, they do not have a list of who voted in *which* primary (the Republican or the Democratic one). Consequently, communicating with voters is less efficient (and therefore costlier). In a strictly closed system in which voters register by party, a ready-made list of voter contacts exists.

The open versus closed nature of the primary may also affect the nature of the message a candidate seeks to deliver. In a strictly closed primary, Republican candidates may be more likely to take more conservative issue positions, while Democratic candidates may espouse a decidedly liberal point of view. After all, the eligible voters in a strictly closed primary are likely to be among the more conservative elements in the Republican primary and the more liberal elements in the Democratic primary. Because independents and others cannot

Table 8.3. Primary Election Systems

Primary system	Open	Semi-open (voter must publicly declare which ballot he chooses)	One-party closed (one party has closed primary; other party permits unaffiliated voters to participate)	Closed	Top-two
States using primary system	Alabama Arkansas Georgia Hawaii Illinois Indiana Iowa Michigan Minnesota Mississippi Missouri Montana N. Dakota Ohio S. Carolina Tennessee Texas Vermont Virginia Wisconsin Wyoming	Arizona Colorado Kansas Maine Massachusetts New Hampshire New Jersey Rhode Island West Virginia	Alaska Connecticut Idaho N. Carolina Oklahoma S. Dakota Utah	Delaware Florida Kentucky Maryland Nevada New Mexico New York Ohio Pennsylvania	California Louisiana Washington Nebraska*
Total	21	9	7	9	4

*Nebraska holds top-two elections only for non-partisan Unicameral (state legislature).
Source: National Conference of State Legislatures, "State Party Election Types," June 2018, http://www.ncsl.org/research/elections-and-campaigns/primary-types.aspx.

participate, the candidates, in essence, preach to the choir—the party faithful. But in open or top-two primary systems, the electorate represents a broader spectrum of policy positions. It was this assumption that led California voters to adopt the top-two primary in 2010. The first election under the new system was held in 2012, and while there have been too few elections under the new system to allow for definitive assessments, the available evidence is decidedly mixed, suggesting at best only a moderate impact on candidate and voter behavior.[36]

5. Voter eligibility and access rules

In some regards, federal policies have diminished the amount of latitude that states have in determining voter eligibility. In particular, several amendments to the U.S. Constitution were adopted to specifically prohibit the discriminatory practices of some states (e.g., the Fifteenth and Nineteenth Amendments, which prohibited the states from denying the right to vote based on race or sex, respectively) or to establish a national standard (e.g., the Twenty-Sixth Amendment, which standardized the legal voting age at eighteen years). Federal influence over voter eligibility and access certainly is not limited to the several constitutional amendments. Congressional actions such as the 1965 Voting Rights Act (and its subsequent renewals) and the 1993 National Voter Registration Act (commonly known as the Motor-Voter Bill) are well-known examples of significant federal mandates. The 2002 Help Americans Vote Act (HAVA), while not specifically targeted at voter eligibility and access, is another example of federal action in the electoral process, in this case seeking to upgrade and partially standardize the mechanics and administration of voting in the states.

In 2013, the U.S. Supreme Court reconsidered certain aspects of the 1965 Voting Rights Act (VRA).[37] A key provision of the 1965 VRA was Section 5, which provided for federal oversight of the administration of electoral laws in states where discriminatory practices had previously existed. For the most part, Section 5 applied to southern states. In striking down the essence of Section 5, the Court reduced federal control over the electoral law decisions of those states. This in turn has led a number of these states to change electoral laws in ways that will likely impact voter participation in some instances. In particular, some states have reduced early voting periods and increased the requirements for registration and voting, arguing such restrictions are necessary to protect electoral integrity.

Meanwhile, other states have expanded voter registration, encouraging greater voter participation. Automatic voter registration (AVR), adopted in full by fifteen states with another three states passing measures similar to it, appears to have had a substantial impact. According to a 2019 analysis, "AVR, markedly increases the number of voters being registered—increases in the number of registrants ranging from 9 to 94 percent."[38] Of course, there are significant partisan implications for all of these changes in voter registration rules. As one analysis noted, "In some states, Republican-led legislatures restricted voting access in ways that experts say would disproportionately affect Democratic voters. In more states, however, Democratic-led legislatures opened access in ways that could help that same voting bloc undermine Republicans."[39]

Rules are never neutral; they always constrain or promote certain behaviors. Electoral rules can encourage or discourage the participation of specific groups or individuals. Therefore, changes in such rules almost always advantage or disadvantage particular groups and political parties. Obviously, changes to electoral rules are easier to push through when one political party controls both chambers of the legislature as well as the governor's office. In other words, changes in electoral law occur more often in times of unified government, especially when the parties are polarized.[40] But it is worth noting that bipartisan reforms do occasionally occur. In 2016, GOP-leaning Alaska voters adopted AVR, and West Virginia lawmakers managed to pass a voter reform bill with support from both parties by combining an automatic registration process of the sort supported by Democrats with voter identification requirements along the lines that Republicans back.[41]

Other sorts of reforms can be important. For example, whether or not a state conducts elections by mail, as Colorado, Oregon, and Washington do, has important consequences beyond just partisan considerations. The consequences for the potential voter are obvious—it makes voting more convenient. A voter can read campaign materials and fill out the ballot at his or her convenience, then slip it in the privacy-protected envelope and drop it in the mail.

For political parties and the candidates, any voting laws that promote early voting add to their planning and strategic burdens. In states where many people vote early, candidates must time their campaigns to coincide with when the ballots are made available to the voters—usually about three weeks prior to the scheduled Election Day. This means media buys and targeted mailings must be undertaken earlier and presumably sustained for a longer period of time.

All of the voting differences discussed do not exhaust the ways electoral rules vary across the states. Nevadans, for example, find a line on their ballots for "None of These Candidates" in U.S. presidential, U.S. Senate, and statewide contests (governor, lieutenant governor, secretary of state, state treasurer, state controller, attorney general, and justice of the supreme court). Relatively few voters vote that line in presidential races, but almost 20 percent do in judicial contests.[42] Vermont law requires that any statewide election for a state office where no candidate secures a majority of the vote is to be determined by the state legislature. Thus, when the incumbent governor, Democrat Peter Shumlin, finished first in the 2014 election with 46.4 percent of the vote, he did not automatically win. Instead because he failed to attain a majority, the contest was turned over to the state legislature to decide. It was the twenty-fourth time the Vermont legislature was forced to pick the winner. In early 2015, the 180 legislators chose Shumlin. (No second-place finisher has been selected by the state legislature since 1853.[43]) The point to keep in mind is that the electoral process differs from state to state in large and small ways.

REDISTRICTING

The American preference for single-member legislative districts and the "one person, one vote" conception of political equality means that redistricting is an important feature of state politics. Redistricting involves the redrawing of legislative district lines after each new federal census is released. It may seem obvious that the state is required to redraw those state legislative districts once new census data are available; after all, since the reapportionment revolution of the 1960s, we require each legislative district to have roughly the same population as every other district within the state. But what may not be so obvious is this: states are also charged with drawing the *congressional* lines within the state as well. In other words, every ten years all congressional districts are redrawn by the states.[44] In most states, the ultimate redistricting authority is the state legislature.[45] In other words, redistricting is achieved through statute—the legislature passes a bill laying out the boundaries of each legislative district and the governor signs it into law. Given the highly political nature of the issue, partisan control of the legislature and the governor's office are important advantages. If one party controls all three points of action—the lower state house, state senate, and governor's office—that party is in a strong position to implement a redistricting plan that benefits its interests and harms the opposition party. This is commonly referred to as a gerrymander, after the way Massachusetts governor Elbridge Gerry's party drew state legislative district lines to its advantage in 1812. These lines are critical because they (usually) stay in effect for a decade—until the next census.[46] And remember also that the state is drawing the lines for both the state legislature and the congressional districts within that state. For these reasons, state elections held in the "zero year" of a decade (2020, 2030, etc.) can have important consequences for partisan fortunes in both the state legislature *and* the U.S. House of Representatives. Because the census data are made available in the "one year" (e.g., 2021) and in most cases have to be used in redrawing district lines for the next decade starting in the "two year" (e.g., 2022), the election in the "zero year" determines who will be in control of the redistricting process.

It is clear that the Republican Party understood the importance of the 2010 state elections for the upcoming redistricting process for both state legislative districts and congressional districts.[47] Employing a strategy they called REDMAP (Redistricting Majority Project), the party identified the legislative chambers most likely to flip party control. They spent more than $30 million on state legislative races in 2010, hoping to turn some Democratic-controlled state legislative chambers into Republican-controlled chambers. They were immensely successful, winning over seven hundred additional legislative seats, gaining control of numerous chambers, and greatly enhancing the party's role in the redistricting process. Republicans gained unified control of eight additional states, including Michigan and Wisconsin—two states that were subsequently considered to have produced clear partisan gerrymanders. Another five states that had been under unified Democratic control shifted to divided control as a result of the 2010 election. The political implication is that under divided control the two parties must negotiate and compromise in a bipartisan manner to reach consensus on a redistricting plan. Had Democrats retained unified control, they would have controlled the redistricting process and been more likely to gerrymander some districts to their partisan advantage. Overall, Republicans added eight states to their list of unified control, and broke Democratic control in another five states, putting the GOP in a strong position to influence the drawing of electoral boundaries for both state legislative and congressional districts in those states. And these district lines typically stay in effect for ten years, until the next census and round of redistricting. Speaking in 2019 about the Republican victories due to their REDMAP strategy, one Democratic leader said, "We're still paying the price for getting wiped out in 2010."[48]

It is important to remember that the state legislature is responsible for redistricting the congressional districts within the state as well as the state legislative districts. That the Democrats were in a worse position to influence the drawing of congressional lines in states such as New York, North Carolina, Michigan, Ohio, and Wisconsin is not a trivial outcome of the 2010 state elections. Some have argued that the Republicans were able to maintain their majority in the U.S. House of Representatives from 2012 through 2016 precisely because the party had gained majorities in so many state legislatures in 2010 and were able to draw favorable congressional district lines in a number of states.[49] There is little doubt that gerrymandering in states like Michigan, North Carolina, and Pennsylvania inflated the Republican advantage in the U.S. House of Representatives after 2012. But other variables were certainly involved, including the fact that Democratic voters are more likely to cluster in urban areas, while Republican voters are more broadly distributed across suburban and rural areas. This is sometimes referred to as a "natural gerrymander," and is a common feature of a political system that relies on single-member districts.[50]

As one recent study concludes, "Without a doubt, gerrymandering makes things worse for the Democrats, but their underlying problem can be summed up with the old real estate maxim: location, location, location."[51] In other words, the spatial distribution of Democrats is less efficient than of Republicans, especially in a single-member legislative district system. Nonetheless, there is little doubt that the 2012 congressional election outcomes were altered by the 2010 shift in state legislative chambers. And, of course, state legislative elections were also affected.[52]

It appears the Democrats learned a costly lesson from the 2010 REDMAP experience. They created the National Democratic Redistricting Committee, under the direction of former U.S. attorney general Eric Holder, and are increasingly focused on fundraising for state legislative elections in targeted states. They now fully appreciate the importance of controlling state legislatures during the redistricting process.

In June 2019, the U.S. Supreme Court gave even greater weight to the partisan implications of the 2020 state legislative elections. In *Rucho v. Common Cause*, a much-anticipated decision, a closely divided Court ruled that partisan gerrymandering was a political question beyond the jurisdiction of the federal courts. The Court determined that questions involving it should be left to the states. [53] There is little doubt that *Rucho* will increase the intensity of legislative elections in states where control over redistricting remains in the legislature's hands, as both parties seek to gain control of drawing the lines.

There are, however, a growing number of states in which the redistricting process has been placed outside the immediate control of the legislature.[54] In these places, the drawing of the lines is usually controlled by an outside (independent) commission that has been granted authority to produce them. About one-third of the states now have some form of independent commission for redrawing lines for state legislative districts, congressional districts within the state, or both legislative and congressional districts.[55]

While these independent commissions are still subject to political and partisan pressures (i.e., they are usually not entirely "independent"), it is usually true that they are not as overtly partisan as the legislature. In other words, in terms of the political stakes for redistricting, the election results in the "zero year" are not quite as crucial in those states with independent redistricting commissions.

Commissions are more likely to be instituted in states with the initiative process, such as Arizona, California, and Washington. In 2018, four states held initiatives or referenda on redistricting commissions and all four passed them; voters in Colorado, Michigan, Missouri, and Utah approved commissions or some other mechanism to facilitate a more independent redistricting process. The specifics of how these commissions operate differ by state. Thus, heading into the next round of redistricting, the mechanics of how the process will play out will vary by state. In some the state legislature will draw the lines and in others a commission or some other external entity will do so.

The States and Direct Democracy

One of the key differences between policymaking at the state level compared to the national level is the potential for direct citizen action in many states. This is largely because of the availability in the states of the instruments of direct democracy known as the initiative, the referendum, and the recall. Virtually all states permit at least one of these instruments and almost one-third of the states allow all three forms. The national government allows none of them. In this sense, the public has a greater ability to inform, direct, or constrain the policy actions of elected officials at the state level than at the national level. It should also be pointed out, however, that in the past few years, elected officials in a number of states have moved to limit the use of these instruments by the public.

The recall. Between March 2011 and June 2012, one of the biggest election stories in the United States played out in Wisconsin. It was quite a tale—arguably unprecedented in American history. As part of the Republican electoral sweep in 2010, Wisconsin flipped from unified Democratic control to unified Republican control. It is unusual for a state government to flip from unified control by one party to unified control by the other in a single election.[56] With the Wisconsin Assembly, the Wisconsin Senate, and the Wisconsin governorship suddenly all firmly in the hands of Republicans, the new governor, Scott Walker, and the legislature made sweeping changes in the collective bargaining rights and the benefits packages of the state's public employee unions. The legislation did not pass without a fight; as the legislation was scheduled for a vote in the state senate, fourteen Democratic state senators actually fled the state to break a quorum and prevent action on the bill in the Senate.[57] At the same time there were mass public protests; according to one news account, "Capitol police estimated 25,000 people, many carrying signs protesting the Republican plan, converged on the state Capitol building . . . including 5,000 packed inside."[58]

Ultimately, the anti-union legislation narrowly passed on strict party line votes in both chambers and was then signed by the governor. Within days, petitions to recall some state senators were being circulated—under state law only those elected officials who had been in office for at least one year could be subject to a recall. By the summer of 2012, recall elections were held against thirteen state senators (ten Republicans and three Democrats), the lieutenant governor, and the governor. Never had there been so many recall elections held in the span of a year as occurred in Wisconsin. Ultimately, only three of the fifteen officials were defeated in the recall elections—all Republican state senators. A fourth Republican state senator resigned rather than face a recall vote. After a brutal and expensive campaign, Governor Walker retained his office with 53 percent of the vote. Over $125 million was spent on the Wisconsin recalls, including at least $75 million on the governor's recall alone.

One of the reasons that so much attention and so much money were lavished on the Wisconsin recalls is that the issues in play had national implications. Collective bargaining, public employee retirement obligations, and state budget constraints were issues playing out not just in Wisconsin, but in Indiana, Michigan, and Ohio as well. In effect, the recall elections in Wisconsin served as a plebiscite on public policy in a way that only happens at the state (or local) level in the United States.

While as many as thirty-nine states allow for the recall of local officials, only nineteen states permit the recall of state officials. The precise offices subject to the recall, and the procedures by which the recall is put into effect, vary among the states. Generally, the process required is that a petition calling for a recall election be circulated and a specific number of valid signatures must be gathered. If the petitioners meet this standard, a special election is called to remove the official from office. The process may be simple to comprehend, but it is rarely successful. As noted in chapter 4, only twice have governors been recalled from office. Since 1990, only twelve state legislators have been recalled (Arizona, California, Colorado, and Wisconsin offering the most recent examples).[59]

While it may be true the recall is only occasionally successfully executed, the mere threat of its use can influence public policy. A recent example involves Alaska, where in 2019 Governor Mike Dunleavy vetoed over $400 million dollars in the appropriations bill passed by the Alaska legislature, then drastically cut state spending to help pay for a higher "permanent fund dividend" (an annual payment to individual Alaska citizens based on an oil severance tax). Most of the cuts imposed by the governor were to higher education and social services. After several unsuccessful attempts by the legislature to override the governor's veto, a recall petition was begun against the governor. The reaction was stunning. Within two weeks, almost thirty thousand signatures were gathered, enough to trigger the next phase in a rather complicated recall process in Alaska.[60] As one of the recall organizers said, "It's fair to say that Alaska has never seen anything quite like this."[61]

By late August, the governor had walked back some of his cuts and reduced his demand to fully fund the annual permanent fund dividend. His initial $135 million cut to the University of Alaska system was scaled down substantially and funds were restored to several programs that had been eliminated under his original budget action. Perhaps predictably, the governor said these changes were not related to the recall effort. [62]

Thus, even with the difficulty in successfully recalling state officials, there appears to be an increase in such efforts. Most such efforts are doomed to failure. But, as the Alaska example demonstrates, these recall efforts may have other motivations, notably getting those officials facing a potential recall to alter their behavior. Moreover, even if such efforts fail to change the behavior of target officials, they have the potential to energize the challenging party's voter base for future campaigns.

Finally, it is important to note that recall efforts are actually more prevalent and more successful at the local government level, in part because the signature requirements to get them on the ballot are lower. The local officeholders most likely to face a recall are city council or school board members. In recent years the number of local officials across the nation who are successfully recalled averages about sixty, with another twenty who resign their office before the recall election is held.[63]

The referendum. While there are several versions of the referendum, the common element is that a policy proposal (a potential law or constitutional amendment) is submitted (referred) to the voting public for approval. It is also a common practice (indeed, it is constitutionally required in some states) to submit any proposal for bonded indebtedness to the public for a vote. None of this, of course, is allowed at the federal level.

The referendum process exists in all states—save, arguably, for Delaware—most commonly for adoption or rejection of amendments to the state constitution.[64] Note that at the federal level, constitutional amendments are not submitted directly to the public for a vote. Additionally, in about half the states, members of the public can directly challenge a law passed by the state legislature by requiring a *popular referendum* on the law. This requires the gathering of signatures on a petition and, if the threshold for the required number of signatures is met, the issue is put to public vote in the next election. As one authority on state politics puts it, "The popular referendum is effectively a public veto of a law."[65]

Granting the right of approval or rejection through a referendum vote is an important form of direct democracy that does not exist at the federal level. In this sense, state governments afford their citizens the opportunity to exert a direct impact on public policy in a way that the national government does not. Indeed, about 30 percent of the items brought forth by referendum are rejected by the citizens. Recently, that figure has trended higher; between 2014 and 2018 there were fifteen veto referenda on various state ballots, and in eleven cases the vote repealed the legislative action. For example, in 2018 Arizona voters used the popular referendum to repeal a law passed by the state legislature that would have expanded the eligibility for scholarships in the state, while in Missouri voters rejected a "right to work" bill passed overwhelmingly by the legislature.

It is important to keep in mind that different states offer different direct democracy options. In 2011, Ohio voters rejected a bill (Senate Bill 5) that the Ohio state legislature had passed earlier in the year. The measure was similar to the one that had passed in Wisconsin that led to the recall frenzy discussed earlier. In the Ohio case, the bill limited collective bargaining options for public employee unions, eliminated the mandatory payment of union dues, and required public workers to contribute more to their pension funds—provisions similar to those that had passed in Wisconsin.[66] But instead of pursuing recall elections of the officials involved—which is not an option under Ohio law—Ohioans sought to repeal the law through the popular referendum process. They were successful, striking down the law by 62 percent to 38 percent. As in Wisconsin, huge sums were spent on the referendum election—about $54 million.[67] Ohio voters had the ability to pursue a straightforward path of holding a referendum election on the anti-union bill. Why did their counterparts in Wisconsin take the recall route on their anti-union bill, a process that required a series of elections strung out over more than a year? The answer is simple: the popular referendum does not exist in Wisconsin. Thus, the only immediate avenue open to challenging the law in Wisconsin was an attempt to recall the public officials involved in passing it.

The initiative. There are also several versions of the initiative, but the most important point is that the initiative can be a powerful instrument of direct democracy. As one expert source on the subject proclaims, initiatives "are the most potent form of direct democracy."[68] Indeed, some of the most important and controversial public policies today—minimum wage laws, immigration, abortion, marijuana use, and gun control—have been the subject of the initiative process in one state or another. State tax limitations and expenditure mandates are also common topics addressed through the initiative process.

Only about half the states (twenty-four, to be exact) provide for the direct initiative. About half the population of the United States lives in states with a direct initiative option, California and Florida being the two largest states with the process. Sponsors of a proposal must gather the requisite number of signatures on petitions in order to get their policy proposal on the ballot in the next regularly scheduled election. The direct initiative, therefore, is an instrument of political participation that allows the public to bypass the state legislature and the legislative process altogether. It can become a tactical weapon for groups that feel unrepresented.

In recent decades, conservatives often turned to the initiative process.[69] In fact, a recent analysis by one authority on the subject of initiatives concludes, "The evidence consistently finds that initiative states adopt more conservative social policies than non-initiative states in the United States, and this finding holds across a wide array of policies."[70] This may be due to the fact that during much of the study period, Democrats controlled more legislatures and were likely to adopt more progressive policies. But with the majority of state legislatures now under more conservative Republican control, some liberal groups "are using state ballot initiatives as their weapon of choice."[71] In other words, the initiative and veto referendum may provide the public with a countervailing instrument in the policymaking process. As one expert points out, "the initiative pushes policy towards the outcome preferred by a majority of citizens, but the direction of that effect varies depending on the relative policy positions of the government officials and voters."[72] Another scholar uses the term "hybrid democracy" to describe the initiative states.[73] We think this an apt term; it captures the idea that these states have a policymaking process that combines the traditional American penchant for representative government by elected officials with the element of direct democracy through the initiative. Clearly, the policy process has the potential to be different in these states.

The ease by which initiatives can be employed varies; in states like California, Oregon, and North Dakota it is much easier to use than it is in Illinois or Wyoming.[74] The most significant difference is the proportion of valid signatures that must be gathered. In some states the requirement is 5 percent of the number of votes in the last statewide election (for governor, typically). In other states the requirement is 10 percent or even 15 percent. In a few states there are requirements that the signatories must be geographically dispersed (a certain number of signatures must come from a certain number of counties or congressional districts, for example), which increases the difficulty of meeting the standards for acceptance onto the ballot. Because of these variables, the use of the initiative as a method of policymaking is more likely in some states than others. It is a common practice in Oregon, Colorado, and Washington.[75] It is particularly popular in California, where since 1912 California voters have considered almost 400 initiatives, passing 135 of them (see figure 8.1).

In about sixteen initiative states, the instrument can be used to amend the state constitution, while in the remaining eight initiative states it can only be used to create a statutory law. This is an important distinction. Any changes made to the state constitution through the direct initiative can only be altered or overturned by the courts or by another constitutional amendment. But initiatives that simply create statutory law can be changed by the legislature, although in some states it might have to wait a certain period before doing so.

A team of scholars provide a useful summation of the role that instruments of direct democracy play in the political environments of some states. They note,

> Direct democracy—specifically, the initiative process—has important effects where it is used. It . . . may alter participation levels and the issues voters use when evaluating candidates. There is some evidence that direct democracy may lead state policies to be more representative of what voters in a state prefer.[76]

There are both positive and negative aspects of direct democracy in the states, and they are frequently debated and discussed among political

Figure 8.1   Initiatives in California, by Decade

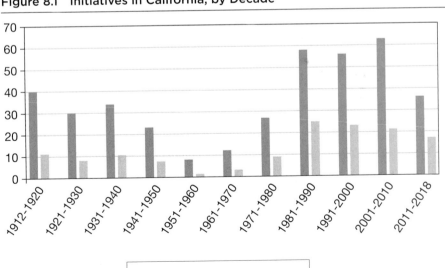

Initiatives   Approved

practitioners, political scientists, and journalists. While the initiative and refer-endum provide opportunities for voters to influence a variety of public policies, sometimes the task can be daunting. California voters found seventeen propo-sitions on their ballot in November 2016. They touched a wide range of issues, including several that conflicted. For example, one proposal proposed to ban capital punishment in California, while another wanted to speed up the execu-tion process for death row inmates. Other measures asked voters to approve a $2 increase in the tobacco tax, to require background checks for the purchase of ammunition, to legalize recreational marijuana, and to overturn a ban on bilingual education in public schools that had been imposed in 1998. As one observer of California politics commented, "It's incredible the amount of sub-stance and complexity in the November ballot. It's going to be overwhelming for voters to deal with."[77] But there are shortcuts available to voters in deciding how to vote on initiatives. They can, for example, use the support or opposi-tion from particular politicians or interest groups to reach what is, from their personal political perspective, the correct voting decision on such measures.[78]

To reiterate, our larger point is that any discussion about direct democracy takes place only in the context of state politics, not national politics. There are no instruments of direct democracy at the national level in the United States. At the state level, as states appear to be realigning or sorting on the basis of political ideology and culture, the initiative, referendum, and recall may be especially useful in fostering innovative policies. They are, in effect, important instruments in the laboratories of democracy. Strikingly different policies in regard to the use of marijuana, end-of-life decisions, abortion, environmental regulation, health care, and the definition of animal cruelty exist among states in part because of the initiative and referendum procedures in some of them. In the current political climate, however, some legislators are wary of the ini-tiative and veto referendum procedures, in part because these instruments can overturn the policy preferences of a legislative majority.

Finally, it is worth noting that the number of initiatives qualifying for the ballot and the number passing are down a bit over the past thirty years.[79] Perhaps this is not surprising. As a number of states have moved to make these instruments more difficult to use by changing the petition signature require-ments to make the process more difficult, getting them on the ballot may be more difficult.[80] But, again, even the threat that an initiative might be mounted may be enough to get the legislature to move in the direction that those con-templating such an effort might want.

TERM LIMITS AND THE STATES

At the end of the 1980s, a movement began to limit the number of terms lawmakers could serve in office. It first met with success with the passage of term limit initiatives in California, Colorado, and Oklahoma in 1990. Two years later, again through the initiative process, limits were placed on legislative terms in Arizona, Arkansas, Florida, Michigan, Missouri, Montana, Ohio, and South Dakota. By the end of 1994, term limits were in place in nineteen states. Almost all of these laws were the product of the initiative process. Several states eventually repealed their term limits, or the state supreme court determined they or the measures that put them on the ballot violated state constitutional provisions, so that currently there are fifteen states with term limits on their state legislators.

In important respects, the term limitation laws that were adopted differed from state to state, with some states imposing stricter limits on state legislative service than other states. But one thing that all the term limit initiatives contained was a term limit on members of Congress as well as on state legislators. Here, then, is a case in which almost 40 percent of the states (and about 80 percent of the states with the initiative from of direct democracy) used a state-based process to define a federal office. While the precise nature of the term limits on state legislatures varied from state to state, almost all of them attempted to place the exact same limit on their members of Congress: six years (three terms) in the House of Representatives and twelve years (two terms) in the Senate. Few people recall that the original term limit laws passed in the states included provisions limiting congressional terms as well. This has been forgotten because in 1995 the U.S. Supreme Court struck down the part of each of state initiative that imposed limits on members of Congress, finding that states (and Congress itself) cannot impose an additional qualification for federal office beyond those in the U.S. Constitution, only a constitutional amendment could do so.[81] Thus what many viewed as an effort to limit congressional terms through the use of a state-based instrument of direct democracy ultimately had no direct effect on the federal office but did have a substantial effect on state legislative office in the states that adopted them.

Nonetheless, it would be a mistake to assume that state legislative term limits have had no impact on Congress; one early report on the impact of term limits found that members of Congress from term-limited states were more likely to be former state legislators than were members from non-term-limited states: 61 percent of members who represented states with legislative term limits were former state legislators compared to only 46 percent of members from non-term-limited states.[82] The presumption is that term-limited legislators who do not want to end their political careers are forced to seek other offices for which to run, and a congressional seat would be an obvious next step.

Because term limit laws differ, the effect of the law is not the same for all the states that impose them.[83] They differ in the length of terms allowed. In those states in which the limit is generous (twelve years in each chamber in Louisiana and Nevada), the effects are different than in states where the limit is especially stringent (six years in the lower chamber and eight in the upper chamber in Michigan). A strict term limit can actually accelerate the already substantial effect of a "wave election," such as that experienced in 2010. A good example is Michigan: when the state legislature convened in January 2011,

54 percent of the state representatives and 76 percent of the senators were newly elected—an extraordinary level of turnover by any standard. Such a high level of turnover was not an isolated event. In 2018, 66 percent of the Michigan state senators were barred from returning due to term limits.[84] Term limits also vary by whether once they are reached the lawmaker can no longer serve in the legislature (a lifetime ban as in Missouri) or simply has to sit out an election cycle (as Nebraska). Thus, although fifteen states have term limits, the details of those limits vary.

THE PRESIDENTIAL ELECTION AND THE STATES

The method by which Americans choose their chief executive is unique. Some might even be tempted to characterize it as bizarre. It consists of two distinct and decidedly different phases—the nomination phase and the general election phase. The two phases evolved separately. But each, in its own way, emphasizes the role of the states in choosing the national executive.

The presidential primaries. The first step—the nomination phase—is actually a series of steps defined by a combination of national party rules, state party rules, and state election laws. There is no mention of any nomination phase in the U.S. Constitution. The system has evolved over time and the current process bears almost no resemblance to the system of 1800, and only faint resemblance to the system of 1900 or even 1950. Indeed, the nomination system continually morphs. For our purposes, the key things to understand about the current nomination system are the following.

First, each state party is allocated a certain number of delegates by the national party. Most of these delegates are pledged to support a particular candidate, and they are authorized to attend the national nominating convention and vote for that candidate. There are several ways delegates may be selected, the most common of which are caucuses or primary elections. In 2016, about a quarter of the state parties used a caucus nominating system, along the lines of Iowa's. In 2020, far fewer states used caucuses. In most states primary elections are now held.

Second, the decision about how many delegates can participate at the nominating convention is a matter for each national political party to decide. Republicans tend to have smaller nominating conventions than Democrats; in 2020 the Republicans planned for roughly twenty-five hundred delegates to their convention, while the Democrats anticipated about forty-five hundred delegates to their convention.[85]

Third, the manner in which the delegates are allocated to each state is different for each party and it is not based solely on state population. The Democratic Party, in particular, allocates additional delegate seats to those states that tend to vote for its candidates—basically, a reward for voting for the party in the past. To a lesser extent, the Republicans do this also.

Fourth, the manner by which delegates within a state are allocated to various candidates also differs. Depending on state law, each party in a state can choose to have nominating caucuses, nominating conventions, or nominating primaries. Over time the system has evolved that most of the nominating events are now primary elections. For the Republicans in 2020 each state party must decide if it will allocate delegates using some form of proportionally or winner-take-all rules.[86] The Democrats only award delegates on a proportional basis to candidates who get at least 15 percent of the vote in a state primary or caucus.[87]

Fifth, there are also differences by state and party as to who can participate in a nominating primary or caucus. Some state parties restrict participation to registered members of the party (a closed system), while other state parties allow independents to participate (open primary). Closed primaries are more common, but there are notable exceptions. Most notably, the New Hampshire presidential primary is a semi-open primary, meaning that independents (nonaffiliated) voters can participate.

Sixth, since 1972, the first two nominating events are the Iowa caucuses, followed within eight days by the New Hampshire primary elections. Because they host the first events in which delegates are allocated, these two states attract a substantial amount of money and attention from the candidates and the media. Usually any candidate who does better than projected in Iowa and New Hampshire is bestowed instant credibility and the appearance of momentum. Any candidate who does worse than expected may find it difficult to recover. In effect, these two small states exert disproportionate influence on the presidential nomination system. In this regard, a noteworthy observation is that in important ways Iowa and New Hampshire are not reflective of the national electorate because they have much smaller racial and ethnic minority populations.[88] To balance these characteristics, the Democrats have put Nevada and South Carolina next on their nomination calendar.

Each state, usually through legislative statute, determines when it will hold its presidential nominating event, sometimes ignoring or challenging national party rules. And within a state, the two parties might not share the same primary date or even method of selection. In 2020, for example, Hawaii Republicans were scheduled to hold their caucuses on March 10, while the Democrats held their primary on April 4. Moreover, when their party has an incumbent running, some state parties will opt not to hold any primary or caucus, as several state Republican parties chose to do in 2020.[89]

Starting in the 1980s, many states have moved their primaries or caucuses to an earlier date, hoping to increase their influence on the nomination process. And as one state moved forward, other states would subsequently move their events even earlier on the calendar. A sort of "calendar creep" occurred, a process known as "frontloading." Increasingly, we see states moving their primaries to the early months of the presidential election year (from, say, April to February). Calendar creep has changed the dynamics of the presidential nominating process. In 1976, only 10 percent of the delegates were selected by early March; by 2008, over 70 percent had been chosen by then.[90]

Overall, one can see that the nomination phase is really a series of state-based political events. And each state (or state party organization, in some cases) makes important decisions about the manner, timing, and mechanics of its particular nominating events. Some states, notably Iowa and New Hampshire, exert disproportionate influence in the process because they get to hold the earliest contests. Without question, states matter when it comes to establishing rules for choosing presidential nominees.

The general election and the Electoral College. In the presidential selection process, the nomination phase and the election phase are distinct. The field of candidates differs, the rules differ, the strategies employed differ, and the length of the campaign differs.[91] But the strategic role of the states is the same. As one political scientist notes,

> Candidate behavior is conditioned by the rules of the game. Presidential elections in the United States are determined by the state-based Electoral College. . . . This electoral structure has enormous implications for advertising strategies. Most candidates . . . focus on the fifteen to twenty states that swing back and forth between the two major parties.[92]

In recent presidential elections, the number of "swing" or "battleground" states has been even smaller. For the 2020 election, perhaps ten states are the focus. At the beginning of this chapter, we noted that the president is not elected by a nationwide popular vote but in a series of fifty-one concurrent elections (each of the fifty states plus the District of Columbia). The purpose of these concurrent elections is to choose each state's electors for the Electoral College. The number of electors from each state is equal to that state's congressional delegation (seats in the House of Representatives plus two senators). Thus, more populous states such as California (fifty-five electors) and Texas (thirty-eight) have many more electors than less populous states such as Montana (three) or South Dakota (three).

One might expect presidential candidates to spend far more time, money, and effort in large states because there are many more electoral votes to be won there. So why is it that in the past few presidential elections the candidates have spent about as much time in New Mexico and Nevada as they have in California and Texas? It is because of a combination of three things: (1) a competitive presidential election where both major parties believe that they can win, (2) a series of noncompetitive state elections where both parties recognize that there are some states they are certain to win and other states that they are certain to lose, and (3) the existence of something called the "unit rule." The unit rule is the same thing as "winner-take-all." It is up to each state to decide how to allocate its Electoral College votes, and all but two states (Maine and Nebraska are the exceptions) choose to assign all their electors to the winner of the popular vote in the state. Thus, the plurality winner in a state gets all of the state's electoral votes.

One of the closest state races for president in 2016 was in Michigan, where Donald Trump received 2.28 million votes to Hillary Clinton's 2.27 million. With more than 4.45 million votes cast, Trump won by about thirteen thousand votes. That is less than one-half of 1 percent of all the votes cast in the state, but because Michigan allocates its electors using the unit rule, Trump received 100 percent of its Electoral College votes—all sixteen electors.

States use the winner-take-all rule because they think it increases their Electoral College clout. But this is only true in those states where the popular vote is expected to be close. If the popular vote in a state—even a large state like California—is expected to be one-sided, then the candidates will not spend much time or money there. For one candidate the state is a given, for the other it is a lost cause. Either way, why spend precious resources pursuing a sure thing or a lost cause when there are states still up for grabs? And in an election in which the Electoral College vote is expected to be close, every state and its electoral votes (even New Hampshire's paltry four votes) can be important. Consequently, while Washington (twelve Electoral College votes) and Virginia (thirteen Electoral College votes) have almost identical value in Electoral College math, if one of them is considered safe for one party and the other is thought to be up for grabs, the candidates will spend their resources in the competitive state. In presidential electoral politics, some states matter more than others simply because the likely outcome in them is uncertain.

Thus, in 2016 candidates Trump and Clinton spent most of their campaign time in just a handful of states: Florida, Michigan, Ohio, North Carolina, Pennsylvania, and Virginia—all more populous states that were competitive. But they also spent considerable time in smaller but also competitive states such as Nevada and New Hampshire. Neither Trump nor Clinton spent much time at all in California, New York or Texas—three of the most populous states—because each of these states were "safe" for one or the other.

The other oft-noted aspect of America's presidential election system is that it is possible for a candidate to receive more popular votes nationwide and still lose in the Electoral College. Indeed, this happened at least five times, including twice in this century (Gore vs. Bush in 2000 and Trump vs. Clinton in 2016).[93] Because of such occurrences many people advocate abolishing the Electoral College and replacing it with a direct national popular vote. But there are others who defend the unique contrivance of the Electoral College, arguing that it is an important reflection of a federal system of government—one in which the states play a key role in the selection of federal officers.[94] It is likely that elected officials who consider the proposals to reform the system will always calculate whether their state stands to win or lose under any changes.

STATE ELECTIONS IN A POLARIZED FEDERAL SYSTEM

In this book, we make the case that states matter in the policymaking process. And in this chapter we argue that states are key electoral units. Logically, then, we might expect that voters are attentive and active participants in state elections. Unfortunately, this is usually not true. State elections, which should be about state issues and holding elected state officials accountable for their record in office, often appear not to be about that at all. There are a series of variables—some perhaps causal, others perhaps confounding—that help explain why this happens. At a minimum, we need to discuss party polarization, electoral competition (or lack thereof), and the effect of national factors.

Polarization. In the past few years, a great deal has been written about party or ideological polarization in the United States.[95] Much of the attention is devoted to polarization at the national level, especially in Congress. But there is ample evidence that political polarization exists at the state level as well. Indeed, some state legislatures appear to be even more polarized than the U.S. Congress.[96] Note that polarization in this context simply means the ideological distance between the political parties in a given legislature. It does not necessarily induce gridlock; in fact, one can have highly polarized political parties but "productive" policymaking, especially if one party holds the governor's seat and large majorities in both chambers of the state legislature. But in terms of electoral choice, polarized parties are likely to offer candidates who are considerably more liberal or more conservative than the median voter. Assuming that the median voter prefers middle-of-the-road or "moderate" policies, he or she may find him- or herself voting for a candidate who does not match his or her policy preferences, but simply meets a "lesser of two evils" criterion. In other words, the median voter may feel dissatisfied and not adequately represented.

Electoral competition. For statewide office, such as governor, elections remain competitive in many states. But in some states, one party dominates. In 2019, there were eight statewide partisan executive offices elected in California and all were held by Democrats. Even more impressive is that year all twenty-seven statewide elected officials in Texas were Republicans.

Below the statewide level, many state legislative districts are so dominated by one party that the other major party does not even bother to try and field a candidate. Depending on the year and circumstance, between 35 percent and 40 percent of state legislative races are uncontested. In some places, the situation is even more dismal. In 2018—a year where many elections were hotly contested—the vast majority of state legislative races were uncontested by one of the two major parties, particularly in Massachusetts (71 percent uncontested), Hawaii (68 percent), and Rhode Island (68 percent).[97] In all three states, it was the Democratic party that benefitted. But there are other states, especially in the South and the Mountain states, where the Republican Party benefited from Democrats failing to mount challenges. In recent elections the state with the least competitive legislative districts may be Georgia: 80 percent of the seats for its state house of representatives were uncontested by one of the major parties in 2014 and again in 2016. In other words, 80 percent of the candidates were effectively elected *before* the general election was even held, leaving general election voters in those districts with no meaningful choice to make. Georgia showed a modest improvement in 2018; "only" 60 percent of the seats in the House and Senate were uncontested by one party or the other!

Even if a legislative race is contested, there is no guarantee that it is actually competitive. One commonly used measure of a "competitive election" is that the winning candidate's margin of victory was no greater than 10 percent of the votes cast. Recent research shows that only about 12 percent of state legislative races across the country are competitive by this standard—that is, only one out of every eight legislative contests.[98] The trends differ by state, but overall the number of competitive districts has declined over the last generation.[99] While elections for governor are usually more competitive than state legislative races, they too have experienced a decline in competitiveness in recent years.[100]

The intertwining of national politics and state elections. We have long known that state elections are influenced by national issues and trends.[101] Presidents have "electoral coattails" that help members of the president's party in down-ticket elections, and those coattails are "withdrawn" in midterm elections, when the president's party usually loses seats in the U.S. House and in state legislatures. The extent of presidential coattails and the subsequent midterm election reaction against the president's party vary by year, state, and political circumstances. But such national forces appear to be growing in state elections, and especially in state legislative elections. One scholar studied the effect of national factors on state legislative elections for the period from 1970 to 2010 and concluded "national contextual factors related to the president's party, evaluations of the president, and the presidential election cycle are important predictors of state legislative election outcomes."[102] Others have reached the same verdict.[103] After examining a variety of variables, including the number of uncontested races, the ideological position of the incumbent legislator, the popularity of the governor and the president, and the condition of the economy, another political scientist concludes,

> Elections do not appear to hold state legislators accountable for state-level policy outcomes, their legislative records, or their general performance . . . instead of serving as a referendum on state legislators' own action, state legislative elections are dominated by national politics.[104]

Other research shows that, for the most part, "legislators do not face meaningful electoral consequences" even if they are more ideologically extreme than the voters in their district.[105]

Why is it the case? There are a series of variables that converge to create this situation. First, many people are not knowledgeable about state politics or about how important states are in the policymaking scheme. Only one of four voters know who their state legislator is. Even more discouraging is the fact that less than half can correctly identify which party controls their state senate or state house.[106] They are better at identifying the governor's party affiliation. Second, some voters appear to have a weak grasp on what the states do, what the national government does, and which officials are elected at which level. Because state elections and national elections are often held at the same time, it appears that issues associated with candidates for the national level seep into the voter's calculus for choosing among candidates in state elections. This has been called "the distraction hypothesis": elections for national offices (especially the presidential election) distract potential voters from state issues and conditions, even when voting for candidates for state office.[107] In other words, the existence of a federal system makes the potential voter's job more difficult. As some have argued, the states are less visible to the average citizen than either the national government or their local governments. This reality is made worse by the diminished media coverage of state politics.[108] All of this is ironic. In chapters 1 and 2, we showed that states matter, especially in a period in which the national government appears polarized and gridlocked. In chapters 4 and 5, we provided evidence that state institutions and officials are more capable and better equipped to be effective policymakers than they were in the past. And in chapter 6, we documented that states set many important public policies and that these policies vary by state. Earlier in this chapter, we made the case that American elections are organized around the states. We also noted that many states have the initiative, referendum, and recall, mechanisms the national government does not have to translate public opinion into public policy. But—and here is the irony—voters often have limited or no real choice at all among candidates for state office and they often appear to be uninterested in or inattentive to state elections. Thus, while states matter, indeed increasingly so, the choices provided for the voters in state elections are either nonexistent (uncontested or uncompetitive elections), distasteful (too ideologically extreme), misunderstood (confused by the complications of federalism), or simply overlooked (lack of knowledge about or lack of interest in state politics).

This is not to say that state legislative elections are unimportant or inconsequential. When national sentiment moves toward or away from a particular party, a "wave election" can shift hundreds of state legislative seats. And, when voters view the stakes as high, they will focus on state legislative races. Virginia is one of the handful of states that holds its state election in odd-numbered years. In 2017, Virginia Democrats were energized by a series of national and state events, and they actively recruited and campaigned for candidates at the state level. They doubled the number of Democratic candidates running for the legislature, and they invested heavily in targeted races. Their efforts proved successful and they flipped fifteen seats from Republican to Democrat and came within two seats of becoming the majority party. Democrats, it seems, were learning the crucial lesson that Republicans had mastered years before.

States elections matter. In November 2019, Democrats finished the job they began in 2017 by winning control of both chambers of the Virginia legislature for the first time this century.

There is one final observation to make about state legislative elections: not every legislative seat gets filled through one. As discussed in box 8.1, state legislative vacancies get filled through a variety of mechanisms other than a special election. The point to keep in mind is that elections are time-consuming and expensive, and some states try to minimize those costs by employing alternative means to fill open elected positions.

Box 8.1	The Rules Governing How States Fill Vacant State Legislative Seats

There are almost seventy-four hundred state legislative seats in the United States. During the course of any given year, some number of them will be vacated because members die, resign, or get removed from office for some reason. One might assume that the voters get to choose their replacements, but the rules under which those seats get filled vary by state. Voters actually get to select the new representatives in only half the states, as Table 8.4 shows. In the other half, local government officials, local political parties, the governor, or state legislators from the same house and party as the lawmaker being replaced make the choices.

Table 8.4.

Method used to fill vacant seat	States using method
Filled by voters through special election (25 states)	AL, AR, CA, CT, DE, FL, GA, IA, KY, LA, ME, MA, MI, MN, MS, MO, NH, NY, OK, PA, RI, SC, TX, VA, WI
Political party of previous incumbent appoints (5 states)	**CO, IL**, IN, NJ, ND
County Board of Commissioners appoint (8 states)	**AZ**, MT, **NV**, NM, **OR**, TN, WA, WY
Governor appoints (11 states)	**AK, HI, ID**, KS, **MD**, NE, NC, SD, UT, VT, WV
Members of same legislative house and party of previous incumbent elect (1 state)	OH

Note: States in bold must appoint new member from the same party as the previous member.

Source: http://www.ncsl.org/research/elections-and-campaigns/filling-legislative-vacancies.aspx.

CONCLUSION

It is a curiosity of the American federal system that each governing level—national and state—has been at the forefront of "democratizing" the political system, but in different ways. Generally speaking, the national government has led the way in opening the franchise—the right to vote—to more classes of people. One need only think of the effects of the Fourteenth, Fifteenth, Nineteenth, Twenty-Fourth, and Twenty-Sixth Amendments on the U.S. Constitution and the effects of the 1965 Voting Rights Act to understand how the national government expanded the definition of citizenry, in terms of who could vote, beyond what the states (or at least some states) were willing to do.

Many states have allowed their citizens greater opportunities to directly influence public policy than what is permitted at the national level. One need only think of the instruments of direct democracy available at the state levels that are unavailable at the national level to appreciate the difference. The multitude of judicial elections at the state level, in contrast to the manner in which federal judges are chosen, is another example of significant differences.

The main theme of this chapter is the variety of ways in which electoral rules and procedures that are defined at the state level impact the way politics plays out at the national level. All federally elected officeholders are chosen under rules influenced by the states. Rules matter, particularly electoral rules. And electoral rules among the states are a hodge-podge. They differ from one state to another in one or more of the following ways:

- Who can vote (voter eligibility).
- The process by which they get registered to vote (and note that they do not register at all in North Dakota).
- How they vote (ballot structure, absentee/mail/early voting rules).
- For whom they can vote (open versus closed primaries, which offices are elected).
- When they vote (presidential year, off-year, odd-year).
- How often they vote (terms of office).
- For what they can vote (just candidates or candidates and issues).

States also differ rather dramatically in terms of the relative strength of each the two major political parties in them. While nationally the two parties are currently roughly equal in strength, that is not the case in many states today. Some states are heavily Republican, some are heavily Democratic, and a smaller number are competitive and hotly contested between the two parties. At the intersection of these two issues—state party strength and state electoral rules—we find the Electoral College and the campaign for the presidency. In numerous ways, some obvious, others less so, state electoral and party systems matter.

9

Why States Matter Now

> The American people are not boiling with concern about the workings of
> their state governments.
>
> —V. O. Key, *American State Politics* (1966)

V. O. Key's comment is just as true today as it was in 1966. Unfortunately, it may be even more the case today that people are not interested is the workings of their state government. In the previous chapters, we have made the case that states matter in the American federal system of government. They are important because many significant policy decisions are made at the state level. They are important because federal policy is often administered through state agencies. They are important because states are often innovative policymakers, in some cases moving well in advance of the national government. They are important because in many instances they offer a greater decision-making role for the individual citizen through the instruments of direct democracy. They are important because the states are the electoral fount of all national elected officials. They are important because they generate and spend billions of dollars on their own and determine how local governments operate. As Thomas Gais, director of the Rockefeller Institute of Government, points out,

> A lot of people don't realize that state and local governments carry out the great bulk of domestic policies in the United States. The federal government administers some big domestic programs such as Social Security, Medicare, SSI and a few others. For the most part, however, when you're talking about the domestic programs, state and local governments make them happen. Out of eight people working for governments in the United States, seven of them are on the state and local payrolls.[1]

While the general public and the media may be slow to recognize this trend, interest groups have and they have responded accordingly. As one public policy expert notes, there is a "fundamental shift underway in lobbying, as interest groups switch their focus from Washington to the states."[2] As evidence, he cites a recent report that the number of organizations with lobbyists declined by 25 percent in Washington, DC, but increased by more than 10 percent in the states.[3] Along the same lines, a government relations firm that represents a variety of clients in the states says that gridlock at the national level has caused many organizations to shift their focus and they are now "taking a renewed interest in state government relations."[4]

Why has this happened? In part because unified government at the national level has become a rare occurrence.[5] In the thirty-nine-year period between 1980 and 2019, the president's party has held a majority in both houses of Congress in only ten years. Remarkably, during this period we had divided government at the national level *75 percent of the time*, punctuated only briefly by instances of unified party control. While one party may capture both the presidency and Congress for one or two electoral cycles, it is difficult for either major party to maintain it for long at the national level. In the 2016 election, the Republicans captured the White House and both houses of Congress, but just two years later, the Democrats took control of the House. Separated powers with different electoral institutions, along with polarized parties and a nonrandom distribution of ideological preferences geographically, means that currently it is difficult to sustain a governing majority at the national level in the United States. Thus, given current political realities, gridlock at the national level is likely to occur more often than not for the foreseeable future. As we noted in chapter 2, under this scenario the states become the default option in the policymaking arena.

STATES IN AN EVER-EVOLVING FEDERAL SYSTEM

The American experiment with federalism was just beginning as the eighteenth century was ending. It was a new political system for a nascent nation, and there was much uncertainty about exactly how the new arrangement would work in practice. Historians and political scientists often characterize the federal arrangement that developed in the nineteenth century as "dual federalism," meaning that each level of government had its own sphere of operation and did not intrude much into what was considered the other's sphere. This characterization is, of course, a simplification. In fact, there was always an ongoing disagreement about the proper roles to be played by each level.

As we discussed in earlier chapters, the New England states resisted some of the federal government's actions surrounding the War of 1812, as illustrated by the Hartford Convention. John C. Calhoun of South Carolina ardently defended slavery and states' rights and was a central figure in the 1832 Nullification Crisis. He argued that states not only had the right to nullify what they considered to be odious federal laws, but that they also had the right to secede from the Union. By 1861, southern efforts to leave resulted in the Civil War. More than six hundred thousand soldiers died in that conflict—more not just as a percentage of the population but also in raw numbers, than any other war in American history.[6] Perhaps "duel federalism" is a more apt description of the period than "dual federalism."

During the latter half of the nineteenth century and continuing into the twentieth century, the nature of the relationship between the national and state governments changed in significant ways. Some of the changes were prompted by the European wave of immigration prior to World War I, the rapid population growth, and the transition from a rural to an urban society brought on by industrialization. Recall that at the beginning of the twentieth century the U.S. population stood at about 100 million. By the close of the century, it was about 300 million. In 1900, a majority, about 60 percent, of Americans still lived in rural areas. By 2000, about 80 percent lived in urban and suburban areas. A huge transformation of American society had occurred. Many local governments, especially cities, adapted to these changes and expanded their service and regulatory functions accordingly.

Meanwhile, after two world wars and a severe economic depression, the national government emerged as a much stronger and more visible presence than it had been before. Thus, both the national and local levels of government adjusted to changing times. Meanwhile, many state governments languished. Still geared toward serving a rural society, many of them resisted making the transition to the new realities. One journalist at the time lamented "the shocking depth to which state government has sunk in the United States."[7]

As the country was urbanizing, many legislatures remained dominated by rural interests, largely due to persistent malapportionment. An observer proclaimed that "state legislatures may be our most extreme example of institutional lag. In their formal qualities they are largely nineteenth century organizations and they must, or should address themselves to twentieth century problems."[8] As a result, as two political scientists observed, "Over the course of a century, the state legislatures evolved from the wellsprings of American government into political backwaters."[9] The president of the U.S. Conference of Mayors in 1949 protested that "American cities are under the control of unsympathetic state legislatures dominated by agricultural oligarchies."[10]

By the mid-twentieth century, then, there was growing pressure to "do something" about state governments generally, and about state legislatures specifically. In response, the American Political Science Association commissioned a study and the Council of State Governments created committees to make reform recommendations.[11] Several other organizations aimed at modernizing state governments became active. One of these organizations was the National Municipal League, which had become frustrated with what they saw as the unsympathetic treatment of cities and their problems from their own state officials.

Consequently, at roughly the same time as the legislative "reapportionment revolution," there began a concerted effort to upgrade and modernize the institution of state government. California was at the forefront of this move-ment, but other states followed quickly. The Eagleton Institute of Politics at Rutgers University provided an institutional locus, often with funding from benefactors such as the Carnegie Corporation and the Ford Foundation. The Eagleton Institute conducted commissioned analyses of state legislatures in at least eight states. Meanwhile, many states pursued their own reform agendas; commissions to review and recommend changes to state legislative practices were created in Pennsylvania, West Virginia, Iowa, Illinois, Idaho, Oregon, and Washington.[12] As we discussed in chapter 5, similar efforts were made on behalf of the executive and judicial branches. Additionally, numerous states transformed their fiscal systems during the last part of the twentieth century. Thus, by the 1980s, most states had emerged as stronger and more capable partners in the federal system, leading to claims about "the resurgence of the states."[13] Their metamorphosis was characterized as a "quiet revolution," and "a phoenix-like resurrection of federalism."[14]

GETTING BEYOND "ZERO-SUM GAMES" AND THE "ALABAMA SYNDROME"

The reemergence of the states as capable governing bodies over the last half century is not a development that is fully recognized or appreciated by the media or the general public. There are several reasons for this. First, there is a tendency to view developments in federalism as a zero-sum game. As Alison LaCroix states, "The debate is nearly always framed in terms of a binary con-frontation" in which either the national government wins or the states win.[15] We have tried to show that federalism in today's world is much more compli-cated than that simple characterization. It is not just about the states versus the national government. In today's polarized political world, one party often dominates policymaking at one level with the other party controlling policy-making at the other level. Under these conditions, the functioning of federalism is complicated by partisan considerations.

Second, even today, despite the irrefutable progress made by states as poli-cymaking and administrative units, there is a lingering tendency to judge them by their lowest common denominator. This phenomenon has been called deri-sively "the Alabama syndrome." The comment was prompted by the reluctance of federal government decision makers in the 1960s to allow any latitude to state administrators in implementing and administering new federal policies such as Medicare or the "War on Poverty" for fear of what a "George Wallace would do" with that sort of authority.[16] (Wallace was Alabama's segregationist governor.) For some, that period still colors their perception of the relationship between the national government and the states. As one expert on the subject wrote, "The tenacity and violence of southern resistance to changes in race relations gave federalism a very bad name."[17] And there is evidence that state administrators in the South still are more likely to resist federal agency edicts than their counterparts elsewhere.[18]

Clearly, not all states are the same and not all states enjoy comparable policymaking capacities. We have sought to document that fact. Some states are innovators and other states are laggards in any given policy arena. Perhaps Americans are reluctant to embrace or even acknowledge an expanded role for the states precisely because they lack confidence in particular states to "do the right thing," on whatever they might perceive that to be on any given policy.

Most people are remarkably inconsistent in their views of the proper federal-state relationship. Both Republicans and Democrats are guilty on this score. Americans will favor a national or state approach depending on the issue at stake, the relative position of the national government and any given state on that issue, and their own opinion on it. Politicians also treat federalism as an "expedient tool."[19] Simply stated, partisans on both sides want decisions made by the level of government they currently control. When in 2006 Congress was debating a constitutional amendment banning same-sex marriage, 56 percent of gay marriage opponents thought it was an issue for the federal government to decide. When in 2015 the Supreme Court was on the verge of issuing a decision that would make same-sex marriage legal across the nation, 72 percent of gay marriage opponents thought it was a matter best left to the states.[20] Similarly, in 2016, with Democrats in control of the White House, 78 percent of Republicans preferred to concentrate political power in state governments. Responding to that same question in 2017, shortly after President Trump took office, only 44 percent of Republicans wanted power concentrated in state governments.[21] So, federalism gets something of a black eye because everyone promotes the level of government that produces the policies they prefer. Americans are all for greater policymaking independence for the states except when they disagree with the policies produced. When it comes to federalism, everyone is a hypocrite.

Keep in mind as well, that similar concerns can be transferred to the relationship between state and local governments, as documented in chapter 7. Again, there is a tendency for Americans to want the level of government that gives them their preferred policy to be empowered to make that decision. Preemption laws are imposed by state governments for many reasons, but mostly they are driven by a desire to control a particular policy outcome and not by any coherent theory about what decisions should each level of government should be authorized to make.

STATES AND THE TASK AHEAD

As one federalism expert notes, "The most appealing reason for courts to enforce limits on Congress and to preserve the role of autonomous states is the prediction that states will in fact experiment with new policies, looking for new ways to serve the public good."[22] This comment, of course, harkens back to Justice Brandeis's "laboratories of democracy" argument. The notion may be pertinent today for several reasons. First, the federal deficit will almost certainly require cutbacks in federal aid, especially outside health care. Second, changes in technology and communication are such that states can be aware of the policy choices made by other states. Policymakers and administrators in one state talk to their counterparts in other states. They are cognizant of the policy options available, especially as some associations, interest groups, think tanks, and others provide such information to them. The executive director of the National Governors Association put it this way:

> You have all these policies going on in the states. They've got K–12 education to run, a university system, and incredible challenges in health care and criminal justice. So we're trying to share ideas, solutions . . . and to analyze what's working and what's not working.[23]

Finally, there is a strong argument to be made for allowing states some policy latitude, because it is obvious that the states still differ in terms of political culture and policy preferences. The party realignment, or partisan sorting, that began in the 1960s and 1970s is largely complete, and many states now appear to be "more red" or "more blue," and as a result fewer of them are experiencing divided government. As Ann Althouse succinctly states, "There are times for the national government to stand back and let policies emerge at the lower level of decision making."[24] This is one of those times.

Not too long ago, the respected British newsmagazine *The Economist* published a special report on how the states were leading the way in search of innovative policies to reinvigorate the United States. The article was aptly titled "Let 50 Flowers Bloom" and noted that:

> America's 50 states are consciously and vigorously competing to find the best formula for regulation and taxes and introducing sweeping reforms to that end. . . . Whether or not Congress puts aside its fiscal vendetta long enough to help with any of this, progress is being made around the country.[25]

The challenges facing state governments and their local governments are many. The biggest will be the financial one, as many states are likely to face, in the words of one observer, "prolonged fiscal austerity."[26] Alice Rivlin, a former head of the federal Office of Management and Budget (OMB), argued that a combination of the current federal deficit and the aging of the population will produce a long-term structural imbalance that is fiscally unsustainable.[27] As federal budget problems mount, there will be an irresistible incentive for national policymakers to push many of the costs of administering programs down to the state level. Indeed, this has been happening for some time. The National Conference of State Legislatures estimated that the administration of

George W. Bush offloaded over $100 billion in program administrative costs onto the states. Such unfunded or poorly funded mandates may help the federal government's budget, but it creates major fiscal problems for the states. In turn, state governments have found it hard to resist the urge to unload some of their costs onto local governments.

In any event, it clear that for the foreseeable future state officials will have to make hard choices between paring back or eliminating programs or raising taxes and fees. In a recent review of American federalism, it was observed that "mounting concern about federal debt, partisan politics, and legislative gridlock at the federal level has also contributed to the need for states to step up and take matters into their own hands."[28] Demography and economics are conspiring to force the states to the policy fore.

THE PUBLIC'S RESPONSIBILITY

Given all this, the first task of the public citizen is to be better informed about the critical role that states play in public policymaking. While states remain essential partners in the American federal system, they are not often presented as such. For one thing, from the media's point of view, there is rarely a natural state constituency. News is usually viewed as being either national or local in scope.[29] Moreover, in recent years there are fewer and fewer reporters covering the "state capitol beat."[30] A recent study found that between 2003 and 2014 the number of full-time newspaper reporters assigned to the nation's statehouses declined by 35 percent.[31] Another analysis observes,

> State governments have more power and more money than ever before. . . . Everyone—political parties, academics, trade organizations, labor unions, corporations—has discovered this. Everyone, that is, except the press.[32]

It should be pointed out, however, that in recent years some excellent online publications covering the politics of particular states, such as *MinnPost* and the *Texas Tribune*, have emerged.[33] But, of course, the burden falls on citizens to find these outlets.

But, even when there is news coverage from the state level, it is usually just about a single state. There is very little comparative state reporting occurring. This is understandable because most news consumers are only interested in what is happening in their own state—if they are interested at all![34] But without a comparative perspective, Americans miss most of the larger trends in state policymaking and miss the bigger picture of changes in the federal-state relationship. There are a few sources of comparative state political news available, such as the Pew Charitable Trusts' stateline.org.[35] Unfortunately, such sources are not well known to the general public. We think that they should be. One gains a greater appreciation for the vitality of state government and politics through such venues.

Moreover, it is only through a comparative framework that we can truly appreciate the advantage of a federal system. The public needs to realize that states only matter if they have the freedom to devise different approaches to solving public problems, and that they have the ability to do so within the political and cultural context of each state. There are limits to such variation, of course. In a compound republic, both individual rights and states' rights have a place. "States' rights" is an easy phrase to toss about, especially when one is frustrated with the current national government. But with rights also come responsibilities for all the citizens of a state, not just the citizens who form the majority. There is a cost to having the states continue to matter as we enter a period of austerity. It may be a cost in the form of reduced services or the elimination of entire programs in some instances. It may be a cost in the form of higher state and local taxes in order to replace federal aid. It will likely be some of both.

An important task for the citizen is to understand that hard choices will have to be made; therefore, there is value in having a variety of policy options explored. It is essential that we recognize there are real policy consequences to state elections. States with unified Republican control will make different decisions than states with unified Democratic control. States with divided control will likely arrive at still other decisions. States matter, and consequently who controls the governing apparatus of them matters. Appreciating this basic fact is fundamental for citizens of the United States.

Notes

CHAPTER 1: MAKING A CASE FOR THE STATES

1. Fox News 13 (Salt Lake City), December 26, 2018. "West Wendover formally adopts recreational marijuana sales ordinance, gives permit to dispensary," https://fox13now.com/2018/12/26/west-wendover-formally-adopts-recreational-marijuana-sales-ordinance-gives-permit-to-dispensary/.

2. Salt Lake City Tribune, "Giant Discount Liquor Store Opens in West Wendover Giving Utah Buyers Another Place to Cross the Border for Cheap Booze," November 11, 2017, https://www.sltrib.com/news/2017/11/08/giant-discount-liquor-store-opens-in-west-wendover-giving-utah-buyers-another-place-to-cross-the-border-for-cheap-booze/.

3. Salt Lake City Tribune, "Giant Discount Liquor Store Opens."

4. These figures are based on the 2019 federal poverty definition of $20,780 for a family of three, and calculated from the percentages in table 1.1.

5. Monica Davey, "Twinned Cities Now Following Different Paths," *New York Times*, January 12, 2014, http://www.nytimes.com/2014/01/13/us/twinned-cities-now-following-different-paths.html? r=0.

6. Lawrence R. Jacobs referred to them as "cousins" in "Right vs. Left in the Midwest," a Sunday Opinion piece in the *New York Times*, November 23, 2013, http://www.nytimes.com/2013/11/24/opinion/sunday/right-vs-left-in-the-midwest.html?_r=0. Roger Feldman called them "two peas in a pod" in an opinion piece called "Minnesota and Wisconsin: How Did Two Peas in a Pod Grow Apart?" in the Minneapolis Star Tribune on March 7, 2015, http://www.startribune.com/minnesota-and-wisconsin-how-did-two-peas-in-a-pod-grow-apart/295426901/.

7. Jacobs, "Right vs. Left in the Midwest."

8. We are not the first to point out the policy differences affecting the citizens of these two cities. See James Gimpel and Jason E. Schuknect, *Patchwork Nation* (Ann Arbor: University of Michigan Press, 2004), 7.

9. Reid Wilson, "Taxes, Marijuana, Legislatures at Stake in November," *Morning Consult*, October 11, 2015, http://morningconsult.com/2015/10/taxes-marijuana-legislatures-at-stake-in-november/. The quote is from Matt Walter, president of the Republican State Leadership Committee.

10. National Conference of State Legislatures, Center for Legislative Strengthening, "State Legislative Policymaking in an Age of Political Polarization," February 2018, 18.

11. Brad McElhinny, "W.Va. House Speaker Condemns Actions Surrounding Anti-Muslim Display Outside Chamber," *MetroNews*, March 1, 2019.

12. The 1790 Pennsylvania Constitution actually required free public education for those who could not afford it on their own, but legislation creating such public schools did not pass for some years.

13. U.S. Census Bureau, "1790 Fast Facts," http://www.census.gov/history/www.through_the_decades/fast_facts/1.

14. https://www.biggestuscities.com/. November 19, 2019.

15. "Population of the largest metropolitan areas in the U.S. as of 2018. November 19, 2019 https://www.statista.com/statistics/183600/population-of-metropolitan-areas-in-the-us/.

16. United States Census Bureau. History. Novembver 19, 2019. https://www.census.gov/history/www/through_the_decades/index_of_questions/1790_1.html

17. Martha Derthick, *Keeping the Compound Republic: Essays on American Federalism* (Washington, DC: Brookings Institution Press, 2001), 3.

18. Derthick, *Keeping the Compound Republic*, 3.

19. The quote is from Daniel Webster, as cited in Samuel Beer, *To Make a Nation: The Rediscovery of American Federalism* (Cambridge, MA: Belknap Press of Harvard University Press, 1993), 12.

20. For a thoughtful summary of these events and the changes they wrought, see Martha Derthick, "Federalism," in *Understanding America*, ed. Peter H. Schuck and James Q. Wilson (New York: PublicAffairs, 2008), 121–45.

21. Robert Allen, ed., *Our Sovereign State* (New York: Vanguard Press, 1949), xxix.

22. See James T. Patterson, *The New Deal: Federalism in Transition* (Princeton, NJ: Princeton University Press, 1969).

23. Terry Sanford, *Storm over the States* (New York: McGraw-Hill, 1967), 21.

24. Robert Allen, "The Shame of the States," in *Our Sovereign State*, ed. Robert S. Allen (New York: Vanguard Press, 1949), i.

25. Allen, "The Shame of the States," iii.

26. Jon C. Teaford, *The Rise of the States* (Baltimore, MD: Johns Hopkins University Press, 2002), 2.

27. See Teaford, *The Rise of the States*.

28. Alan Rosenthal, *Heavy Lifting: The Job of the American Legislature* (Washington, DC: CQ Press, 2004), 7–8.

29. Peverill Squire, *The Evolution of American Legislatures: Colonies, Territories and States, 1619–2009* (Ann Arbor: University of Michigan Press, 2012), chap. 7.

30. An even larger proportion (71 percent) of respondents held a positive view of their local governments. For all three levels of government, the question posed was "how much trust and confidence to you have in [level] of government?" For federal government, the question was specific to domestic policy. November 19, 2019. https://news.gallup.com/poll/5392/trust-government.aspx.

31. Justin McCarthy, "Majority in U.S. Prefer State Over Federal Government Power," July 11, 2016, http://www.gallup.com/poll/193595/majority-prefer-state-federal-government-power.aspx?version=print.

32. Andrew Gelman, David Park, Boris Shor, Joseph Bafumi, and Jeronimo Cortina, *Red State, Blue State, Rich State, Poor State* (Princeton, NJ: Princeton University Press, 2008), 21–22.

33. This point is often made in the context of the growing polarization in the United States. See, e.g., Alan Abramowitz, *The Disappearing Center* (New Haven, CT: Yale University Press, 2010).

34. Gimple and Schuknecht, *Patchwork Nation*, 9.

35. Bill Bishop, *The Big Sort: Why the Clustering of Like-Minded Americans Is Tearing Us Apart* (New York: Mariner, 2009). A good discussion of the evidence, pro and con, of sorting can be found in Steven Schier and Todd Eberly, *Polarized: The Rise of Ideology in American Politics* (Lanham, MD: Rowman & Littlefield, 2016), esp. 47–62.

36. Harry Enten and Nate Silver, "Migration Isn't Turning Red States Blue," August 29, 2014, http://fivethirtyeight.com/features/immigration-isnt-turning-red-states-blue/.

37. Gerald Wright and Nathaniel Birkhead, "The Macro Sort of the State Electorates," *Political Research Quarterly* 67 (2014): 436.

38. The quote is from Illinois state senator Toi Hutchinson in November 2018. At the time, Senator Hutchinson was the president of the National Conference of State Legislatures. See David Lieb and Geoff Mulvihill, "New Power, New Laws," *The Denver Post* (November 12, 2018), p. 13A.

39. https://www.newyorker.com/cartoons/issue-cartoons/cartoons-from-the-may-2-2016-issue.

40. Daniel Elazar, *American Federalism: A View from the States* (New York: Thomas Crowell, 1966), 6.

41. See https://howmuch.net/articles/comparing-us-states-to-entire-countries-by-gdp-2019; http://statisticstimes.com/economy/countries-by-projected-gdp.php. June 19, 2019.

42. Mackenzie Bean, "50 States Ranked by Opioid Overdose Death Rates," *Becker's Hospital Review*, January 17, 2019. The data reported are based on the Centers for Disease Control statistics for 2017.

43. Frank Newport, "State of the States: Importance of Religion," October 20, 2012, http://www.gallup.com/poll/114022/state-states-importance-religion.aspx.

44. Michael S. Lewis-Beck and Peverill Squire, "Iowa: The Most Representative State?" *PS: Political Science and Politics* 42 (2009): 39–44.

45. Dante Chinni, "With Gridlock in Washington, Lobbyists Turn to Statehouses," *Wall Street Journal*, January 14, 2016.

46. Shanna Rose, "State Legislatures as National Actors," *PS: Political Science and Politics* 52:3 (July 2019), 436.

47. Bill Bishop, *The Big Sort*, 222.

48. Alan Greenblatt, "All or Nothing," *Governing,* January 2019, https://governing.com/topics/gov-state-politics-governors-2019.html.

49. The Congressional Budget Office, "A Visual Summary of the The Budget and Economic Outlook: 2019 to 2019." January 29, 2019, https://www.cbo.gov/system/files/2019-03/54918-Outlook-VisualSummary_0.pdf.

50. Dan Hopkins, "All Politics Is National Because All Media Is National," June 6, 2018, https://fivethirtyeight.com/features/all-politics-is-national-because-all-media-is-national/.

51. Johns Hopkins University., December 18, 2019. https://www.newswise.com/articles/jhu-survey%3A-americans-don%E2%80%99t-know-much-about-state-government.

52. https://www.pewresearch.org/fact-tank/2014/07/10/5-key-takeaways-from-our-census-of-statehouse-reporters/.

53. Jeffrey Lyons, William Jaeger, and Jennifer Wolak, "The Roots of Citizens' Knowledge of State Politics," *State Politics & Policy Quarterly* 13 (2012) 183–202.

54. Steven Michael Rogers, "Accountability in a Federal System" (PhD dissertation, Princeton University, 2013).

55. Seth Masket, "Why We're Not Holding State Legislators Accountable," *Pacific Standard*, September 2, 2014, http://www.psmag.com/politics-and-law/voting-accountability-state-legislators-politics-election-89974.

CHAPTER 2: STATES AND THE FEDERAL SYSTEM

1. Steve Harrison, "Charlotte City Council Approves LGBT protections in 7–4 vote," *Charlotte Observer*, http://www.charlotteobserver.com/news/politics-government/article61786967.html.

2. Michael Gordon, Mark S. Price, and Katie Peralta, "Understanding HB2: North Carolina's Newest Law Solidifies State's Role in Defining Discrimination," *Charlotte Observer*, March 26, 2016, http://www.charlotteobserver.com/news/politics-government/article68401147.html.

3. Matt Zapotosky and Mark Berman, "Justice Dept. to North Carolina: Law Limiting Protections for LGBT People Violates Federal Law," *Washington Post*, May 4, 2016, https://www.washingtonpost.com/politics/justice-dept-to-north-carolina-law-limiting-protections-for-lgbt-people-violates-federal-law/2016/05/04/c11fa75a-1237-11e6-81b4-581a5c4c42df_story.html.

4. Alan Blinder, Richard Pérez-Peña, and Eric Lichtblau, "Countersuits over North Carolina's Bias Law," *New York Times*, May 9, 2016, http://www.nytimes.com/2016/05/10/us/north-carolina-governor-sues-justice-department-over-bias-law.html?_r=0.

5. Blinder, Pérez-Peña, and Lichtblau, "Countersuits over North Carolina's Bias Law."

6. Nolan McCaskill and Caitlin Emma, "11 States Sue Obama over Transgender Bathroom Directive," *Politico*, May 25, 2016, http://www.politico.com/story/2016/05/texas-lawsuit-obama-transgender-bathroom-223569.

7. Emery Dalesio and Jonathan Drew, "AP Exclusive: 'Bathroom bill' to cost North Carolina $3.76B." March 30, 2017, https://www.apnews.com/e6c7a15d2e16452c8dcbc2756fd67b44.

8. http://www.governing.com/templates/gov_print_article?id=486250301; https://www.tennessean.com/story/news/politics/2016/04/18/tennessee-set-sue-federal-government-over-refugee-resettlement/83205430/; https://hrwatchdog.calchamber.com/2019/02/california-challenges-federal-preemption-of-meal-and-rest-break-laws/; https://nashp.org/as-states-take-the-lead-to-address-drug-costs-federal-action-follows/.

9. Alison LaCroix, "How the Noisy Debate Over States' Rights Distorts History and the Intent of Federalism," *Washington Post*, March 25, 2010. http://voices.washingtonpost.com/political-bookworm/2010/03/how_the_noisy_debate_over_stat.html.

10. Sixty-First Legislature of the State of Idaho, HB 117, page 2, lines 39–44.

11. *Florida v. Sibelius* (2010), No. 3:10-CV-91-RV-EMT (N.D. Fla. March 23, 2010).

12. *National Federation of Independent Businesses v. Sibelius*, 132 S.Ct. 2566 (2012).

13. These data were taken from https://www.kff.org/health-reform/state-indicator/state-activity-around-expanding-medicaid-under-the-affordable-care-act/?currentTimeframe=0&sortModel=%7B%22colId%22:%22Location%22,%22sort%22:%22asc%22%7D.

14. Mahalley D. Allen, "Federalism," in *Political Encyclopedia of U.S. States and Regions*, ed. Donald Haider-Markel (Washington, DC: CQ Press, 2009), 766.

15. John D. Donahue, *Disunited States* (New York: Basic Books, 1997), 17.

16. David Brian Robertson, *Federalism and the Making of America*, 2nd ed. (New York: Routledge, 2018) 11.

17. See, e.g., Ilya Somin, "No More Fair-Weather Federalism," National Review online, August 18, 2017, https://www.cato.org/publications/commentary/no-more-fair-weather-federalism.

18. For purposes of simplicity, we use the term "states" here as the conventional term for regional government; it is not necessarily the term used in some of the federal systems we have identified. on

19. Nicole Bolleyer and Lori Thorlakson, "Beyond Decentralization—the Comparative Study of Interdependence in Federal Systems," *Publius: The Journal of Federalism* 42, no. 4 (2012): 576. The eleven countries that meet their criteria are Argentina, Australia,

Austria, Belgium, Canada, Germany, India, South Africa, Spain, Switzerland, and the United States.

20. Ronald L. Watts, "Federalism, Federal Political Systems, and Federations," *Annual Review of Political Science* 1 (1998): 123–24.

21. The four are the United States, Switzerland, Canada, and Australia. David E. Smith, *Federalism and the Constitution of Canada* (Toronto: University of Toronto Press, 2010), 17.

22. Campbell Gibson and Kay Jung, "Historical Census Statistics on Population Totals By Race, 1790 to 1990" (U.S. Census Bureau, Working Paper #56, September 2002).

23. The figure is from Russell Thornton, *American Indian Holocaust and Survival: A Population History Since 1492* (Norman: University of Oklahoma Press, 1987), 133.

24. Thomas S. Kidd, *Patrick Henry, First Among Patriots* (New York: Basic Books, 2011), 183.

25. This discussion relies, in part, on William J. Bennett, *American Theories of Federalism* (Tuscaloosa: University of Alabama Press, 1964), 128, chap. 3.

26. "The General Court of Massachusetts on the Embargo, February 22, 1814," in *State Documents on Federal Relations* (Department of History, University of Pennsylvania, Philadelphia, 1911), 71–72.

27. Bennett, *American Theories of Federalism*, 92–100.

28. John Dinan, "Contemporary Assertions of State Sovereignty and the Safeguards of American Federalism," *Albany Law Review* 74 (2011): 1665.

29. See Christian G. Fritz, "Interposition and the Heresy of Nullification: James Madison and the Exercise of Sovereign Constitutional Powers" (Washington, DC: Heritage Foundation, 2012). This is Number 41 of the "First Principles" series of the Heritage Foundation and can be found at http://report.heritage.org/fp41. See also Bennett, *American Theories of Federalism*, especially 98–100.

30. Lydia Wheeler, "States Rise Up Against Washington," *The Hill*, February 10, 2015, thehill.com/regulation/legislation/232255-states-rising-up-against-washington.

31. Adam Olson, Timothy Callaghan and Andrew Karch, "Return of the 'Rightful Remedy': Partisan Federalism, Resource Availability, and Nullification Legislation in the American States." *Publius* 48:3 (Summer 2018), 495–522.

32. See, e.g., Jack N. Rakove, *Original Meanings* (New York: Vintage Books, 1996), chap. 7.

33. Cecelia M. Kenyon, ed., *The Antifederalists* (Indianapolis: Bobbs-Merrill, 1966), xxi–cxvi.

34. 17 U.S. 316.

35. Kenyon, *The Antifederalists*, xliii.

36. There is also the issue of national supremacy in this case, but for our purposes the question of the meaning of the necessary and proper clause is most important.

37. *McCulloch v. Maryland*, 17 U.S. 316 (1819), 405.

38. *McCulloch v. Maryland*, 406.

39. *McCulloch v. Maryland*, 421.

40. Martha Derthick, "Federalism," in *Understanding America*, ed. Peter H. Schuck and James Q. Wilson (New York: Public Affairs, 2008), 127.

41. Kenyon, *The Antifederalists*, xliii.

42. 317 US 111 (1942).

43. *United States v. Lopez*, 514 US 549 (1995).

44. Joseph F. Zimmerman, *Contemporary American Federalism: The Growth of National Power*, 2nd ed. (Albany: State University of New York Press), 119.

45. Katherine Loughead, "Which States Rely the Most on Federal Aid?" *The Tax Foundation*, January 9, 2019. The analysis relies on U.S. Bureau of Census data from FY 2016. https://taxfoundation.org/federal-aid-reliance-rankings/.

46. Ibid.

47. http://www.deseretnews.com/article/865649135/Legislature-passes-resolution-calling-for-repeal-of-17th-Amendment.html?pg=all.

48. *The Federalist* (Cleveland: World Publishing Co., 1961), 417.

49. The German federal system retains a system similar to that originally established in the U.S. Senate. In the German instance, the upper chamber, the Federal Council, is composed of members chosen by the legislatures of the *Länder* (states).

50. Martha Derthick and John J. Dinan, "Progressivism and Federalism," in *Progressivism and the New Democracy*, ed. Sidney M. Milkis and Jerome M. Mileur (Amherst: University of Massachusetts Press, 1999), 81.

51. https://www.huffpost.com/entry/alec-legislation_n_4652051.

52. This is their phrase, as found on the American Heritage website at https://www.heritage.org/about-heritage/mission. Accessed July 3, 2019.

53. John York, "Would Repealing the 17th Amendment Revive Federalism?" July 2018, https://www.heritage.org/the-constitution/report/would-repealing-the-17th-amendment-revive-federalism.

54. "Noble but quixotic" is the phrase used by the vice president of the conservative Cato Institute in an assessment of the movement to repeal the Seventeenth Amendment. See http://www.cato.org/publications/commentary/repeal-17th-amendment. July 3, 2019.

55. L. Sandy Maisel and Mark Brewer, *Parties and Elections in America*, 5th ed. (Lanham, MD: Rowman & Littlefield, 2008), 47.

56. These figures are reported in James T. Patterson, *The New Deal: Federalism in Transition* (Princeton, NJ: Princeton University Press, 1969), 31, 47.

57. Patterson, *The New Deal*, 38.

58. Derthick, "Federalism," 128.

59. Patterson, *The New Deal*, 198.

60. As quoted in Christopher Sullivan, "1963 at 50: A Year's Tumult Echoes Still," *Associated Press*, January 14, 2013.

61. This was especially the case in Mississippi. For a history of the resistance to segregation in Mississippi, see Joseph Crespino, *In Search of Another Country: Mississippi and the Conservative Counterrevolution* (Princeton, NJ: Princeton University Press, 2007), or Neil McMillen, *The Citizens Council* (Champaign: University of Illinois Press, 1994).

62. See footnote 16 in Dinan, "Contemporary Assertions of State Sovereignty and the Safeguards of American Federalism."

63. Joseph F. Zimmerman, *Contemporary American Federalism: The Growth of National Power* (Westport, CT: Praeger, 1992), 11.

64. See table 4 of the Congressional Research Service report, "Federal Grants to State and Local Governments: A Historical Perspective on Contemporary Issues," March 3, 2015, https://www.fas.org/sgp/crs/misc/R40638.pdf.

65. Derthick, "Federalism," 130.

66. Ann O'M. Bowman and Richard Kearney, *The Resurgence of the States* (Englewood Cliffs, NJ: Prentice Hall, 1986).

67. Congressional Research Service, "Federal Grants to State and Local Governments," table 3.

68. While most Republican presidents at least pay some lip service to restoring the role of the states in the federal system, George W. Bush seemed reluctant to even make the symbolic gesture. As one observer noted, "He paid no honor to federalism." In addition to meeting substantial state resistance to his efforts to nationalize education policy and to create a national identification card, the cost of the expansion of prescription drug benefits to Medicare resulted in substantial cost increases to the states. See Derthick, "Federalism," 136.

69. https://www.dallasnews.com/news/politics/2012/06/07/atty-gen-greg-abbott-says-his-job-is-simple-sue-the-federal-government-then-go-home.

70. Paul Nolette and Colin Provost, " Change and Continuity in the Role of State Attorneys General in the Obama and Trump Administrations," *Publius* 48:3 (Summer 2018), 470.

71. Elizabeth Mann Levesque, "Waiving Goodbye to Congressional Constraints: Presidents and Subnational Policy Making," *Presidential Studies Quarterly* 49 (2019), 358–93.

72. Derthick, "Federalism," 123.

73. Daniel J. Hopkins, *The Increasingly United States: How and Why American Political Behavior Nationalized* (Chicago: University of Chicago Press, 2018), 2.

74. Larry N. Gerston, *American Federalism: A Concise Introduction* (Armonk, NY: M. E. Sharpe, 2007).

75. Gerston, *American Federalism*, 32.

76. Martha Derthick, *Keeping the Compound Republic* (Washington, DC: Brookings Institution Press, 2001), 140.

77. David Walker, *The Rebirth of Federalism* (Chatham: Chatham House, 1995), xii.

78. John D. Nugent, *Safeguarding Federalism: How States Protect Their Interests in National Policymaking* (Norman: University of Oklahoma Press, 2009).

79. Jennifer M. Jensen, "Governors and Partisan Polarization in the Federal Arena," *Publius: The Journal of Federalism,* 47:3 (Summer, 2017), 329. Also see *Jennifer M. Jensen, The Governors' Lobbyists* (Ann Arbor: University of Michigan Press, 2016).

80. Nugent, *Safeguarding Federalism*, 225.

81. Zimmerman, *Contemporary American Federalism*, 196.

82. These and other examples are discussed in Sean Nicholson-Crotty, "Leaving Money on the Table: Learning from Recent Refusals of Federal Grants in the American States," *Publius: The Journal of Federalism* 42 (2012): 449–66.

83. Derthick, "Federalism," 140.

84. Robert McCartney, "How States and Localities Are Filling the Gaps Left by Washington Gridlock," *Washington Post*, September 26, 2015, https://www.washington-post.com/local/how-states-and-localities-are-filling-the-gaps-left-by-washingtons-grid-lock/2015/09/26/e43c5b58-63b8-11e5-b38e-06883aacba64_story.html.

85. Elizabeth Fredericksen, Stephanie Witt, and David Nice, *The Politics of Intergovernmental Relations*, 3rd ed. (San Diego: Birkdale Publishers, 2016), chap. 6.

86. Zimmerman, *Contemporary American Federalism*, 164.

87. Zimmerman, *Contemporary American Federalism*, 176. Also see chapter 7 of this volume.

88. Robertson, "American Federalism as a Political Weapon," 23.

89. Alice Rivlin, "Rethinking Federalism for More Effective Governance," *Publius: The Journal of Federalism* 42 (2012), 299.

90. See, e.g., Erin Ryan, *Federalism and the Tug of War Within* (New York: Oxford University Press, 2011).

CHAPTER 3: STATE FISCAL SYSTEMS

1. Josiah Bates, "Alaska's State Budget is Slumping." *Time Magazine*, July 10, 2019, https://time.com/5623042/alaska-budget-cuts/.

2. On Pennsylvania, see Karen Langley, "Pennsylvania's Budget Impasse Comes to an End: 'We Need to Move On,'" *Pittsburgh Post-Gazette*, March 24, 2016.

3. http://triblive.com/news/allegheny/10157118-74/million-district-budget.

4. Sophia Tareen, "Awkward: Illinois Governor Sued by Wife's Non-Profit," *St. Louis Post-Dispatch*, June 9, 2016.

5. See, e.g., "The Great Kansas Tax Cut Experiment Crashes and Burns," *Forbes Magazine*, June 2017, https://www.forbes.com/sites/beltway/2017/06/07/the-great-kansas-tax-cut-experiment-crashes-and-burns/#65763a3e5508.

6. See, e.g., Irene Rubin, *The Politics of Public Budgeting*, 7th ed. (Washington, DC: CQ Press, 2014).

7. Phil Kabler, "West Virginia Heads into Special Session to Close Budget Shortfall," *Tribune News Service*, May 12, 2016, http://www.governing.com/topics/finance/tns-west-virginia-budget-session.html. The senator quoted is Mike Hall.

8. Tracy Gordon, Megan Randall, Eugene Steuerle, and Aravind Boddupalli, "Fiscal Democracy in the States: How Much Spending Is on Autopilot?" Urban Institute, July 2019.

9. Center on Budget and Policy Priorities, "Federal Aid to State and Local Governments." April 19, 2018, https://www.cbpp.org/research/state-budget-and-tax/federal-aid-to-state-and-local-governments.

10. Another way to think about this is that the calendar year is divided into four quarters and these quarters are often important reporting periods for businesses and economic analysis (e.g., "second quarter sales were up by 5 percent"). Only Texas does not operate off one of the four economic quarters.

11. National Association of State Budget Officers, Summary: Spring 2019. "Fiscal Survey of States," https://higherlogicdownload.s3.amazonaws.com/NASBO/9d2d2db1-c943-4f1b-b750-0fca152d64c2/UploadedImages/Fiscal%20Survey/Summary_-_Spring_2019_Fiscal_Survey.pdf.

12. The National Bureau of Economic Research (NBER) has determined that the Great Recession actually began in December 2007 and bottomed out in June 2009.

13. National Conference of State Legislatures (NCSL), "Update on State Budget Gaps: FY 2009 & FY 2010," Denver: National Conference of State Legislatures, February 20, 2009, 2.

14. These and subsequent figures are from the Center on Budget and Policy Priorities, June 27, 2012, "States Continue to Feel Recession's Impact," https://www.cbpp.org/research/states-continue-to-feel-recessions-impact.

15. NCSL, "Update on State Budget Gaps: FY 2009 & FY 2010."

16. Pamela Prah, "States Balance Budgets with Cuts, not Taxes," *Stateline*, June 15, 2011, http://www.pewstates.org/projects/stateline/headlines/states-balance-budgets-with-cuts-not-taxes-85899375037.

17. http://www.usatoday.com/news/nation/2009-05-04-fed-states-revenue_N.htm.

18. Pew Charitable Trust, Fiscal 50: State Trends and Analysis, "Federal Funds Provide 30 Cents of Each Dollar of State Revenue," February 25, 2015. It should be noted that different reports cite different figures for a variety of reasons. The most important difference is that some calculate federal aid as a percent of state and local revenues and some report it as percent of state revenues only. Because states receive more federal aid than do local governments, the "percent of state revenue" figure is always higher than the "percent of state and local revenue." E.g., while federal aid comprised 35.5 percent of state revenue, it comprised only about 26 percent of state and local revenue.

19. National Association of State Budget Officers, "Summary: Spring 2019 Fiscal Survey of States," June 13, 2019, https://higherlogicdownload.s3.amazonaws.com/NASBO/9d2d2db1-c943-4f1b-b750-0fca152d64c2/UploadedImages/Fiscal%20Survey/Summary_-_Spring_2019_Fiscal_Survey.pdf.

20. Katherine Barrett and Richard Greene, "Rainy Day Fund Strategies," The Volcker Alliance, July 10, 2019, https://www.volckeralliance.org/publications/rainy-day-fund-strategies-call-action.

21. Pew Charitable Trusts, "'Lost Decade' Casts a Post-Recession Shadow on State Finances," June 4, 2019. https://www.pewtrusts.org/en/research-and-analysis/issue-briefs/2019/06/lost-decade-casts-a-post-recession-shadow-on-state-finances.

22. Ron Snell, "States' Experiences with Annual and Biennial Budgets," April 2011. http://www.ncsl.org/research/fiscal-policy/state-experiences-with-annual-and-biennial-budgeti.aspx.

23. With the exception of the last four years of the Clinton administration, the federal government spent more than it received in every year since 1970. In other words, the federal government has run a deficit in 90 percent of its budgets over the past forty years.

24. John Kincaid, "The Constitutional Frameworks of State and Local Government Finance," in *The Oxford Handbook of State and Local Government Finance*, ed. Robert D. Ebel and John E. Petersen (New York: Oxford University Press, 2012), 62–63.

25. See David M. Primo, *Rules and Restraint: Government Spending and the Design of Institutions* (Chicago, IL: University of Chicago Press 2008), chap. 5.

26. NCSL Fiscal Brief: "State Balanced Budget Provisions." October 2010. http://www.ncsl.org/documents/fiscal/StateBalancedBudgetProvisions2010.pdf.

27. See Carl E. Klarner, Justin H. Phillips, and Matt Muckler, "Overcoming Fiscal Gridlock: Institutions and Budget Bargaining," *Journal of Politics* 74 (2012): 992–1009.

28. "What's Open, What's Closed: Your Guide to the Shutdown," *Star-Tribune*, July 12, 2011, http://www.startribune.com/politics/statelocal/124952649.html.

29. See W. Mark Crain, *Volatile States* (Ann Arbor: University of Michigan Press 2003), especially chap. 8. For an alternative point of view, see Thad Kousser, Mathew D. McCubbins, and Ellen Moule, "For Whom the TEL Tolls: Can State Tax and Expenditure Limits Effectively Reduce Spending?" *State Politics and Policy Quarterly* 8 (2008): 331–61.

30. Katharine Bradbury, "State Government Budgets and the Recovery Act," Public Policy Briefs, No. 10–1, February 17, 2010, Federal Reserve Bank of Boston, 3.

31. http://www.tennessean.com/story/news/politics/2016/05/20/gov-bill-haslam-signs-hall-income-tax-cut-repeal-into-law/84044810/.

32. Legislative Analysts' Office, "California Tax System: A Visual Guide," April 10, 2018.

33. *South Dakota v. Wayfair, Inc.* 585 U.S.___(2018)

34. Liz Farmer, "A Year After Online Sales Tax Ruling, Are States Reaping More Revenue?" *Governing*, June 21, 2019, https://www.governing.com/week-in-finance/gov-anniversary-wayfair-sales-tax-ruling-state-revenues.html.

35. David Brunori, *State Tax Policy: A Political Perspective*, 2nd ed. (Washington, DC: Urban Institute Press, 2005), 53.

36. Brunori, *State Tax Policy: A Political Perspective*, 54.

37. Michael Leachman and Michael Mazarov, "State Personal Income Tax Cuts: Still a Poor Strategy for Economic Growth," Center for Budget and Policy Priorities, May 14, 2015, http://www.cbpp.org/research/state-budget-and-tax/state-personal-income-tax-cuts-still-a-poor-strategy-for-economic.

38. Federation of Tax Administrators. November 19, 2019. https://www.taxadmin.org/current-tax-rates.

39. https://www.pewtrusts.org/en/research-and-analysis/blogs/stateline/2019/08/19/vaping-craze-prompts-new-state-taxes.

40. Carina Julig, "Colorado Surpasses $1 billion in Marijuana Tax Revenue," *Denver Post*, June 12, 2019.

41. Tanyua Basu, "Colorado Raised More Tax Revenue from Marijuana than from Alcohol." Time Magazine. May 18, 2016. https://time.com/4037604/colorado-marijuana-tax-revenue/.

42. Kate Smith, "Washington Expects Pot Sales Tax Revenue Siurge to $1 Billion," Bloomberg News. October 23, 2015. http://www.bloomberg.com/news/articles/2015-10-23/washington-expects-pot-sales-tax-revenue-surge-to-1-billion.

43. See page 15 in https://lcb.wa.gov/sites/default/files/publications/annual_report/2017-annual-report-final2-web.pdf.

44. In addition, as of 2020, thirty-three states permitted the use of medical marijuana under certain conditions.

45. Federation of Tax Administrators. August 11, 2019. https://www.taxadmin.org/assets/docs/Research/Rates/corp_inc.pdf.

46. https://taxfoundation.org/state-corporate-rates-brackets-2019/; Prah, "States Balance Budgets with Cuts, not Taxes."

47. Mike Maciag, "How States' Dependence on Corporate Taxes Has Declined," *Governing*, January 6, 2016, http://www.governing.com/topics/finance/gov-state-corporate-income-tax-revenues.html.

48. Jonathan Mattise, Associated Press. "With Coal and Gas Down, West Virginia Faces Budget Quandary." March 7, 2016. http://www.wvgazettemail.com/news/20160307/with-coal-and-gas-down-west-virginia-faces-budget-quandary/.

49. Alex DeMarban and Yereth Rosen, "Days of Reckoning", Anchorage Daily News. June 30, 2016. http://www.adn.com/politics/2016/06/29/walker-budget-vetoes-include-capping-permanent-fund-divdends-at-1000/.

50. See, e.g., Ernest Scheyder, "In North Dakota's Oil Patch, a Humbling Comedown." Reuter's. May 18, 2016. http://www.reuters.com/investigates/special-report/usa-northdakota-bust/.

51. James McPherson, "North Dakota Revenue Estimate Expects Rising Oil." Associated Press, January 7, 2019, https://www.apnews.com/b200edb6f060494ab5355b5c1e8a3d75.

52. https://www.taxadmin.org/2016-state-tax-collection-by-source; Mary Murphy, Akshay Iyengar, and Alexandria Zhang, "Tax Revenue Volatility Varies Across States, Revenue Streams." PEW, August 29, 2018, https://www.pewtrusts.org/en/research-and-analysis/articles/2018/08/29/tax-revenue-volatility-varies-across-states-revenue-streams.

53. Vehicle Title, Tax and Registration Costs by State. March 15, 2019. https://www.compare.com/auto-insurance/coverage/vehicle-costs.

54. Governors' Highway Safety Association, "Seat Belts." November 21, 2019. https://www.ghsa.org/state-laws/issues/seat%20belts.

55. Donna Leinwand, "Cities, States Tack on More User Fees," *USA Today*, March 18, 2009, http://www.usatoday.com/news/nation/2009-03-17-user-fees_N.htm; Katherine Barrett and Richard Greene, "The Risks of Relying on User Fees," *Governing*, April 2013.

56. Grace Marion, "Lottery Scratch-Off Ticket Sales Start Dec. 1 with Multi-State Games Expected to Follow in Early 2020," *Mississippi Today*, July 19, 2019. Also see Frances S. Berry and William D. Berry, "State Lottery Adoptions as Policy Innovations: An Event History Analysis," *American Political Science Review* 84 (1990): 395–414.

57. Olivia Berlin and Jackson Brainerd, "Keeping State Lottery Revenue Alive," National Conference of State Legislatures, September 2017, http://www.ncsl.org/research/fiscal-policy/keeping-state-lottery-revenue-alive.aspx.

58. Lee Davidson, "Utahns Buy 19% of Idaho's Lottery Tickets," *Salt Lake City Tribune*, April 6, 2012, http://www.sltrib.com/sltrib/news/53862915-78/lottery-idaho-utah-sales.html.csp.

59. These figures, as well as state-specific figures discussed in the text, are based on information from the National Conference of State Legislatures, "Chart of Lottery Payouts and Revenue, By State," http://www.ncsl.org/issues-research/econ/lottery-payouts-and-state-revenue-2010.aspx.

60. See American Gaming Association. "State of Play." August 12, 2019. https://www.americangaming.org/state-of-play/, commercial gaming states.

61. See https://www.americangaming.org/state-of-play/, tribal gaming states.

62. *Murphy v. National Collegiate Athletic Association*, 584 US___ (2018).

63. Ryan Rodenberg, "United States of Sports Betting: An Updated Map of Where Every State Stands," espn.com, August 2, 2019, https://www.espn.com/chalk/story/_/id/19740480/the-united-states-sports-betting-where-all-50-states-stand-legalization.

64. Associated Press, "Why Sports Betting Won't Make States a Lot of Money," Marketwatch, January 2, 2019, https://www.marketwatch.com/story/why-sports-betting-wont-make-states-a-lot-of-money-2019-01-02.

65. National Alcohol Beverage Control Association, "Control States Directory and Information. November 19, 2019. https://www.nabca.org/control-state-directory-and-info.

66. https://bnd.nd.gov/history-of-bnd/; Chester Dawson, "Shale Boom Helps North Dakota Bank Earn Returns Goldman Would Envy," *Wall Street Journal*, November 16, 2014.

67. The Morrill Land Grant Act (1862) is usually noted as the first actual example of fiscal federalism, transferring federal lands to states to sell for the establishment of land grant colleges.

68. Another six states adopted lotteries between 2000 and 2009.

69. See State and Local Government Finance Data Query System, the Urban Institute-Brookings Institution Tax Policy Center, http://www.taxpolicycenter.org/taxfacts/displayafact.cfm?DocID=528&Topic2id=90&Topic3id=92; http://www.taxpolicycenter.org/briefing-book/what-are-sources-revenue-state-governments.

70. See Congressional Budget Office, "Actual ARRA Spending Over the 2009–2011 Period Quite Close to the CBO's Original Estimate," www.cbo.gov/publication/42682.

71. Not all of these funds went directly to state and local governments, as some were directed to small businesses and qualifying individuals. Moreover, ARRA yielded at least an additional $200 billion in tax reductions to individuals and corporations, making the "value" of the total stimulus package in excess of $700 billion.

72. There were at least half a dozen governors (all Republicans) who announced they would refuse ARRA funds that extended unemployment benefits, arguing that certain strings attached to these funds would obligate their state to offer extended benefits in the future. Ultimately, the funds were accepted in most of these states.

73. But it does happen from time to time. For an explanation of the causes of such refusals to accept the federal funds, see Sean Nicholson-Crotty, "Leaving Money on the Table: Learning from Recent Refusals of Federal Grants in the American States," *Publius* 42 (2012): 449–66.

74. Marilyn Rubin and Katherine Willoughby, eds., *Sustaining the States: The Fiscal Viability of American State Government* (Boca Raton, FL: CRC Press, 2015), 10.

75. The remainder (17 percent) is categorized as "other." See OMB, "Fiscal Year 2013 Analytical Perspectives," Table 18-2, "Trends in Federal Grants to State and Local Governments," http://www.whitehouse.gov/sites/default/files/omb/budget/fy2013/assets/spec.pdf.

76. See Katharine Loughead, "Which States Rely the Most on Federal Aid?" January 9, 2019. The Tax Foundation. Data are from FY 2016. Explanation of "general revenue" appears below map on the website, https://taxfoundation.org/federal-aid-reliance-rankings/.

77. Note that we refer to state spending, not state and local combined. Medicaid funds are part of the state appropriations process.

78. Rachel Brand, "Medicaid: The 800-Pound Gorilla," *State Legislatures* (October/November 2011), 15; Dan Boyd, "State Medicaid Costs Called a 'Runaway Train,'" *Albuquerque Journal*, October 28, 2015, http://www.abqjournal.com/666735/state-medicaid-costs-a-runaway-train.html.

79. Center for Colorado's Economic Future, "Issue Brief: Colorado's State Budget Tsunami," University of Denver, July 2009, 6.

80. Congressional Budget Office, "The Underfunding of State and Local Pension Plans," Economic and Budget Issue Brief, May 2011.

81. Pew Charitable Trusts. June 4, 2019. https://www.pewtrusts.org/en/research-and-analysis/issue-briefs/2019/06/lost-decade-casts-a-post-recession-shadow-on-state-finances.

82. Michael Cembalest, "The ARC and the Covenants, 2.0: An Update on the Long-Term Credit Risk of US States," *Eye on the Market*, J. P. Morgan, May 19, 2016.

83. Pew Charitable Trusts, "The State Pension Funding Gap: 2017," June, 2019

84. Heather Gillers, "Bull Market Isn't Helping Pensions," *Wall Street Journal*, April 11, 2019.

85. Urban Institute, "State and Local Government Pensions." August 10, 2019. https://www.urban.org/policy-centers/cross-center-initiatives/state-and-local-finance-initiative/projects/state-and-local-backgrounders/state-and-local-government-pensions.

86. See "Hybrid Public Pension Plans," Pew Charitable Trusts, April 2015.

87. Timothy Conlan and Paul Posner, "Federalism Trends, Tensions and Outlook," in *The Oxford Handbook of State and Local Government Finance*, ed. Robert Ebel and John Petersen (New York: Oxford University Press, 2012), 98.

88. American Society of Civil Engineers. 2017 Infrastructure Report Card. November 19, 2019. http://www.infrastructurereportcard.org/.

89. John Schoen, "Rebuilding America Will Be Harder than it Sounds," *CNBC*, May 17, 2016, http://www.cnbc.com/2016/05/17/rebuilding-america-will-be-harder-than-it-sounds.html.

90. http://www.governing.com/topics/transportation-infrastructure/is-this-the-way-states-can-sell-tax-hikes-for-transportation.html.

91. Chris Isidore, "Gas Taxes are rising because Americans are driving more fuel-efficient cars," *CNN Business*, July 1, 2019, https://www.cnn.com/2019/07/01/business/state-gas-taxes-increase/index.html.

92. U.S. General Accountability Office, "State and Local Governments' Fiscal Outlook: 2018 Update. December 13, 2018. https://www.gao.gov/products/GAO-19-208SP.

93. D. Roderick Kiewiet and Mathew McCubbins, "State and Local Government Finance: The New Fiscal Ice Age," *Annual Review of Political Science* 17 (2014): 105.

94. Norton Francis and Frank Sammartino, "Governing with Tight Budgets," September 10, 2015, http://www.urban.org/research/publication/governing-tight-budgets.

CHAPTER 4: THE POLICYMAKING ENVIRONMENT IN THE STATES

1. See the discussion in Peverill Squire, *The Evolution of American Legislatures: Colonies, Territories, and States, 1619–2009* (Ann Arbor: University of Michigan Press, 2012), 72–83.

2. James Madison, Alexander Hamilton, and John Jay, *The Federalist Papers* (New York: New American Library, 1961), 303–4.

3. Horst Dippel, "The Changing Idea of Popular Sovereignty in Early America Constitutionalism: Breaking Away from European Patterns," *Journal of the Early Republic* 16 (1996): 21–45; Gordon S. Wood, *Creation of the American Republic 1776–1787* (Chapel Hill: University of North Carolina Press, 1969), 446–53.

4. John W. Burgess, "The American Commonwealth: Changes in Its Relation to the Nation," *Political Science Quarterly* 1 (1886): 9–35.

5. Peverill Squire and Keith E. Hamm, *101 Chambers: Congress, State Legislatures, and the Future of Legislative Studies* (Columbus: Ohio State University Press, 2005), 68.

6. See the discussion in Squire, *The Evolution of American Legislatures*, 243–48.

7. Squire, *The Evolution of American Legislatures*, 271–73.

8. Jonathan Elliot, *Debates on the Adoption of the Federal Constitution, in the Convention Held at Philadelphia, in 1787; with a Diary of the Debates of the Congress of the Confederation; as Reported by James Madison, a Member and Deputy from Virginia* (Washington, DC: Jonathan Elliot, 1845), 327.

9. See the discussion in Leslie Lipson, *The American Governor from Figurehead to Leader* (Chicago, IL: University of Chicago Press, 1939), 17–30.

10. The following discussion is drawn from Rui J. P. de Figueredo Jr., "Budget Institutions and Political Insulation: Why States Adopt the Item Veto," *Journal of Public Economics* 87 (2003): 2677–701; John A. Fairlie, "The Veto Power of the Governor," *American Political Science Review* 11 (1917): 473–93; National Conference of State Legislatures, *Inside the Legislative Process*, Table 98-6.10, http://www.ncsl.org/documents/legismgt/ILP/98Tab6Pt3.pdf, and various state constitutions.

11. It appears in Article 1, Section 7 (2). See https://avalon.law.yale.edu/19th_century/csa_csa.asp.

12. It appears in Article III, Section 2 (6). See https://vault.georgiaarchives.org/digital/collection/adhoc/id/365.

13. See the discussion in Peverill Squire and Gary Moncrief, *State Legislatures Today: Politics Under the Domes* (Boston: Longman, 2010), 216–18.

14. See Wisconsin Legislative Council, *Wisconsin Legislator Briefing Book 2019–2020*, chap. 25. See also Lawrence Andrea, "Tony Evers Proves Once Again That Wisconsin Governors Have the Broadest Veto Powers in the U.S.," *Milwaukee Journal Sentinel*, July 3, 2019; and Kelly Meyerhofer, "Republicans Propose Constitutional Amendment Limiting Governor's Veto Power," *Wisconsin State Journal*, July 10, 2019.

15. http://www.ncsl.org/research/fiscal-policy/gubernatorial-veto-authority-with-respect-to-major.aspx.

16. See Peverill Squire and Gary Moncrief, *State Legislatures Today: Politics under the Domes*, 3rd ed. (Lanham, MD: Rowman & Littlefield, 2020), 174.

17. Tim Lockette, "Alabama Constitutional Commission Debates Veto Override Power," *Anniston Star*, July 1, 2013.

18. See the discussion of gubernatorial power in Margaret Ferguson, "Governors and the Executive Branch," in *Politics in the American States*, ed. Virginia Gray, Russell L. Hanson, and Thad Kousser, 11th ed. (Thousand Oaks, CA: Sage, 2018).

19. This discussion was taken from Finla Goff Crawford, *State Government* (New York: Henry Holt, 1931), 181–82. See also Legislative Reference Bureau, *Constitutional Convention Bulletin No. 9, The Executive Department* (Springfield: Legislative Reference Bureau, 1920), 623–25.

20. Alan Greenblatt, "From 42 Agencies to 15: How Arkansas Overhauled State Government without Laying Anyone Off," *Governing.com*, July 2019.

21. This list is taken from *The Book of the States, 2018 Edition* (Lexington: Council of State Governments, 2018), 124–28.

22. JoyAnna S. Hopper, "The Regulation of Combination: The Implications of Combining Natural Resource Conservation and Environmental Protection," *State Politics & Policy Quarterly* 17 (2017): 105–24.

23. https://www.ourcampaigns.com/CandidateDetail.html?CandidateID=4365.

24. See Mark L. Early, "'Special Solicitude': The Growing Power of State Attorneys General," *University of Richmond Law Review* 52 (2017–2018): 561–67; Paul Nolette, "The Duel Role of State Attorneys General in American Federalism: Conflict and Cooperation in an Era of Partisan Polarization," *Publius* 47 (2017): 342–77.

25. Lawrence M. Friedman, *A History of American Law* (New York: Touchstone, 1973), 122–23.

26. Friedman, *A History of American Law*, 123–24.

27. Charts of current state court structures can be found at http://www.courtstatistics. org/Other-Pages/State_Court_Structure_Charts.aspx.

28. http://www.vermontjudiciary.org/court-divisions.

29. http://www.ncsc.org/conferences-and-events/4th-symposium/~/media/Files/PDF/ Conferences%20and%20Events/4th%20Symposium/Davenport-VT.ashx; https://www. courts.state.nh.us/circuitcourt/index.htm.

30. The number adds to fifty-two because Oklahoma and Texas each have two courts of last resort.

31. Don Willett, "Chalices, Jack-o'-Lanterns and Other State Court Tiebreakers," *Wall Street Journal*, May 31, 2016.

32. Russell Berman, "Arizona Republicans Try to Bring Back Court-Packing," *The Atlantic*, May 10, 2016; Alan Greenblatt, "Does Size Matter? The Latest Battle Over State Supreme Courts," *Governing*, May 12, 2016; Mark Joseph Stern, "Arizona's Governor Is Leading Republicans' Quiet, Radical Takeover of State Supreme Courts," *Slate*, August 29, 2019, https://slate.com/news-and-politics/2019/08/arizona-supreme-court-rigging-doug-ducey-bill-montgomery.html.

33. Evan H. Caminker, "Thayerian Deference to Congress and Supreme Court Majority Rules: Lessons from the Past," *Indiana Law Journal* 78 (2003): 73–122.

34. Maria L. La Ganga, "Nebraska Supreme Court Rules on Keystone XL Pipeline," *Los Angeles Times*, January 9, 2015.

35. Whitney Woodworth, "Oregon Legislature Considers if Voters Should Decide Fate of Non-Unanimous Jury Law," *Salem Statesman Journal*, May 10, 2019.

36. Melinda Deslatte, "Unanimous Jury Verdict Requirement among New Louisiana Laws," *Advocate*, December 31, 2018.

37. On the complexity of the judicial selection at the state level, see Greg Goelzhauser, "Classifying Judicial Selection Institutions," *State Politics & Policy Quarterly* 18 (2018): 174–92.

38. Peverill Squire and Eric R. A. N. Smith, "The Effect of Partisan Information on Voters in Nonpartisan Elections," *Journal of Politics* 50 (1988): 169–79.

39. Phil Kabler, "Spending Sparks Criticism in Supreme Court Race," *Charleston Gazette-Mail*, May 12, 2016.

40. Thomas Gray, "The Influence of Legislative Reappointment on State Supreme Court Decision-Making," *State Politics & Policy Quarterly* 17 (2017): 275–98.

41. See https://www.ncsc.org/microsites/judicial-salaries-data-tool/home/Special-Reports/Salary-Reductions.aspx.

42. Jeff Jenkins, "Amendment Would Withhold Retirement Fund Payments Until Controversial Impeachment Ruling Overturned," *WV MetroNews*, February 11, 2019.

43. See G. Alan Tarr, "The Past and Future of the New Judicial Federalism," *Publius* 24 (1994): 63–79.

44. See "New Judicial Federalism," http://encyclopedia.federalism.org/index.php/ New_Judicial_Federalism.

45. Robert W. Williams, "Introduction: The Third Stage of New Judicial Federalism," *NYU Annual Survey of American Law* 59 (2003): 211–19.

46. Joshua Sharpe, "Georgia High Court Strikes Down Part of DUI Law," *Atlanta Journal-Constitution*, February 18, 2019; Jonathan Shorman and Lara Korte, "Abortion Protected by Kansas Constitution, State Supreme Court Rules," *Wichita Eagle*, April 26, 2019.

47. Alan Blinder, "Alabama Judge Defies Gay Marriage Law," *New York Times*, February 8, 2015.

48. See Carl T. Bogus, "The Battle for Separation of Powers in Rhode Island," *Administrative Law Review* 56 (2004): 77–134.

49. William C. Dawson, *A Compilation of the Laws of the State of Georgia, Passed by the General Assembly, Since the Year 1819 to the Year 1829, Inclusive* (Milledgeville, GA: Grantland and Orme, 1831).

CHAPTER 5: THE POLICYMAKING CAPACITY OF STATE GOVERNMENTS

1. See Larry Sabato, *Goodbye to Good-Time Charlie*, 2nd ed. (Washington, DC: CQ Press 1983).

2. James Reston, "Boston: Big Problems and Little Men in State Capital," *New York Times*, October 5, 1962.

3. Martin F. Nolan, "The City Politic: Rocky's Road to Albany," *New York Magazine*, August 31, 1970.

4. Alan Rosenthal, *The Best Job in Politics* (Washington, DC: CQ Press, 2013).

5. Rosenthal, *The Best Job in Politics*, 3.

6. Rosenthal, *The Best Job in Politics*, 5

7. Bryan Lowry, "Kansas Gov. Sam Brownback Cuts Medicaid Reimbursements, Higher-Ed Spending," *Kansas City Star*, May 18, 2016.

8. See Margaret Ferguson, "Governors and the Executive Branch," in *Politics in the American States*, ed. Virginia Gray, Russell L. Hanson, and Thad Kousser, 11th ed. (Thousand Oaks, CA: Sage, 2018).

9. Quoted in Louis Jacobson, "Experience Preferred," *State Legislatures Magazine*, January 2016.

10. Bernard Schoenburg, "Former Gov. Jim Edgar Urges Gov. Bruce Rauner to Quit Holding Budget Hostage," *State Register-Journal*, October 16, 2015.

11. Kerry Lester, "Thompson Says State in 'Worst Position Ever,' " *Arlington Heights Daily Herald*, October 20, 2015.

12. Keviun McDermott, "Budget Showdown Looming in Illinois as Rauner's First Session Ticks Down," *St. Louis Post-Dispatch*, June 1, 2015.

13. Anthony Izaguirre, "Schedules Show West Virginia Governor Largely Absent in Job," AP News, May 11, 2019, https://www.apnews.com/f080da8d7189476e91062c69483166a1.

14. See John A. Hamman, "Career Experience and Performing Effectively as Governor," *American Review of Public Administration* 34 (2004): 151–63.

15. Margaret Ferguson, "Governors and the Executive Branch," in *Politics in the American States*, ed. Virginia Gray and Russell L. Hanson, 11th ed. (Thousand Oaks, CA: Sage, 2018), 238.

16. Peverill Squire, "Electoral Career Movements and the Flow of Political Power in the American Federal System," *State Politics and Policy Quarterly* 14 (2014): 72–89.

17. These data were calculated by the authors from gubernatorial salary data found in various editions of the *Book of the States* and the Bureau of Labor Statistics CPI Inflation Calculator.

18. Mackinac Center for Public Policy, "Government Transparency Groups Announce Database of Public Employee Salaries," March 23, 2017.

19. Emily Bohatch, "Here's Who Makes More Money than SC Gov. Henry McMaster (Hint: The List Is Long)," *The State*, May 15, 2019.

20. See Steve Berkowitz, "Alabama Football Coach Nick Saban Set to Make $8.3 Million This Season under New Contract," *USA Today*, July 27, 2018. Saban was scheduled to make $8.7 million in 2019. The governor was paid $120,395.

21. James Salzer and Greg Bluestein, "Top Aides Benefit as Kemp Shuffles Pay Structure in Governor's Office," *Atlanta Journal-Constitution*, February 8, 2019.

22. Kevin Hardy and Barbara Rodriguez, "Here's What Kim Reynold's Top Appointees Make—and Who Got a $50,000 Bonus," *Des Moines Register*, January 29, 2019.

23. Peter Holley, "'She's an Amazing Employee': Wife of Maine Governor Takes Waitressing Job to Make Ends Meet," *Washington Post*, June 25, 2016.

24. *Bangor Daily News*, "Maine Hasn't Raised the Governor's Pay in More Than 20 Years. It Should Now," April 8 2019.

25. Lee Davidson, "Salary for Utah Governor May See 36 Percent Bump," *Salt Lake Tribune*, February 12, 2015.

26. Theo Francis, Hanna Sender, and Russell Adams, "The WSJ CEO Pay Rankings," *Wall Street Journal*, May 18–19, 2019.

27. Amber Phillips, "Terry Branstad Just Became the Longest Serving Governor in American History," *Washington Post*, December 14, 2015.

28. See Ann O'M. Bowman, Neal D. Woods, and Milton R. Stark II, "Governors Turn Pro: Separation of Powers and the Institutionalization of the American Governorship," *Political Research Quarterly* 63 (2010): 304–15.

29. These numbers were calculated by the authors from various editions of the *Book of the States*.

30. Missouri State Auditor, "Findings in the Audit of the Office of the Governor," April 2015; see also Mark Brunswick, "Governor's Staff Partly Paid by State Agencies," *Star Tribune*, March 9, 2009; John O'Connor, "Illinois Agencies Cover Half the Pay for Gov. Rauner's Staff," *St. Louis Post-Dispatch*, August 10, 2015; "Governor Reynolds Paying Staff with Money from Other Agencies; Staff Says It's Nothing New," WhoTV.com, July 25, 2019.

31. These data are taken from United States Census Bureau, Annual Survey of Public Employment & Payroll, "State Government Employment & Payroll Data."

32. These data are taken from Cynthia J. Bowling and Deil S. Wright, "Public Administration in the Fifty States: A Half-Century Administrative Revolution," *State and Local Government Review* 30 (1998): 52–64.

33. These data are taken from the American State Administrators Project.

34. See Cynthia J. Bowling, "State Bureaucracies," in *Politics in the American States*, ed. Virginia Gray, Russell L. Hanson, and Thad Kousser, 11th ed. (Thousand Oaks, CA: Sage, 2018), 512–13.

35. These data were calculated by the authors from http://www.calhr.ca.gov/state-hr-professionals/Pages/workforce-planning-statistics.aspx. The workforce data are from December 2018.

36. Mark Pazniokas, "Change is Coming, Whether People Like It or Not," *Connecticut Mirror*, July 24, 2019.

37. Center for State & Local Government Excellence, "State and Local Government Workforce: 2018 Data and 10 Year Trends," May 2018, 6; Center for State & Local Government Excellence, "State and Local Government Workforce: 2019 Survey," July 2019, 6.

38. Mike Maciag, "The 'Silver Tsunami' Has Arrived in Government," *Governing*, May 31, 2016.

39. These data were taken from NASCA, accenture, and NEOGOV, "'Job One' Reimagine Today's State Government Workforce," March 2019, 3–4, 7.

40. Center for State & Local Government Excellence, "State and Local Government Workforce: 2019 Survey," July 2019, 5.

41. Katherine Barrett and Richard Greene, "Think Federal Workers Have It Bad? It's Worse for State and Local Employees," Governing.com, February 11, 2019.

42. CBIZ Talent & Compensation Solutions, "Compensation and Benefits Study Report: State of Missouri," April 26, 2019, 21.

43. Katherine Barrett and Richard Greene, "To Keep Public Workers, States Offer New Salaries and Benefits," Governing.com, July 22, 2019.

44. NASCA, accenture, and NEOGOV, "Job One" Reimagine Today's State Government Workforce," March 2019, 5.

45. Bill Lucia, "State Lowers Degree Requirements for Child Welfare Case Workers," RouteFifty.com, May 29, 2019.

46. Jonna Lorenz, "State of Kansas Employees Shift Dramatically from Classified to Unclassified Status," *Topeka Capital-Journal*, January 30, 2019.

47. Data from 1957 can be found in John C. Wahlke, Heinz Eulau, William Buchanan, and LeRoy C. Ferguson, *The Legislative System* (New York: Wiley, 1962), 489. Data for 2015 are from http://www.ncsl.org/research/about-state-legislatures/who-we-elect.aspx and http://www.pewtrusts.org/en/research-and-analysis/blogs/stateline/2015/12/10/state-legislatures-have-fewer-farmers-lawyers-but-higher-education-level.

48. These data are taken from the Center for American Women in Politics, https://www.cawp.rutgers.edu/women-state-legislature-2019.

49. Data on African American and Hispanic American state legislators http://www.ncsl.org/research/about-state-legislatures/legislatures-at-a-glance.aspx. See Peverill Squire and Gary Moncrief, *State Legislatures Today: Politics under the Domes*, 3rd ed. (Lanham, MD: Rowman & Littlefield, 2020), 78–80.

50. These figures are from Duane Lockard, "The State Legislator," in *State Legislatures in American Politics*, ed. Alexander Heard (Englewood Cliffs, NJ: Prentice Hall, 1966), Table 1. The figures are for lower houses. Turnover was often even higher in state senates, but many of the "newcomers" in the senates had come over from the house, so it is difficult to get a good historical measure of true turnover in the upper chambers.

51. On turnover over the several decades, see Gary Moncrief, Richard G. Niemi, and Lynda W. Powell, "Time, Term Limits, and Turnover: Membership Stability in U.S. State Legislatures," *Legislative Studies Quarterly* 29 (2004): 357–81; Richard G. Niemi and Laura R. Winsky, "Membership Turnover in U.S. State Legislatures: Trends and Effects of Districting," *Legislative Studies Quarterly* 12 (1987): 115–23; and Kwang S. Shin and John S. Jackson III, "Membership Turnover in U.S. State Legislatures: 1931–1976," *Legislative Studies Quarterly* 4 (1979): 95–114.

52. On turnover in recent years and the difference between states with term limits and states without term limits, see Peverill Squire and Gary Moncrief, *State Legislatures Today: Politics under the Domes*, 2nd ed. (Lanham, MD: Rowman & Littlefield, 2015), 50–51.

53. Clint S. Swift and Kathryn A. VanderMolen, "Term Limits and Collaboration Across the Aisle: An Analysis of Bipartisan Cosponsorship in Term Limited and Non-Term Limited State Legislatures," *State Politics and Policy Quarterly* 16 (2016): 198–226.

54. Marjorie Sarbaugh-Thompson, "Measuring 'Term-Limitedness' in U.S. Multi-State Research," *State Politics and Policy Quarterly* 10 (2010): 199–217.

55. See Daniel C. Lewis, "Legislative Term Limits and Fiscal Policy Performance," *Legislative Studies Quarterly* 37 (2012): 307; David R. Berman, "Legislative Climate," in *Institutional Change in American Politics*, ed. Karl Kurtz, Bruce Cain, and Richard Niemi (Ann Arbor: University of Michigan Press, 2007),107–18; and Thad Kousser, *Term Limits and the Dismantling of State Legislative Professionalism* (New York: Cambridge University Press, 2005).

56. Lewis, "Legislative Term Limits and Fiscal Policy Performance."

57. This discussion of legislative professionalization is derived from Peverill Squire, "Measuring Legislative Professionalism: The Squire Index Revisited," *State Politics and Policy Quarterly* 7 (2007): 211–27 and Peverill Squire, "A Squire Index Update," *State Politics & Policy Quarterly* 17 (2017): 361–71.

58. See the discussions in Squire, "Measuring Legislative Professionalism," and Squire, *Evolution of American Legislatures*, chap. 7.

59. Frederick J. Boehmke and Charles R. Shipan, "Oversight Capabilities in the States: Are Professionalized Legislatures Better at Getting What They Want?" *State Politics and Policy Quarterly* 15 (2015): 366–86.

60. Michelle Cole, "ALEC Gains Foothold in Oregon, with One-Fourth of Legislators as Members," Oregonian, May 26, 2012.

61. See Alexander Hertel-Fernandez, "Who Passes Businesses 'Model Bills'? Policy Capacity and Corporate Influence in U.S. State Politics," *Perspectives in Politics* 12 (2014): 582–602. Recent evidence of this behavior can be found at https://www.usatoday.com/in-depth/news/investigations/2019/04/03/abortion-gun-laws-stand-your-ground-model-bills-conservatives-liberal-corporate-influence-lobbyists/3162173002/. For an intriguing look at how interest group model legislation is disseminated as policy innovation, see Kristin Garrett and Joshua Jansa, "Interest Group Influence in Policy Diffusion Networks," *State Politics and Policy Quarterly* 15 (2015): 387–417.

62. Melinda Gann Hall, "State Courts," in *Politics in the American States*, ed. Virginia Gray, Russell Hanson, and Thad Kousser, 11th ed. (Thousand Oaks, CA: Sage, 2018), 280.

63. The federal court data were taken from. Federal Judicial Caseload Statistics 2016, https://www.uscourts.gov/statistics-reports/federal-judicial-caseload-statistics-2016. The state court data were taken the National Center for State Courts, Court Statistics Project, http://www.courtstatistics.org/NCSC-Analysis/National-Overview.aspx.

64. See Lawrence M. Friedman, *A History of American Law* (New York: Touchstone, 1973), 525–38; Robert A. Kagan, Bobby D. Infelise, and Robert R. Detlefsen, "American State Supreme Court Justices, 1900–1970," *American Bar Foundation Research Journal* (1984): 371–408.

65. See the qualifications listed in *The Book of the States, 2018 Edition* (Lexington: Council of State Governments, 2018), 198–99.

66. These data are taken from National Center for State Courts, "Survey of Judicial Salaries," Vol. 40, No. 2, as of July 1, 2015.

67. The chief justice is actually paid slightly more than the other four justices.

68. James M. Anderson and Eric Helland, "How Much Should Judges Be Paid? An Empirical Study of the Effect of Judicial Pay on the State Bench," *Stanford Law Review* 64 (2012): 1316–19; Jonathan Remy Nash, "Judicial Laterals," *Vanderbilt Law Review* 70 (2017): 1914–15.

69. For 2019 see, e.g., Dan Boyd, "Chief Justice Tells Legislators Courts can 'Breathe' Again," *Albuquerque Journal*, January 17, 2019; Jamie Lovegrove, "SC Supreme Court Chief Justice Again Asks Lawmakers to Raise Pay for Judges," *Post and Courier*, February 27, 2019; Jessica Miller, "Utah's Chief Justice Asks Lawmakers to Fund New Judges, While Touting Efforts to Make Civil Courts More Accessible to Those Intimidated by the Legal System," *Salt Lake Tribune*, January 29, 2019; Emma Platoff and Jolie McCullough, "Texas Supreme Court Chief Nathan Hecht Calls for Nonpartisan Judicial Elections, Bail Reform," *Texas Tribune*, February 6, 2019; Betsy Z. Russell, "Idaho's Courts Face 'Critical' and 'Dire' Needs," *Post Register*, January 16, 2019; Sherman Smith, "Chief Justice Lawton Nuss Highlights Impact of Kansas Courts, Desire for More Funds," *Leavenworth Times*, February 7, 2019.

70. See Stephen J. Choi, Mitu Gulati, and Eric A. Posner, "Are Judges Overpaid? A Skeptical Response to the Judicial Salary Debate," *Journal of Legal Analysis* 1 (Winter 2009): 47–117. For examples of controversy, see Michael Cooper, "New York's Top Judge Threatens Suit to Get Raises for Bench," *New York Times*, April 10, 2007; "On Oklahoma Judicial Pay Issue, Politics Needs to Take a Back Seat," *The Oklahoman*, October 7, 2013; http://blogs.wsj.com/law/2012/07/24/state-courts-concerned-about-losing-judges-after-no-salary-growth/.

71. https://www.ncsc.org/Topics/Human-Resources/HR-Management/State-Links.aspx?cat=Judicial%20Clerkship%20in%20State%20Trial%20and%20Appellate%20C.

72. These data are from https://www.nawj.org/statistics/2018-us-state-court-women-judges and http://www.nawj.org/us_state_court_statistics_2016.asp.

73. These data are taken from Ciara Torres-Spelliscy, Monique Chase, and Emma Greenman, "Improving Judicial Diversity" (Brennan Center for Justice, 2010).

74. Tracey E. George and Albert H. Yoon, "The Gavel Gap" (American Constitution Society, 2016).

75. Ricardo Lopez, "Dayton Selects McKeig as Next Supreme Court Justice," *Star Tribune*, June 28, 2016.

76. Alicia Bannon and Laila Robbins, "Two Women of Color Won State Supreme Court Races—and Sadly, That's Progress," Brennan Center for Justice, November 12, 2018; Will Doran, "A First in North Carolina: Black Woman Named Chief Justice of State Supreme Court," Governing.com, February 14, 2019.

77. Laila Robbins and Alicia Bannon, "State Supreme Court Diversity," Brennan Center for Justice, July 23, 2019, 4.

78. See Robert A. Kagan, Bliss Cartwright, Laurence M. Friedman, and Stanton Wheeler, "The Evolution of State Supreme Courts," *Michigan Law Review* 76 (1977): 961–1005.

79. See Peverill Squire, "Measuring the Professionalization of U.S. State Courts of Last Resort," *State Politics and Policy Quarterly* 8 (2008): 223–38.

80. G. Marcus Cole quoted in Louis Jacobson, "Obscure, Yet Influential, Jobs in State and Local Government," *Governing*, September 30, 2015.

81. Data on judges per state were gathered in Melinda Gann Hall, "State Courts," in *Politics in the American States*, ed. Virginia Gray, Russell Hanson, and Thad Kousser, 11th ed. (Thousand Oaks, CA: Sage, 2018), 280.

82. Alan Rosenthal, *Engines of Democracy: Politics & Policymaking in State Legislatures* (Washington, DC: CQ Press, 2009), 8.

CHAPTER 6: PUBLIC POLICY AND THE ROLE OF THE STATES IN A CHANGING FEDERAL SYSTEM

1. Pamela Prah attributes this assessment to an analyst at the Cato Institute. See Pamela M. Prah, "Uncertainty from Washington Continues for States," Stateline.org, January 4, 2013, http://www.i360gov.com/local-government-news/2013/jan/04/uncertainty-from-washington-continues-for-states.

2. https://www.al.com/news/2019/03/9-issues-to-watch-during-the-2019-alabama-legislative-session.html.

3. https://www.thegazette.com/subject/news/government/des-moines-iowa-capitol-traffic-cameras-issues-legislative-session-2019-supreme-court-ipers-sexual-harassment-20190113.

4. https://www.spokesman.com/stories/2019/jan/13/washington-legislative-preview-issues-to-watch-in-/.

5. https://www.vpr.org/post/6-issues-watch-during-2019-vermont-legislative-session#stream/0.

6. *Governing*, "Issues to Watch: 18 of the Biggest Policies and Problems Legislatures Will Confront in 2019," https://www.governing.com/topics/politics/gov-2019-legislative-issues-to-watch.html.

7. Martha Derthick, *Keeping the Compound Republic* (Washington, DC: Brookings Institute Press, 2001), 28.

8. This is actually a paraphrase. In his dissent in *New State Ice Co. v. Liebmann* 285 U.S. 311 (1932), Brandeis wrote, "It is one of the happy incidents of the federal system that a single courageous State may, if its citizens choose, serve as a laboratory; and try novel social and economic experiments without risk to the rest of the country."

9. Michael Gormley, "Cuomo Signs NYS Legislation Outlawing Declawing of Cats," *Newsday*, July 22, 2019; Brendan Kiley, "Washington Becomes First State to Allow Human Composting," *Seattle Times*, May 22, 2019; Louis Sahagun and Phil Willon, "California Becomes First State to Ban Fur Trapping After Gov. Newsom Signs Law," *Los Angeles Times*, September 4, 2019; N'dea Yancey-Bragg, "Maine Becomes First State to Ban Styrofoam Food Containers, Effective 2021," *USA TODAY*, May 1, 2019.

10. Chris Chieppo, "'Pay for Success': An Idea with Bipartisan Appeal," *Governing*, March 1, 2016.

11. http://www.socialinnovationcenter.org/archives/3176.

12. Luke Keele, Neil Malhotra, and Colin McCubbins, "Do Term Limits Restrain State Fiscal Policy?" *Legislative Studies Quarterly* 38 (2013): 292.

13. This discussion is based in part on Todd Donovan, Christopher Mooney, and Daniel Smith, "Morality Policy," in *State and Local Politics: Institutions and Reform*, 3rd ed. (Boston, MA: Wadsworth/Cengage, 2013), chap. 13, Rebecca J. Kreitzer, "Politics and Morality in State Abortion Policy," *State Politics & Policy Quarterly* 15 (2015): 41–66, and Justin Phillips, "Public Opinion and Morality," in *Politics in the American States*, ed. Virginia Gray, Russell Hanson and Thad Kousser, 10th ed. (Los Angeles: Sage, 2013), 440–58.

14. Virginia Gray, "The Socioeconomic and Political Context of States," in *Politics in the American States*, ed. Virginia Gray, Russell Hanson and Thad Kousser, 10th ed. (Los Angeles: Sage, 2013), 6.

15. http://www.ghsa.org/html/stateinfo/laws/cellphone_laws.html.

16. The policy diffusion literature is too extensive to review here, but one should begin with Jack Walker, "The Diffusion of Innovation in the American States," *American Political Science Review* 63 (1969): 830–99 and Virginia Gray, "Innovation in the American States: A Diffusion Study," *American Political Science Review* 67 (1973): 1174–85. For recent treatments, see Fabrizio Gilardi, "Four Ways We Can Improve Policy Diffusion Research," *State Politics & Policy Quarterly* 16 (2016): 8–21; Andrew Karch, *Democratic Laboratories: Policy Diffusion Among the States* (Ann Arbor: University of Michigan Press, 2007); Sean Nicholson-Crotty, "The Politics of Diffusion: Public Policy in the American States," *Journal of Politics* 71 (2009): 192–205; Frederick J. Boehmke and Paul Skinner, "State Policy Innovativeness Revisited," *State Politics and Policy Quarterly* 12 (2012): 304–30; and the special issue on policy diffusion, edited by Frederick Boehmke and Juliana Pachecho, *State Politics and Policy Quarterly* (March 2016).

17. Graeme Boushey, *Policy Diffusion Dynamics in America* (New York: Cambridge University Press, 2010), 5.

18. Nicholson-Crotty, "The Politics of Diffusion," 199–200.

19. See Boehmke and Skinner, "State Policy Innovativeness Revisited," and Melissa Maynard, "Which States Are Most Innovative?" Stateline.org, November 19, 2012.

20. Italics added by authors to emphasize relevant phrases.

21. http://www.hawaiipublicschools.org/ConnectWithUs/Pages/Home.aspx.

22. Mike Maciag, "States That Spend the Most (and the Least) on Education," Governing. com, June 4, 2019, https://www.governing.com/topics/education/gov-education-funding-states. html; National Association of State Budget Officers, *State Expenditure Report*, 2018, 22.

23. https://www.census.gov/data/tables/2017/econ/school-finances/secondary-education-finance.html.

24. Center for Budget and Policy Priorities, "K-12 Funding Up in Most 2018 Teacher-Protest States, but Funding still Well Below a Decade Ago," March 6, 2019.

25. C. Kirabo Jackson, "Does School Spending Matter? The New Literature on an Old Question," NBER Working Paper Series, December 2018, https://www.nber.org/papers/w25368.

26. http://schoolfunding.info/litigation-map/.

27. Michael Berkman and Eric Plutzer, "The Politics of Education," in *Politics in the American States*, ed. Virginia Gray, Russell Hanson, and Thad Kousser, 11th ed. (Thousand Oaks, CA: Sage, 2018), 405.

28. Jonathan Shorman and Dion Lefler, "After Nine Years, Could Kansas School Funding Lawsuit be Over? Justices Will Decide," *Wichita Eagle*, May 9, 2019.

29. Jonathan Shorman and Dion Lefler, "Kansas School Funding is Adequate, High Court Says. But Justices Will Still Oversee Case," *Wichita Eagle*, June 14, 2019.

30. https://www.census.gov/data/tables/2017/econ/school-finances/secondary-education-finance.html.

31. Maciag, "States That Spend the Most (and the Least) on Education."

32. http://nces.ed.gov/programs/coe/indicator_coi.asp, "Public High School Graduation Rates," updated May 2019.

33. See http://www.corestandards.org/standards-in-your-state/.

34. See https://www.aft.org/ae/summer2018/shapiro_brown.

35. http://blogs.edweek.org/edweek/state_edwatch/2015/08/eight_states_add_citizenship_test_requirement_for_grads.html.

36. See https://joefossinstitute.org/our-programs/civics-education-initiative/.

37. University of Pennsylvania Graduate School of Education, "Is There an NCLB Curriculum?" http://www.gse.upenn.edu/features/research/de_facto. The article cites work by Andy Porter, Morgan Polikoff, and John Smithson in mapping curriculum content from state to state.

38. Lauren McGaughy, "Texas Board Votes to Eliminate Hillary Clinton, Helen Keller from History Curriculum," *Dallas Morning News*, September 14, 2018. See also www.csmonitor.com/USA/Education/2015/1120/Texas-textbook-vote-highlights-disputes-over-US-history-and-how-to-teach-it.

39. Valerie Strauss, "Federal Judge Tells Arizona It Can't Ban Mexican American Studies," *Washington Post*, December 28, 2017. See also http://www.theatlantic.com/education/archive/2015/07/how-one-law-banning-ethnic-studies-led-to-rise/398885/.

40. Casey Leins, "These States Require Schools to Teach LGBT History," *U.S. News & World Report*," August 14, 2019; Sarah Schwartz, "Four States Now Require Schools to Teach LGBT History," *Education Week*, August 12, 2019, https://blogs.edweek.org/teachers/teaching_now/2019/08/four_states_now_require_schools_to_teach_lgbt_history.html.

41. *Oklahoma Historical Society's Encyclopedia of Oklahoma History and Culture*, "Anti-Evolution Movement," https://www.okhistory.org/publications/enc/entry.php?entry=AN011.

42. Elizabeth Flock, "Law Allows Creationism to be Taught in Tenn. Public Schools," *Washington Post*, April 11, 2012.

43. See Ann Reid, "Op-Ed: It's Still Hard to Teach Evolution in Too Many Public School Classrooms," *Los Angeles Times*, November 18, 2018. See also the 2014 updated discussion at http://www.pewforum.org/2009/02/04/fighting-over-darwin-state-by-state/; and the National Center for Science Education list of legislation through 2017, https://ncse.com/library-resource/chronology-academic-freedom-bills.

44. Pew Research Center for the People and the Press, "Reading the Polls on Evolution and Creationism," September 28, 2005; https://news.gallup.com/poll/21814/evolution-creationism-intelligent-design.aspx; https://ncse.com/library-resource/polls-creationism.

45. Pew Research Center, "America's Changing Religious Landscape," May 12, 2015, 143–46.

46. Michael Berkman, Eric Plutzer, and Nicholas Stark, "Teaching Evolution: State Institutions, Public Opinion and Science Curriculums," paper presented at the 2006 State Politics and Public Conference, Texas Tech University, May 2006.

47. https://www.guttmacher.org/state-policy/explore/sex-and-hiv-education.

48. https://www.leg.state.mn.us/lrl/guides/guides?issue=charter.

49. https://www.publiccharters.org/latest-news/2017/10/23/annual-enrollment-share-report-finds-charter-school-enrollment-has-tripled.

50. See https://data.publiccharters.org/ and https://nces.ed.gov/fastfacts/display.asp?id=65.

51. Mark Berends, "Sociology and School Choice: What We Know After Two Decades of Charter Schools," *Annual Review of Sociology* 41 (2015): 159–80; Julian R. Betts and Y. Emily Tang, "The Effects of Charter Schools on Student Achievement," in *School Choice at the Crossroads: Research Perspectives*, ed. Mark Berends, R. Joseph Waddington and John Schoenig (New York: Routledge, 2019).

52. Susan Dynarski, "Where Charter Schools Outperform," *New York Times*, November 22, 2015, http://www.nytimes.com/2015/11/22/upshot/a-suburban-urban-divide-in-charter-school-success-rates.html?_r=0.

53. Loren Collingwood, Ashley Jochim, and Kassra A. R. Oskooii, "The Politics of Choice Reconsidered: Partisanship, Ideology, and Minority Politics in Washington's Charter School Initiative," *State Politics & Policy Quarterly* 18 (2018): 87.

54. https://www.educationnext.org/public-support-climbs-teacher-pay-school-expenditures-charter-schools-universal-vouchers-2018-ednext-poll/#charters.

55. On the general topic, see https://www.edchoice.org/school-choice/school-choice-in-america/#.

56. National Council on Disability, "School Choice Series: Choice & Vouchers—Implications for Students with Disabilities," November 15, 2018, 11.

57. https://dpi.wi.gov/sites/default/files/news-release/dpinr2018-91.pdf.

58. https://www.edchoice.org/school-choice/programs/louisiana-scholarship-program/.

59. https://www.edchoice.org/resource-hub/fast-facts/#taxcredit-scholarship-fast-facts.

60. For background, see Stephanie Saul, "Public Money Finds Backdoor to Private Schools," *New York Times*, May 21, 2012.

61. https://www.edchoice.org/resource-hub/fast-facts/#taxcredit-scholarship-fast-facts.

62. https://nces.ed.gov/programs/digest/d17/tables/dt17_206.10.asp.

63. https://hslda.org/content/laws/.

64. Congressional Research Service, "Federal Support for Academic Research," report 7-5700, October 18, 2012.

65. Sandy Baum, Michael S. McPherson, Breno Braga, and Sarah Minton, "Tuition and State Appropriations: Using Evidence and Logic to Gain Perspective," Urban Institute, updated March 2018; Jung-cheol Shin and Sande Milton, "Rethinking Tuition Effects on Enrollment in Public Four-Year Colleges and Universities," *Review of Higher Education* 29 (2006): 213–37; and James Hearn, Carolyn Griswold, and Ginger Marine, "Region, Resource, and Reason: A Contextual Analysis of State Tuition and Student Aid Policies," *Research in Higher Education* 37 (1996): 241–78.

66. College Board Advocacy and Policy Center, "Trends in Tuition and Fees, Enrollment, and State Appropriations for Higher Education By State," July 2012. See 4–6.

67. https://publicaffairs.vpcomm.umich.edu/key-issues/tuition/general-fund-budget-tutorial/.

68. State Higher Education Executive Officers Association, "State Higher Education Finance: FY 2018," 2019, 22.

69. College Board Advocacy Center, "Trends in Tuition and Fees," Table 2-9.

70. State Higher Education Executive Officers Association, "State Higher Education Finance: FY 2018," 8.

71. Jon Marcus, "Americans Don't Realize State Funding for Higher Ed is Falling, New Poll Finds," *The Hechinger Report*, February 25, 2019.

72. See Katherine Barrett and Richard Greene, "States Start Making Colleges Work for Funding," *Governing*, April 2016.

73. Amy Y. Li, "Lessons Learned: A Case Study of Performance Funding in Higher Education," thirdway.org, January 25, 2019.

74. https://lawcenter.giffords.org/scorecard/#FL.

75. https://lawcenter.giffords.org/scorecard/#FL.

76. Lynn Bartels and Kurtis Lee, "3 New Gun Bills on the Books in Colorado Despite Its Wild West Image," *Denver Post*, March 21, 2013; Ron Scherer, "Connecticut Responds to Newtown with Groundbreaking Gun Control Laws," *Christian Science Monitor*, April 2, 2013.

77. Michael Luca, Deepak Malhotra, and Christopher Poliquin, "The Impact of Mass Shootings on Gun Policy," Harvard Business School Working Paper 16-126, May 2016.

78. https://lawcenter.giffords.org/scorecard/#FL.

79. Zusha Elinson, "'Red Flag' Gun Provisions Gather Bipartisan Support," *Wall Street Journal*, June 3, 2019; Ryan Foley, "Gun-Seizure Laws Grow in Popularity Since Parkland Shooting," *Sun Sentinel*, February 10, 2019.

80. Matt Vasilogambros, "Hundreds of New State Gun Laws: Most Expand Access," Stateline.org, March 2, 2018.

81. See the list provided in https://www.gunstocarry.com/ccw-reciprocity-map/.

82. Jason Clayworth, "Register Investigation: 99.6% of Iowa Gun Permits Approved," *Des Moines Register*, March 10, 2013.

83. https://www.gunstocarry.com/ccw-reciprocity-map/.

84. See H.R. 38, Concealed Carry Act of 2017, https://www.congress.gov/bill/115th-congress/house-bill/38/actions?q=%7B%22search%22%3A%5B%22concealed+carry+reciprocity+act%22%5D%7D.

85. https://lawcenter.giffords.org/gun-laws/policy-areas/who-can-have-a-gun/domestic-violence-firearms/.

86. https://www.nraila.org/gun-laws/. Select Castle Doctrine.

87. https://lawcenter.giffords.org/gun-laws/policy-areas/guns-in-public/stand-your-ground-laws/; http://www.ncsl.org/research/civil-and-criminal-justice/self-defense-and-stand-your-ground.aspx.

88. Max Brantley, "Sen Ballinger Retreats—Gives Up on 'Stand Your Ground' Bill for this Legislative Session," *Arkansas Times*, April 8, 2018.

89. Adam Cohen, "Will States Lead the Way to Legalizing Marijuana Nationwide?" *Time Magazine*, January 28, 2013, http://ideas.time.com/2013/01/28/will-states-lead-the-way-to-legalizing-marijuana-nationwide/.

90. http://www.ncsl.org/research/health/state-medical-marijuana-laws.aspx.

91. https://no-smoke.org/materials-services/lists-maps/#1518200878061-ebc83fdc-2d6c.

92. https://www.lung.org/our-initiatives/tobacco/cessation-and-prevention/tobacco-21-laws.html.

93. Jorge L. Ortiz, "No Smoking? Hawaii Lawmaker Wants to Say Goodbye to Cigarettes Forever," *USA TODAY*, February 5, 2019.

94. See Pew Charitable Trusts, "The Punishment Rate," March 2016.

95. https://sentencingproject.org/wp-content/uploads/2016/01/Trends-in-US-Corrections.pdf.

96. Calculated by authors from data in Wendy Sawyer and Peter Wagner, "Mass Incarceration: The Whole Pie 2019," Prison Policy Initiative, March 19, 2019.

97. Bureau of Justice Statistics, "Key Statistic: Prisoners," https://www.bjs.gov/index.cfm?ty=kfdetail&iid=488.

98. N. C. Aizenman, "New High in U.S. Prison Numbers," *Washington Post*, February 29, 2008.

99. Pew Charitable Trusts, "The Punishment Rate."

100. E. Ann Carson, "Prisoners in 2014," Bureau of Justice Statistics, September 2015.

101. Calculated by the authors from data in Danielle Kaeble and Mary Cowhig, "Correctional Populations in the United States, 2016," Bureau of Justice Statistics, April 2018, 11–12.

102. The Sentencing Project, "Top Trends in State Criminal Justice Reform, 2018," January 2019.

103. Legislative Analyst's Office, "A Primer: Three Strikes—The Impact After More Than a Decade," October 7, 2005, http://www.lao.ca.gov/2005/3_strikes/3_strikes_102005. htm.

104. Calculated by the authors from data in Erica E. Phillips, "'Three-Strikes' Prisoners Drawing a Walk," *Wall Street Journal*, March 30–31, 2013.

105. Radha Iyengar, "I'd Rather Be Hanged for a Sheep than a Lamb: The Unintended Consequences of 'Three-Strikes' Laws," National Bureau of Economic Research, Working Paper 13784, February 2008.

106. Stanford Law School, Three Strikes Project, "Proposition 36 Progress Report: Over 1,500 Prisoners Released Historically Low Recidivism Rate," April 2014.

107. Tom James, "Lifer Inmates Excluded from Washington '3 Strikes' Changes," *Seattle Times*, May 22, 2019.

108. John Wooldredge, "State Corrections Policy," in *Politics in the American States*, ed. Virginia Gray, Russell Hanson, and Thad Kousser, 10th ed. (Los Angeles: Sage, 2013), Table 9-1; and Richard C. Fording, "State Corrections Policy," in *Politics in the American States*, ed. Virginia Gray, Russell Hanson, and Thad Kousser, 11th ed. (Thousand Oaks, CA: CQ Press, 2018), Table 10-2.

109. Wooldredge, "State Corrections Policy," 283.

110. See the timeline at https://deathpenalty.procon.org/view.resource.php?resourceID =001172#timeline.

111. Dan Frosch, "Republicans Push to End Executions," *Wall Street Journal*, February 20, 2019. See also Marin Cogan, "Meet the Red-State Conservatives Fighting to Abolish the Death Penalty," *Washington Post*, June 3, 2016; Alan Greenblatt, "The Death Penalty's New Skeptics," *Governing*, June 2016.

112. Statistics are from the Death Penalty Information Center, "Facts About the Death Penalty," May 31, 2019.

113. Jennifer Bronson and E. Ann Carson, "Prisoners in 2017," Bureau of Justice Statistics, April 2019, 16.

114. E. Ann Carson, "Prisoners in 2016," Bureau of Justice Statistics, January 2018, 14.

115. Michael Cohen, "How For-Profit Prisons Have Become the Biggest Lobby No One Is Talking About," *Washington Post*, April 28, 2015; Justice Policy Institute, "Gaming the System: How the Political Strategies of Private Prison Companies Promote Ineffective Incarceration Policies," June 2011; Ciara O'Neill, "Private Prisons Pour Millions into Lobbying State Lawmakers," FollowTheMoney.org, July 2, 2018, https://www.followthe-money.org/research/blog/private-prisons-pour-millions-into-lobbying-state-lawmakers.

116. Rebecca Boone, "Private Prison Company Escapes Idaho Following Scandal, Lawsuits," *Idaho State Journal*, October 3, 2013.

117. Jamie Lovegrove, "SC Supreme Court Abolishes 'Common Law Marriage,' Couples Now Required to Get a License," *Post and Courier*, July 25, 2019; https://www.unmarried. org/common-law-marriage-fact-sheet/.

118. 32 Cal. 2d 711 (1948). See the discussion in R. A. Lenhardt, "Beyond Analogy: Perez V. Sharp, Antimiscegenation Law, and the Fight for Same-Sex Marriage," *California Law Review* 96 (2008): 839–900.

119. 388 U.S. 1 (1967).

120. "President Bush's Remarks on Same-Sex Marriage," *New York Times*, February 24, 2004.

121. 576 U.S. ___ (2015).

122. http://www.al.com/news/birmingham/index.ssf/2016/03/alabama_supreme_court_dismisse.html.

123. http://www.al.com/news/index.ssf/2016/05/alabama_chief_justice_roy_moor_10.html.

124. Leada Gore, "Marriage Licenses End in Alabama? What's Next, What It Means If You're Getting Married," al.com, May 24, 2019.

125. Everdeen Mason, Aaron Williams, and Kennedy Elliott, "The Dramatic Rise in State Efforts to Limit LGBT Rights," *Washington Post*, June 10, 2016.

126. Tony Cook, Tom LoBianco, Brian Eason, "Gov. Mike Pence Signs RFRA Fix," *Indianapolis Star*, April 2, 2015.

127. Kate Royals, "Senate Passes 'Religious Freedom' Bill," *Clarion-Ledger*, April 15, 2016.

128. See the list provided in https://www.aclu.org/anti-lgbt-religious-exemption-legislation-across-country.

129. Jimmie E. Gates, "ACLU Files Lawsuit to Declare HB 1523 Unconstitutional," *Clarion-Ledger*, May 9, 2016; Neely Tucker, "U.S. District Judge Strike Down Mississippi's 'Religious Freedom' Law," *Washington Post*, July 1, 2016.

130. Anita Lee and Justin Mitchell, "Supreme Court Says 'No' to LGBT Supporters Appealing Mississippi's 'Religious Freedom' Law," *Sun Herald*, January 8, 2018.

131. See https://www.hrc.org/state-maps/employment.

132. See https://www.hrc.org/state-maps/conversion%20therapy; and Kevin Miller, "Bill Signing Makes Maine the 17th State to Ban 'Conversion Therapy" for Minors," *Portland Press Herald*, May 30, 2019.

133. 410 U.S. 113 (1973).

134. See Barbara Hinkson Craig and David M. O'Brien, *Abortion and American Politics* (Chatham: Chatham House, 1996), 74–75; Roy Lucas, "Federal Constitutional Limitations on the Enforcement and Administration of State Abortion Statutes," *North Carolina Law Review* 46 (1967–1968): 730–78; Karen O'Connor, *No Neutral Ground?* (Boulder, CO: Westview Press, 1996), 46–47; A. A. Smyser, "Hawaii's Abortion Law 30 Years Old," *Hawaii Star-Bulletin*, March 21, 2000.

135. Craig and O'Brien, *Abortion and American Politics*, 75.

136. *Planned Parenthood of Southeastern Pennsylvania v. Casey*, 505 U.S. 833 (1992).

137. Cindy Dampier and Chad Yoder, "Changing Abortion Rights: How Illinois' New Law Compares with What Others States Are Doing," *Chicago Tribune*, June 5, 2019.

138. "North Dakota Governor Approves 6-Week Abortion Ban," *St Louis Post Dispatch*, March 26, 2013.

139. Nina Liss-Schultz, "The Supreme Court Just Rejected the Country's Most Extreme Abortion Ban," *Mother Jones*, January 25, 2016.

140. Amber Phillips, "14 States Have Passed Laws This Year Making It Harder to Get an Abortion," *Washington Post*, June 1, 2016.

141. Christine Vestal, "New Laws Deepen State Differences over Abortion," RouteFifty.com, July 30, 2019.

142. Emma Green, "The New Abortion Bills Are a Dare," *The Atlantic*, May 15, 2019.

143. Kate Smith, "Tennessee to Push for Total Abortion Ban with Sights on Supreme Court," cbsnews.com, August 12, 2019, https://www.cbsnews.com/news/tennessee-abortion-laws-tennessee-to-push-for-total-abortion-ban-with-sights-on-supreme-court/.

144. https://reproductiverights.org/what-if-roe-fell.

145. https://www.guttmacher.org/state-policy/explore/abortion-policy-absence-roe.

146. Rosemary Westwood, "How Health Officials in Pro-Life States Are Quietly Dismantling Abortion Access," *Pacific Standard*, July 31, 2019.

147. The Guttmacher Institute provides a useful compendium of state abortion laws: https://www.guttmacher.org/state-policy/explore/overview-abortion-laws.

148. https://www.guttmacher.org/state-policy/explore/targeted-regulation-abortion-providers.

149. The case was *Whole Woman's Health v. Hellerstedt*, 579 U.S. ___ (2016). See the discussion https://www.governing.com/topics/health-human-services/tns-planned-parenthood-abortion-ruling.html. For the Louisiana case, see Mark Ballard, "Law That Will Soon Close More Louisiana Abortion Clinics Goes into Effect Next Week," *The Advocate*, January 22, 2019; Adam Liptak, "Supreme Court Blocks Louisiana Abortion Law," *New York Times*, February 7, 2019.

150. Gardiner Harris, "In Hawaii's Heath System, Lessons for Lawmakers," *New York Times*, October 16, 2009.

151. Christine Vestal, "Utah's Health Insurance Exchange in Limbo," *Stateline*, January 11, 2013.

152. See https://www.kff.org/state-category/health-coverage-uninsured/.

153. Rabah Kamal, Cynthia Cox, Rachel Fehr, Marco Ramirez, Katherine Horstman, and Larry Levitt, "How Repeal of the Individual Mandate and Expansion of Loosely Regulated Plans Are Affecting 2019 Premiums," kff.org, October 26, 2018, https://www.kff.org/health-costs/issue-brief/how-repeal-of-the-individual-mandate-and-expansion-of-loosely-regulated-plans-are-affecting-2019-premiums/.

154. https://www.tangohealth.com/blog/california-individual-mandate-signed-into-law/.

155. http://kff.org/medicaid/state-indicator/federal-matching-rate-and-multiplier/.

156. https://www.kff.org/health-reform/state-indicator/state-activity-around-expanding-medicaid-under-the-affordable-care-act/?currentTimeframe=0&sortModel=%7B%22colId%22:%22Location%22,%22sort%22:%22asc%22%7D.

157. Boris Shor, "Ideology, Party, and Opinion: Explaining Individual Legislator ACA Implementation Votes in the States," *State Politics & Policy Quarterly* 18 (2018): 371–94.

158. Charles Courtemanche, James Marton, Benjamin Ukert, Aaron Yelowitz, and Daniela Zapata, "Early Impacts of the Affordable Care Act on Health Insurance Coverage in Medicaid Expansion and Non-Expansion States," *Journal of Policy Analysis and Management* 36 (2017): 178–210; Rachel Garfield, Anthony Damico, and Kendal Orgera, "The Coverage Gap: Uninsured Poor Adults in States that Do Not Expand Medicaid," Kaiser Family Foundation, June 12, 2018.

159. https://www.census.gov/content/dam/Census/library/publications/2019/demo/p60-267.pdf. See Table 6, "Number and Percentage of People Without Health Insurance Coverage by State: 2017 and 2018."

160. These figures were taken from the Kaiser Family Foundation, "Where Are States Today? Medicaid and CHIP Eligibility Levels for Adults, Children, Pregnant Women, and Adults" March 2019.

161. Kaiser Family Foundation, "Where Are the States Today?" March 31, 2019, https://www.kff.org/medicaid/fact-sheet/where-are-states-today-medicaid-and-chip/.

162. Rick Pluta, "A Michigan State-Federal Health Care Exchange Killed by Senate Republicans," March 22, 2013, http://www.michiganradio.org/post/michigan-state-federal-health-care-exchange-killed-senate-republicans.

163. https://www.kff.org/health-reform/state-indicator/state-health-insurance-marketplace-types/?currentTimeframe=0&sortModel=%7B%22colId%22:%22Location%22,%22sort%22:%22asc%22%7D.

164. These data were taken from Christine Heffernan, Benjamin Goehring, Ian Hecker, Linda Giannarelli, and Sarah Minton, *Welfare Rules Databook: State TANF Policies as of July 2017*, Washington, DC: The Urban Institute, October 2018, 198–99, 259–60.

165. See Heather Hahn, David Kassabian, and Sheila Zedlewski, *TANF Work Requirements and State Strategies to Fulfill Them*, Urban Institute, Brief #05, March 2012; Center on Budget and Policy Priorities, "Policy Basics: An Introduction to TANF," August 15, 2018, 4–5.

166. See the NCSL compilation of these laws: http://www.ncsl.org/research/human-services/drug-testing-and-public-assistance.aspx.

167. Mark Carl Rom, "State Health and Welfare Programs," in *Politics in the American States*, ed. Virginia Gray, Russell L. Hanson, and Thad Kousser, 10th ed. (Los Angeles: Sage, 2013).

168. National Partnership for Women & Families, "State Paid Family and Medical Leave Laws," June 2019; https://www.natlawreview.com/article/oregon-passes-paid-family-and-medical-leave-law.

169. http://www.ncsl.org/research/energy/renewable-portfolio-standards.aspx.

170. Galen L. Barbose, "U.S. Renewables Portfolio Standards: 2018 Annual Status Report," Lawrence Berkeley National Laboratory, November 2018, https://emp.lbl.gov/publications/us-renewables-portfolio-standards-1.

171. Liz Farmer, "States Forge Ahead of Feds to Address Retirement Crisis," *Governing*, July 16, 2015; Liz Farmer, "States Step In for Retirees," *Wall Street Journal*, September 8, 2015; https://www.naifa.org/advocacy/state-issues-positions-(2014-2017)/sinp/state-sponsored-retirement-plans.

172. Liz Farmer, "No 401(k)? No Problem. States Have You Covered," Governing.com, February 8, 2017, https://www.governing.com/topics/finance/gov-states-look-close-private-sector-retirement-gap.html.

173. https://www.stopbullying.gov/laws/index.html; Lisa Baumann, "Gov. Bullock Signs Montana Anti-Bullying Bill into Law," *Great Falls Tribune*, April 21, 2015.

174. Marie Szanizslo, "'Most Comprehensive' Opioid Bill Becomes Law," *Boston Herald*, March 15, 2016.

175. http://www.ncsl.org/research/health/prescribing-policies-states-confront-opioid-overdose-epidemic.aspx.

176. Jason Hildago and Seth A. Richardson, "Nevada, Once a Leader for Self-Driving Cars, Is Now Playing Catch Up with Other States," *Reno Gazette Journal*, April 20, 2017; http://www.ncsl.org/research/transportation/autonomous-vehicles-self-driving-vehicles-enacted-legislation.aspx.

177. http://www.ncsl.org/research/transportation/state-unmanned-aircraft-systems-uas-2016-legislation.aspx.

178. http://www.ncsl.org/research/transportation/current-unmanned-aircraft-state-law-landscape.aspx.

179. Monica Nickelsburg, "Washington State Greenlights Delivery Robots on Sidewalks," Geek Wire, April 30, 2019.

180. Tim Henderson, "State Battle Big Tech Over Data Privacy Laws," July 31, 2019, https://www.pewtrusts.org/en/research-and-analysis/blogs/stateline/2019/07/31/states-battle-big-tech-over-data-privacy-laws.

181. Elaine S. Povich, "'Fake Meat' Battle Spread to More States," Stateline, January 25, 2019.

182. Povich, "'Fake Meat' Battle Spread to More States."

183. Kelsey Piper, "ACLU, Tofurkey Ask for an Injunction on Arkansas's Anti-Veggie Burger Law," vox.com, August 14, 2019, https://www.vox.com/future-perfect/2019/7/22/20706073/arkansas-tofurky-veggie-burger-ban-aclu.

184. https://www.lexology.com/library/detail.aspx?g=621e8ee0-0067-4bff-941d-9a4f-29b80bb1.

185. Wallis Watkins, "'Truth in Labeling' Law Is a Win for Louisiana Farmers, But Key Questions Remain," New Orleans Public Radio, June 26, 2019.

186. Jack Nicas and Joe Palazzolo, "Pro-Gun Laws Gain Ground," *Wall Street Journal*, April 4, 2013; http://www.governing.com/blogs/view/gov-advancing-the-debate-guns-teachers-and-classrooms-in-south-dakota.html.

187. Brady Dennis and Juliet Eilperin, "State's Aren't Waiting for the Trump Administration on Environmental Protections," *Washington Post*, May 19, 2019.

188. Louise Radnofsky, "States Harden Views over Laws Governing Abortion," *Wall Street Journal*, April 1, 2013.

189. Donald F. Kettl, "Split Ahead," *Governing* (August 2019), 16.

190. See http://www.cc.com/video-clips/zpomqm/the-daily-show-with-jon-stewart-law---border. The comment comes at 1:14.

191. http://www.theatlantic.com/business/archive/2016/07/vermont-gmo-food-companies/490553/.

192. Malcolm Gay, "The Catfish Are Biting (and It Hurts)," *New York Times*, July 28, 2007; Chris Lawrence, "Catfish 'Noodling' Now Legal in West Virginia," *WV MetroNews*, June 21, 2018; Missouri Department of Conservation, "Why 'No' to Noodling," http://mdc.mo.gov/fishing/regulations/why-no-noodling.

193. See Marissa Sulek, "Davenport 'Fish Guy' Charged for Illegally 'Noodling' a Mississippi Catfish," wqad.com, April 1, 2019.

CHAPTER 7: STATES AND THEIR LOCAL GOVERNMENTS

1. Christine Martell and Adam Greenwade, "Profiles of Local Government Finance," in Robert Ebel and John Petersen, ed. *The Oxford Handbook of State and Local Government Finance* (New York: Oxford University Press, 2012), 177.

2. One township in Pennsylvania (Northern Liberties Township) came close. The 1790 census listed the population there at 9,913. Northern Liberties Township became part of the city of Philadelphia around 1850. See Table 2, "Population of 24 Urban Places: 1790." Us Census Bureau, https://www.census.gov/population/www/documentation/twps0027/tab02.txt.

3. See, e.g., Edward T. Howe, "The Connecticut Poll Tax," November 9, 2018, https://connecticuthistory.org/the-connecticut-poll-tax/.

4. See US Department of Commerce, Bureau of the Census, "Population of States and Counties of the United States: 1790 to 1990, ix, https://www.census.gov/population/www/censusdata/PopulationofStatesandCountiesoftheUnitedStates1790-1990.pdf.

5. "A Brief History of Georgia Counties," September 10, 2019. https://georgiainfo.galileo.usg.edu/topics/history/article/progressive-era-world-war-ii-1901–1945/a-brief-history-of-georgia-counties.

6. John Joseph Wallis, "American Government Finance in the Long Run: 1790 to 1990," *Journal of Economic Perspectives* 14 (2000): 66.

7. See, e.g., *Bayless v. Knox County*, 286 S.W. 2d 579 (Tenn. 1955).

8. Part of the discussion of the types of local governments is based on pp. 3–6 of US Census Bureau, "Governments—Individual State Descriptions, 2012", https://www2.census.gov/govs/cog/2012isd.pdf.

9. "City Government Structure: An Overview," September 10, 2019. https://www.stlouis-mo.gov/government/about/city-government-structure.cfm.

10. City and County of San Francisco, "Board of Supervisors," November 20, 2019. sfbos.org

11. These figures are from the State of California Department of Finance and represent estimates as of January 2019. Published May, 2019, https://www.census.gov/population/www/censusdata/PopulationofStatesandCountiesoftheUnitedStates1790-1990.pdf.

12. These figures are 2019 estimates from http://worldpopulationreview.com/us-counties/tx/.

13. Ohio History Central, "Township," https://www.ohiohistorycentral.org/w/Township.

14. Michigan Township Association, "What Townships Do," https://www.michigan-townships.org/whattwpdo.asp.

15. United States Census Bureau. September 19, 2019. https://www.census.gov/govs/definitions/index.html#s.

16. See ACIR Report, "The Problem of Special Districts in American Government," May 1964, https://library.unt.edu/gpo/acir/Reports/policy/A-22.pdf.

17. Chicago Historical Society, Encyclopedia of Chicago, "Special Districts," September 10, 2019 .www.encyclopedia.chicagohistory.org/pages/1181.html.

18. Richard Florida, "Rise of the Fragmented City," April 28, 2015. https://www.citylab.com/equity/2015/04/rise-of-the-fragmented-city/391556/.

19. Richard Florida, 2015. https://www.citylab.com/equity/2015/04/rise-of-the-fragmented-city/391556/.

20. City and County of Honolulu. September 10, 2019. https://www.honolulu.gov/.

21. See Tax Policy Center, "The State of State and Local Tax Policy." September 10, 2019. https://www.taxpolicycenter.org/statistics/state-and-local-own-source-general-revenue. See also Ronald Fisher and Andrew Bristle, "State Intergovernmental Grant Programs," in *The Oxford Handbook of State and Local Government Finance*, ed. Robert Ebel and John Petersen (New York: Oxford University Press, 2012), Table 9.2, 218–20.

22. Tax Policy Center, September 2019. https://www.taxpolicycenter.org/briefing-book/what-are-sources-revenue-local-governments.

23. These data were calculated by the authors from U.S. Census Bureau data at https://www.census.gov/data/datasets/2016/econ/local/public-use-datasets.html.

24. Tax Policy Center, "Tax Policy Briefing Book," https://www.taxpolicycenter.org/briefing-book/what-are-sources-revenue-local-governments.

25. Mike Maciag and J.B. Wogan, "A Thousand Cuts," *Governing* (February 2017), 36.

26. Presentation by Scott Pattison, Executive Director of the National Association of State Budget Officers (NASBO) on July 30, 2014.

27. Macaig and Wogan, "A Thousand Cuts," 34–35.

28. Janna Herron, "Which States Have the Highest and Lowest Property Taxes?" *USA TODAY*, June 27, 2019. See also http://taxfoundation.org/blog/how-high-are-property-taxes-your-state.

29. The Pew Charitable Trusts, "The Local Squeeze" (Washington, DC, 2012), 8, http://www.pewstates.org/research/reports/the-local-squeeze-85899388655. Also see Federal Funds Information for the States, "State Policy Reports," 30, no. 10 (July 2012); and Lucy Dadayan, "The Impact of the Great Recession on Local Property Taxes," State University of New York at Albany: The Rockefeller Institute, July 2012.

30. Susan Landes, "Financing Recreations and Parks," Commonwealth of Pennsylvania (2005), 10, http://www.dcnr.state.pa.us/brc/publications/Pubs/Finance_Handbook.pdf.

31. Chapter 36.95 of the Revised Code of Washington and RCW 36.95.100.

32. Barrett and Greene, "The Risks of Relying on User Fees."

33. Mike Maciag, "Addicted to Fines," *Governing*, September 2019, https://www.governing.com/topics/finance/gov-addicted-to-fines.html.

34. Maciag, "Addicted to Fines."

35. Jared Walczak and Scott Drenkard, "State and Local Sales Tax Rates, 2018." Tax Foundation, February 13, 2018. https://taxfoundation.org/state-and-local-sales-tax-rates-2018/.

36. The phrase, "the system for distributing authority" is from Joseph F. Zimmerman, *Contemporary American Federalism*, 2nd ed. (Albany: State University of New York Press, 2008), 164.

37. The discussion of relative powers of local governments and charters is drawn primarily from Joseph F. Zimmerman, *Contemporary American Federalism*, 2nd ed., chapter 8; and Patricia Fredericksen, Stephanie Witt and David Nice, *The Politics of Intergovernmental Relations*, 3rd ed. (San Diego: Birkdale, 2016), chapter 6.

38. Fredericksen, Witt, and Nice, *The Politics of Intergovernmental Relations*, 3rd ed., 194.

39. The quote appears in footnote 5, p. 7 of Jesse J. Richardson Jr., Meghan Zimmerman Gough and Robert Puentes, "Is Home Rule the Answer? Clarifying the Influence of Dillon's Rule on Growth Management." Brookings Institute, Center of Urban Metropolitan Policy, January 2003, https://www.brookings.edu/wp-content/uploads/2016/06/dillonsrule.pdf.

40. See Candy Woodall, "Who Has the Most Lobbyists in PA?" PennLive.com (2016), https://www.pennlive.com/news/2016/04/who_has_the_most_lobbying_powe.html.

41. National League of Cities, "Cities 101—Delegation of Powers," https://www.nlc.org/resource/cities-101-delegation-of-power.

42. See University of Tennessee, Municipal Technical Advisory Service, "Private Act Charter," https://www.mtas.tennessee.edu/reference/private-act-charter.

43. Fredericksen, Witt, and Nice, *The Politics of Intergovernmental Relations*, 204.

44. Illinois Lt. Governor Evelyn Sanguinetti, quoted in May 2017, https://www.riverbender.com/articles/details/bill-calculating-cost-of-unfunded-mandates-on-local-governments-passes-general-assembly-20997.cfm.

45. New York State Association of Counties, "State of Mandates," report published January 2019. Quotation is from page 2, https://www.nysac.org/files/Mandate%20Whitepaper%20 1_18_19.pdf.

46. Ross Ramsey, "Analysis: Unfunded State Mandates Have a New Enemy—the Governor of Texas." *Texas Tribune*, January 22, 2019, https://www.texastribune.org/2019/01/22/unfunded-mandates-new-enemy-governor-texas/.

47. "Jason Mercier, "State Law Prohibits Unfunded Mandates, yet Local Governments Continue to Be Burdened by Them." Washington Policy Center, April 10, 2018, https://www.washingtonpolicy.org/publications/detail/state-law-prohibits-unfunded-mandates-yet-local-governments-continue-to-be-burdened-by-them.

48. William L. Spence, "Unfunded State Mandates Likely to Lead to Lawsuit," https://dnews.com/local/unfunded-state-mandates-likely-to-lead-to-lawsuit/article_42d75c3e-fef9-5465-8107-c29af601817b.html.

49. Jessica Bulman-Pozen, "State-Local Preemption: Parties, Interest Groups and Overlapping Government," *PS: Political Science and Politics* 51 (2018): 27.

50. Luke Fowler and Stephanie Witt, "State Preemption of Local Authority: Explaining Patterns of State Adoption of Preemption Measures," *Publius* 49 (2019): 552.

51. Tim Henderson, "Age Gap Fuels City-State Clashes," *Stateline*, July 12, 2016, http://www.pewtrusts.org/en/research-and-analysis/blogs/stateline/2016/07/12/age-gap-fuels-city-state-clashes.

52. Alan Blinder, "When a State Balks at a City's Minimum Wage," *New York Times*, February 21, 2016. See also http://laborcenter.berkeley.edu/minimum-wage-living-wage-resources/inventory-of-us-city-and-county-minimum-wage-ordinances/.

53. Blinder, "When a State Balks at a City's Minimum Wage."

54. Associated Press, "New Mexico Blocks Right to Work Ordinances." April 1, 2019. https://www.governing.com/topics/mgmt/New-Mexico-Blocks-Right-to-Work-Ordinances.

html; Dan Petrella, "In Yet Another Rebuke to His Republican Predecessor, Gov. J. B. Pritzker Signs Bill Banning Local 'Right-to-Work' Zones," *Chicago Tribune*, April 12, 2019.

55. Anna Staver, "Colorado Cities Can Raise Minimum Wages Starting in January 2020," *Denver Post*, May 28, 2019.

56. Samantha J. Gross, "Plastic Straws Are Out: Ron DeSantis Vetoes Prohibition of Local Straw Bans," *Tampa Bay Times*, May 10, 2019, https://www.tampabay.com/florida-politics/buzz/2019/05/10/plastic-straw-are-out-ron-desantis-vetoes-prohibition-of-local-bans/.

57. Jack Suntrup, "Columbia City Council Members Take On State Lawmakers' Proposals," *Columbia Missourian*, April 20, 2015.

58. Valerie Bauerlein and Jon Kamp, "Cities, States Clash on Social Policy," *Wall Street Journal*, July 8, 2016.

59. Tom Coulter, "New CAFO Law Divides Farmers over Future of Agriculture, Environment in Missouri," *Columbia Missourian*, August 7, 2019.

60. Bauerlein and Kamp, "Cities, States Clash on Social Policy."

61. Tim Cromartie, "Understanding State Mandates and Suspended Mandates: Local Government Impacts," *Western City*, March 1, 2014, http://www.westerncity.com/article/understanding-state-mandates-and-suspended-mandates-local-government-impacts.

CHAPTER 8: ELECTIONS AND POLITICAL PARTIES

1. Theda Skocpal, quoted in Ella Nielsen, "The Important 2020 Elections Not Talked About: State Legislatures," *Vox*, July 5, 2019, https://www.vox.com/policy-and-politics/2019/7/5/20680124/state-legislatures-gerrymandering-redistricting.

2. The official results were 6,019,422 votes for Feinstein (54.2 percent) and 5,093,942 for De Leon (45.8 percent). See https://elections.cdn.sos.ca.gov/sov/2018-general/sov/2018-complete-sov.pdf.

3. In Australia, where the system is common in several Australian states, it is called the "Alternative Vote," while elsewhere it is known as the "Instant Runoff Vote" (IRV).

4. The observant reader will note that over twenty-three thousand first-place votes were cast for Bond and Hoar but just over fifteen thousand votes transferred in the second round. This is because about eight thousand voters chose a first-place preference but did not rank the other candidates.

5. While Cruz had never run for office before, it would be inaccurate to describe him as a political novice. A Harvard-educated lawyer, he had clerked for former U.S. Supreme Court Chief Justice Rehnquist and had been appointed Solicitor General of Texas.

6. http://www.politifact.com/texas/statements/2015/apr/27/ted-cruz/ted-cruz-says-half-presidents-were-previously-gove/. Five former presidents served in both the governor's office and the U.S. Senate.

7. Doreen Barrie and Roger Gibbins, "Parliamentary Careers in the Canadian Federal State," *Canadian Journal of Political Science* 22 (1989): 137–45.

8. Klaus Stolz, "Moving Up, Moving Down: Political Careers across Territorial Levels," *European Journal of Political Research* 42 (2003): 223–48.

9. Peverill Squire, "Electoral Career Movements and the Flow of Political Power in the American Federal System," *State Politics and Policy Quarterly* 14 (2014): 72–89.

10. "Voting Wrongs," *The Economist*, May 28, 2016, 13.

11. In 1992 there were 510,497 elected officials, a figure that almost certainly has increased over the years. The figure is reported in Frank Shelly, J. C. Archer, F. M. Davidson, and S. D. Brunn, *Political Geography of the United States* (New York: Guilford Press, 1996), 123.

12. There are some excellent discussions of these matters, however. See Douglas Rae, *The Political Consequences of Electoral Laws* (New Haven, CT: Yale University Press,

1967). Also see David M. Farrell, *Electoral Systems: A Comparative Introduction*, 2nd ed. (New York: Palgrave, 2011); Pippa Norris, *Electoral Engineering: Voting Rules and Political Behavior* (New York: Cambridge University Press, 2004); and Michael Gallagher and Paul Mitchell, eds., *The Politics of Electoral Systems* (New York: Oxford University Press, 2005).

13. A recent study of the electoral laws and how they influence partisan outcomes in the United States is Jonathan A. Roden, *Why Cities Lose: The Deep Roots of the Urban-Rural Political Divide* (New York: Basic Books, 2019).

14. North Carolina also has a run-off rule, but it only applies if no candidate receives at least 40 percent of the primary vote. It is not, therefore, a majoritarian requirement.

15. See Peverill Squire and Gary Moncrief, *State Legislatures Today*, 3rd ed. (Lanham, MD: Rowman & Littlefield, 2020), 23–25.

16. Richard G. Niemi, Jeffrey S. Hill, and Bernard Grofman, "The Impact of Multimember Districts on Party Representation in U.S. State Legislatures," *Legislative Studies Quarterly* 10 (1985): 441–55.

17. http://ncsl.typepad.com/the_thicket/2012/09/a-slight-decline-in-legislatures-using-multimember-districts-after-redistricting.html.

18. Stephen Calabrese, "Multimember District Congressional Elections," *Legislative Studies Quarterly* 25 (2000): 611–43.

19. Elizabeth Kolbert, "Drawing the Line," *New Yorker*, June 27, 2016, 70; Jamie Carson, M. Crespin, C. Finocchiaro, and D. Rohde, "Redistricting and Party Polarization in the U.S. House of Representatives," *American Politics Research* 35 (2007): 878–904.

20. In fact, history reveals that MMDs were eliminated by some states because they led to one party dominating elections. See Thomas Schaller, "Multi-Member Districts: Just A Thing of the Past?" http://www.centerforpolitics.org/crystalball/articles/multi-member-legislative-districts-just-a-thing-of-the-past/.

21. See Didi Kuo, "Electoral System Reform in the United States," Conference Report, Program on American Democracy in Comparative Perspective, Stanford University, Center on Democracy, Development, and the Rule of Law, June 3, 2014, https://fsi.stanford.edu/sites/default/files/electoral_system_report.pdf.

22. Bobby Harrison, "Mississippi Sole State Where Popular Vote Only One Factor in Winning Statewide Office," *Mississippi Today*, June 9, 2019; https://mississippitoday.org/2019/06/09/mississippi-sole-state-where-popular-vote-only-one-factor-in-winning-statewide-office/.

23. James Langan, "A Cure That Is Likely Worse than the Disease." *William and Mary Law Review* 46 (2005): 1569–95, http://www.uvm.edu/~dguber/POLS125/articles/langan.htm.

24. See Fairvote, "Where is Ranked Choice Voting Used?" https://www.fair-vote.org/where_is_ranked_choice_voting_used?gclid=EAIaIQobChMItppPXmOmP5A IVh6_sCh0ZrAwXEAAYASAAEgKLpPD_BwE.

25. L. Sandy Maisel and Mark D. Brewer, *Parties and Elections in America*, 5th ed. (Lanham, MD: Rowman & Littlefield, 2010), 199.

26. One expert finds that 87 percent of judges in state court systems face the electorate in one way or another. See Roy A. Schotland, "Judicial Elections," in *Guide to Political Campaigns in America*, ed. Paul Herrnson (Washington, DC: CQ Press, 2005), 391.

27. The Brennan Center, "Wisconsin's Most Expensive Judicial Election in a Decade," https://www.brennancenter.org/blog/wisconsin-most-expensive-supreme-court-election-decade.

28. Jon Frandsen, "Cash Flows into Judicial Races: What's Being Bought?" *Stateline*, June 14, 2016, http://www.pewtrusts.org/en/research-and-analysis/blogs/stateline/2016/06/14/cash-flows-into-state-judicial-races-whats-being-bought.

29. Schotland, "Judicial Elections," 394.

30. David Rottman, "Judicial Elections in 2008," Council of State Governments, *Book of the States 2009*, 291.

31. Rottman, "Judicial Elections in 2008," 391.

32. "2010 Judicial Elections Increase Pressure on Courts," *Legal News*, November 9, 2010. http://www.legalnews.com/Detroit/776290.

33. Sam Zeff, "Get Ready for a Raucus Kansas Supreme Court Retention Race," *KCUR Radio*, May 24, 2016, http://kcur.org/post/get-ready-raucous-kansas-supreme-court-retention-race#stream/0. The quote is from KU political science professor Burdette Loomis.

34. National Conference of State Legislatures, http://www.ncsl.org/research/elections-and-campaigns/primary-types.aspx.

35. Maisel and Brewer, *Parties and Elections in America*, 211–12.

36. Douglas J. Ahler, Jack Citrin and Gabriel S. Lenz, "Do Open Primaries Improve Representation? An Experimental Test of California's 2012 Top-Two Primary," *Legislative Studies Quarterly* 41 (2016): 237–68; Benjamin Highton, Robert Huckfeldt and Issac Hale, "Some General Election Consequences of California's Top-Two Primary System," *California Journal of Politics and* Policy 8:2 (2016); Eric McGhee and Boris Shor, "Has the Top Two Primary Elected More Moderates?" *Perspectives on Politics* 15 (2017): 1053–66.

37. *Shelby County v. Holder*, 570 U.S. 529 (2013).

38. Kevin Morris and Peter Dunphy, "AVR Impact on State Voter Registration," Brennan Center for Justice, April 11, 2019.

39. Matt Vasilogambros, "Voter Access Matters in 2020, and These Lawmakers Know It." Stateline.org, August 1, 2019, https://www.pewtrusts.org/en/research-and-analysis/blogs/stateline/2019/08/01/voter-access-matters-in-2020-and-these-lawmakers-know-it.

40. Nancy Martorano Miller, Keith Hamm, Maria Aroca, and Ronald Hedlund, "An Alternative Route to Voting Reform: The Right to Vote, Voter Registration, Redistricting and U.S. State Constitutions," *Publius* 49 (Summer 2019), 465–89.

41. http://www.governing.com/topics/politics/gov-week-politics-voter-registration-wisconsin-primary.html.

42. Adam Brown, "Losing to Nobody? Nevada's 'None of These Candidates' Ballot Reform," *Social Science Journal* 48 (2011), 364–70.

43. http://www.governing.com/topics/politics/gov-vermont-peter-shumlin-election.html; "Shumlin Defeats Milne in Legislature Governor Vote," *Burlington Free Press*, January 9, 2015.

44. To be completely accurate, only 428 districts are currently redrawn by the states because seven states have only one congressional district each. In those instances, the congressional district is the entire state and does not have to be redrawn.

45. At least twelve states now have laws in place for the next round of redistricting that will require that some entity other than the state legislature draw the congressional boundary lines within the state. Moreover, there are some states in which a commission is used to draw state legislative lines but in which the legislature has responsibility for drawing congressional districts within the state. See Associate Press, "Number of States Using Redistricting Commissions Growing," March 21, 2019. https://apnews.com/4d2e2aea7e224549af61699e51c955dd.

46. While this is generally true, it is possible for redistricting to be done more than once every decade. Perhaps the best known instance of this was when the Republican Party won majority control of the Texas Legislature in 2003 and moved to redistrict despite the fact that the legislature had just effected a new redistricting plan (under the then-majority Democrats) in 2002.

47. This discussion relies in part on Herman Schwartz, "Democrats: It's the States, Stupid!" *Reuters*, July 14, 2013, http://blogs.reuters.com/great-debate/2013/07/14/

democrats-its-the-states-stupid/; and Elizabeth Kolbert, "Drawing the Line," *New Yorker*, June 27, 2016, 68–70.

48. The quote is from Matt Harringer, communications director for the Democratic Legislative Campaign Committee, an organization charged with increasing the number of Democrats in state legislatures. Quoted in Amber Phillips, "The Democratic Party's Future Is at Stake in State Legislative Races." *Washington Post*, August 14, 2019.

49. See, e.g., Sam Wang, "The Great Gerrymander of 2012," *New York Times*, February 2, 2013, http://www.nytimes.com/2013/02/03/opinion/sunday/the-great-gerrymander-of-2012.html?pagewanted=all.

50. Nicholas Goedert finds that the urban concentration of Democrats currently creates a persistent natural, or geographic, bias that favors Republicans, and that this bias is more important than partisan gerrymandering in explaining the distribution of seats compared to votes in the U.S. See Nicholas Goedert, "Gerrymandering or Geography? How Democrats Won the Popular Vote but Lost the Congress in 2012," *Research and Politics*, April–June 2014: 2053168014528683.

51. Johnathan Rodden, *Why Cities Lose* (New York: Basic Books, 2019), 5.

52. See "Not Gerrymandering, but Districting: More Evidence on How Democrats Won the Popular Vote but Lost the Congress," *The Monkey Cage*, http://themonkeycage.org/2012/11/15/not-gerrymandering-but-districting-more-evidence-on-how-democrats-won-the-popular-vote-but-lost-the-congress/, accessed March 27, 2013.

53. 588 U.S. ___ (2019).

54. By our count, eighteen states fit under this definition. But there is some latitude for interpretation of the phrase "outside the control over the legislature." E.g., in Maine, New York, Rhode Island, Vermont, and Virginia, the redistricting commissions are advisory; they recommend plans but the legislature has the authority to reject the recommendation and adopt a different plan.

55. See National Conference of Legislatures, "Redistricting Commissions" at http://ncsl.org/research/redistricting/2009-redistricting-commissions-table.aspx. Also see Associated Press, "Number of states using redistricting commissions growing," https://www.apnews.com/4d2e2aea7e224549af61699e51c955dd.

56. Even in 2010, when the Republicans picked up multiple governorships and over seven hundred state legislative seats in states across the country, only one state other than Wisconsin flipped from unified Democratic to unified Republican. That state was Maine. The more common practice is for a state to move from unified for one party to divided to unified for the other party over the course of several elections.

57. On breaking quorum in this case and others, see Peverill Squire, "Quorum Exploitation in the American Legislative Experience," *Studies in American Political Development* 27 (2013): 142–64.

58. Jeff Mayers, "Democrats Flee Wisconsin to Protest Union Curbs," *Reuters*, February 17, 2011.

59. For a list of recalled state legislators, see http://www.ncsl.org/legislatures-elections/elections/recall-of-state-officials.aspx.

60. Alex DeMarban, "Recall Dunleavy Group Says It Passed a 28,000 Signature Threshold in Two Weeks," *Anchorage Daily News*, August 16, 2019, https://www.adn.com/politics/2019/08/16/recall-dunleavy-group-says-it-passed-a-28000-signature-threshold-in-two-weeks/.

61. Scott Kendall, quoted in Emma Coleman, August 12, 2019. "Recall Effort for Alaska Governor Collects Two-Thirds of Necessary Signatures in a Single Week." RouteFifty.com, https://www.routefifty.com/management/2019/08/roundup-aug-13–2019/159098/.

62. https://www.nbcnews.com/news/us-news/embattled-alaska-governor-scales-back-budget-cuts-approves-oil-wealth-n1044446.

63. These figures are calculated by the authors from information in Joshua Spivak, "Opinion: The Republican Party's Recall Bonanza Could Backfire—Badly," August 13, 2019, *Newseek*, https://www.newsweek.com/recall-elections-democrats-gop-1454052.

64. According to Jennie Drage Bowser, formerly of the National Conference of State Legislatures, Delaware's referendum authority is extremely limited, applying only to the question of whether or not "Bingo" should be licensed or prohibited. See NCSL, "Legislative Referendum: Constitutional Provisions," information sheet dated January 2012.

65. Donovan, Mooney, and Smith, *State and Local Politics*, 114–15.

66. Initiative & Referendum Institute, *Ballotwatch*, December 2011, No. 2, 1.

67. Unlike Wisconsin, where the pro-union forces were outspent in the effort to recall Governor Walker, in Ohio they held a commanding advantage in campaign expenditures. The pro-union groups outspent the anti-union coalition by more than 3:1.

68. Initiative and Referendum Institute, http://www.iandrinstitute.org/BW%20 2008-3%20Results%20v4.pdf, accessed August 27, 2010.

69. Arthur Lupia and John Matsusaka, "Direct Democracy: New Approaches to Old Questions," *Annual Review of Political Science* 7 (2004): 474–74.

70. John G. Matsusaka, "Public Policy and the Initiative and Referendum: A Survey with Some New Evidence," *Public Choice* 174 (2018): 137.

71. Liz Essley Whyte, "How Democratic are Ballot Initiatives," *The Atlantic*, http://www.theatlantic.com/politics/archive/2016/01/ballot-initiatives-2016/422385/.

72. Matsusaka, "Public Policy and the Initiative and Referendum," 137.

73. Elizabeth Garrett, "Hybrid Democracy," *George Washington University Law Review* 73 (2005): 1096–130.

74. Shaun Bowler and Todd Donovan, "Measuring the Effect of Direct Democracy on State Policy: Not All Initiatives Are Created Equal," *State Politics and Policy Quarterly* 4 (2004): 345–63.

75. Squire and Moncrief, *State Legislatures Today: Politics under the Domes*, 3rd ed. (Lanham, MD: Rowman & Littlefield, 2020), 171.

76. Donovan, Mooney, and Smith, *State and Local Politics*, 148.

77. Mark Baldassare, president of the Public Policy Institute of California, quoted in www.sfgate.com/bayarea/article/November-ballot-crowded-with-weighty-measures-8335746.php.

78. Arthur Lupia, "Shortcuts versus Encyclopedias: Information and Voting Behavior in California Insurance Reform Elections," *American Political Science Review* 88 (1994): 63–76.

79. See Initiative and Referendum Institute, "Overview of Initiative Use, 1900–2018" (January 2019), www.iandrinstitute.org.

80. Kerri Milita, "Election Laws and Agenda Setting," *State Politics & Policy Quarterly* 15 (2015): 119–46.

81. *U.S. Term Limits, Inv. v. Thornton*, 514 U.S. 779 (1995).

82. Karl T. Kurtz, "An Unexpected Benefit of Term Limits," *The Thicket* (National Conference of State Legislature's blog), April 23, 2009, http://ncsl.typepad.com/the_thicket/2009/04/an-unexpected-benefit-of-term-limits.html.

83. Marjorie Sarbaugh-Thompson, "Measuring 'Term-Limitedness' in U.S. Multi-State Research," *State Politics and Policy Quarterly* 10 (2010): 199–217.

84. Jonathan Oosting, "Term Limits Force Michigan into American's Biggest Legislative Turnover," Detroit News, https://www.detroitnews.com/story/news/local/michigan/2018/11/25/term-limits-michigan-largest-legislative-turnover-country/2017865002/.

85. At this writing (mid-August 2019) the precise number of delegates per state is uncertain due to the awarding of bonus delegates based on several factors.

86. https://www.270towin.com/content/republican-primary-and-caucus-delegate-allocation-methods.

87. https://www.270towin.com/content/thresholds-for-delegate-allocation-2020-democratic-primary-and-caucus.

88. Stephen Wayne, *Is This Any Way to Run a Democratic Election?* 4th ed. (Washington, DC: CQ Press, 2011), 179.

89. Alex Isenstadt, "Republicans to Scrap Primaries and Caucuses as Trump Challengers Cry Foul," Politico, September 6, 2019, https://www.politico.com/story/2019/09/06/republicans-cancel-primaries-trump-challengers-1483126.

90. Barry Burden, "The Nominations: Rules, Strategies, and Uncertainty," in *The Elections of 2008*, ed. Michael Nelson (Washington, DC: CQ Press, 2010), 25.

91. Maisel and Brewer, *Parties and Elections in America*, 319.

92. Darrell West, *Air Wars*, 5th ed. (Washington, DC: CQ Press, 2010), 19.

93. The elections of 1824, 1876, and 1888 all resulted in the selection of a president who had not won the popular vote. While the evidence is not definitive, the 1960 election might also fall into this category. See, e.g., Stephen Medvic, *Campaigns and Elections* (Boston: Wadsworth/Cengage, 2010), 48.

94. Martin Diamond, *The Electoral College and the American Idea of Democracy* (Washington, DC: American Enterprise Institute, 1977).

95. A good summary is provided in Steven Schier and Todd Eberly, *Polarized: The Rise of Ideology in American Politics* (Lanham, MD: Rowman & Littlefield, 2016).

96. See, e.g., Boris Shor, "Party Polarization in America's State Legislatures: An Update," in *The State of the Parties*, ed. John Green, Daniel Coffey, and David Cohen, 7th ed. (Lanham, MD: Rowman & Littlefield, 2014), 121–36. See also https://research.bshor.com/category/polarization/.

97. Jennifer McDermott, Steve LeBlanc, and Audrey McAvoy, "In 3 States, Two-Thirds of Statehouse Races Were Uncontested." Associated Press, March 21, 2019, https://www.apnews.com/a5f8eaadeb9b4c04a1bc3a52f5c7ea66

98. Carl Klarner and Heather Evans, "The Polarization and Nationalization of State Elections, 1971–2014," http://klarnerpolitics.com/.

99. Klarner and Evans, "The Polarization and Nationalization of State Elections, 1971–2014." Also see Keith Hamm and Gary Moncrief, "Legislative Politics in the States," *Politics in the American States*, ed. Virginia Gray, Russell Hanson, and Thad Kousser, 10th ed. (Washington, DC: CQ Press, 2013), 172–75, for a similar interpretation using a different measure of "competitive."

100. Klarner and Evans report that since 2003, only about 40 percent of all gubernatorial elections qualify as competitive. See Klarner and Evans, "The Polarization and Nationalization of State Elections, 1971–2014."

101. See, e.g., James E. Campbell, "Presidential Coattails and Midterm Losses in State Legislative Elections," *American Political Science Review* 80 (1988): 45–63; John Chubb, "Institutions, the Economy, and the Dynamics of State Elections," *American Political Science Review* 82 (1984): 133–54. Also see William Berry, Michael Berkman, and Stuart Schneiderman, "Legislative Professionalism and Incumbent Reelection," *American Political Science Review* 94 (2000): 859–74. For the role of gubernatorial coattails, see Robert Hogan, "Gubernatorial Coattail Effects in State Legislative Elections," *Political Research Quarterly* 58 (2005): 587–97.

102. Katharine Javian, "The Influence of National Contextual Factors on State Legislative Election Outcomes," paper prepared for the 2012 American Political Science Association annual meeting scheduled for New Orleans in September 2012. Also see Katharine Javian, "Party Voting in the American States: How National Factors and Institutional Variation Affect State Elections" (PhD dissertation, Temple University, August 2012).

103. See Klarner and Evans, "The Polarization and Nationalization of State Elections, 1971–2014." Also see Carl Klarner and C. Lockwood Reynolds, "Driven to Distraction: State

and National Forces in State Legislative Elections," paper prepared for the 2014 annual meeting of the State Politics and Policy Conference, Iowa City, May 2014.

104. Steven M. Rogers, "Accountability in a Federal System" (PhD dissertation, Princeton University, 2013), 4.

105. Steven Rogers, "Electoral Accountability for State Legislative Roll Calls and Ideological Representation." *American Political Science Review* 111 (2017): 555.

106. Rogers, "Accountability in a Federal System," 34–35.

107. Klarner and Reynolds, "Driven to Distraction," 22.

108. Jeffrey Lyons, William Jaeger, and Jennifer Wolak, "The Roots of Citizens' Knowledge of State Politics," *State Politics and Policy Quarterly* 13 (2012): 185–86.

CHAPTER 9: WHY STATES MATTER NOW

1. "Institute Q&A," The Nelson Rockefeller Institute of Government, University of Albany, New York, September 2010.

2. Donald Kettl, "Lobbyists Leave Capitol Hill for the States," *Governing*, June 2016, http://www.governing.com/columns/potomac-chronicle/gov-lobbying-states   -washington. html.

3. Kettl, "Lobbyists Leave Capitol Hill." The report is from The Center for Public Integrity, "Amid Federal Gridlock, Lobbying Rises in the States," https://www.publicintegrity. org/2016/02/11/19279/amid-federal-gridlock-lobbying-rises-states.

4. Mike Macaig, "Louisiana's Budget Crisis Empowers an Unusual Group," *Governing*, July 2016, http://www.governing.com/topics/politics/gov-louisiana-budget.html.

5. Shanna Rose and Cynthia Bowling, "The State of American Federalism 2014–15: Pathways to Policy in an Era of Party Polarization," *Publius* 45 (2015): 351–79.

6. Anne Leland and M-J Oboroceanu, "American War and Military Operations Casualties: Lists and Statistics," Washington, DC: Congressional Research Service Report 7-5700, February 26, 2010.

7. Robert S. Allen, "The Shame of the States," in *Our Sovereign State*, ed. Robert S. Allen (New York: Vanguard Press, 1949), xiii.

8. Alexander Heard, "Introduction—Old Problem, New Context," in *Our Sovereign State*, ed. Allen, 3.

9. Stephen Ansolabehere and James Snyder, *The End of Inequality: One Person, One Vote and the Transformation of American Politics* (New York: Norton, 2008), 88.

10. Quoted in Allen, "The Shame of the States," xxii.

11. See the discussion in Peverill Squire, *The Evolution of American Legislatures, Colonies, Territories, and States, 1619–2009* (Ann Arbor: University of Michigan Press, 2012), 291–97; and Belle Zeller, *American State Legislatures* (New York: Thomas Y. Crowell, 1954).

12. Jon Teaford, *The Rise of the States* (Baltimore: Johns Hopkins University Press, 2002), 199–200; Squire, *The Evolution of American Legislatures*, 297–307.

13. Ann O. Bowman and Richard Kearney, *The Resurgence of the States* (Englewood Cliffs, NJ: Prentice Hall, 1986).

14. Carl Van Horn, ed., *The State of the States* (Washington, DC: CQ Press, 1989), 1–12; Teaford, *The Rise of the States*, chap. 8.

15. Alison LaCroix, "How the Noisy Debate Over States' Rights Distorts History and the Intent of Federalism," http://voices.washingtonpost.com/political -bookworm/2010/03/ how_the_noisy_debate_over_stat.html. Also see Alison LaCroix, *The Ideological Origins of American Federalism* (Cambridge, MA: Harvard University Press, 2010).

16. There are numerous references to the "Alabama syndrome," but it is generally attributed to James L. Sundquist, *Making Federalism Work* (Washington, DC: Brookings Institution,

1969), 271. Also see Ira Sharkansky, *The Maligned States*, 2nd ed. (New York: McGraw-Hill, 1978), 7; Kimberly Johnson, *Governing the American State: Congress and the New Federalism, 1877–1929* (Princeton, NJ: Princeton University Press, 2006), 159; and John D. Nugent, *Safeguarding Federalism: How States Protect Their Interests in National Policymaking* (Norman: University of Oklahoma Press, 2009), 221.

17. Martha Derthick, *Keeping the Compound Republic* (Washington, DC: Brookings Institute Press, 2001), 148.

18. Nicholas G. Napolio and Jordan Carr Peterson, "Their Boot in Our Face No Longer? Administrative Sectionalism and Resistance to Federal Authority in the U.S. South," *State Politics & Policy Quarterly* 19 (2019): 101–22.

19. David Brian Robertson, *Federalism and the Making of America* (New York: Routledge, 2011), 9.

20. Aaron Blake, "Gay Marriage Opponents Are Suddenly All about States' Rights. Wonder Why," *Washington Post*, June 11, 2015.

21. Ariel Edwards-Levy, "Both Parties Seem to Be Having a Change of Heart about Federal Power," *Huffington Post*, February 15, 2017; https://www.huffpost.com/entry/democrats-republicans-views-federal-power_n_58a4cf0be4b07602ad515dec.

22. Ann Althouse, "Vanguard States, Laggard States, Federalism and Constitutional Rights," *University of Pennsylvania Law Review* 152 (2004): 1745–1827.

23. Louis Jacobson, "New Head of Governors Group Talks Future of States," *Governing*, March 28, 2016, http://www.governing.com/topics/politics/gov-scott -pattison-national-governors-association.html.

24. Althouse, "Vanguard States, Laggard States," 1746.

25. "Let 50 Flowers Bloom," *The Economist*, March 16–22, 2013, 16.

26. Virginia Gray, "The Socioeconomic and Political Context of States," in *Politics in the American States*, ed. Virginia Gray, Russell Hanson, and Thad Kousser, 10th ed. (Thousand Oaks, CA: CQ Press, 2013), 26.

27. Alice Rivlin, "Rethinking Federalism for More Effective Governance," *Publius* 42 (2012): 390.

28. Shama Gamkhar and J. Mitchell Pickerill, "The State of American Federalism 2011–2012: A Fend for Yourself and Activist Form of Bottom-Up Federalism," *Publius* 42 (2012): 378.

29. Nugent, *Safeguarding Federalism*, 215–16.

30. Alan Rosenthal, *The Decline of Representative Democracy* (Washington, DC: CQ Press, 1997); Peverill Squire and Gary Moncrief, *State Legislatures Today: Politics Under the Domes*, 2nd ed. (Lanham, MD: Rowman & Littlefield, 2015), 211–13.

31. http://www.journalism.org/2014/07/10/americas-shifting-statehouse-press/.

32. Jennifer Dorrah, "Statehouse Exodus," *American Journalism Review* (April/May 2009), www.ajr.org/article.asp?id=4721.

33. https://www.minnpost.com/; https://www.texastribune.org/.

34. Nugent, *Safeguarding Federalism*, 216.

35. See, e.g., https://www.pewtrusts.org/en/research-and-analysis/blogs/stateline/2019/01/28/state-of-the-states-2019.

Index